THE LIFE AND TIMES OF

T. H. GALLAUDET

EDNA EDITH SAYERS

Gallaudet

sapere aude

THE LIFE AND TIMES OF

T.H. Gallaudet

ForeEdge

ForeEdge
An imprint of University Press of New England
www.upne.com
© 2018 Edna Edith Sayers
All rights reserved
Manufactured in the United States of America
Designed by Mindy Basinger Hill
Typeset in Garamond Premier Pro

For permission to reproduce any of the material in this book,
contact Permissions, University Press of New England, One Court Street,
Suite 250, Lebanon NH 03766; or visit www.upne.com

Library of Congress Cataloging-in-Publication Data

NAMES: Sayers, Edna Edith, author.

TITLE: The life and times of T.H. Gallaudet / Edna Edith Sayers.

Description: Lebanon NH : ForeEdge, 2018. | Includes bibliographical
references and index.

IDENTIFIERS: LCCN 2017019075 (print) | LCCN 2017033226 (ebook) |
ISBN 9781512601411 (epub, mobi, & pdf) | ISBN 9781512600513 (cloth)

SUBJECTS: LCSH: Gallaudet, T. H. (Thomas Hopkins), 1787–1851. |
Teachers of the deaf—United States—Biography.

CLASSIFICATION: LCC HV2426.G3 (ebook) | LCC HV2426.G3 S29 2018
(print) | DDC 371.91/2092 [B]—dc23

LC record available at https://lccn.loc.gov/2017019075

5   4   3   2   1

FOR HARLAN LANE

Contents

THOMAS HOPKINS GALLAUDET (1787–1851) is well known today as the founder of deaf education in the United States, but few can say precisely just what it was that he did or why he did it. To those who know just his name (and more often than not mispronounce it: the name is properly GAL-uh-det), the man is a shadowy figure behind Gallaudet University in Washington, DC, where deaf students surprised a nation of television watchers in 1988 by marching in the streets to demand a "Deaf President Now!" Gallaudet University had its beginnings, however, some years after T. H. Gallaudet's death, when it was established in Washington as a school for the "deaf and dumb and blind"; it was named for him only decades later.

For the sign-language community of Deaf Americans and their friends, in contrast, Gallaudet is the beloved first principal of the American School for the Deaf in West Hartford, Connecticut, incorporated in 1816 as the Connecticut Asylum for the Education and Instruction of Deaf and Dumb Persons. More importantly for this group, he is the man associated with two signal Deaf people: Laurent Clerc, cherished as the founder of American Sign Language (ASL), whom Gallaudet brought to our shores from Paris in 1816, and Sophia Fowler, whom Gallaudet married in 1819 and who was known much later, at Gallaudet College where she was Matron, as the Queen of the Deaf. It is widely believed in the Deaf community that he was motivated to do all of this out of benevolence inspired by a little deaf girl who lived next door to his parents.

For everyone who knows anything of him today, Gallaudet was a secular saint, a man of disinterested benevolence and unflappable mild manner, admired by the general public, adored by the deaf people who knew him during his lifetime, revered by the many who have benefited from his work, and honored by the United States Post Office with a 20¢ stamp.

Why would anyone question this story? Well, for one thing, historians recognize this sketch as an egregious example of "Great Man" historiography, the now discredited view that social, political, and scientific progress is achieved by daring paradigm shifts made by lone (male) visionaries of genius. In a similar fashion, historians of Deaf culture have been misled in the past by what sociologist Paddy Ladd calls the "Grand Narrative," in which every nation's Deaf community is constructed as the product of a distinguished hearing (male) educator.[1] For historians inspired by Ladd it is rather Gallaudet's Deaf mentor and assistant Laurent Clerc who was the major player, and so it seemed to me.

Even more disturbing than the currency of the "Great Man" and "Grand Narrative" models, however, is the copious evidence that our hero was deeply invested in both white nationalism and a regressive creed of exclusionary Protestantism, evidence that has always been readily available to anyone who wanted to look at it, though precious few have done so. Such incontrovertible evidence for a radically reactionary belief system sat uncomfortably for me with the notion that Gallaudet was also a warm advocate for the dignity of deaf people and the legitimacy of sign language. In the present day, American Sign Language, Deaf culture, and Deaf rights are understood to be elements of a broadly liberal agenda that celebrates diversity and enshrines the dignity and rights of the individual as among the highest of public virtues. How can one be an advocate *for* the Deaf and *against* every other minority?

As it turns out, in 1817 when Hartford's crony capitalists opened the nation's first sign-language school for the deaf, respect for diversity, dignity, and rights were the last things anyone thought of. To the contrary, the school's founders regarded deaf education and sign language as tools for strengthening the Yale-educated ruling class and advancing its agenda and social hegemony. That the immortal souls of countless deaf Americans could be thereby granted salvation, and that Connecticut could be assisted to usher in the long-awaited Millennium, were convenient rationales for most of the school's backers, although Gallaudet and a handful of others sincerely believed in these aims. He was, therefore, indeed earnest in his support of sign language education and the dignity of deaf people, albeit for reasons I had not previously imagined. And as for the "Great Man" and "Grand Narrative" histories that I had at first regarded as patent mythography, these models turned out, much to my surprise, to get it exactly right. Gallaudet couldn't have done it without Clerc, of course, but once the school was open, the fight for sign language was his alone. It was not so much that Roman Catholic Clerc didn't have the standing in Calvinist Hartford to have made any social impact on his own, although that was certainly true. It's rather largely that Clerc just wasn't interested in the fight. He had his pupils, his family, his little signing community, and he was content to leave the public stage to Gallaudet. So it was Gallaudet, and Gallaudet alone, who sowed the seed of sign language, nursed it in his residential school, and kept away the crows who would have devoured the emerging Deaf community before it had a chance to root.

Can we, then, celebrate this very great man for the blessings he conferred on two centuries of Deaf Americans, in light of what we learn of his support for principles and interests that virtually all present-day users of ASL regard as racist and bigoted? That's a decision every reader has to make individually. Gallaudet was for thirty years an active participant in the American Colonization Society (ACS), dedicated to racial cleansing by deporting free black Americans to ACS–run colonies in West Africa. Gallaudet believed that Americans of African ancestry had no legitimate place in the United States of America, and he fought with all the resources he could muster against the abolition movement's increasingly forceful and confident arguments for a multiracial nation. That he could hold such views as a minister of the gospel will strike some readers as inexplicable: Christians today take as given that African Americans are, in the words of abolitionist William Jay, among our brethren for whom Christ died. For Calvinist Connecticut, however, that Christ died for Africans did not imply that He wanted them to live in Hartford. And as for our constitutionally guaranteed freedom of conscience, for Gallaudet and his associates, that amounted to the freedom to choose correct (Calvinist) doctrinal beliefs while ushering the Church of Rome into the oblivion they believed had been prophesized for it in the Book of Revelation. Gallaudet invested his own money, mostly from book royalties, into a secret society, LUPO, that he hoped would expunge Catholicism from the nation.

In other endeavors, he did less harm and some good. As chaplain at the Retreat for the Insane, his belief that "the insane" needed divine salvation rather than medical treatment was safely marginalized by the physicians who ran the hospital, and he seems to have provided some of the more tractable patients with real services. His very considerable volunteer efforts to professionalize teaching influenced Horace Mann and eventually resulted in the establishment of state normal schools, or teachers' colleges, in Massachusetts and Connecticut. Gallaudet believed that the normal schools would create a body of theory and best practices that would elevate the profession. He would probably be surprised to learn that two hundred years later, we got the theory without any of the elevation.

Perhaps he came closest to a real contribution to educational practice in *The Mother's Primer* (1836), a book he wrote for beginning readers. Here, Gallaudet boldly eschewed traditional phonetic instruction with its endless strings of nonsense syllables and urged the teaching of simple whole words in a child's first lessons. If only he had stuck to his guns, we could applaud his courage, but he proved an apostate to the whole-word method and in subsequent publications turned out the accustomed "ba be bi bo bu by" drivel. Before he lost his nerve, though, his understanding of how children learn to read was brilliantly inspired by his classroom interactions with deaf learners, and this was recognized by colleagues during his lifetime.[2]

Given all these interests and efforts — the good, the bad, and the very ugly indeed — what would Gallaudet himself say if asked about his life's vocation? He would say he was a writer — a writer of children's books who might have been a poet had circumstances (always unspecified) been other than they were. He wrote dozens of poems, mostly unpublished, over his lifetime, as well as book reviews and essays on various topics that were published in both general-readership newspapers and academic journals. But it was his books for children, for parents and schools, and for missionaries to use with beginning readers in the so-called heathen East that provided him and Sophia, their eight children, and Sophia's sister Parnell a comfortable life in Hartford, if a rather frugal one by our standards. In all these efforts, Gallaudet's ability to lay open the most complicated topics was never matched by his contemporaries, and his prose remains to this day instantly recognizable. Whether it strikes the reader as beautifully lucid or unctuously patronizing is another question.

Several flattering though regrettably fanciful biographies of Gallaudet were written for children in the course of the twentieth century: insofar as they relate what history knows of Gallaudet, they are derivative of three nineteenth-century biographies. The first biography, *Tribute to Gallaudet,* was begun just months after his death in the fall of 1851, as an oration at a memorial service in Hartford presided over by Henry Barnard, a fellow Yale graduate, then principal of the Connecticut State Normal School. It's tempting to see Barnard's efforts as deriving from admiration for a man we might consider his mentor, but Barnard similarly hosted a memorial and compiled a book fourteen years later for Samuel Colt, the Hartford manufacturing genius whose fortune was made by manufacturing and selling guns to the U.S. Army.[3] So it seems that Barnard was simply the man to turn to for memorials. Barnard's lengthy remarks and the orations of other speakers (including Laurent Clerc) were published as a book for the express purpose of generating some income for the "deaf and dumb widow." Fortunately for us, *Tribute* appended a good number of primary documents, the value of which was understood even by contemporary readers. Gallaudet's children hoped for a wide distribution and were gratified that the book sold out quickly.[4]

Apparently not satisfied with Barnard's Herculean effort, Gallaudet's children asked Heman Humphrey, a Yale classmate of Gallaudet's, to make another effort. Humphrey was a Congregationalist minister, a driving force in the temperance movement, and the president of Amherst College. Again fortunately for us, Humphrey's *Life and Labors of Thomas Hopkins Gallaudet* takes as its format the reproduction of all the letters, sermons, and addresses that the Gallaudet offspring could find, strung together with minimal intrusion of Humphrey's own voice or views.

Then in 1887, Edward Miner Gallaudet, the youngest child and at the time the president of Gallaudet College, undertook a biography that would clinch the saintly image of his father. Because Edward Miner had been a child when his father died, he had to rely on the miscellany of papers collected from his father's desk by his oldest brother, Thomas, and on the memories of his seven older siblings (his mother had died a decade earlier), grown a bit dim more than thirty-five years after Gallaudet's death. In any case, no one in the family knew much about Gallaudet's work outside of deaf education. Of all of Gallaudet's other fields of endeavor, his children were largely ignorant, for Father had been assiduous in protecting the sacred family circle from contact with the wider world in which only the male heads of families properly moved, and Edward Miner Gallaudet had little recourse but to defer to his father's colleagues Barnard and Humphrey on most points. Between that circumstance and Edward Miner's hagiographic purpose, not to mention his own tendency toward family aggrandizement (he alleged that the Gallaudets were descendants of the Doge of Venice, that they had a family coat-of-arms, and so on), this is the least reliable of the three nineteenth-century biographies. In that same year, which was the centennial of Gallaudet's birth, Henry Winter Syle, a Deaf man who had entered the Episcopal priesthood under the guidance of Gallaudet's oldest son, Thomas, published a brief sketch of T. H. Gallaudet's life featuring Thomas's impressions.

Twentieth-century historians who have taught us a great deal about Gallaudet were all focused on the history of deaf education. Harlan Lane's groundbreaking *When the Mind Hears,* first published in 1984, tells the story of the founding of the Asylum and its earliest decades through the eyes of Laurent Clerc. Covering the beginnings of deaf education in France and elsewhere, along with Gallaudet's exploratory trip to Europe, his return with Clerc, and his fourteen years as principal of the American Asylum, Lane's meticulously detailed and magisterial account remains basic to our understanding of these years of Gallaudet's life. I am sure I speak for many other readers in attesting that this book single-handedly radicalized my thinking on what it means to be Deaf, and my dedication of the present book to Harlan is a small return on what so many of us owe him.

Phyllis Valentine's 1993 doctoral dissertation, "American Asylum for the Deaf: A First Experiment in Education, 1817–1880," includes valuable discussion of how Gallaudet's views of Scottish Common Sense philosophy shaped his decision to use sign language as the medium of instruction and on some gritty details of exactly how the Asylum was funded. More recently, R. A. R. Edwards's *Words Made Flesh* (2012) asks important questions about the specific (undocumented) signed language actually used at the school and explores the newly formed Deaf community from the perspective of the pupils.

Two doctoral dissertations address specific aspects of Gallaudet's thought, but both range a bit more widely than their announced topics. James Fernandes's 1980 "The Gate to Heaven: T. H. Gallaudet and the Rhetoric of the Deaf Education Movement" examines sermons, addresses, and publications by Gallaudet on deaf education, as well as some writings from his formative years at Yale College and Andover Theological Seminary. Nathan Chang's 2016 "Legacy of Jonathan Edwards in the Founder of American Deaf Education" examines a wide range of Gallaudet's writing in an effort to better understand his (evolving) theological views.

The books Gallaudet wrote are all held by the Gallaudet University Archives, and many are widely and inexpensively available from used book dealers, although the *Mother's Primer* seems to have been read to shreds by almost anyone who acquired a copy, and it is now extremely rare. Some of his sermons were published in pamphlet form or in newspapers and are therefore readily available, often digitally, though others, such as those he preached at the Talcott Street Congregational meeting house to an African American congregation, are lost. The Annual Reports of the American Asylum that he penned for fourteen years are available in some libraries but not electronically. His many newspaper and magazine articles were often published under pseudonyms and thus can be difficult to identify and locate. Ascription of some such articles can be made only from contemporary references to his authorship, confirmed by Gallaudet's very distinctive prose style. The letters and diaries that remain to us are untranscribed and unpublished, aside from scattered extracts appearing in the Barnard, Humphrey, and E. M. Gallaudet biographies and elsewhere.

A twentieth-century descendant donated to the Library of Congress the collection she had inherited, which seems to have come chiefly from what Gallaudet's son Thomas removed from his father's desk after his death. This collection includes three journals, a collection of poetry, and an undergraduate notebook, as well as a large selection of letters and miscellaneous notes. Gallaudet did not make copies of the letters he sent, even on official business, and he did not systematically save those received; that we nevertheless have a great deal of primary material is something of a minor miracle, despite the lack of deeply regretted items, such as the journal Gallaudet kept as a tutor at Yale and which his son Edward Miner excerpted in his 1887 biography. Many letters concerning the founding and administration of the Asylum are archived at the American School for the Deaf in West Hartford and in the Mason Fitch Cogswell papers at the Beinecke Library, Yale University. Otherwise, letters are scattered among a score of archives ranging from the John Hartwell Cocke Family Papers at the University of Virginia, to the Kentucky School for the Deaf, to the Massachusetts Historical Society, and back to several collections at Yale and around Hartford.

My greatest debt is to Diana Moore, who worked with me to locate and secure primary source material from all these scattered repositories. Diana traveled to the University of Virginia to photograph the trove of letters Gallaudet wrote to his planter friend General Cocke and accompanied me on several weeklong trips to archival holdings in Hartford and New Haven and in Boston, Newton, and Amherst, Massachusetts; it is indeed regrettable that she had to leave the project before drafting was well begun. A comparable debt is owed to generations of unsung archivists and cataloguers who have made it possible for anyone today to locate and consult the manuscripts that constitute our national heritage. These include staff at the Sterling and the Beinecke Libraries at Yale, the Connecticut Historical Society, the Watkinson Library at Trinity College, the Hills Library at Andover-Newton Theological Seminary (special thanks to Diana Yount there), the Harriet Beecher Stowe House, the Massachusetts Historical Society, the American Antiquarian Society, the Small Special Collection Library at the University of Virginia, the archives at Gallaudet University and the American School for the Deaf (thank you, Maria Jacovino), and, last but not least, the Library of Congress (special shout-out to Eric Eldritch). Thanks also to Suzanne Schwartz at the Olin Library, Cornell University, and to the people at the New York Public Library, the Boston Public Library, the Presbyterian Historical Society in Philadelphia, and the Miner Library of the University of Rochester Medical Center who kindly responded to emailed requests for records. Michael Olson and Jamie Smith at the Gallaudet University Archives, Peter D. Rawson at the Watkinson Library, Danielle Johnson and Karen DePauw at the Connecticut Historical Society, Regina Rush at the University of Virginia, Claryn Spies and Jessica Becker of the Sterling Library MSSA, Robin Duckworth at the Congregational Library in Boston, and June Can at the Beinecke kindly and efficiently responded to follow-up questions. The First Church of Christ in Hartford opened its holdings to me, and I thank church historian Roberta L. Roy for her gracious welcome. The Institute for Living, formerly the Retreat for the Insane and now a division of Hartford Hospital, does not maintain an archive, but all its *Annual Reports* were found to have been stored in a closet, and I was kindly permitted free access to these rare and fragile documents. I am likewise deeply grateful to the archivists who assisted in locating, reproducing, and granting permission to use the images here.

My interest in pursuing the life of T. H. Gallaudet began in my study of the poet and essayist Lydia Sigourney, who had quite a bit to say about Gallaudet and his pupils, but it was not until that interest was later piqued by a stray reference in Lawrence Goodheart's *Mad Yankees* to Gallaudet's use of opium that I was able to glimpse what a fascinating study his life might be. I thank Larry, and also Stephen Ross at the Sterling Library, for helping me locate that letter. Subsequently, a casual reading of a new book by Edward Baptist, *The Half Has Never Been Told*, proved a road-to-Damascus moment as it suddenly dawned on me — how could I have been so naive? — that the American Asylum's endowment derived from the profitability of slave-labor plantations in Alabama. I thank Ed for several enlightening email chats, and Jennifer Faubert at the American School for the Deaf for electronic copies of the relevant documents.

It has been my personal pleasure, and my professional profit as well, to have worked with Phyllis Valentine and Nathan Chang over the last several years. Both were engaged in their own research, yet both generously shared electronic copies they had made of various primary sources I was lacking, as well as their expertise as it bore on various aspects of my own research. I came to this project with little understanding of Calvinism and no understanding of the theological controversies that explain so much of Gallaudet's thought, and I'm grateful to Nathan and also to Kirk VanGilder for patient answers to the often pathetically uninformed questions.

Four scholars I have never met kindly responded to my questions about their work, and I thank them here: Craig Steven Wilder, Eric Schlereth, Christopher L. Webber, and James Stewart. Thanks also to Gary Wait, past archivist at the American School for the Deaf, and to two scholars in Deaf history who responded to my questions and musings: Christopher Krentz and R. A. R. Edwards. Concerning Rebecca Edwards in particular, I wish to state here my full awareness that my departures from her interpretations of the documentary evidence she assembled, and on which I rely, were made at my extreme peril, and I trust that her generosity is not too poorly repaid by my reconsideration of all that her data might lead one to conclude. I've also benefited from chats with others in the Deaf community, including Stephen Nover, Stephen Weiner (who was so charmingly delighted to learn that Gallaudet's paternal ancestors were Sephardic Jews), John Lee Clark, and Joan Naturale. William Sayers was a signal resource in many respects and provided broad support during the eight years largely invested in this biography. Douglas C. Baynto, John V. Van Cleve, and Brian Greenwald read the entire manuscript in draft; they all made thoughtful suggestions, which I hope I have taken full advantage of. I thank you all.

Edna Edith Sayers

THE LIFE AND TIMES OF T. H. GALLAUDET

Sometime in the year 1800, a twelve-year-old boy arrived in Hartford by coach. He was small for his age — he would grow to be just five feet six and a half inches tall, according to the passport he obtained when he was twenty-eight, and "thin in his person," 120 pounds by his own account.[1] Nearly thirteen, he would already have been out of a child's loose pantaloons and into knee breeches and hose like his father, although his hair was probably cut short, not worn in a queue like a man's. He may already have been wearing the trademark spectacles from which his ASL name sign derives, the sign by which he was, and is, known to people who use American Sign Language. At the end of his life, we find him asking his son Thomas to teach his nine-month-old granddaughter "the sign of spectacles for her grandfather."[2] He had traveled, alone, from Philadelphia, where he had been born and raised and where he had been left by his family to finish school when they moved to Hartford. It is not known whether his parents knew of or agreed to his decision to join them, or whether, instead, his appearance in Hartford was a surprise. But Hartford was surely a surprise to young Thomas Hopkins Gallaudet. With a population of something over five thousand, it was dwarfed by Philadelphia and its eighty-one thousand residents. And it wasn't just the relative size that made Hartford so provincial.

City demographics usually differ from those of the surrounding countryside, not only in residents' educational levels and occupations but also in their religion and even ethnicity and language. This is due to constant in-migration of multifarious outsiders for employment and trading. In Connecticut, however, this was not the case. None of its cities was large enough to attract even in-state college graduates let alone outsiders, and none was an international port where various strangers would have washed up. Even Yale College in New Haven hired only from within the state to avoid theological contamination. In 1800, the state was virtually 100 percent conservative Calvinist in religion, as it was nearly 100 percent conservative Federalist in politics.[3] Hartford's population still comprised almost in its entirety the descendants of the Puritans of Newtowne, Massachusetts, as Cambridge was then called, who founded it in 1635, and the slaves they purchased over the next 150 years.

To see how odd this must have seemed to outsiders, we can compare Hartford to a nearby city about the same size, Albany, where Gallaudet's contemporary James Fenimore Cooper came to study shortly before his twelfth birthday in 1801. Albany, like Hartford, had been founded in the seventeenth century, and both cities were river ports that relied on trade between the interior and the Long Island Sound. There the similarities stopped. Albany had been a polyglot settlement of "composite cultural heritage," in the words of a Cooper biographer, the home of soldiers, Indian traders and Indians, Catholics, free blacks, and many persons of mixed blood. The African American community was vibrant and was left to go its own way, for example with the Afro-Dutch celebration of Pinkster (Pentecost) gone off in a decidedly African direction in the black communities of New Netherland. Here Cooper and William Jay, son of John Jay and future abolitionist, prepared for Yale under the Episcopalian rector Thomas Ellison, who had himself studied at Oxford University. Whatever Cooper learned from Ellison, and he claimed it wasn't a lot, he didn't miss a thing in Albany — it would all pour out again in his novels years later.[4] In contrast, Gallaudet's two years spent preparing for Yale at the Hartford Grammar School, from 1800 to 1802, seem to have vanished from his psyche. As well they might have. Although or perhaps partly because the Hartford Grammar School employed as teachers young Yale men getting some practice in the classroom before returning to Yale as tutors, the city itself could only have been a great bore to a boy who had been reared in cosmopolitan Philadelphia, the seat of the fledgling government of the United States.[5]

At Gallaudet's birth in December of 1787, the Constitutional Convention had already submitted its draft of the U.S. Constitution for state ratification. When Gallaudet was eighteen months old, George Washington was inaugurated as the first president of the new nation. In 1792, when he was not yet five, riots erupted when freethinker Elihu Palmer advertised that he would give a public lecture against the divinity of Jesus Christ.[6] In response to this brazen demonstration of infidelity, many residents secured memberships in their churches, and Peter Wallace Gallaudet, commission merchant, and his wife, the former Jane Hopkins, took the step of publicly professing their beliefs and having their names inscribed in the rolls of the church they had been attending, the Second Presbyterian.[7]

In July of the following year, 1793, Philadelphia saw a flood of refugees from the slave revolt in the French colony of Saint-Domingue, present-day Haiti, and Philadelphians responded generously to what they saw as white victims of Negro atrocities. Mathew Carey, writing that year, said that in just a few days the sum of $12,000 was raised in donations for the relief of the dispossessed French sugar planters.[8] That same month, an especially virulent form of the yellow fever pathogen was introduced into the city, leading to an epidemic that played out over four months and left five thousand people dead, about 10 percent of the population. As vividly described by historian Billy G. Smith in *Ship of Death*, the *Hankey,* which had carried infected mosquitoes and sailors from the west African island Bolama, docked in Philadelphia for one week in July. During that week, seamen from other ships who came aboard the *Hankey* were bitten by infected mosquitos, and infected men among the *Hankey's* crew who were well enough to whore visited brothels where they infected Philadelphia mosquitoes. By late July, yellow fever had broken out at a brothel next to the pier at which the *Hankey* was docked. Illness among prostitutes garnered little attention, and the disease spread; three weeks later, respectable residents such as the merchants and their families living near the docks began to fall ill. The Gallaudets were on Second Street, two doors from the corner of Chestnut, a prime location in which to meet the mosquitoes from the *Hankey.*[9]

Many physicians urged quarantine for ships coming from the West Indies, but Dr. Benjamin Rush, civic leader and signer of the Declaration of Independence, which still assured him of a great deal of local clout, was convinced that the disease sprang from city-generated garbage, and he successfully argued against the need for a quarantine. By mid-August, the church bells were tolling for funerals so many times a day as to seem almost continuous, and doctors urged residents to leave town. Fires burned at every street corner to purify the air, and residents walked in the streets with handkerchiefs soaked in vinegar held to their noses. By August 27, the bells tolled no longer, for there were far too many deaths to bother with funerals, and corpses were dumped into mass graves. City government collapsed, then the federal government. Jefferson fled to Monticello; Treasury Secretary Alexander Hamilton stayed at his post and contracted the fever. Private hospitals closed their doors to victims; Bush Hill, established as an emergency public hospital, soon found itself with no medical supplies, food, or blankets, and definitely no medical care. By mid-September, President Washington himself left for the safety of Mount Vernon, and mail service shut down. Captains refused to dock their ships, farmers and fishermen refused to enter the city to sell food, and all shops were closed, leaving survivors with neither employment nor anything to eat. Philadelphia native Charles Brockden Brown, a journalist and novelist who lived through these events, had one of his characters in *Ormond* point out that money was of no avail to those who had perforce to stay in the city: "Supposing provisions to be had at any price, which was itself improbable, that price would be exorbitant."[10] Tales circulated of sick people shoved into mass graves while still alive, and of others locked out of their own homes by their families.

Brockden Brown brings the plague-ridden city to life in his 1799 novel, *Arthur Mervyn, or, Memoirs of the Year 1793.* Like most Philadelphians, most of Brown's characters mistakenly believe that the disease is contagious, which causes them, in their fright, to flee the city. Brown's novel vividly describes the roads leading from Philadelphia clogged with terrified refugees: "Families of weeping mothers, and dismayed children, attended with a few pieces of indispensable furniture, were carried in vehicles of every form. The parent or husband had perished; and the price of some moveable, or the pittance handed forth by public charity, had been expended to purchase the means of retiring from this theatre of disasters; though uncertain and hopeless of accommodation in the neighbouring districts."

In the city, the title character overhears two men, going door to door in search of dead bodies to haul away, talking about their last pick-up: "Damn it, it wasn't right to put him in his coffin before the breath was fairly gone. I thought the last look he gave me, told me to stay a few minutes." "Pshaw! He could not live. The sooner dead the better for him; as well as for us."[11]

Houses are left open to looters who steal furniture and jewelry from under the noses of people on their deathbeds. Arthur Mervyn, searching for the effects of a certain Wallace, which he wishes to return to Wallace's family, wanders through a deserted house, noting evidence of what had passed the previous evening: "The bed appeared as if some one had recently been dragged from it. The sheets were tinged with yellow, and with that substance which is said to be characteristic of the disease, the gangrenous or black vomit." At that moment, a "ghost-like" footstep is heard: "The door opened, and a figure glided in. [Wallace's] portmanteau dropped from my arms, and my heart's-blood was chilled. If an apparition of the dead were possible, and that possibility I would not deny, this was such an apparition. A hue, yellowish and livid; bones, uncovered with flesh; eye, ghastly, hollow, woe-begone, and fixed in an agony of wonder upon me."[12]

It is Wallace, a miraculous survivor of both the fever and the hospital at Bush Hill. Mervyn and the novel's frame narrator, a physician, know that yellow fever is not transmitted by contact with the sick (though neither they nor their author Brockden Brown had any idea that it was transmitted by mosquitoes) and thus bravely do what's right to their fellow man while all around them are either fleeing for their lives or looting the homes of those who have fled. Such is the terror that Brown is easily able to carry off a fully fledged gothic novel with no crumbling castle or secret passages, only ordinary colonial homes on Chestnut, Walnut, and Market Streets: "The door was ajar; and the light within was perceived. My belief, that those within were dead, was presently confuted by a sound."[13]

We don't know what the Gallaudets did during the fall of 1793. They likely believed, as most Presbyterians did, that the epidemic was God's punishment for the Sabbath-breaking, theater-going, and deism-proclaiming residents of the city. Indeed, Elihu Palmer was blinded by his bout with the fever, which the devout claimed was divine retribution, although Palmer used his new condition to effect in presenting himself as the blind man who yet could see through the flimsy claims of church. Jane and Peter Wallace Gallaudet must have thanked God that none of their children succumbed — and patted themselves on the back for having safely ensconced themselves in the church the previous year. P. W. Gallaudet (thus did he style himself professionally, though he was always known as Wallace) may have stayed in the city along with other merchants to refute the suspicion that trade was to blame. Whether he had the wherewithal to send his wife, who would have been pregnant with Catherine, and two small sons, Thomas Hopkins and Charles, to friends in the country or even to Jane's family in Hartford, whether Jane and her children found themselves on the road fruitlessly seeking lodgings, or whether they all stayed in the city behind locked doors and shuttered windows eating down their larder, whatever they did would have been one of Gallaudet's earliest memories. In 1810, Gallaudet would tell a friend that during a later epidemic of 1797, the family rented lodgings in Lancaster.[14] His silence on the more severe epidemic of 1793 may suggest that they stayed in the city. Epidemics recurred in Philadelphia seven times over the next fifteen years, threatening the city's survival as an urban center.[15] P. W.'s business prospects must have dimmed after each outbreak.

In 1794, the first part of Thomas Paine's refutation of the Bible as divine revelation, *The Age of Reason,* appeared in Philadelphia, as elsewhere, and with the newly established French Directory, French deistical books became available in translation. The French were already suspect among many Anglo-Philadelphians for what appeared to be their role in the yellow fever epidemic — post hoc, propter hoc: the fever had arrived on the heels of the French refugees from Haiti, who appeared to be immune. Brockden Brown criticizes this belief when he has a character justify himself on these grounds for leaving a young French woman next door to bury her father alone in her backyard.[16] But the xenophobic hysteria was only beginning. When Volney, who had argued in his 1791 *The Ruins, or, A Meditation on the Revolutions of Empire,* that no religion based on revelation could withstand scrutiny by reason, arrived in Philadelphia as a diplomat for the Directory, President Adams was sure that he was a spy. The Alien and Sedition Acts were signed into law in 1798, and with the arrival of Irish radicals fleeing their failed uprising that year, paranoia over Catholic immigration was in full swing.

In 1799, Washington died at Mount Vernon, and in 1800 the federal government left for Washington City. It is not known why P. W. Gallaudet moved his family to Hartford that same year. His wife was a native of the city, a daughter of sea captain Thomas Hopkins who had plied the West Indies line and a descendant of the same founder-generation stock as virtually every other white resident of Hartford. They had been married in Hartford, in the Center Church by the Rev. Nathan Strong ten months before Gallaudet's birth, and Jane must have found Philadelphia, with its endless round of atheism and epidemics, unnerving.[17] As well, everyone knew that the way to escape yellow fever epidemics was to get away from the coast, and Hartford was far enough up the Connecticut River to be spared. Washington Irving, for example, was sent as a boy from his home in Manhattan in 1798 to Tarrytown, twenty-five miles up the Hudson, to escape yellow fever (and there encountered the Dutch folklore that inspired so much of his later writing), and the Gallaudets may well have had something like this in mind for all their children.

On the other hand, it's hard to see how P. W. could have moved his business so far inland. P. W.'s account book and the newspaper ads he placed show that a least a sizable portion of his rather miscellaneous commissions, which included cloth, nails, snuff, and the odd harpsichord, was in slave-grown Caribbean sugar and sugar's distilled product, rum.[18] This trade was also conducted in Hartford, which is situated at the head of the navigable stretch of the Connecticut River. However, international cargo passed through Hartford only after transfer at ports more accessible to the Atlantic. The most likely explanation for his move is that his business in Philadelphia had failed and he was seeking a healthful location from which to reestablish it, albeit on a somewhat more modest scale. But exactly in what trade P. W. engaged in Hartford is unknown.

What can be safely surmised about the Gallaudets in Hartford is that they were snubbed. It would not be fair to argue from the lack of any ephemeral evidence like invitations to dine or drink tea with this or that leading family. However, when in 1814, local mogul Daniel Wadsworth established an invitation-only school for girls in his mother's mansion, taught by Lydia Huntley (soon to become internationally known as the poet and essayist Mrs. Sigourney), he invited all three daughters of the not particularly wealthy physician Mason Fitch Cogswell, one of whom was deaf, but did not invite Gallaudet's younger sister, who was of an age with the Cogswell girls and lived next door to them. Little Jane Gallaudet didn't even make Wadsworth's waiting list. Why Mrs. Gallaudet's family would have been treated like this can be surmised: ability to pay was not the criterion that put a girl on Wadsworth's invitation list, but rather, as Lydia Sigourney would later explain, "similarity of station." Mrs. Gallaudet may have been a direct descendent of at least two of the original hundred settlers who followed the Rev. Thomas Hooker west and were gathered in Hartford as the First Church — in fact, she was descended from Hooker himself — but her husband was, in the eyes of Hartford, a man of question-able origins, most likely seen as an odd duck to boot.[19]

The surname Gallaudet was enough of a stigma in a town otherwise peopled with the families bearing the names of English Puritans. Hart-ford residents had likely never met a descendant of French Huguenots, or realized that the Huguenots were as much followers of John Calvin's theological doctrines as the Puritans were. And although P. W. was active as treasurer and accountant in the Center Church, as the First Church came to be called, and bought a half-share in a pew when the new brick meeting house was built in 1807,[20] he was perhaps by now too demonstratively pious. His personal commitment to temperance was so "rigid," in the words of William A. Alcott, a friend of his famous son who could only have had the story from Thomas Hopkins Gallaudet himself, that "he abstained even from animal food."[21] P. W. would not have been the only man in Hartford advocating temperance while living off the rum trade, but it's not likely that there were many other vegetarians in the city in those years. A few decades later, vegetarianism would become something of a fad in Massachusetts, but for Connecticut Congregationalists of 1800, abstaining from animal food was unorthodox. Worse, with regard to eccentricity, P. W. was depressive, and his piety took the form of prostrate ramblings as he spent many hours, at least in the later years for which we have diaries, pouring his heart and soul onto page after page after page — he even "crossed" his pages, turning the book ninety degrees when a page was full and writing at right angles across what he had written — in attempts to understand a Bible verse or descry God's plan for him and in lamenting outright that depression kept him in bed from afternoon to late morning.[22] The diaries are distressingly pathetic to read today and must surely have been excessive even by the standards of the day. Such religious and moral excesses, insofar as they were public knowledge, would have been regarded by the Hartford and the Center Church elite as unseemly.

Perhaps the Hartford beau monde was right to be suspicious, for the Gallaudets had not always been Calvinists, and their byzantine history of religious affiliations over centuries of displacement goes some way toward fleshing out the facts of both the father's and the son's overzealous piety and inflexible commitment to the doctrines of the Reformed denominations, as well as the intense struggles with religious doubts each experienced before finally entering the church. As for Gallaudet's later stands against Episcopalians and Catholics, his casual exclusion of Jews from consideration for civic life, and the compromises with Baptists and Methodists that he would make as principal of the American Asylum for the Education and Instruction of the Deaf and Dumb, a look back into family history is instructive.[23]

When P. W. and Jane Gallaudet joined the Second Presbyterian Church in Philadelphia in 1792, their oldest son was four, so there is no doubt about his having been reared from earliest memory in the Calvinist tradition. Philadelphia's Second Presbyterian was known for its "well-ordered" revivals, the pastor, Ashbel Green, employing effective but not "excitable" methods of moving his auditors to repentance and conversion, very like the Gallaudets' Hartford pastor Nathan Strong. We know, therefore, that Gallaudet was raised in the evangelical branch of American Calvinism.[24] But while his mother had been born into a centuries-long line of Calvinists, his father had not.

P. W.'s father, Thomas Gallaudet (no middle name), a tobacconist in New York, bequeathed to his son his own copy of the Anglican Book of Common Prayer, described in P. W.'s will as the "Common Prayer Book of the Episcopal Church, with my Father's name Thomas Gallaudet on the cover." Supporting this evidence that P. W.'s father was an Anglican rather than a Presbyterian is an 1825 letter from a second cousin of Gallaudet, Peter Lewis De St. Croix, in which the writer says this about his grandmother Leah Gallaudet, sister of the Thomas Gallaudet in question: "My grandmother Leah was a strict Episcopalian, so strict that she could hardly admit any other denomination to be orthodox." Leah and her brother Thomas were the children of the Huguenot immigrant Pierre Elisée Gallaudet, and it would seem illogical for someone who fled his homeland because of his Calvinist beliefs to then bring up his family in America in the Church of England, a much different tradition in Protestantism that is much closer to the Roman Church he had fled, but that seems to have been the case.[25] There are numerous examples of Huguenot immigrants converting to the Anglican Church in America when they left their settlement, New Rochelle, for Manhattan.[26] In any case, this Thomas Gallaudet, who wrote his name on his Book of Common Prayer and was the brother of the ultraorthodox Episcopalian Leah, was buried in the "Old Brick Presbyterian Church Yard on Beeckman Street" in New York, while his wife, P. W.'s mother, was buried in her family plot in the "Presbyterian Church Yard, Woodbridge, N.J." It looks, then, as though Thomas joined the Presbyterians as an adult, very possibly in connection with his marriage.[27]

Going back another generation, we find the expected church of the Huguenots, the Reformed Church of France. The father of Thomas Gallaudet, Pierre Elisée (Peter Elisha)[28] Gallaudet, had been born in Mauzé-sur-le-Mignon, a small town near the Atlantic coast of France twenty miles east of La Rochelle, about 1690. He left his homeland in 1711 with other Huguenots and sailed to America, where he was a founder of New Rochelle. So far, all this agrees with Gallaudet family tradition: the Huguenot Pierre Elisée emigrates to America, his American son is raised as an Anglican (this passed over silently but never denied), but marries a Presbyterian and returns at some point to the Reformed Church (Presbyterian rather than Reformed Church of France, but close enough), and his grandson Peter Wallace lives and dies a Presbyterian.[29]

What did not make it into family tradition was that Pierre Elisée's grandfather back in France was one Isaac Galladite, who appears to have been a Sephardic Jew — that is to say, descended from Jews who had fled the Iberian Peninsula in or soon after the 1490s. The surname Gallaudet is not French, as is usually supposed, but rather Breton, a Celtic language long spoken in Brittany; considering Isaac Galladite's origins, it is probably a translation of a Sephardic surname.[30] Isaac's son Josué (Joshua) Gallaudet had been baptized in a Catholic church in Mauzé as an infant and thus was assuredly a Catholic at the time he converted to the French Reformed Church, but previous generations, according to Robert Munro Erwin, another descendant of Pierre Elysée, were members of a small synagogue in Brittany. Erwin says that the names Josué, Jacob, and Joseph Galladite, as well as Isaac, appear as members of this synagogue.[31] It is not clear how this could have been so, as Jews had been expelled from Brittany in 1240 and did not (openly) return until the eighteenth century, but if the Galladite family indeed came to Brittany directly from Spain or Portugal around the turn of the sixteenth century, they would have come as conversos and would have lived in Brittany in the sixteenth century as crypto-Jews. There are two known Jewish grave stones from the sixteenth century found in Brittany, dated 1574 and 1594, and giving the names, on the one, Solomon son of Jacob, and, on the other, Isaac of Leon.[32] It's unlikely that Solomon and Isaac were strangers merely passing through when they died — how would anyone have known that one was from Leon and the other was a son of Jacob? The Galladite ancestors Josué, Jacob, Joseph, and Isaac were contemporaries of these two, and they bear Hebrew names that would have been extraordinary, if not impossible, in Catholic France. But Isaac Galladite married a Catholic, only to see his son Josué renounce the Roman church for French Calvinism and his grandson Pierre Elisée emigrate to New York, where he raised an Anglican family.

This history of ever-changing religious affiliation is not unusual in American families, nor is the forgotten, then shockingly rediscovered Jew in the family tree, but then it is extremely unlikely that Thomas Hopkins Gallaudet had any inkling of his Jewish forebears. The string of Hebrew names among Gallaudet's pre-Protestant ancestors — Isaac, Josué/Joshua, and indeed Elisée/Elisha — is a tip-off to us that these ancestors were not the Catholic Frenchmen they were purported to have been, but it perhaps would not have been so obvious to anyone immersed, as Gallaudet was, in an Old Testament–based theocracy like Connecticut's, where the given names Ashbel, Barzillai, Eliphalet, and Elihu were to be found in the same families as Thomas, John, George, and Charles. Had he known all this, would he have been so eager, thirty or forty years after his arrival in Hartford as an under-grown boy, to want to block immigration on the basis of religious affiliation, or to deport Americans on the basis of complexion? But he did know much of the story, and he clearly wanted to pull the ladder up behind his great-grandfather.

So the Gallaudets arrived in Hartford traumatized and probably broke, and although they joined the Center Church they were not otherwise greeted with open arms. And what did Hartford look like to the Presbyterian child from Philadelphia, Thomas Hopkins Gallaudet? For one thing, a sea change in men's fashion had just been getting underway in Philadelphia, where a few bold men were wearing long trousers and their natural hair, having shockingly discarded their wigs and hair powder. None of this would have been evident in Hartford, where men like the Gallaudets' new neighbor Dr. Cogswell continued to wear knee breeches and silk hose through the 1820s. Women's fashion, too, had undergone a remarkable change in Philadelphia, with the Revolutionary-era woman's décolletage (filled in with a scarf), the voluminous skirts, the stays, the high-heeled shoes, and the huge mob caps giving way to a simpler empire-waist gown, but that was surely not yet true in Hartford. The men and women, boys and girls Gallaudet met in school and in church would have looked quite old-fashioned to him. He would rail against fashion for his whole life and dress himself always in somber black.

Meals, too, even for the rich, were still as unvaried in Hartford as they had been everywhere in colonial times. Salt beef was boiled with root vegetables, dried beans were boiled with onion and salt pork, and Indian pudding — cornmeal mush served with molasses — was ubiquitous. Farmers brought seasonal produce to residential neighborhoods in carts, as Hawthorne describes in *The House of the Seven Gables:* "the countryman's cart of vegetables, plodding from door to door, with long pauses of the patient horse while his owner drove a trade in turnips, carrots, summer-squashes, string-beans, green peas, and new potatoes, with half the house wives of the neighborhood."[33] Hartford housewives purchased their beef and pork in bulk in the fall and butchered, salted, or smoked it at home. Baking was done either without any leavening at all, resulting in an awfully hard cookie or corn pone, or with homegrown yeast, which took twenty-four hours and involved hops, malt, rye, and molasses. In *Seven Gables*, as late as 1850 when the novel is set, Hepzibah Pyncheon is discombobulated when a customer expects to buy yeast at her shop. It's easy to see why families would employ a cook if they could afford it, for feeding a family was not a matter of airy dumplings or flakey biscuits: it was a lot of heavy lifting.

P. W. surely employed — or, in Philadelphia, owned — a black woman to cook for the family.

Throughout the first two decades of Gallaudet's life in Hartford, all this home mush making, meat salting, bean boiling, and yeast growing would give way to something new: groceries. By the 1830s, one could buy not only the usual salt, sugar, molasses, tea, and coffee, but also white and whole-grain wheat flour, oranges, lemons, olives, figs, and raisins, all available year-round, which would prompt Gallaudet, in 1835, to warn darkly against unnamed "luxurious dainties" and "curiously compounded preparations." The colonial diet he encountered in Hartford in 1800 was what his household ate until the family broke up after his death from dysentery, a diarrheal disease caused by contamination of a family's backyard well by their backyard privy. Small lot sizes and the poor understanding of infectious disease made contaminated water commonplace, and the temperance movement eliminated the traditional options of far safer beer and cider. Dysentery was a fact of life — or of death — for those with feeble immune systems, as Gallaudet's clearly was.[34]

P. W. Gallaudet was in Hartford for the opportunities he believed it would offer in trading on commission, and trade was indeed still the major source of income in Hartford, as it was in all American cities at this time. It would not be long before manufacturing and, especially, banking and insurance, would become Hartford's economic engine, but these were as yet in their infancies. Jeremiah Wadsworth had a woolen mill in the city, but Samuel Colt would not open his gun factory in Hartford until 1848. The Hartford Bank had been incorporated in 1792, with Wadsworth as the largest subscriber,[35] to handle exchanges in bank notes and different specie, of which there were still many. And there was a county jail to handle debtors. Built in 1793 at the western end of Pearl Street, the jail had a tavern on the second floor for use by the more respectable prisoners. Gallaudet would one day preach in this jail.[36] The Hartford Fire Insurance Co. (later the Hartford), would be organized in 1810 with Eliphalet Terry as president and Nathaniel Terry, Henry Hudson, and Daniel Wadsworth among the directors — the latter three would also be directors of Gallaudet's school. But P. W. Gallaudet would have been only minimally aware of where the 1 percent was putting its money.

What was visible to any resident was the steady stream of farm wagons bringing flour, corn, potatoes, onions, salted beef, and barrel staves overland to Hartford to be shipped to the West Indies, where the food would provide enslaved Africans with a coarse diet and the staves would be made into barrels to ship island rum. It was also easy to see that manufactured goods imported from England — including such gewgaws as fans, earrings, toothpowder, cotton and silk cloth, as well as essentials like paper, sealing wax, buttons and buckles, forks, knives, scissors, nails, fishhooks, hammers, screws, shovels, shot and powder, sugar and tea — were also unloaded in Hartford for retail distribution in city shops and farther inland. Advertisements in Hartford newspapers trumpeted these items for sale on "Jew Street," which cannot be identified today but which suggests that Jews, who, the state supposed in 1818, had never officially resided in Connecticut, had in fact traded here in colonial times.[37] (Unless, indeed, the street was named with the epithet, already in use for two hundred years, for traders who drive hard bargains.) P. W. must have carved out a place for himself in this trade.

Hartford did not readily admit to having a demographic living in poverty (although it did), but it could not deny that it had a small number of residents of African ancestry, and these were uniformly poor. There were no educated black leaders like James Forten, Absolom Jones, and Richard Allen, who made Philadelphia a center for abolition and civil rights in the early years of the century. Already in 1787, when Allen and Jones were told to sit in the church balcony of St. George's Methodist Church where they were members, they walked out and formed a mutual aid society for black churches that became the African Methodist Episcopal (A.M.E.) denomination in 1816. In contrast, black members of Hartford's Center Church, who had sat with their owners while still enslaved but were banished to the balcony at emancipation, did not make any effort on their own behalf until 1819 — when they moved to the church basement. A ban on the importation of enslaved persons had been in place since 1774, but well into the 1820s they were still legally sold off the auction block on New Haven's Center Green.[38] P. W. would have been accustomed, in Philadelphia, to hiring other people's slaves or black day laborers when he needed them to haul the merchandise he was buying for resale. In Hartford, he may have found a tighter market due to the smaller demographic. White day laborers, if he had to resort to such, would have been an additional expense for him.

For Hartford residents white and black, public life would have been very dull by Philadelphia standards. There were two public holidays: the Fourth of July and Washington's birthday, both celebrated in Hartford with sedate public lectures. Thanksgiving was a state holiday in Connecticut and Massachusetts, celebrated privately by families. Christmas and Easter were not celebrated at all: the state-established Congregational Church regarded celebration of the birth or resurrection of Jesus as Roman Catholic practices and passed over these days in silence. We will see Gallaudet making a regular diary entry on December 25, 1810, from the road in western Pennsylvania, with no mention of the day's significance elsewhere in Christendom.[39]

In Hartford, a theater built in 1795 and offering three shows a week had kept its offerings and audiences in good order and had been patronized by "respectable" people, but in 1800 the state legislature prohibited theatrical performances, along with circuses, traveling jugglers, acrobats, and the like, and the building would thereafter be used for lectures. P. W. Gallaudet would not have patronized dramatic productions in Philadelphia, of course, and he would have been as innocent of the theater as Jethro Coffin, the Nantucket trader in the 1835 novel *Miriam Coffin, or, The Whale-Fishermen*, who receives an invitation in London, along with the playbill, to attend the evening's performance and imagines the playbill to be an invoice, the address to be a warehouse, and the curious goods offered for sale to be paintings. It's not until he arrives at the theater that he realizes he's in "the very temple of Sathanas — the playhouse of Beelzebub!" Jethro figures he might as well stay for the show; P. W. would surely have hotfooted it right out of there.[40]

In the first decade of the nineteenth century, as throughout the eighteenth, there was not much to read in Hartford other than the Bible and religious works such as John Bunyan's 1678 *Pilgrim's Progress*, which, as we learn in *Little Women*, was still wildly popular among the generation of Gallaudet's children. If one had more intellectual interests, there were books of history (but not that infidel Gibbon!) and the poetry of Milton and Pope. By the 1810s and 1820s, newspapers and magazines to suit every taste were widely available, and even respectable people would drop their guard to the extent of enjoying the novels of Walter Scott and James Fenimore Cooper. Before those decades, though, one had to go out of state to purchase the masterpieces of English fiction. Samuel Richardson's novel of seduction, *Pamela; or, Virtue Rewarded* was the first book that the journalist Benjamin Franklin ever printed, and even the most pious parents in most parts of the United States permitted their daughters to read both "the Holy bible and *Clarissa Harlowe*," another Richardson novel of seduction that ends in the instructive death of the heroine.[41] Matthew Lewis's anti-Catholic novel *The Monk* (1796) had started a rage for the gothic, picked up by Philadelphia novelist Brockden Brown, and the picaresque and satiric novels of Henry Fielding were perennially popular, especially with male readers. But all that was elsewhere.

Connecticut residents steered clear of fiction because they believed that reading a novel was "like falling asleep in a snowdrift"; it "destroy[ed] the power of the mind for any strong and useful exercise."[42] Worse, novels implanted false ideas about life. These views were so widespread and so often articulated by Gallaudet that we can safely assume that he never read an actual novel, and what's more, that the literary culture in which he was educated was so full of holes that he remained blissfully ignorant his whole life of the import of much of the literature he *did* read. We will see Gallaudet making a major gaffe in a Yale commencement speech about a Shakespearean play he knew only from bowdlerized excerpts, and it seems pretty clear that no one in the audience of parents and state-established clergy would have caught his gross misinterpretation. Even with literary texts of approved morality that Gallaudet and his peers were permitted to read whole, knowledge of a wider literary culture was often crucial to even basic comprehension. When in Goldsmith's 1766 *Vicar of Wakefield,* for example, Olivia is said to be "very well skilled in controversy" because she has read "the disputes between Thwackum and Square," the reader must know that Thwackum, Square, and their disputes were created by Henry Fielding in *Tom Jones* as objects of satire. If the reader does not know that, then he fails to grasp Goldsmith's meaning: Olivia is *not* familiar with disputation. Gallaudet quite literally had no idea what he was missing — and misunderstanding — in favorite books such as *The Vicar.* Until his dying day, he continued to assert that novels had no place in a family library because they fail "to sustain the cause of truth, uprightness, and industry."[43] He did not similarly warn against Shakespeare's oeuvre, but surely only because he never suspected what his plays were actually about.

Poetry was acceptable everywhere in Connecticut, and even the English Romantics Wordsworth and Coleridge, whose *Lyrical Ballads* had appeared in 1798, were popular in some circles. Far more popular in the state, however, was the poetry of Yale president Timothy Dwight and his cohort, the Hartford Wits, who objected to the Romantics and consciously harked back to the Augustan writers of a century past: Pope, Dryden, and

Swift. Seemingly every educated man in Connecticut wrote such poetry, and Gallaudet himself did so throughout his life. Dr. Mason Fitch Cogswell, the Gallaudets' new neighbor in Hartford, had been one of the minor Wits before his 1800 marriage. It's unlikely that young Gallaudet knew of Cogswell's anonymous contributions to satires published in Hartford newspapers before his family moved to the city, but the social assumptions of the Hartford elite who snubbed the Gallaudets were reflected in — and to some extent shaped by — this literary work. Furthermore, Dr. Cogswell's character, tastes, politics, and cultural mindset were to assume such vast importance in Gallaudet's venture into deaf education as to make his poems worth a look.

Between 1791 and 1798, five of the Wits — Richard Alsop, Theodore Dwight, and the physicians Lemuel Hopkins, Elihu Hubbard Smith, and Mason Fitch Cogswell — were gleefully collaborating on a twenty-number run of poems that they called *The Echo,* in which they mocked those leery of scientific progress — one number hilariously ridicules a state resident's claim to have disproven Newton's law of universal gravitation — and counterintuitively from our perspective loudly declaimed regressive political and cultural ideologies, inveighing against democracy as "hostile to good government" and Romanticism as simply the uncultivated taste of low-life rhymesters.[44] They called their verses satires, but these pieces were mostly vicious ad hominem mockeries of named individuals whose political visions ran counter to those of Connecticut's Yale-educated ruling class. "Echo No. 10," a piece for which we have indubitable evidence of Cogswell's collaboration,[45] ridicules Virginians as descendants of "Pokahontas, a celebrated Squaw," and excoriates John Hancock, at the time governor of Massachusetts, for having hosted an Equality Ball to which free blacks were invited. The connection between Hancock's Equality Ball and Pocahontas appears tenuous to our eyes, but it was clear to the Connecticut readers of *The Echo:* this all added up to racial "amalgamation," which was everything from socializing to marrying across racial lines, as both cause and outcome of coddling democrats and poor people. Cogswell and his collaborators appended a footnote in which they dilate on the odor of persons of African ancestry and the degrading speech patterns they were alleged to use: "Ah! Massa Gubbernur! . . . Me grad to see you," a character they call "Cuffey" is made to say to Governor Hancock.[46]

The Echo was the last, inglorious gasp of the Connecticut literati, and the

Wits had all moved on from humor to scolding, if they were still writing at all — Cogswell, for his part, wrote only for medical journals after his marriage. By the turn of the nineteenth century, Connecticut understood literature's job to be unambiguous didacticism. Gallaudet would not have thought *The Vicar of Wakefield* suitable for his own children because it leaves readers to figure out on their own which way the satire is cutting, and one needed a Yale degree to that! But even a Yale degree did not avail Gallaudet in regard to this slippery text. In a letter to Yale professor James L. Kingsley, Gallaudet shows that he seriously misunderstood Goldsmith's passage on how an ill turn always seems much worse at first than it will later appear because one's mind's eye becomes accustomed to the new gloom. Again, he could have had no idea how severely he was hampered by the ideologically imposed deficiency of his cultural tool chest.[47]

One day's boat ride down the Connecticut and west through the Long Island Sound would have brought any Hartford resident to New York, where, in 1802, Washington Irving launched a satiric column as Jonathan Oldstyle. Quite unlike the *Echo* collaborators, "Oldstyle" satirized the social institutions taken for granted by churches and middle-class residents, including even the subjugation of women in marriage — a topic also taken up in Philadelphia by Brockden Brown. Gallaudet, as we shall see, would later refer to even the mildest emancipation of married women as "disgusting." Irving's column would have been unthinkable in 1802 Hartford, but elsewhere it made a big splash, attracting even the out-of-town interest of Brockden Brown, who hoped to steal Oldstyle for his own Philadelphia magazine. In fact, the bolder Irving became in his satire and japes, the more the New York public ate it up. To create some buzz for his first book, *The History of New York*, which he wrote under the name Diedrich Knicker-bocker, Irving placed phony missing-person ads in New York newspapers for this supposed historian, and the public fell hard for the hoax, then laughed at the stunt and bought the book. All this is to say that we of the present day are separated from young Thomas Hopkins Gallaudet and the Hartford society in which he lived not only by two centuries but also by the sometimes unfathomably and often deeply disturbing set of regressive principles that he and his cohort held.

Arriving in Hartford, young Thomas (was he ever called Tom?) found a city far less diverse and far more monolithically Presbyterian than Philadelphia, for, although the Calvinist devout constituted the same small minority in Hartford that they did in Philadelphia, here they were legally established by the state constitution and thus controlled city government and kept the public atmosphere to their liking. It took a year or two for young Gallaudet to settle into this strange new world. He was never an athlete — he liked battledore and probably ice-skated but never engaged in anything more strenuous — and was definitely not the studious type, although that may have been only because he was too advanced for the curriculum on offer at Hartford Grammar School. Still, he definitely wasn't a reader, nor was he much interested in religion. The scraps of evidence we have from these years show him, instead, playing parlor games and generally goofing off. In the undated poem "On Chess," he lists riddles, jokes, ice-skating, dancing, backgammon, speculation, whist, and chess as enjoyable pastimes. He could later disapprove of most of these and would proscribe many for his children, so it's surprising to see that at one time in his life he approved even of speculation — a simple, low-stakes kind of poker with a trump suit that was especially popular with ladies but increasingly frowned upon by respectable people. In an 1800 novel, *Julia and the Illuminated Baron* by Maine author Sally Sayward Wood, the heroine's virtuous lover is aghast to see Boston women at a card table, "occup[ying] their time . . . in this shameful manner."[48] In Jane Austen's *Mansfield Park* (1813), the dastardly Henry Crawford, shamelessly flirting with our heroine Fanny Price, attempts "to inspirit her play, sharpen her avarice, and harden her heart" in a game of speculation.[49] In contrast, the young Gallaudet has nothing but good-natured smiles for ladies who speculate at cards: "'who bids ladies' - six Sir — 'here' — / Bless me, 'tis but a deuce; How hard."[50]

An undated personal essay tells us a bit about his boyhood outside of school: "I used to steal away from my companions, and find out a lonely spot in the fields or woods where we were sporting, and seating myself under the shade of some venerable tree, and drawing a thousand strange figures in the sand before me, and ever and anon whistling a simple air of the nursery, give up my youthful fancy to any drams of future happiness or greatness, which it might choose to form."[51]

Whatever Gallaudet's difficulties accommodating himself to Hartford life, he became accustomed to it quickly enough that by the time he entered Yale at the end of 1802 as a sophomore, he was a model Yankee.

GALLAUDET'S CAREER as a reformer was shaped by the worldview and guiding principles of the end-stage Puritan society that he first met in Hartford as a boy and that he adopted as his own at Yale College. Or, perhaps more precisely stated, it was his outsider status to this worldview and these guiding principles and his consequent convert's zeal that shaped his career. At the heart of this society were the Calvinist doctrines preached by its Congregational churches, so called because each had been, originally, answerable only to its congregation. In Connecticut, church and state had always worked hand in glove: the seventeenth-century colonial churches had determined which of the male members of the community were eligible for the franchise and had run the elections for township governments, while the post-Revolution state built the churches and paid the clergy, assigning them governmental powers. It was the role of the clergy in state government that made Connecticut not just a state with an officially established church but a true theocracy. By the turn of the nineteenth century, Connecticut's Congregational churches were subject to a state association of ministers and were frequently referred to, for this reason, as Presbyterian. Hartford had four churches: two Congregational/Presbyterian, one Baptist, and one Episcopal. Property-owning members of the Baptist and Episcopal churches could apply for the franchise and for exemptions to the state taxation for support of the Congregational clergy and meeting houses, and that's about as far as freedom of religion went in 1800 Connecticut.[1]

Six thousand residents, four churches: it doesn't take a lot of math to see that a very large majority of Hartford residents were not attending church at all. Despite establishment, Connecticut's rate of church membership was about the same as those of states without established churches: about 12 percent of Americans belonged to a church at the time of the Revolution.[2] In Hartford, however, unlike in Philadelphia, the unchurched 88 percent did not leave much of a public record, for the Congregationalists controlled every aspect of city life. It was the time of the Second Great Awakening, but Connecticut's revivals were "calm" — no unseemly enthusiasm was tolerated — and were led by its settled pastors, for the itinerant preachers active elsewhere were regarded threats to public order and run out of the state.[3] That revivals of any sort took place at all, however, is odd, because the bedrock notion of the revival — that salvation is granted by divine grace to individual sinners when they profess their faith in Christ's atonement — is irreconcilable with Calvin's predestination doctrine, which had been a keystone of the Congregational churches since the arrival of the Mayflower. This was the first step on the slippery slope that should have been evident during Gallaudet's lifetime: revivals resulted in the fading away of Calvin's soteriology, which in turn bled academic theology of its rigor, resulting finally in the clergy's loss of their accustomed pride of place among the educated elite. Not that anyone at the time saw what was happening. Gallaudet's pastor in Hartford, Nathan Strong, and his mentor at Yale, Timothy Dwight, both died before the church was disestablished; survivors, including Gallaudet, simply proceeded as though nothing in particular had changed.

But in the first decade of the century, the established clergy were still the gatekeepers to public offices and a legal counterweight to democracy such as it was under Connecticut's limited franchise — the white male residents who met the franchise requirements and were able to spend a full day casting their votes in any given election typically comprised less than 10 percent of the population. The state was easily managed, therefore, by the so-called Standing Order of established clergy and the Yale men they boosted into monopolized public offices. Liberty was understood in New England to be restrained by "equitable laws, and by the religion of the scriptures."[4] Against this Standing Order, neither Episcopalians, who did not regard Calvinist doctrines as "the religion of the scriptures," nor Jeffersonian Democratic-Republicans, who did not regard Connecticut's laws as "equitable," had as yet made so much as a dent.[5]

Federalist standard-bearer John Adams, in his fourth year as president, was immensely popular in Hartford for his support of the strong national government needed to protect New England's mercantile economy, but the party spirit, against which Washington had warned, was already firmly entrenched. Connecticut's Federalist Standing Order regarded the Democratic-Republicans as "infidels" who would welcome a French takeover of the United States. The Democratic-Republicans, who could be found in small numbers in New Haven, regarded the Federalists as admiring sycophants of Great Britain who planned to impose a monarchical government on the country. The presidential election of 1800, a rematch between Adams and Jefferson, was taking place through the spring, summer, and fall, each state on its own schedule. In Connecticut, however, hardly anyone was paying attention because electors were chosen by the state legislature, which answered to the Standing Order, not the voters.

HARTFORD

It would not be much of an exaggeration to say that for Hartford in 1800, the demonization of France had become the new patriotism. Every July 4th, the city celebrated the anniversary of the Declaration of Independence with a public lecture by a leading citizen, chosen by a committee of leading citizens, of course. In 1798, Theodore Dwight, a lawyer, a major contributor to *The Echo* (as discussed in the previous chapter), and close friend of Dr. Cogswell's, took the rostrum, where he tore straight into France and, for good measure, Franklin, Jefferson, Madison, the Bavarian Illuminati, "savage hordes" from Ireland, and the Jesuits. Dwight wrapped up his patriotic diatribe against toleration and accommodation with the usual comforting image of Connecticut: "Here every man is the sovereign proprietor of his little farm, and the happy master of his peaceful dwelling."[6]

The blithe assumption that the typical male resident owned his own prosperous farm was pure myth, the social reality for most families being rural poverty and high levels of out-migration for their children. But the rural poor, if any of them happened to be admitted to this celebratory oration, and the Standing Order alike would have responded to Dwight's paranoid tendency, because it was rooted in a pervasive culture of fear, shared by residents across class lines.[7]

A few months later, Nathan Strong of the First Church of Hartford preached a Thanksgiving sermon that was essentially a pulpit version of Dwight's oration — minus the Illuminati, which, because Strong is such a likeable character, one would like to think he found a bit over the top. Strong was earlier known for his "worldliness, wit, and social aptitudes" as well as his gin distillery, and at the turn of the century he was still "a man of wit and worldly taste" who wore his gray hair "turned back and rolled in waves upon his shoulders." He published two volumes of sermons, but his reputation as "a very able divine" lay more in his impressive delivery. It is evident, however, that he fell for Dwight's paranoid conspiracy theories hook, line, and sinker.[8]

Taking as his text Revelation 17:4, "And I heard another voice from heaven, saying, Come out of her, my people, that ye be not partakers of her sins, and that ye receive not of her plagues," Strong recast the apocalyptic warning given by Theodore Dwight in terms of the actual Apocalypse and the approaching Millennium, the thousand-year reign of peace preceding the return of Christ and the end of the world. The verse was a popular text to bolster just about any argument, perhaps the best known being the come-outer doctrine of William Lloyd Garrison's abolition campaign. Here, however, Strong uses it to warn that if the infidels — that is, the French and their American converts to deism — ever got ahold of our government, "America must drink the cup of Babylon."[9]

The following year, the city's July 4th oration was given by one William Brown, who fleshed out the warnings of Dwight and Strong with juicy details.[10] A scheme to revolutionize the entire world, Brown alleged, "was engendered in the malignant minds of a certain description of self-called philosophers, the zealous idolaters of vice, in all its hideous forms, and the determined foes to Christianity, in all its various denominations" — Brown is referring to the philosophers of the European Enlightenment. The plan, originated by Voltaire, is to "disturb . . . the established order of thought" by establishing "jacobinic clubs" in the United States, circulating seditious pamphlets, fomenting treasonous conspiracies and insurrections, profaning Washington and Adams, and so on. What Brown called the "jacobinic clubs" were the Democratic-Republican societies established to inform the public about the actions of government (newspapers had not yet taken over this job) and to bring the will of the people to bear on governmental policies. They had all but disappeared by the time of Brown's oration, but this did not stop Federalists from warning America about them.[11] By "seditious pamphlets," Brown meant pamphlets and newspaper articles arguing for the opposition view; for "conspiracies to treason," one can take one's pick, because the word "treason" appeared at any hint of opposition; "insurrections" referred to events like the Whiskey Rebellion of 1791, a tax protest staged by farmers in western Pennsylvania who found the whiskey tax unfair, and which Federalists saw as the result of "preaching up the rights of man."[12] The word "insurrection" was widely applied, however, like "treason," to any opposition to government policy. Presidents Washington and Adams both responded to "rebellions" like these with force, and seeing to it that the leaders were tried for treason.

William Brown sounds a lot like General Jack Ripper in *Dr. Strangelove* warning of the communist plot to fluoridate our drinking water, because like the fictive General Ripper, he saw every progressive cause as part of a grand conspiracy to undermine our national government. His conclusion, however, is truly bone-chilling today, though not in the sense he intended.

France, he asserts, plans to reach "the borders of Georgia or Carolina" with an army of Frenchmen and "furious Africans" to sack and burn villages and make American virgins "a prey to more than demoniac lust and barbarity," and he invites his audience to imagine "Frenchmen, mingled with negroes . . . joining in the impure and shocking death-dance of Africa."

NEW HAVEN

Yale president Timothy Dwight, brother of Hartford lawyer Theodore, was a Congregational minister whose church was the Yale College chapel. Here, he preached every Sunday to Yale students in mandatory attendance — over his career, that would be 1,301 students who heard him every week during their formative college years and, as one alumnus put it, "had their principles, literary, political, moral, and religious, settled for life."[13] Dwight was a major player in the American Counter-Enlightenment, instrumental in effecting the profound shift in American thought that would break the historical link between the new nation's founding principles and their historical roots in the Enlightenment. Counter-Enlightenment views presented as patriotism drew conservative Americans of every stripe, from pious Presbyterians to luddites and xenophobes, all under one big tent of paranoia. And although Dwight had supported the American Revolution, he was, by the time Gallaudet met him, a leading figure in the American Counter-Revolution, preaching that the Revolutionary cries of liberty and equality were but masks for a plot to annihilate "the right of property, marriage, natural affection, chastity, and decency," just as, he believed, they had been in France.[14]

Dwight's Counter-Revolutionary and Counter-Enlightenment efforts were on display in a sermon he gave in New Haven on July 4, 1798, the same day his brother was speaking in Hartford. "The Duty of Americans, at the Present Crisis" created a sensation far beyond the confines of Yale College in its claims that every alarming cultural manifestation from Diderot's *Encyclopédie* to American Freemasonry was part of a colossal plot perpetrated by the Bavarian Illuminati. The Illuminati conspiracy may seem a sideshow of passing social insanity, but it was at "the epicenter" of the American Counter-Revolution, the major vehicle of the reactionary worldview sweeping the nation.[15] As kooky as it looks, the putative conspiracy was a most serious affair, and because Dwight continued to harp on it well into the nineteenth century, it would have had a profound effect on the teenaged Thomas Hopkins Gallaudet.

According to Dwight, Adam Weishaupt, a professor at the University of Ingolstadt, created the Illuminati to overthrow all civil and religious institutions in the world and to bring mankind to believe that chastity was a groundless prejudice, adultery was lawful, and "the possession of property was . . . robbery." The Illuminati, Dwight avers, insinuated themselves as teachers, journal editors, booksellers, and printers of "obscene" books. In the 1960s, when Robert W. Welch Jr., alleged Illuminati infiltration into banking, communism, the IRS, and White House, he founded the John Birch Society; Dwight's remedy was even more radical, for he urged frightened Americans to observe the Sabbath and support the Adams administration's tax plans. This incendiary sermon closes on a personal note as, speaking of his family, Dwight declares that "I would far rather follow them one by one to an untimely grave, than to behold them, however prosperous, the victims of philosophism," a neat adumbration of the twentieth-century motto, "Better dead than Red."[16]

Today, we know that Weishaupt was a harmless eccentric with a messianic complex whose goals were the perfection of morals, human happiness, and the elimination of superstition and tyranny. But, lest we be too hard on Dwight, even Mary Shelley associated Weishaupt with unholy science experiments when she portrayed Victor Frankenstein's intention to "unfold to the world the deepest mysteries of creation" as having been taught by a chemistry professor at Ingolstadt.[17] In any case, Weishaupt's secret society cost him his university position and resulted in the proscription of his group in Bavaria. He was living in exile, and the erstwhile Illuminati had moved on to other interests, within just a few years of the secret society's founding, more than a decade before Dwight's sermon. It is true that at one point the Illuminati claimed six hundred members, including Goethe and, what's really interesting, the Swiss education reformer Pestalozzi, whose theories and practices would influence both Gallaudet and his father. One assumes they never suspected Pestalozzi's Illuminati past. But after 1785, Weishaupt, penning Illuminati apologetics in exile, was certainly the sole remaining Illuminatus.[18]

Fortunately for the credibility of this unlikely conspiracy theory, it depended not on the facts — there weren't any — but rather on the bizarre Francophobia we saw in the Hartford orations. In 1798, American cities on

the eastern seaboard were fortifying against an expected French invasion,
and Adams named Washington commander of the armed forces just in case.
Citizen Genêt, French ambassador to the United States, had attempted to
recruit American volunteers to fight against Great Britain and was thought
by many to be behind those pesky Democratic-Republican societies that
President Washington had taught citizens to see as un-American. And in
the end, Washington had given Genêt Asylum after all: he was now living
in New York, having suspiciously married a daughter of Governor Clinton.
Everywhere in Federalist New England there was fear of spies, secret agents,
and nefarious networks. There was talk about the Tub Plot, in which French
agents were said to have sailed to America with secret documents hidden in
false bottoms of two tubs, and about a tailor in Philadelphia who was making
large numbers of French uniforms to have them ready when France invaded.
It's no coincidence that Congress passed the Alien and Sedition Acts in
1798, and that President John Adams set about enforcing them selectively
against French residents and sympathizing Americans. In this atmosphere,
Dwight's assertions concerning a hitherto unknown secret society plotting
a French-fueled overthrow of the Congregational Church easily failed to
strike his listeners as ridiculous and, instead, created a sensation.

Dwight appears to us to have been unsinkable, but not everyone was
bamboozled. John Cossens Ogden, an Episcopal priest in Portsmouth, New
Hampshire, in a bitter satire of 1799 paradoxically entitled "A View of the
New-England Illuminati: Who Are Indefatigably Engaged in Destroying
the Religion and Government of the United States; under a Feigned Regard for Their Safety — and under an Impious Abuse of True Religion,"
referred to Dwight as the head of this network of secret clubs, the so-called
Ministers' Meetings, whose aim was to defeat religious toleration in the
United States. Ogden is particularly hard on Yale, which he says prosely-
tizes students, grants degrees to men who can't read Latin if their politics
are sufficiently orthodox, lines its pockets at the expense of public primary
education, and, despite being public property and a state institution, is
controlled by a corporation that meets in secret, names its own successors,
and answers to no one.

Abraham Bishop, also an Episcopal priest, was another critical voice sati-
rizing Dwight and the Yale establishment. Like Odgen, he complained about
public dollars going to privately controlled Yale and about the formation of
a church/state aristocracy kept in place through marriage and Yale degrees

handed out to the politically correct. Unlike Ogden, however, Bishop lived in New Haven, where, as collector of customs after 1800, he would pull down a salary nearly double that of Dwight's, and he had a platform at events sponsored by the tiny but growing Democratic-Republican party. His progressive ideas found little support, however: he was unsuccessful in his attempts to admit girls to New Haven's Hopkins Grammar School, and his support for the slave insurgents in Haiti actually provoked backlash against the uprising.[19]

Bishop's remarks on Dwight's Yale in his 1802 satire *Proofs of a Conspiracy* are well worth reading for the light they shed on P. W. Gallaudet's decision to send his oldest son to college there and on what happened to Gallaudet during his undergraduate years. Gallaudet was admitted to Yale the year these remarks were published.

> To gain the side of those men, who do not fight, but who plan engage-ments — of those who do not labor, but who enjoy in luxury, the fruits of labor, is considered here a great point gained. Parents are ambitious to place their sons in the way to attain this. Colleges are the fortresses, which command the entrance into this land of promise, and these have been mostly officered by church and state men from their institution. . . . It is a fact that the youth are sent there in order to prepare for success in this world, and *pious* parents consider an education given to a son, equal to a farm, or a trade, given to his brethren, and really, if the educated son succeeds, he will enter into the public field, which is in better cultivation, than the fields of his brethren. It will not be denied, that these colleges are now totally opposed to the general government [i.e., the Jefferson administration], and that thence have issued the most virulent attacks on the officers of it. It will not be denied, that officers of the church, and officers of the state, are associated at the head of them, and that these have been careful to support instructors, hostile to our present government. Under such auspices, a young man, without any appeal to his passions, is very likely to follow the track of his superiors. To him they appear to be men of the first magnitude, because of the narrow compass of his vision, none are greater. He imputes their elevation to the system which they have adopted. This fires his ambition. He sees these men connected with other great men in church and state — and that all the promotions, and honors of life are in their gift.[20]

Bishop, by the way, was a Yale alumnus himself, having graduated in 1778 with Noah Webster — and the renegade Hartford Wit, Joel Barlow.

Gallaudet entered Yale College as a sophomore at the start of the 1803 academic year, right about the time of his fourteenth birthday in December 1802 — the academic year ended in September, giving a long vacation in the autumn until lectures started again for the new year in the winter. Fourteen was not an unusual age at the time to start college — James Fenimore Cooper, who started the same year but as a freshman, was thirteen, but some, like John C. Calhoun, who had enrolled the previous year at age twenty, were grown men. At this time, Yale's admission requirements included demonstrated ability with Cicero and Virgil, the Greek New Testament, and arithmetic. Noah Webster had complained about the old-fashioned curriculum, exclaiming at the requirements in Greek and conic sections, "Life is too short!" By the time Gallaudet began at Yale, English had replaced Latin as the language of the classroom, but the classical curriculum was still undertaken by all students in its entirety. Only in their senior year did students read works written in English — by John Locke and William Paley.[21]

As yet, the college had no actual classrooms, so half Gallaudet's class of sophomores met in the library and the other half in a dormitory, Connecticut Hall. During Gallaudet's first year, however, the Connecticut Lyceum was built for class meetings. Tuition was $33 a year, plus $7.32 per quarter for room rental and sweeping of the rooms, which were "defaced and dirty," plus board, the charge for which is buried in time. In addition, there were fees assessed to students from time to time — when the catalogue needed to be printed or the yard cleaned — and there were fines for cutting classes (2¢) and being late (1¢), though these were perhaps rarely imposed. As modest as the fees appear, and although the college was subsidized by state taxes, many students had trouble meeting the cost and took long leaves of absence to earn money by teaching school. Gallaudet's father was at this time in "narrow pecuniary circumstances," but P. W. somehow found enough money for Gallaudet to matriculate at Yale for three years without any lapses.[22]

Like modern administrators today, the president was paid an outsize salary: $2,000 a year, which was double the salary of the governor of the state. Among the professors were President Dwight himself, who handled theology as well as administration; Jeremiah Day, professor of natural philosophy (physics) and mathematics; and Benjamin Silliman, who would be appointed professor of chemistry after he professed religion during an 1803

Yale College revival. Silliman had been something of a religious holdout and had even been regarded by some as a deist, but as soon as he made his public profession of belief President Dwight sent him to study chemistry at the University of Pennsylvania and made him a professor upon his return. Silliman lived outside New Haven on a farm he had inherited, complete with slaves to work it for him so that he could teach. Elizur Goodrich taught law, and although undergraduates would not have studied with him, he and Gallaudet became friends. Two tutors, Moses Stuart and David A. Sherman, bore much of the responsibility for hearing recitations and marking papers for the class of 1805.[23]

When Dwight succeeded to the presidency after the death of the (slightly) more open minded Ezra Stiles, he regarded "as his first task the eradication of the Enlightenment ideas and latitudinarian spirit so pervasive at Yale."[24] Even as a tutor, Dwight had been able to change student behavior by dropping Yale's system of fines and replacing it with fear: Dwight called his method "the system of a parental government.... I governed by the eye and the tongue."[25] As president, he banned amateur theatricals and rigidly enforced Sabbath observance. For amusement, there were still two debating societies — Gallaudet belonged to and became president of one, Brothers in Unity. Here he spoke to fellow students about the conscience, the Barbary pirates, and the emancipation of slaves; what he argued on these topics can only be guessed. His memorial doorway still stands in the Brothers in Unity Court. Phi Beta Kappa, of which Gallaudet was also a member, was active, and there were many other student societies formed for serious social, religious, musical, and literary purposes. Students played football on the Public Green, wearing stovepipe hats, swallow-tailed coats, and knee breeches. And drinking parties on the Fourth of July continued until temperance took a firm hold after Dwight's death.[26]

Poetry was almost the only art to have survived Dwight's housecleaning, and nearly everyone with any pretensions to education and culture dabbled in verse, including both Gallaudet and Timothy Dwight. Dwight was known as an accomplished poet long before a Yale presidency was even dreamed of, and his three long narrative poems illustrate his increasingly reactionary views. The third of these, *Greenfield Hill* (1794), treating chiefly of social issues, posits life in the New England village as the ideal and offers homespun advice in the character of a Yankee yeoman farmer, that putatively ubiquitous Connecticut man we met in Dwight's brother's 1798 Fourth of July oration in Hartford.

Let order o'er your time preside,
And method all your business guide.
Early begin, and end, your toil;
Nor let great tasks your hands embroil.
One thing at once, be still begun,
Contrived, resolved, pursued, and done.
Hire not, for what yourselves can do;
And send not, when yourselves can go,
Nor, till tomorrow's light, delay
What might as well be done today.

What thus your hands with labor earn,
To save, be now your next concern.
With steady hand your household sway,
And use them always to obey,
Always their worthy acts commend;
Always against their faults contend;
The mind inform; the conscience move;
And blame, with tenderness, and love.

Teach them, with confidence, t'impart,
Each secret purpose of the heart.[27]

The advice in this poem is not different in its essentials from that which many of us were still hearing from our parents as recently as the mid-twentieth century and that is sometimes referred to as the Protestant ethic. Many of these maxims recall Franklin: early to bed, early to rise; persevere; don't put off until tomorrow what you can do today; a penny saved is a penny earned; father knows best — or perhaps we can't credit Franklin with that one. And what's so striking is that while the advice is essentially the same given in *Poor Richard's Almanac,* it is here offered straight up, not, like Franklin's aphorisms, in the mouth of his comic creation Poor Richard Saunders and presented to readers with a wink and a dash of cynicism. Like Washington Irving, Benjamin Franklin would never have made it in Connecticut. The stanza beginning "With steady hand your household sway" gives some idea of what was behind the sense of entitlement we see again and again in the Standing Order, who never doubted their right — their duty! — to legislate where and when others might come and go, what they might read, and how they might even think.

Dwight's fearmongering and indoctrination in entitlement gave Gallaudet — a first-generation college student and the only Yale student in the class of 1805 to have a non-Anglo-Saxon surname — a lot to think about. Family pride in its Huguenot heritage notwithstanding, this heritage, like his origins in the mercantile class, was likely seen as a drag on a fourteen-year-old's ambitions to the "honors of life" dangled before his eyes at Yale. His classmate Heman Humphrey, later his biographer, remembers Gallaudet this way: "More youthful in appearance than even in age; modest, unobtrusive, and strictly correct in all his habits. . . . In his studies he was remarkably systematic, and was scrupulously punctual in his attendance upon all college exercises. [But] his voice was not strong, and he was too modest to do himself full justice on the college stage."[28]

Samuel Griswold Goodrich, a bookseller in Hartford, remembers Gallaudet as having "a mind of no great compass." Goodrich clearly liked Gallaudet a good deal, concluding his sketch with the observation, "How wide and ample a field may be harvested by a good man, even though he may not be a giant or a genius!"[29] But whatever Gallaudet's mental powers, the reason he did well in college was that he learned to be a Federalist and to gain the favor of those who, as Bishop said, hold all the honors of life in their gift. The friendships he formed were not with classmates but with tutors and professors: Jeremiah Day, who would succeed Dwight in the presidency, Elizur Goodrich, and later, James L. Kingsley. But his model was Dwight.

Dwight's senior class on disputation, or debate, was a kind of capstone course for graduating students. Each week, he selected two students to take assigned positions, affirmative or negative, on a topic he chose. In 1801, for example, the topics had included "Ought slaves to be immediately emancipated?" "Ought foreign immigration to be discouraged?" and "Are the novel and the theater beneficial?" The right answers were, respectively, negative, affirmative, negative. The purpose of these debates was to teach students to discuss *among themselves* philosophical and theological ideas that might lead to the horrors of egalitarian democracy if allowed to take root among the populace.[30] Like Mustafa Mond and other members of the Controllers' Council in *Brave New World,* Dwight encouraged free and open discussion — behind closed seminar doors. Gallaudet, who was new to all this, copied down or anticipated Dwight's positions and arguments into a notebook that he kept for the rest of his life; the positions he was assigned and the arguments he came up with to support those assigned positions are no longer extant and were probably never saved.[31] Gallaudet did a lot of direct transcribing for Dwight, too, when all the members of his senior class served as volunteer amanuenses for Dwight's four-volume *Travels in New England and New York* and his seven volumes of collected *Sermons*.[32] The class of 1805 was the last Yale class thus to serve Dwight, and Gallaudet must have been grateful for the opportunity to work so closely with the great man. Following are some of the topics for disputes and responses from Gallaudet's notebook.

"Ought Homicide by Duelling [sic] to be punished by death?" Affirmative. Gallaudet must have written this out before July 1804 when Dwight's cousin Aaron Burr killed Alexander Hamilton in a duel, because he makes no mention of that shocking event. As he could have predicted, Dwight's affirmative view on this question was not altered by the death of the Federalist icon Hamilton, and Gallaudet later copied Dwight's argument into an oration, discussed in the next chapter, that he gave on the occasion of his master's degree. Hamilton was to blame, Dwight believed and Gallaudet parroted, for having accepted Burr's challenge.[33]

"Are theaters beneficial?" Negative. Drawing on Dwight's attitudes toward the general population, Gallaudet notes that plays are "attended more numerously by the illiterate and vulgar than by persons of learning and discernment." Men of "learning and discernment" understand that "in most plays Vice is not exhibited in its native deformity"; "the illiterate and vulgar," in contrast, were not able to distinguish between life and art.[34]

"Can the Existence of the Deity be proved from the light of Nature?" Affirmative. This may well have been a trick question, and Gallaudet muffed it the first time he tackled it, crossing out and rephrasing several times as though he wasn't sure how the argument went. He seems to have been following William Paley's 1802 *Natural Theology* when he wrote, "Everything acts from certain principles which are so intricate yet so perfect that it must have required possessed [sic] infinite wisdom to have formed them." The topic was much in discussion, and Paley's take on it was strictly orthodox for Calvinists.

But there were complicating factors. One was that deism's central tenet was the claim that God is evident in the created world and that therefore there never was any divine revelation, or need for it. An affirmative response therefore had to walk a fine line to be acceptable to Trinitarian Christians.

A second complicating factor was that the question could be interpreted to refer to the proof required by so-called primitive peoples such as Africans or deaf Americans. If that's what the question meant, then the correct answer was negative. Gallaudet would spend the rest of his life experimenting with deaf pupils at his school and with any untaught African or Pacific Islander he was able to interrogate, as, for example, the imprisoned Africans from the *Amistad,* whom he grilled on their beliefs. (The *Amistad* captives were one of his most spectacular failures, because Gallaudet refused to use their interpreter and they grossly misunderstood his sign language.)[35]

Another way to interpret the question, however, was with regard to the proof required by educated people in the present day who were entertaining deism. Paley's book was designed for English youths entertaining Enlightenment precepts but who had already been immersed in divine revelation by way of the Bible. If that is what the question meant, then the correct response was a resounding affirmative: for such persons, the existence of God is easily proved by the natural world. In his second stab at this question, he stipulated this interpretation and years later made essentially the same argument as Paley's in one of his best-selling books for children.

"Would it be politic for the United States to establish a National University?" Negative. A national university was endorsed by every president from Washington to John Quincy Adams, Federalists and Democratic-Republicans alike, and Washington himself had offered the nation a donation of 150 shares of James River and Potomac Canal stock as seed money for raising the funds through public and private donation. But Dwight called this a mistake, understandable only insofar as Washington "was not educated at an university; and it is to be presumed that he was not intimately acquainted with this subject." His argument focused on the inevitable location of a national university in the nation's capital: "I would much rather send my children to a state prison . . . than allow them to mingle with such companions" as are to be found in the federal government, he stated. Gallaudet phrased this idea somewhat less dramatically: the capital would lead students into "prodigality and ruin." Dwight additionally argued that "students do not want the books of a large library [such as would be assembled in a national university]; they are totally unable to read them." Gallaudet's version reads, "In this and other colleges we have more books than we can read, of what benefit then would a more extensive collection be."[36]

"Would a monarchical form of government (similar to that of G. Britain) for the united [sic] States be preferable to our present form of government if

both could be established with equal practicableness?" Affirmative. We would be happier without the party politics, bribery, and excessive number of elections, he asserted. Gallaudet would consider this question again in this notebook, citing Montesquieu on the inevitable instability of republics and Paley on their unworkable complexity, before proceeding to compare the constitutions of the United States and Great Britain. In the British legislative branch, for example, Gallaudet argued that the "pernicious effects of [the common people's] impetuosity [is] restrained by a body of nobles and the king. Much as the sovereign will of the people has been advocated, much as their wisdom has been applauded and themselves flattered, I still advocate the doctrine that they are frequently their worst enemies. . . . the popular principle should be restrained within due bounds."

How many Yale undergraduates were openly admitting to being monarchists? The answer is at the bottom of the page, where Gallaudet has written, in large letters, "Unanimously." There really is little question that Connecticut Federalists, and Thomas Hopkins Gallaudet, indeed would have preferred a monarchical form of government. As Abraham Bishop sardonically exclaimed, "Here is a sentiment for the sons of the heroes of 1776."[37]

"Would it be politic in the UStates [sic] to encourage manufactures[?]" Negative. "Manufactures decrease our wealth, virtue and knowledge," and "besides, is it reasonable, is it just that laws should be enacted either imposing heavy duties on imported goods, or prohibiting men from buying the cheapest." The bottom line here is that New England's wealth came from trade, and domestic manufactures would diminish it. Dwight, however, qualified his answer by noting that factories "would furnish employment to many children who now run about the streets, as well as to many men and women who do nothing. . . . Our lowest wages will sustain a man," he said.[38]

"Ought divorces to be granted except in case of Adultery or incontinency?" Negative. Desertion and "illegitimate" children cause suffering for individuals, but "individual happiness must ever be sacrificed to public good or utility," wrote the hard-hearted teenager. Divorce "materially injures the welfare of society," and thus, while it may "gratify the feelings of private persons," general expediency, being the scale on which all laws are measured, is the reason for these "supposed hardships on individuals."

"Would it be just and politic for the nations of the earth to combine and extirpate the Barbary Pirates?" Negative. The United States had been paying

protection money since the early 1790s — $20,000 per annum to Tunis alone, $27,576.96 to Algiers — to avoid any contraction of international trade caused by the pirate depredations, as well as the enslavement of American sailors and passengers, who were sold on the auction block unless they converted to Islam or were wealthy enough to pay ransom.[39] This was widely understood. When the Gallaudets were still living in Philadelphia in 1794, *Slaves in Algiers,* Susanna Rowson's play about an American girl who must elude the sexual advances of her Muslim captor, premiered at the Chestnut Street Theater. And possibly at the very hour Gallaudet was writing his answer, the ship on which Washington Irving was traveling near Elba was boarded by pirates, who allowed it to sail on after relieving the passengers of their possessions — and giving them each a receipt![40] The fate awaiting captive Americans in the Muslim slave markets was so well understood that Franklin, in the last satire he penned before his death, employed this common knowledge to get readers to think about American enslavement of Africans. Franklin's mouthpiece, a fictional Algerian, asks, "If we cease our cruises against the Christians, . . . who in this hot climate are to cultivate our lands? Who are to perform the common labors of our city, and in our families? Must we not then be our own slaves? . . . [O]ur lands will become of no value for want of cultivation; the rents of houses in the city will sink one half; and the revenue of government arising from its share of prizes be totally destroyed!"[41]

Putting the shoe on the other foot was not a mode of thought typical of the Connecticut establishment, and the analogy never occurred to young Gallaudet, or presumably to Dwight. Gallaudet's argument against "extirpation" of the pirates marshals such arguments as embarrassments to commerce and the dangers of any nation having a monopoly on trade, although how this would follow is not made clear. Christian principles emerge only when he contemplates "lay[ing] aside every feeling of humanity, every principle of Christianity" to "extirpate" the pirates "man, woman and child."

A grand, stylized signature with a motto nested in the large flourish from the final "t" of his name concludes the notebook. The motto, *sapere aude*, "Dare to be wise," "Dare to discern," "Dare to find out," or, as Nathan Chang translates, "Have courage to use your own reason!"[42] is a quotation from Immanuel Kant, who used the phrase in his 1784 *Age of Enlightenment* to encourage questioning of civic authority. It became the Enlightenment's motto. That Gallaudet tucked *sapere aude* into his signature in a notebook recording the ideas of Timothy Dwight is beyond odd. Could he have thought that *Dwight* was daring to use his reason to question Enlightenment authority?

We know little else about Gallaudet's undergraduate years. Jefferson's Louisiana Purchase, which thrilled or infuriated Americans everywhere, seems never to have risen to any level of awareness at Yale, although in Hartford the *Courant* was fuming over the aid that the purchase price supplied to Napoleon. In Gallaudet's senior year, another student stuffed a rag filled with gunpowder into the keyhole of a classmate's dormitory room, set the rag on fire, and almost blew off the whole door. That was James Fenimore Cooper "display[ing] the sort of immaturity one would expect of the youngest member of his class."[43]

Gallaudet was just as immature, but his immaturity took the form of imitating Authority, not challenging it. He wrote an imitative mock-heroic poem about wedding cake and "Fairy revelry" on the occasion of the marriage of a classmate, Samuel F. Jarvis. (Jarvis was to become an Episcopal priest and would write about the religion of North American Indians, but he and Gallaudet did not keep in touch after they left Yale.) A month before commencement, Gallaudet wrote an imitative pastoral poem, apparently just for fun, and a short poem in rhymed couplets for the ending of his last address to his debating society, Brothers in Unity, wishing his classmates a life of aiming at truth and virtue in a happy home far from worldly ambition, and, at the ends of their lives, that they all be "kindly" admitted to heaven.[44] This scanty evidence shows that while he had learned to imitate models, he was still attending Episcopal weddings and had not yet fully absorbed the predestination doctrine of Calvinism — else why wish that everyone in his debating club was going to get into heaven?

At the 1805 commencement exercises in September, Gallaudet spoke "On the Increase of Luxury in Connecticut, and It's [*sic*] Destructive Consequences." Gallaudet wasn't valedictorian or even salutatorian (though he may have been the "Latin Salutatorian," as a teacher trained at the deaf school believed) but merely one of many speakers.[45] The conspicuous consumption or "luxury" that is Gallaudet's topic was fueled by economic innovations such as land speculation, but the Standing Order, to which Gallaudet would be admitted upon graduation, blamed a putative decline in morals and religion and regarded it as a serious threat to New England virtue.[46] Dwight had used the topic for student disputes, so Gallaudet would have known the correct answer and best approach to take. He begins,

Amid the general wreck of morality and virtue, occasioned by the political convulsions, which have shaken not only the eastern, but even this western continent, the finger of the politician is often pointed towards Connecticut as standing alone — an example to her sister states, and to the world. But the purity of her morals, the simplicity of her manners, and the happiness of her citizens, however great in comparison with other republics, have diminished to an alarming degree within a century past. To what cause these unhappy effects are to be attributed, is a subject of investigation, which must be deeply interesting to every friend of virtue, and lover of his country. This cause must undoubtedly be looked for in a change of some of the prominent traits of her character. Her political and religious institutions still remain the same; they have been guarded with an anxious care. But her increase in luxury and profusion, her propensity to show and extravagance, have been constantly and rapidly progressing. This, it is believed, will be found the cause of those evils, which, if they do not already threaten her destruction, ought at least to awaken her to a sense of danger.

This opening is a textbook example of the paranoid style ("sense of danger"), the Puritan exceptionality myth ("standing alone [as] an example"), the Dwight brothers' blindness to the wretched lives of the sizable underclass ("happiness of her citizens"), and the obligatory pat on the back for the guardians of political and religious traditions. As he has learned to do, he pins the blame on "the meanest citizen" and on a too-egalitarian government — Jefferson is now in the White House — that makes the underclass "eligible to all the honors and dignities of those in a more exalted station." Formerly, Gallaudet alleges, the "statesman revered his plough" but now regards it with "contempt." He is pulling out all the stops to position himself as a Connecticut Yankee, and we cannot but wonder, firstly, to what extent he understood that his own ancestors were urban craftsmen, mariners, and merchants who wouldn't have known a plow if they'd tripped over one on the way to the counting table, and secondly, what the commencement audience would have thought of his effort, for surely everyone there would have known that this boy's father was "in trade." Yale commencements were social events for the Standing Order; Democratic-Republicans refused to attend, and the established clergy and business magnates came expecting to hear orthodox orations of its new members.[47] Gallaudet was presenting himself as one of these new members.

Such wholesale adoption of the Standing Order's worldview was not a certain outcome for Yale graduates, despite what Abraham Bishop believed and bemoaned. Bishop himself did not buy into it, and neither did Cooper, who said many years later that the Yale community's conviction of their superiority over those not of Puritan stock created "the lowest, the most degraded, the most vulgar wickedness." Nothing, Cooper said, is "more vicious than self-righteousness, and the want of charity it engenders."[48]

Gallaudet left Yale with his BA degree all of seventeen years old to return to his father's house and read law.

Fresh out of Yale College, Gallaudet landed a plum position reading law in the offices of Chauncey Goodrich, a brother of the Yale law professor. Chauncey Goodrich had served three terms in the U.S. House of Representatives before returning to Hartford to practice law in 1802; in 1807, he would be named to a vacancy in the U.S. Senate and subsequently be elected for one full term before returning to Connecticut to serve, simultaneously, as mayor of Hartford and lieutenant governor of the state.[1] In 1805, however, Goodrich was in Hartford practicing law, and he agreed to take seventeen-year-old Gallaudet into his office to learn the profession. There is no reason to doubt that Goodrich was genuinely happy to get a promising young college man like the ever-punctual and punctilious T. H. Gallaudet, but the Yale network surely didn't hurt the young man's chances.[2]

Law was a popular career choice for young men with literary tastes — Charles Brockden Brown and James Fenimore Cooper both began by reading law, while Washington Irving was admitted to the New York bar — and Gallaudet apparently did very well in Goodrich's office because he was also occasionally able to work for Thomas S. Williams, another prominent Hartford lawyer who would serve in the U.S. House of Representatives and as mayor of Hartford. Had Gallaudet stayed with Goodrich and been admitted to the Connecticut bar, he would have been boosted by this network into similarly prominent political office. Instead, he lasted only one year, and what caused him to abandon his studies can only be guessed.

Gallaudet's admirers would assume that his health broke down, and a look at the years ahead will tell us why they thought so. The earliest extant instance of Gallaudet claiming ill health appears in a letter declining an interview with the Portsmouth, New Hampshire, church in 1814, in which he makes what seems an unnecessarily detailed explanation: "I have been very much of an invalid for these nine or ten years and still labour under the pressure of considerable bodily infirmity. My eyes and lungs are both weak and my general health is such that I can devote but little time to study."[3] However, in the ten years previous to this letter, he had completed two degrees at Yale and a three-year course of study at Andover Theological Seminary, a two-year tutoring position at Yale, a year in a law office and another in a bookkeeping office in Manhattan, a trip on horseback, alone, across the Appalachians and back, and would, within two years, embark on a fact-finding trip to Europe. The claim of ten years of invalidism can therefore hardly be right. Gallaudet simply did not want the kind of responsibilities that devolve upon a pastor or, perhaps more accurately, had judged himself unfitted for such responsibilities. The unusual detail about his eyes reminds us a bit of Dwight, whose poor eyesight combined with what were likely migraines caused him to lament his poor health; both men certainly needed to wear their spectacles, which were still unusual at the time, especially for younger people. As for his lungs, Gallaudet assuredly did not have tuberculosis, as his intended readers in New Hampshire would have assumed; allergies, however, much rarer at the time than they are today, would fit this claim.[4] So this 1814 letter was, at a minimum, misleading.

Usually, Gallaudet kept his excuses less specific. In an undated letter to the Yale chapter of Phi Beta Kappa, he declined a request, probably for a poem, by saying merely that "indifferent health, and other circumstances, which it is unnecessary to mention, are the reasons of my declining the performance of the duty they have seen fit to confer on me."[5] The excuse of "indifferent health" to explain his unwillingness to write a poem suggests a polite fiction: today, we excuse ourselves with claims of being too busy or having a scheduling conflict, but in the nineteenth century, ill health was the most common way to get out of doing something one didn't want to do.

Why he didn't want to write a poem for Phi Beta Kappa or serve as pastor in Portsmouth are different questions, the answers to which are, in part, suggested by his behavior over the next forty years. He was one of those people who does not work well under supervision or an imposed timetable, yet who blossoms when given the space to produce original work on his own. There is no doubt that Gallaudet had a chronic illness, observed by people who knew him, but we need to untangle accounts of this illness from boilerplate excuses he typically made for not taking — or sticking with — paid employment.

Gallaudet seems to have been extraordinarily prone to infectious diseases. For example, he could not attend a meeting in 1838 because of "Erysipelas in my face,"[6] an infection now treated with antibiotics, and he died of an infectious disease, dysentery, which was also afflicting his wife and some of his children, who went on to recover. He also suffered from chronic constipation, "my old and stubborn complaint, which I have always considered the foundation of my indisposition."[7] How long his constipation continued is unclear, but most likely it stayed with him as long as did the psychological conditions, to which we now turn.

The earliest extant expression of his psychological troubles dates to early

1818, when he told a correspondent that for three days he had been in bed "weak and exhausted." At the time, he had been serving as principal of the American Asylum for the Deaf and Dumb for nine months. In May of the same year, his friend and assistant at the school, Laurent Clerc, told Dr. Cogswell that while Gallaudet was sure to feel better after a few days in New Haven, his ill health would certainly return when he got back to Hartford, "especially with his disappointment at finding nothing improved in the Asylum." In fact, when Gallaudet did return to work that month, he spoke to the directors about "the great bodily debility which almost unfits me for the discharge of these momentous duties." A year later, in June of 1819, he told a professional correspondent, "Your letter of the 10th of May should have met with an earlier answer, had I not been so unwell, that it was really out of my power to give any satisfactory reply to your inquiries. And now, I can but just endure the fatigue of thinking in general what to say to you, and to express my thoughts in a manner that will be at all intelligible."[8]

How usual it would have been at this time to respond with personal details of this nature to a *professional* inquiry is difficult to say. These examples suggest, nevertheless, not so much excuses as references to a real condition observable by those close to him. This condition he termed "melancholy," "gloom," or, occasionally, "hypochondria," which in the early nineteenth century still bore its original meaning in English, "A morbid state of mind, characterized by general depression, melancholy, or low spirits, for which there is no real cause." James Boswell, the Scotsman with whose writings Gallaudet may well have been familiar from his *Life of Samuel Johnson*, called his own depression "the black dog" and wrote a monthly essay on the topic in the *London Magazine* called *The Hypochondriack,* which continued over seventy months in 1777–1783. References to people having the "hips" were common in the literature of the period, and public admissions to this illness were less remarkable than they are today, when mental illness confers greater stigma. The disease seems to have been especially common among New England clergymen, and it was perhaps the reason they became clergymen to begin with.[9]

There is only one piece of evidence that Gallaudet ever consulted a physician about this inability to carry on with his daily life due to a "morbid state of mind." This was in an 1828 letter to Eli Todd, a medical doctor who was interested in psychiatry and, in 1823, became the founding director of the Hartford Retreat for the Insane. Gallaudet was to work at the

Retreat many years later as chaplain, but in 1828 the two men knew each other professionally as the heads of the two big "benevolent" institutions in Hartford: a school for the deaf and a psychiatric hospital. Apparently, however, they also had a doctor/patient relationship. In this 1828 letter, Gallaudet reported to Dr. Todd that his health was improving, but "I still suffer from debility, and especially from the want of sleep. Notwithstanding the fatigue that each day produces, I cannot get, on an average, more than four or five hours of rest during the night."[10]

After this letter, such health assessments from Gallaudet grow scarce enough to disappear, eventually, from the record, later mentions of his health having to do only with this or that infection he has picked up. He seems to have been sick pretty frequently anyhow, but the "debility" complaints subsided. From this paper trail, it's reasonable to conclude that Gallaudet, beginning soon after his undergraduate years at Yale and into his twenties and thirties, suffered not from a disabling physical ailment of the lungs but rather from something like what we would call depression and anxiety, which eased for him after consultation with Dr. Todd — or perhaps merely with age. Gallaudet would have known that his father treated his prostrating, lifelong depression with exercise, and he came to recognize outdoor exercise as effective against his own depression a few years after his aborted law career.[11]

One more factor affecting Gallaudet's health was his opium habit, though when this began and exactly how long it continued we cannot say. When in 1820 he arrived in Hartford by coach from a trip out of town, he was so high that he couldn't walk, and the incident created a sensation on the Hartford gossip circle. A young lady of the city included the juicy tale in a letter to a friend, from which the following is a lengthy quote. "To turn to a very different subject," Emily Baldwin breathlessly tells her correspondent,

> have you heard the unhappy story circulated about Mr. Gallaudet since his return from New Haven? I should not mention it, but it is in the mouths of every child here, and you may have heard the wild exaggerations. The report which flies about town was this — that he got into the stage considerably disordered and at every house they stopped took a glass of brandy and water. Ere long before they reached Hartford he was completely intoxicated. — and in this state was carried into the stage office. — His friends seem grieved to the heart at this report — but say little about it,

and leave the main features of it uncontradicted. As far as I can learn the truth it is this, that he was so imprudent as to leave New Haven, being much fatigued and quite ill, as to have thought for the ride [illegible] had taken a large quantity of opium — This affected him so unpleasantly that he thought it necessary to take some brandy — altogether it over-powered his reason, and when he arrived in Hartford, he was utterly unable to stand or sit. — Much that has been said of his situation has been reported to him, and I trust this severe lesson will guard him against the use of opium — I ascribe all his indisposition to this, for he takes it at times in large quantities.[12]

Opium could be had from any druggist without a prescription, often in liquid form as laudanum and widely used as a home remedy for just about any ailment — including depression.[13] Habitual use would certainly account for much of his lethargy and possibly all of his constipation. One thing seems certain: he didn't derive the pleasure from the drug that a fellow indulger and British contemporary, Thomas De Quincey, described in his *Confessions of an English Opium-Eater* in 1821.

Back to 1806, with Gallaudet walking away from Chauncey Goodrich's law office and, it will turn out, heading back to New Haven, we find an amusing example of the state of scientific incuriosity in Connecticut when a solar eclipse took place on June 16. Noah Webster was excited and provided each of his three school-aged daughters with a piece of smoked glass to take to school so that they could look directly at the sun during the eclipse. Their teacher, however, shuttered the windows and would not let the children outside. Did Gallaudet get a piece of smoked glass and have a look? Or keep his head down at his desk? Or was he too depressed to care? Also in 1806, the election results surprised Federalist Hartford when some Democratic-Republicans from the city gained seats in the State Assembly, though this was probably viewed as an aberration rather than the portent it was.

We do know that in September, Gallaudet wrote another amateurishly mannered poem on a shipwreck that had occurred several years previous, entitled "Written on Reading the Account of the Shipwreck of the 'Rose in Bloom'":

Hark! in the storm,
That o'er the troubled bosom of the deep,
Fraught with the dread artillery of Heav'n.[14]

Like his undergraduate efforts, it's a schoolboy's exercise, devoid of anything that might suggest personal emotion, or even a personal experience — Gallaudet had never been closer to a storm at sea than a rainy day on the Long Island Sound. But it demonstrates that Gallaudet was not taking as models the best that was being written at the time: *The Rime of the Ancient Mariner,* to stay with the maritime theme, had been published in 1798, and Scott's *Lay of the Last Minstrel,* which would establish his career, had come out in 1805. These works were available in Hartford. But, like the *Echo* contributors, Gallaudet took his models from a century earlier. More interesting from this year, although we unfortunately do not know the month or whether it was written while he was working in Goodrich's law office or at his parents' house after he quit, is a poem called "To a Lady on Being Asked for Some Pensive Verses." Its opening lines confront Gallaudet's own chronic melancholy:

> I'd rather give thee
> Some more cheerful, sportive lay;
> Melancholy's gloom believe me,
> Should be drove full far away.
>
> 'Tho she sings a soothing song
> Mild as Zephyr's vernal breath,
> 'Tho the notes steal sweet along,
> 'Tis the syren song of death.

This reads today like thoughts of suicide, although we cannot make so much of one line in a poem, especially when the word "death" is needed for the rhyme. But he was certainly considering an imminent demise: "Since his lyre so soon must prove / Dread oblivion's silent slumbers." The "mirthful" tale that follows concerns a man named Flippant who "tripp'd lightly o'er the lawn, / Bound to Belinda in the grove," with "fashionable forms of strutting, / His most bewitching grace on putting." If the comically inverted syntax and off-rhyme lead the reader to expect a parody, she is soon disabused. Gallaudet didn't write parody. Instead, he has Belinda lecture Flippant like a good Calvinist maiden:

> Must lovers, now, t'ensure success,
> From folly's storehouse <u>steal</u> their dress,
> <u>Pilfer</u> the monkey's odd grimace,
> And like the jack-daw prate apace?[15]

The poet has painted himself into a corner: he can't write pensive verse because he needs to drive away melancholy, but he can't write frivolous verse either because it makes him look like a monkey and sound like a crow. The next dated poem was not written until 1810.

By January of 1807, Gallaudet was back at Yale, reading for a master's degree. As with the bachelor's degree that he took in 1805, the master's requirements would have been prescribed for all students with no choice of focus on particular disciplines, although there must have been a choice between pursuing one's classical education and, instead, studying English thinkers, for that is what he did. All of Gallaudet's nineteenth-century biographers refer to his study of "English literature," but at this date, the reference is to what was then called moral philosophy — psychology, political science, economics, ethics, and the like — written in England and Scotland during the seventeenth and eighteenth centuries. Such a course of reading would have included the work of poets such as Alexander Pope, Oliver Goldsmith, and John Dryden, in addition to philosophers such as Thomas Hobbes and John Locke and essayists such as Samuel Johnson, but any verse was studied as discourse, strictly for the philosophy to be distilled from it. Gallaudet emerged from his MA with a sound understanding of the work of doctrinally orthodox British thinkers but no appreciation of literature as we know it today, as we shall see when he tackles Shakespeare in his MA oration.[16]

That summer, Gallaudet visited Saratoga, perhaps with a classmate's family. "A respectable farmer of that place," he later wrote, "whom curiosity prompted me to visit, although entirely deaf, possessed the faculty of conversing so readily and correctly with others by watching the motions of their lips, that scarce a suspicion of his deafness would be entertained by one unacquainted with the fact."

The nameless farmer had been deafened fourteen years before, and Gallaudet thought it "remarkable" that his "utterance was clear and distinct, and his accentuation generally correct." The recital of this man's story, he concluded, would encourage deaf people "to attempt the acquisition of an art, which can restore to them one of the sweetest enjoyments of life." The narrative itself is undated, but Gallaudet's naïveté suggests that it was written before he had any contact with deaf, rather than deafened, people. At this date, he could not tell the difference between the abilities of a native speaker of English who suddenly lost his hearing in adulthood and a person who had never heard the language.[17]

In the fall, a large meteor rather spectacularly landed in Weston, Connecticut, sending Professors Benjamin Silliman and James L. Kingsley to the site to salvage chunks of it. The Weston meteorite was the first recorded in the United States, and people flocked to smash up the stone fragments in search of gold. Silliman and Kingsley brought a twenty-eight-pound fragment back to New Haven, which can still be seen in Yale's Peabody Museum of Natural History, and the following year published both a popular report on the event and a scientific paper that included a chemical analysis. Due to their diligence, the Weston meteorite is one of the best attested in the world.[18]

The year 1807 also saw the imposition of the Embargo Act by President Jefferson. The *Courant* thought it the work of Virginians bent on destroying New England, and most Hartford residents agreed. Connecticut Democratic-Republicans had made some gains in the 1806 election, but the Embargo Act cost them whatever goodwill they had gained.[19] Also in 1807, the Center Church moved into the new brick meeting house on Main Street that it still occupies today, and this was the occasion on which P. W. Gallaudet bought a half-share of a pew.

The Yale commencement exercises for 1808 were held on Wednesday, September 14, with an all-day program of sermons and lectures given by more than twenty graduates, recipients of both bachelor's and master's degrees. Gallaudet's address, "On the Use of Ambition as a Motive in the Education of Youth," was scheduled at the end of the day, immediately before the valedictory oration. The audience must have been exhausted, probably hot, and not very receptive at this moment to an oration that promised to speak of educational innovation but instead sounded a lot more like a sermon on Christian virtue. But then again, 1808 was the year of a major, statewide revival, and the audience was stuffed with Congregational clergy from across the state, so perhaps those gathered for the commencement pricked up their ears.

Gallaudet starts off with a bang: ambition's "influence is directly repugnant to the real spirit of christianity." While the type of ambition "which aims at greater excellence and perfection of character; for the sake of rendering the sphere of usefulness more extensive" is justifiable, ambition aiming at "self-gratification in the attainment of glory" is "productive of many evil and unhappy consequences." Humility is Christianity's prominent characteristic: but we teach children pride and envy when we rank them in school. Children should be given direction, encouragement, and discipline as needed, led along by curiosity, and taught the Christian sense of duty. An undated poem, a parable called "Rival Roses," is Gallaudet's clearest expression of this idea. A gardener has lovingly tended a garden abounding in beautiful roses. When each blossom claims to be the fairest of them all, the gardener protests that he has cared for each of them and they should not be vying with one another: "Thus shall a modest loveliness / Each rose with sweeter graces dress / Each borrow beauty from the rest, / And in the general joy be blest."[20]

Some members of the audience may have recognized that behind Gallaudet's anodyne remarks on raising Christian children was an attack on Adam Smith's *Wealth of Nations* — specifically, its postulate that self-interest and competition together act as the "invisible hand" of the market. No Calvinist could accept the notion that a private vice like self-interest could conduce to public benefit, so Smith was not taught at Yale, or practically anywhere else in the United States. His ideas were instead retailed in simplified form. Gallaudet would have been under the impression that Smith argued for "competitive individualism," and it was this notion he was disproving with the Gospel.[21]

Two curious passages are worth closer looks. One is a reference to Alexander Hamilton: "the great, the splendid, and patriotic Hamilton ... in whose melancholy death, an immense sacrifice was made of resolute and dignified independence to the accursed requisitions of a ruinous public opinion. If ambition ever can be noble his was such; yet had his love of glory, and sensibility to what is deemed honourable reputation been less lively, he might now have lived the first among his countrymen."

Spoken like a true Federalist! Or, more specifically, like Burr's cousin Timothy Dwight, who, as we saw in the previous chapter, blamed Hamilton for the duel.

The other curiosity in this oration is the insertion of some lines from Shakespeare's *Troilus and Cressida,* a text Gallaudet had clearly not read. In his argument against "competition, or a spirit of rivalry," he quotes,

Take the instant way;

For honor travels in a strait so narrow,

That one but goes abreast: keep then the path,

For Emulation hath a thousand sons,

That one by one pursue; if you give way,

Or hedge aside from the direct forthwright [*sic*],

Like to an enter'd tide, they all rush by,

And leave you hindmost.[22]

These lines he believed to support his point that schools wrongly teach children that honor's path is only one man wide. However, that is not the point of the speech in *Troilus and Cressida,* where the wily Ulysses is manipulating Achilles' pride in an effort to get him to return to battle. Ulysses' plan hinges on the observation that

Pride hath no other glass

To show itself but pride, for supple knees

Feed arrogance and are the proud man's fees. (III, iii, 48–50)

In other words, Achilles' pride must be fed by the deference of everyone else, and Ulysses therefore suggests to Achilles that his reputation requires the adulation of his comrades. Oddly, Shakespeare's point here foreshadows Adam Smith's *Theory of Moral Sentiments,* that it is only the opinion of others that makes us moral, and Gallaudet could have done something with this congruence if he'd understood the speech he was quoting.

Gallaudet's study of English letters, focused as it was on moral philosophy rather than aesthetics, would have been heavily reliant on anthologies that collected famous literary speeches or improving passages from Shakespeare, all taken completely out of context and meant to be read for the wisdom therein. To clinch the argument that Gallaudet knew only the passage he quoted, not the play, we note that the lines he quoted appear immediately after Cressida's uncle Pandarus arranges for her and Troilus to have sexual relations without any intent to marry:

I will show you a chamber with a bed; which bed, because it shall not
    speak of your pretty encounters, press it to death: away!

And Cupid grant all tongue-tied maidens here
Bed, chamber, Pandar to provide this gear! (III, ii, 214–218)

Surely Gallaudet did not know he was quoting from a text with a plot like this!

Gallaudet was one of several young men among those awarded the MA in 1808 to be elected college tutor, a common route to a professorship, and he served in that capacity for two years before resigning with the 1810 commencement.[23] Unfortunately, we have next to no extant documentation of those two years. The diary he kept as a tutor and entitled "Prayers, Meditations and Reflections" is known only from excerpts that his son Edward Miner Gallaudet transcribed into his biography. Otherwise, there is a single undated letter concerning an undergraduate he tutored. The boy, whose peculiar given name was D'Kay, had not been well enough prepared for Yale and was returning home for private tutoring. Gallaudet's letter is addressed to that private tutor.

> I have sometimes caught him equivocating. Indeed unless he is reformed in this particular, I fear he will want somewhat of that ingenuous frankness, which is so pleasing in youth, which, if they did but know it, is their greatest security, even in error, and which, I am sure, is the most certain mark of a noble and independent spirit. But college ethics, I know, places falsehood to a Tutor, in the chapter of whiter lies; and perhaps D'Kay has fallen lower in my opinion, in this respect, than he ought in justice to have done — he has also been profane. He should I think be kept from promiscuous society, and be constrained to spend most of his time and especially his evenings at home. His main defect of character is "<u>fickleness</u>", and to check it in his morals, you will have to use a watchful eye, and in his studies to proceed very cautiously and accurately.[24]

Whatever a tutor's official duties at Yale, Gallaudet was taking his role directly from Dwight's *Greenfield Hill:* "With steady hand your household sway,

> And use them always to obey,
> Always their worthy acts commend;
> Always against their faults contend;
> The mind inform; the conscience move;
> And blame, with tenderness, and love.

The excerpts from the lost diary "Prayers, Meditations and Reflections" in E. M. Gallaudet's biography suggest a deeply disturbed mind during the years as a tutor. This biography is in error on several points concerning this period of Gallaudet's life: it is completely ignorant of the master's degree and erroneously states that "On Ambition" was delivered in Hartford rather than New Haven, an error difficult to understand as twenty-year-olds do not typically rent halls to give speeches in their hometowns. But even with this caveat, the excerpts cannot show anything other than that Gallaudet was suffering pretty badly during these years. One can only agree with Edward Miner that these entries are, in many cases, "tragic."[25]

The entries E. M. Gallaudet transcribed actually begin when Gallaudet was still reading for his MA. On New Year's Day of 1808, he wrote of his character defects, which added up, he thought, to being "too much occupied by the world, too negligent of cultivating a Christian temper," and he resolved to adhere to a rigid schedule of prayer and Bible reading. Among the specific character defects he identified are laziness, indulgence in food and drink, and irritability.[26] Laziness was probably what he would later term "debility," which would dog him into middle age; overindulgence, which he would come to term "intemperance," he would overcome; but the third, irritability, he would never correct, and it was mentioned by many people who knew him throughout his life. So far, the diary seems unremarkable — everyone has character defects similar to these, and New Year's resolutions are a common opportunity for vows to change them.

To get an idea of what Gallaudet meant when he wrote that he was "too much occupied by the world, too negligent of cultivating a Christian temper," his son offers two stories he had from an old man who, in his youth, had known Gallaudet when he was a tutor. In the first story, Gallaudet got drunk at a social event. "His mortification and distress were so great that he could have no peace of mind until he had repaired to Hartford and made public confession to the officers of the [Center Church]." We can imagine that the Rev. Nathan Strong, the worldly wit who had been in the distillery business from 1790 until creditors shut him down, may well have been amused by a twenty-one-year-old Yale tutor making an overland trip by coach to Hartford to confess to having gotten drunk at a party.[27] The second story concerns a dancing party one winter in Hartford. Someone came to the hall while the dancing was in progress and told Gallaudet, at the door, that a young man known to everyone there had just fallen through the ice while skating on the Connecticut River and had drowned. Gallaudet told the messenger not to announce the news because "it would break up the dance." However, he immediately saw that his first impulse was heartless and he left the party never to dance again. E. M. Gallaudet traces his father's strict temperance and strenuous opposition to dancing to these incidents, but both were in widespread disrepute in Connecticut by the 1810s.[28]

Gallaudet's diary soon turned from personal failings to theological matters. He wrote that "God has taken His Holy Spirit from me," leaving him to "the infidelity of my own mind," "infidelity" meaning skepticism about the truth of divine revelation. "Man's free agency, his natural depravity, the impracticability of his effecting a radical change of character, the immediate and exclusive and supernatural agency of the Holy Spirit in regeneration, the necessity of publicly professing one's belief in Christ, and of partaking of the Lord's Supper, and the eternity of future punishment."

Gallaudet is here stating what are known today as the five points of Calvinism expressed as the acronym TULIP.[29] His son blamed "the exigeant and extreme doctrines given forth from the pulpits" and the "embarrassing speculations in theology" current at Yale for having produced his father's despondency, but Gallaudet himself, referring to the depression he experienced at Yale during these years, spoke of his "hypochondriachal wailings" at Kingsley's fireside, suggesting that he saw depression, not worry about salvation, as his trouble, the tenets of Calvinism having put the condition of his soul out of his hands.[30]

According to Edward Miner Gallaudet, the only two entries in this lost diary for the year 1810 occur after a ten-month gap. Both are brief, and in Latin. On February 4, 1810, Gallaudet wrote, "*Hoc opus, hic labor est*" — a quotation from the *Aeneid* referring to the task of getting out of the underworld, so easy to enter, so difficult to leave. Edward Miner seems not to have recognized the line; Nathan Chang, who did, believes that Gallaudet was thinking about everlasting torment in hell. But there are other situations that might explain quotation of this line, such as a contract to tutor at Yale that ran until September and that simply could not be gotten out of. We'll never know. The final entry came a few days later: a single word, "*Rursus*," which Edward Miner gives as "Backward," but which Chang translates "Again." Gallaudet's son thought the word spoke of "fruitless struggles after peace of mind," while Chang believes it refers to a recurrence of spiritual anxiety. It could also quite reasonably be taken as referring to a return of depression or of yet other troubles, and there was indeed an "unfortunate affair" that occurred at Yale and perhaps drove him from the college.[31]

Writing to Professor Kingsley four or five months after leaving Yale, Gallaudet apostrophized the mythological river of forgetfulness, saying, "spirit of the Lethean stream give me a whole urn full of thy composing draught, 'till I drown the remembrance of <u>it</u> in sweet oblivion." In another letter, he told Kingsley,

> I hesitate at mentioning another subject, which always brings with it a
> train of unpleasant thoughts, and which I am sensible I ought to endeav-
> our to banish from my mind. Were it not attended with such a host of
> inexplicable circumstances, many of which seem to me to prove that I have
> never had a fair hearing at the proper tribunal, I would forget it forever.
> My own regard for my own dignity would demand this. As it is, a reliance
> upon the word of a gentleman whose honor I can confide in, and my own
> word pledged not to prosecute the matter, should conspire, I confess, to
> obliterate all remembrance of this unfortunate affair.[32]

This "unfortunate affair" could have been anything: a love affair, an insult, an assault, a debt. Whatever it was, Gallaudet was still agonizing over it many months later.

So he decided to travel to Kentucky on horseback across the Appala-chians in the middle of winter. E. M. Gallaudet, realizing that readers would think this decision pretty odd, takes great pains to explain that this trip was made for reasons of health, and of course he is right, in a way, because Gallaudet was clearly treating his depression with the time-honored cure of exercise. Long trips by horseback were actually quite common remedies for a variety of mental disturbances. Louis Dwight, for example, who followed Gallaudet to Yale and then preceded him to the Andover Theological Sem-inary, set off on such a trip two months after his wedding, claiming a lung ailment he had acquired years earlier from inhaling laughing gas in Professor Silliman's chemistry course. At least Gallaudet was single and accountable to no one but his father, who seems to have at least partially sponsored the trip. But while the horseback cure proved effective for Louis Dwight, who returned to his wife and found fulfilling work in prison reform, it didn't seem to do much for Gallaudet.[33]

Gallaudet's pretext for his trip was to assess land that his father had bought as a business investment. He mentions this matter in a letter to Kingsley and refers to it obliquely in his trip diary. His biographers Henry Barnard and Heman Humphrey were both unaware of any of this, however, and assumed, logically but incorrectly, "a business commission for a large house in New York, the prosecution of which took him over the Alleghanies [*sic*], into the States of Ohio and Kentucky." Gallaudet makes no mention anywhere of any commission.[34]

He left Philadelphia on horseback on November 28, 1810, stayed overnight with his family's 1798 summer landlord in Lancaster, and traveled overland to Pittsburgh "accoutred [*sic*] with pistols" and wearing a "woolen wig."[35] Proceeding past the decommissioned Fort Pitt, he rode through forests where he marveled at the age and size of the trees and at grapevines that seemed to grow up into the air without support. At Marietta, he took the Ohio River to Cincinnati, then continued overland through Frankfort, where he observed "the august legislature of Kentucky," as he sardonically termed it to Kingsley. "I saw with my own vision one of the senators, enter the inn where I lodged heading two black fiddlers, who were followed by a goodly cavalcade of representatives, and townsmen and boys. They were parading the streets thro the mud almost the whole night. Don't publish this in any newspaper; for it is deemed as most glorious frolic here, and the Kentuckians if they knew I had spoken of it disrespectfully, would let me feel the length of some of their dirks."[36]

He arrived in Lexington on February 1, picked up mail forwarded from New York by his brother, and by the next day, February 2, would have been ready to continue to his father's land, located on the Green River, if the weather had permitted. On March 5, he traveled to Stanford for reasons unknown, returning to Lexington on the 8th. Finally, on the 21st he left Lexington to arrive in Philadelphia at the end of May. He must therefore have visited his father's Green River lands sometime in March. In 1840, when P. W. wrote his will, he assigned the land to a Philadelphia man to settle a debt.[37]

The trip journal and letters to Kingsley largely concern Gallaudet's health and religious doubts. At first, he wrote of melancholy, gloominess, and being "considerably indisposed"; by the end of the first week, he was "taken with a fainting and obliged to retire immediately to bed." He told Kingsley in February, "Activity and enterprise must be my cure, and they have done much for me on my long journey. My health is considerably improved, and my spirits, save an occasional relapse into morbid apathy, for I have little of fearful anxiety, have recovered in a considerable degree their native cheerfulness."

He also told Kingsley that his constipation cleared up once he got to Kentucky, and credited a diet of corn, "introduced at every meal, prepared in a great variety of shapes and always very palatable."[38]

As for his religious doubts, devotional expressions in his journal began merely as boilerplate prayers for a safe journey and gratitude that that's been the case so far: "Preserve me safe during the journey," "spare me to see our little circle [his family] once more," "Accept, my Father who art in Heaven, my humble and hearty thanks," and so on, until the day's page is filled. Entries end with some version of "For X's sake," the abbreviation for "Christ" that has now fallen out of favor in most Protestant denominations. After five or six weeks of the westward journey, however, Gallaudet drifted into a confessional mode, transcribing his most personal thoughts and feelings, although often in such coded language that it's hard to tell whether he is talking about sexual sins (masturbation comes immediately to mind on a first reading, or perhaps, like Jimmy Carter, committing adultery in his heart) or not about sex at all, as his times, and the man himself, don't seem much interested in agonizing over that topic, and salvation is, instead, the worry of the day: "How much, O my God, do I owe to thy goodness, that my days have been prolonged another year; and that I am still permitted to enjoy the opportunity to becoming reconciled unto thee, ere I am removed from this probationary state."

There are no diary entries for the weeks spent in Lexington, but we do have one poem, transcribed into the February 22nd letter to Kingsley and copied into the notebook of poems now at the Library of Congress, where it is entitled "To a friend likely to be married: written in Kentucky, 1810, and sent to Professor James L. Kingsley." The poem itself is unremarkable, recycling clichéd tropes on romantic love, but one feature stands out: the poem opens with six stanzas not about Kingsley but about the poet, giving us a glimpse into what Gallaudet thought about himself as a writer of verse. Poetry has soothed his "lonely hours," he says, and has been shown only to close friends, never for praise. And then, speaking of himself in the third person, he says,

Had Heav'n propitious bless'd
His morn of life with hours more gay,
Nor on his aching brow press'd
Hope-chilling Hypochondria

Perchance, a nobler son of song,

In riper years he might have been

And, bards of sweet renown among,

With bay-encircled brow been seen.

Did he really think he could have been a renowned poet if he hadn't been afflicted with hypochondria (which he apparently pronounced "hip-o-con-dry-ay")? These stanzas have the feel of real autobiographical comment, not a poetic conceit.

A second bit of evidence we have for what Gallaudet was doing while he waited out the winter weather in Lexington is a May 10th letter written to him by an unknown person he had met in Lexington. This person evidently shared Gallaudet's deep interest in soteriology and was probably affiliated with Transylvania University, which in 1811 was in the throes of doctrinal disputes that would eventually sever its affiliation with the Presbyterians and give it a Unitarian president. Gallaudet had given him an excerpt from one of Dwight's sermons, which must have been handy in his saddlebags and which the acquaintance found "precisely to my mind." The May letter from this unknown person very helpfully, for us, paraphrases Gallaudet's views on "the operations of the spirit": because God works his providences, his plans for us, through our shifting feelings, which depend upon the bodies we have from birth and are as constituted by social norms, the same must be true for God's bestowal of grace. Don't physical causes, Gallaudet asked, affect not only our day-to-day decisions but also our intellectual views of our souls?[39]

Three days after leaving Lexington on his return trip, Gallaudet filled four pages of his journal, confessing that "I discern nothing but death, final and eternal death at thy hands.... I believe that I have deserved at the hands of God eternal banishment from his presence and a consignment to endless misery," and so on. In that same lengthy entry, however, was a "recital of my belief" that included a trust in God's mercy for "a happy immortality beyond the grave." Did this not constitute confidence in salvation?

Primary sources again disappear. Henry Barnard wrote that "on his return, with the intention of pursuing a mercantile life, he entered as clerk a counting-room in the city of New York"; Heman Humphrey followed Barnard, adding that the counting room was "respectable"; E. M. Gallaudet turned this "respectable counting room" into "a permanent engagement . . .

with the firm for which he had been traveling," a patently erroneous conjecture, because Gallaudet told Kingsley from Kentucky that "my present
situation affords no prospect . . . of establishing myself in any regular business for life." All we can say for sure about this position was that Gallaudet
learned — or boned up on — double entry bookkeeping, which he would
use for his own household accounts to the end of his life.[40]

Eight months later, he was enrolled at Andover Theological Seminary
in Andover, Massachusetts. Since he had not yet been divinely assured of
regeneration, he must have enrolled in the expectation that his studies
would nudge the Holy Spirit to action on his behalf. Or he may simply have
found himself unfit to be a bookkeeper and regarded seminary studies as
a respectable out, whether regeneration was granted or not. He had been
painfully conscious, on the Kentucky trip, of his moral obligation to his
father for an education "greater than I, as one of nine children, am entitled
to," and Andover "offer[ed] gratuitous instruction, and the gratuitous use
of such books, as are fitted to this purpose," and it provided students with
"the necessary expenses of living."[41]

Andover had been established only a few years earlier by conservative
Calvinists responding to the shocking appointment of a Unitarian at Harvard College, and it was Timothy Dwight himself who delivered the sermon
at the opening ceremonies in 1808. His topic was the imminent demise
of Roman Catholicism and Islam, the signal importance of "the church
of God . . . which keeps this putrid world from absolute corruption," and
the expected arrival of the Millennium, when the Jews would gather in
Israel, the heathen would "*cast their idols to the moles,*" and the whole world
would "become one vast temple of JEHOVAH."[42] Dwight's choice of the
Millennium as his topic was pitch-perfect, because the seminary's students
were overwhelmingly intending to fit themselves as missionaries to take
an active part in ushering in the thousand-year reign of peace that would
precede the Second Coming of Christ. The notion that godly men could
hasten the Millennium by working to evangelize and reform human beings
worldwide may seem counterintuitive, because Calvinists generally believed
that history was predetermined in God's Providence. Yet the belief that one
could — and in fact had the duty to — expedite the thousand-year reign
of peace and the subsequent Second Coming of Christ was nevertheless
ironically the linchpin in all the reform efforts of the day and would become
the chief motivation for all of Gallaudet's reform efforts in the coming years.

The entire seminary was lodged in a single building on the Phillips Academy campus. There were thirty dormitory rooms, each with its own wood stove for heat, and students fetched their water in pitchers from an outdoor pump. There were to have been five professors, but as yet the faculty comprised only three: one in Sacred Literature, one in Ecclesiastical History, and one in Eloquence of the Desk, which was the composition and delivery of sermons. The planned professorships of Natural Theology and Christian Theology were unfilled. The professors took an oath, renewed every five years, to oppose atheists, infidels, Jews, Papists, "Mohametans," Unitarians (as bad as deists but not as honest, one of the founders said), and Universalists, as well as any belief contrary to the doctrines of original sin, the election or predestination of souls, and other tenets of Calvinism. The three professors advocated "social improvement" in the cause of the Millennium, but they warned that any attempt to change the social order or advocate any action that might produce civil discord was unchristian. Andover students, most of whom had Yale degrees of considerably more recent mint than Gallaudet's and who were thus some years younger than he, absorbed their professors' views and spent their lives advocating snail's-pace amelioration in all social matters.[43]

The annual reports produced by the faculty during Gallaudet's years at Andover give us some idea of the curriculum. Ebenezer Porter, who taught Eloquence of the Desk, met with seniors three times a week to lecture on rhetoric, composition, and delivery; his students wrote skeletons — outlines or plans — of sermons and submitted these for his criticism. In addition, Porter reported giving minute attention to delivery: articulation, pauses, and gestures, as students practiced in the chapel with the published sermons of others and were critiqued by their classmates. Gallaudet was never to be regarded as a mesmerizing preacher — his forte was clarity — so perhaps Porter's methods were not very effective with all students.

Moses Stuart, professor of Sacred Literature, had been one of two tutors assigned to Gallaudet's Yale class of 1805; whether or not he was Gallaudet's tutor, they would have known one another from Yale. In 1812, Stuart reported that the class of which Gallaudet was a member regularly heard him lecture on sacred literature, and under his direction they studied Hebrew two days a week, reading twenty chapters of Genesis, sixty chapters of Psalms, and the first ten chapters of Proverbs, and New Testament Greek two days a week, reading twenty-five chapters in the Evangelists. They also engaged in "minute, grammatical, critical and hermeneutic investigation of the sacred text" at hand, with the goal of producing a "correct interpretation of the Word of God," and in weekly discussions with him of their work.

The third professor, Leonard Woods, who taught Ecclesiastical History, was in poor health, so his reports are skimpy and he did not teach at all in 1813. Woods's lack of interest in the logical inconsistencies of doctrinal matters such as free will and redemption, however, was said to have significantly influenced students, so Gallaudet most likely had Woods to thank for letting go of his difficulties with Calvinist doctrine. In any case, he was ready to profess his beliefs at the Center Church of Hartford at the end of his first year of classes.[44]

The year had been momentous outside the confines of the seminary, as the United States declared war on the United Kingdom. Both Timothy Dwight and Nathan Strong saw the declaration of war as a de facto decision to join forces with the "Anti-Christ" (France) and warned of divine chastisement. The Standing Order and its spokesmen Dwight and Strong hoped to provoke outrage among the citizenry, but although it's safe to assume that Andover students were as opposed to "Mr. Madison's War" as everyone else in Federalist New England, the war seems to have been felt largely as a difficulty in getting textbooks, and life went along much as usual for students who barely noticed the battles roaring through the St. Lawrence and breaking out in spots along the Atlantic Coast.[45]

Professor Stuart told the directors that the library did not hold sufficient numbers of New Testament Greek and Hebrew dictionaries or of the Septuagint, and that it held no Hebrew grammar at all. In 1813, he told the directors it was impossible to buy some of these books because they were available only from England; in 1814, he was able to report that Hebrew Bibles and New Testament lexicons were being published in the United States.

As for the students, they too were desperate for books during the war — or at least some of them were. The Society of Inquiry, an invitation-only student group focused on foreign missions, saw the lack of books as its chief difficulty. In an 1813 letter, apparently to someone with London connections, the committee sought an agent there who would purchase books and mail them to Andover. The committee then naively added, "We are aware of the difficulties that at present obstruct all communications between Europe and this Country, but we trust they will not entirely frustrate our wishes." In fact, as the young men were penning this letter, Newark was being burned and Fort Niagara captured by the British, so one would say they did indeed have a problem. Six months later the students had scaled back their hopes and were seeking a book-buying agent in Boston, asking for discounts and considering terms of credit. Their naive proffers bring a smile today, but in truth, specie was so scarce that they had little choice. A loose sheet now in the Society Records tells us exactly what they wanted to buy: mostly dictionaries and grammars of "Hindoostanee" and "Sanskrita." Gallaudet was not a member of this group, perhaps simply because he had no intention of leaving the country on a foreign mission, but he would have known about his classmates' worries concerning the missionaries' language barrier, and in just a few years he would come up with a neat, all-purpose solution: Sign.[46]

The only firsthand information we have on Gallaudet as an Andover student shows him to have been one of the "noisy idle fellows" who "with unavailing battle / Disturb the quiet by our rattle" — by playing battle-dore while others were trying to study. His poem, "The Petition of the Battledores, Written while a member of the Theolog. Sem. at Andover, Mass. 1813 — when some found fault with some of us who used battledore for exercise,"[47] is written in the voice of a battledore, a racket strung with parchment, gently mocking the killjoy students: "Dread Sirs! incline a patient ear / You humble battledores to hear, / With parchment-rending grief who learn / Their healthful aid ye 'gin to spurn."

At the 1814 anniversary exercises in September, Gallaudet gave a valedictory oration that clearly had been composed by a committee of students. None of it sounds anything like Gallaudet, or like anyone else in particular, but reads rather like a hodgepodge that aims to include each student's hobbyhorse. There is a nod to William Wilberforce, who had sponsored a bill that abolished the British slave trade but had left slavery intact in the British West Indian colonies — his full conversion to abolition would not occur until the 1820s. There is also a nod given to the War of 1812: while "others have been stunned with 'the confused noise' of the 'battle of the warrior,' and seen 'garments rolled in blood,' *we* have heard at a distance 'the noise of the seas, the noise of their waves, and the tumult of the people.' Our employment has been the delightful one of 'inclining the ear onto wisdom, and applying the heart to understanding;' of 'searching for the hid treasures' of that divine knowledge, into which 'angels desire to look.'"[48]

And there are the customary remarks about the students' immediate futures as "the busy and momentous scenes of untried action" and "a course which, though arduous, is delightful," which cannot be understood as Gallaudet's own expectations — there is no evidence whatever that he himself actually contemplated a life as a missionary to foreign lands or anything else either busy or momentous or untried or arduous or, sad to say, delightful.

The valedictory address, like Gallaudet's entire three years at Andover, gives the impression of a total lack of engagement, of disconnect, of playing battledore rather than angling to procure a "Hindoostanee" dictionary at a reasonable discount. Now in his late twenties, he was licensed to preach upon presenting a "Theological Discourse, Together with His Views of the Natural and Revealed Religion" and answering questions put to him.[49] Ordination was the affair of the congregation that hired a minister (or the mission society that sent him abroad), and Gallaudet would much later claim to have been ordained by the Rev. Mr. Nathan Perkins, pastor of the Fourth Church of Hartford, at an Ecclesiastical Council convened in 1834. Unfortunately, as far as the Congregational Library Obituary Database is concerned, this never happened: he was never ordained. Unless Perkins, who was well into his eighties at the time, misfiled his record of the ordination, it's hard to explain Gallaudet's claim. He was certainly licensed to preach in 1814, however, and he preached both as a guest and as a chaplain until his death.[50]

And now, Thomas Hopkins Gallaudet returned to his father's house in Hartford, next door to Dr. and Mrs. Cogswell and their five small children. The Gallaudets also had five small children. When they had moved to Hartford fourteen years earlier, they had already buried three children in Philadelphia and had five still living. The next child, Ann Watts, was born the year of the move. Jane the younger was born in 1801 while Gallaudet was finishing grammar school, Theodore in 1805 when Gallaudet was graduating at Yale, Edward in 1808 when Gallaudet was speaking about ambition at the Yale commencement, and Wallace the younger in 1811 when Gallaudet was completing his trip to Kentucky and working in the "respectable counting room." In 1814, then, when Gallaudet returned to his parents' home, Jane Gallaudet, now forty-nine — her last child was born when she was forty-six — would have had at least the five younger children in the house. What's worse was the prospect of the imminent failure of the family business — they would leave Hartford within two years for New York, where P. W. would open a Christian bookstore, a significant downscaling of his business aspirations. But in the meantime, they were hanging on in Hartford, and however much they loved their firstborn, one can imagine how little pleased they were to see him unpack his bags.

As for the Cogswells next door, former Hartford Wit Mason Fitch Cogswell was now a father of a family and a surgeon whose reputation derived chiefly from cataract surgery. Cogswell had been training in New York in 1784–1785 when the German surgeon Frederick William Jericho, who had pioneered the removal of a cataract from the lens of the eye, visited the city as part of a tour of the United States to train other doctors in the technique.[51] The operation was still regarded as sensational when Cogswell became one of the first American cataract surgeons. Now married to the step-daughter of the owner of the Federalist *Courant,* Cogswell was the father of five. His oldest child, Mary, was the same age as Gallaudet's youngest sister Jane, and his youngest, Catharine, was the same age as little Wallace Gallaudet. It must have been a lively neighborhood when the children were out of school.

But the Cogswell children were usually in school. The summer before Gallaudet came home, Daniel Wadsworth had established an invitation-only private girls' school in his mother's mansion, taught by the young poet and schoolteacher from Norwich, Lydia Huntley. Fifteen girls of the very first families in Hartford had been selected as Miss Huntley's pupils, with Mary, Elizabeth, and Alice Cogswell among the fifteen. As Lydia Huntley explained in her autobiography many years later, writing as the internationally known poet Mrs. Sigourney, "As his [Wadsworth's] influence in society gave him an almost unlimited choice of pupils, he kept in view the similarity of station and of attainments," so as to eliminate "disparities that might cause jealousies and impede friendships."[52]

The fact that Alice Cogswell had been deaf since age two apparently made no difference to Wadsworth as he considered her "attainments." Alice and her family used so-called home signs, a vocabulary of signs invented by a deaf child for persons, objects, and activities specific to the household, with minimal to no grammar. But we can deduce from the word-for-word English glosses of Alice's signed utterances that Miss Huntley jotted down at the time that the Cogswells' home signs were sophisticated enough to have served for fairly detailed narratives, and, more importantly for Alice's prospects of education, they exhibited a grammar very like that of a genuine sign language. Alice and her sisters taught these signs to Miss Huntley and the other girls in the class.

The Cogswells also used a finger alphabet, which Mrs. Sigourney describes as two handed and that was probably the so-called Old Alphabet, descended, in America, from an eighteenth-century form of the British finger alphabet. It was published in the *Pennsylvania Magazine* in 1776 as an amusement that could also be used by the deaf. A 1793 observer described it thus: "Many of the dumb learn to communicate by their fingers, forming an alphabet, by pointing at each finger, by shutting them separately, by laying various numbers of fingers upon the other hand, first on one side, then on the other, and by different signs, passing through the whole scale of sounds — and composing words by visible motions, which are agreed upon by a friend." This, too, was adopted in Miss Huntley's classroom. The third and final element in Alice's communications skill set was speech, which she uttered "with a guttural intonation," and Mrs. Sigourney tells us that Alice spoke when she signed, though her words were probably not well understood, for her father describes her as able "neither to hear nor speak."[53]

It's certain that Alice's mother had taught her at least the basics of reading. Children were expected to have learned the letters of the alphabet and to have a simple, basic reading vocabulary before they started school, and Wadsworth would not have invited Alice if she had not been at least minimally prepared. The finger alphabet alone demonstrates her literacy, since it can be used only among people who can read. Less than one year after Miss Huntley's school opened, Alice wrote this, without help or correction, in a letter to Gallaudet: "I am very glad you write to me. You stay long in the ship on the waves," and "I hope, I shall learn to read well before you Come back. — I love my arithmetic and my school." It's not flawlessly idiomatic English, but neither is it remarkably out of the range of early writing samples of any child, which suggests that Alice, who could not have learned the English language by ear, began reading well before she started with Miss Huntley. The Cogswells were delighted with Miss Huntley and with Alice's progress in her classroom; Miss Huntley was effusively delighted with Alice; and Alice was delighted with everyone.

Nevertheless, it surely occurred to all involved with Alice Cogswell and Miss Huntley's school, including the other twelve girls and their parents, that while language diversity — or Christian charity, as they probably saw it — was all well and good, the girls would be learning more efficiently if Alice were in a full-time communication-accessible classroom and the other fourteen had a full-time spoken-language, recitation-centered school day. Dr. Cogswell was convinced that there were many deaf Americans in just as much need of literacy as his daughter was and that he was uniquely positioned to help them. How Cogswell proceeded is discussed in the next chapter.

This chapter ends with the return of Thomas Hopkins Gallaudet to his parents' home and his acquaintance with Alice. What was he doing in the months after September 1814? Certainly not waiting for job offers; these came but were declined on grounds of ill health, as we have seen in the previous chapter: "I have been very much of an invalid for these nine or ten years." Gallaudet's stated plans were "to preach only occasionally as my strength will permit, to journey at frequent intervals, and to decline being settled, unless indeed some situation should offer cares and duties far less numerous than must be attached to the ministry among as large a congregation as [Portsmouth's]." How he planned to earn his bread, he never said.

Gallaudet's friend, William A. Alcott, perhaps got it right when he said that Gallaudet "seemed unwilling to engage; perhaps he knew not why."[54] Years later, Gallaudet's family and those among his colleagues who undertook to secure his legacy, claimed that God's plan for him was his reason for dithering: as Henry Barnard put it, "his Master had work for him" not yet disclosed. Tales of his teaching Alice were intertwined with this explanation, as Heman Humphrey, Gallaudet's second biographer, followed Barnard and one-upped him, so to speak: Gallaudet's "Master" not only had a plan but actually "visited one of the most prominent and worthy families in Hartford, with a sore and lasting affliction," making their daughter deaf so that Gallaudet could enter onto his life's work, "unstopping the ears of thousands, and pouring the light of knowledge and salvation into their dark minds." Like Barnard, Humphrey says that Gallaudet began to teach Alice "in his vacations at home." Edward Miner Gallaudet, writing as an old man and looking back fondly on the father he hardly knew, can do no better than to quote Barnard and Lewis Weld, a man who taught at the Hartford school for the deaf while Gallaudet was principal — in fact, Gallaudet had recruited him for the job fresh out of Yale — and who later married Alice's sister Mary.[55]

Lewis Weld seems to have been the originator of the now famous hat myth, and I use the word "myth" deliberately of the many foundation stories that grew up around Gallaudet, some of which may well contain elements of historical truth. While Alice "was amusing herself with other children at his father's house," Weld wrote, Gallaudet noticed that she was "deaf and dumb" and took a "compassionate interest in her situation, with a strong desire to alleviate it."

> He at once attempted to converse with and instruct her and actually suc-
> ceeded in teaching her the word *hat* before she left this garden where the
> interview took place. This led to a very intimate intercourse with the child
> and her father's family during intervals of relaxation from professional
> studies extending through several years, and resulted in her acquiring,
> chiefly through his agency, so much knowledge of very simple words and
> sentence as satisfied her friends that she might learn to write and read, and
> that Mr. Gallaudet of all in the circle of their acquaintance, was the person
> best qualified to undertake her instruction.... Dr. Cogswell ... hesitated
> no longer, but resolved that by the leave of a kind Providence his daughter
> should be educated.[56]

Edward Miner Gallaudet, in improving on Weld's foundation myth, declared that Alice was wholly uneducated, in "deplorable condition" when Gallaudet met her.[57] It's the Deaf American origin story, the "Grand Narrative," as British sociologist Paddy Ladd calls it, in which "Deaf communities are constructed solely as the individual end product of a lineage of distinguished hearing educators" rather than as the communal efforts of Deaf people and their families.[58] In this myth, Alice is passive and disadvantaged; her father is helpless; both await Gallaudet's wise intervention.

None of this bears any relation to what we know of Gallaudet, the Cogswells, or the society in which they lived. Weld was still a child on his father's farm outside of Hartford at the time the hat story was supposed to have happened. Gallaudet was vague on *what* he taught Alice — there is no hat — but he is quite definite about *when:* it was during that idle winter of 1814–1815 — when Alice was in school with Miss Huntley, though he doesn't say that.[59] Mrs. Sigourney, for her part, everywhere and entirely fails to mention either that Alice had previously had any other teachers than her own family before enrolling in Wadsworth's school, or that Gallaudet even knew Alice until he was hired by the committee of benefactors to research deaf education and set up a school. What we know or can be reasonably confident is true is that the Cogswells signed at home, Alice learned her letters, the finger alphabet, and simple words from her family, and she was mainstreamed into an exclusive girls' school by 1814. We should therefore have some serious questions about the hat myth.

One question would be just when it was still possible for Alice not to know the word "hat," a three-letter, monosyllabic word of the kind common in primers used by mothers to teach young children their letters. Even without a primer, it was the sort of word that anyone might have chosen in an early lesson. Charlotte Elizabeth Phelan, for example, writing in 1823, described a first lesson for a deaf child using the words "dog," "man," and "hat," all made with cardboard letters arranged on a rug.[60] Mrs. Cogswell would have had a primer in the house, one that she had used with her two older children. Such primers were all based on a premodern form of phonics, not exactly suited to teaching a deaf child who could not associate letters with sounds but easy enough to adapt to a whole-word reading approach. Mrs. Cogswell clearly did something like that, because Alice was spelling words on her fingers when she arrived in Miss Huntley's classroom. Alice having been born in 1805, her mother would have been spending time with her and a basic primer by, perhaps, 1809, and certainly before 1811. A classmate of Alice's at the Asylum, George Loring, in official remarks made years later after the deaths of Alice and her parents and *at a ceremony honoring Gallaudet and Clerc,* stated that Dr. and Mrs. Cogswell "used every means they could contrive to teach her the simplest rudiments of written language, and, in the attempt, they partially succeeded."[61]

A second question concerning dates would be how much time Alice would have had for anything but the most casual of exchanges with Gallaudet after she began school with Miss Huntley, school being a six-day-a-week endeavor with only Saturday afternoons free. Sundays were not days on which children could play outside, and Mrs. Sigourney tells us that her pupils returned to school on Saturday afternoons to make clothing for the poor.

A third question would involve what exactly a twenty-seven- or twenty-eight-year-old man was doing outside watching children play. Had his father no work for him in accounts, his mother no odd jobs for him around the house or errands in town? What was going on in the Gallaudet family?

The answers to the first two questions are deducible from the record. Alice already knew the English word "hat" and was probably trying to teach Gallaudet the sign for the concept when he scratched the word in the ground, if indeed the hat incident ever really took place at all. And Alice certainly was not available for any sort of regular hours with another teacher. The answer to the third question concerning why Gallaudet was hanging around his parents' backyard remains a mystery. On that note, we begin the next chapter by looking into what else was going on next door, at the Cogswell residence.

WHEN ALICE COGSWELL LOST her hearing to spinal meningitis in November of 1807, three months after her second birthday, the Cogswells were presented with a challenging communication puzzle. With the parents initially baffled, it was left to Alice and her older sisters to develop a functioning system of home signs, which they did.

The Old Alphabet, with which one could spell English words on one's fingers, would have come to the family from an outside source after Alice started learning to read. Cogswell's father, James, who had been living with his son's family in Hartford until his death the previous year, had had his portrait painted some years previous by the deaf limner John Brewster, who had lived in the elder Cogswell's home while the portrait was in progress. Brewster, who as a fifty-year-old would later be Alice Cogswell's oldest classmate at the Asylum, used a sign language of some sort, never documented, and he probably also used the indigenous Old Alphabet to spell words on his fingers: he was literate in English, perhaps only minimally so but enough to have made use of a finger alphabet with patrons. Alice's parents were unlikely to have met Brewster themselves but would certainly have heard James Cogswell's stories about this singular figure. Alternately, Dr. Cogswell could have known the Old Alphabet from boyhood. Finger alphabets were in widespread use among schoolboys and clerics long before the establishment of deaf education; the founder of deaf education in France, Charles Michel de l'Épée, for example, had been acquainted with the French finger alphabet before he ever met a deaf person. More than the Old Alphabet, however, the Cogswells appeared not to know.[1]

It is widely accepted that Alice's family had, as Henry Barnard averred, "a publication of the Abbe Sicard, which Dr. Cogswell had procured from Paris," but this is highly unlikely. Cogswell did not read French (nor did Gallaudet at this date), and in any case Roche-Ambroise Sicard's 1800 and 1808 books on deaf education were so exclusively focused on teaching pupils to read French as to have been worthless to a monolingual American family beyond the general lesson that such instruction was possible. Barnard could have confused Sicard with his predecessor at the Paris school for the deaf, the Abbé Charles Michel de l'Épée, from having half-remembered a claim Gallaudet made 1818 that he had perused "a treatise on the mode of instructing deaf-mutes, by the Abbé de l'Épée, providentially in the possession of [Alice's] father" before 1816. Of course that would have had to be in translation.[2] That Gallaudet could not read French despite a Yale and Huguenot heritage may seem remarkable, but this deficiency was common, indeed willful, in the early republic, where a new nationalism prompted even intelligent people such as Dr. Benjamin Rush to say that learning French was not worthwhile because "the English language certainly contains many more books of real utility and useful information than can be read without neglecting other duties."[3] In other words, as Gallaudet said in one of his Yale disputes, we already have enough books here. The instant case is an example of how Connecticut's provincial suspicions of the larger world hampered Cogswell's efforts.

Ironically, a treatise by de l'Épée had been translated by the Bostonian Francis Green as *The Method of Instructing the Deaf and Dumb, Confirmed by Long Experience,* and it could have been obtained if Cogswell had known about it. Green was a father who had been through everything Cogswell was to go through in seeking education for his child and for other deaf children, and he left a significant paper trail on his research in the form of two books and numerous newspaper articles. It is one of the fascinating ironies of the history of deaf education in America that while Green had undertaken the translation for the very purpose of "enabl[ing] every person, who is disposed, to become an instructor of the Deaf and Dumb,"[4] his two books and all of his journalistic efforts were so mysteriously forgotten that no English-language reader seems to have benefited from them. Cogswell and Gallaudet could have saved significant time, effort, and money if they had known Green's work.

Green was a Boston merchant who, because he was a Loyalist, settled in Halifax for a time after the Revolution. In 1780, he sent his son Charles to the Braidwood Academy in Edinburgh, where the boy was given artic-ulation lessons (speech therapy), excelled in drawing, and learned a signed language that he used with classmates. Green's visits to Charles in Edin-burgh impressed him deeply, and he documented his views in *Vox Oculis Subjecta*, which outlined the Braidwoods' "art." Noting that information on deaf education was difficult to find, Green hoped his work would doc-ument the Braidwoods' "ingenious method" and "excite the attention of the public" to a plan for a free school for children who were born deaf.[5] Published anonymously in England in 1783, the book was reviewed in the *Boston Magazine* in 1784 and was published in the United States in 1785, back in the days when a bachelor Cogswell was chortling over his rhyming mockeries with fellow Wits.

What happened next is not precisely known, but something surprised Green into a rupture with the Braidwoods, whom he never mentioned again, subsequently referring to *Vox Occulis Subjecta* as a "*hasty pamphlet.*"[6] Alexander Graham Bell concluded, in 1900, that the Braidwoods regarded Green's publication of their methods to be a violation of their intellectual property rights, and Gallaudet's subsequent experience with the Braidwoods suggests that Bell is correct in that conjecture. Charles Green drowned while hunting near Halifax in 1787, the year of Gallaudet's birth, but Francis Green continued his research: within three years, he was in Paris visiting de l'Épée's school for the deaf and in London agitating for a charity school to be established along the same lines. In 1801, when Gallaudet was still a pupil at the Hartford Grammar School, Green undertook the translation of de l'Épée's *Method of Educating the Deaf and Dumb.* In the translator's preface, Green again notes the difficulty of finding books on deaf education; he lists all the books known to him and marvels that none of the authors knew anything at all about their predecessors in this field. Green praises de l'Épée's efforts to remedy that strange disconnect and condemns the conduct of unnamed others — the Braidwoods — who adhered to the practice "like the Jewish Talmudist, who dealt in secret writings, *of allowing no persons to be professed practical conjurers but the Sanhedrim themselves.*"[7] With this turn toward de l'Épée's pedagogical approach, Green ceases to speak of deaf education as an "art" or an "ingenious method" and instead writes of de l'Épée's book as a kind of vade mecum that enables "every person" to teach the deaf by any method deemed suitable.

Green concludes his interesting preface by acknowledging the difficulty of translating into English a work on teaching French, admitting that where he has been unable to provide English analogues to de l'Épée's explanations of how to teach French in sign language — where his text was "out of the reach of translation" — he simply omitted sections, although a perusal of the translation shows that he also left many such instances stand in French. A similar work "formed upon the structure of the English tongue," Green wrote, is needed before deaf education can properly be undertaken in Anglophone nations.[8] This was the case because de l'Épée was teaching in a system for encoding French, rather than in a natural sign language; more on this point follows.

While Gallaudet was pursuing undergraduate studies at Yale, Green, now back in Boston, pleaded for a free school for deaf children, so that

"the translator . . . will not have lived, *altogether*, in vain," and appealed to
the Massachusetts clergy for a count of deaf residents of the state, all in
letters published in the *New England Palladium* in 1803 and the *Medical
Repository* (New York) in 1804. The Massachusetts clergy, who were state
officials of the established Congregational Church, responded with a list
of seventy-five names, from which Green extrapolated the figure of five
hundred deaf residents in the country as a whole. Green's numbers were
severe undercounts. Today's deaf demographic is around .10 percent of
the population, but Green's count was less than .02 percent of the state's
population; there should have been at least four hundred deaf people in
Massachusetts alone and more than five thousand in the nation (counting
enslaved residents).[9] But whatever the numbers, nothing came of Green's
ideas or his efforts to establish a free school, and he died in Medford in
1809. Interestingly for present-day students of Deaf foundation mythology,
in these newspaper articles Green also recounted, for perhaps the first time
in English, the story of de l'Épée's initial instruction of "two twin sisters,
Deaf and Dumb from their birth," whose mythological significance is un-
derscored by their namelessness.[10]

As for Green's translation of de l'Épée, Gallaudet's memory of perus-
ing the book before 1816 was surely faulty. For one thing, Cogswell never
mentioned the book to Alice's teacher Lydia Huntley, who stated flatly that
neither the sign language nor the one-handed alphabet (as was used at de
l'Épée's school in Paris) had as yet "crossed the ocean to the western world":
"Having no guide in this species of instruction," she wrote, "I earnestly labored to enlarge the number of signs."[11] Had Cogswell actually owned and
read Green's translation of de l'Épée before sending Gallaudet to Europe, he
would scarcely have let Miss Huntley flounder in the classroom inventing
signs with his three daughters as she did. For another thing, on the eve of
sailing for England "on the deaf and dumb business," as Gallaudet called it,
Gallaudet was telling Jedidiah Morse, an Illuminati conspiracy theorist and
cofounder of Andover Theological Seminary, that "the mss. of Mr. Green
of which Mrs. Morse spoke to me, on the subject of instruction [*sic*] the
deaf and dumb, in case it is of value, could be secured for me against my
return, or it could be sent to me now, it might perhaps contribute to the
success of my undertaking."[12]

Why the Morses would have a copy of any of Green's manuscripts is not
clear. But it is perfectly plain in this letter that Gallaudet knew nothing

about Green and that, if Mrs. Morse read the manuscript in question, it must have related to Green's work on *Vox Occulis Subjecta* — otherwise, she would have told Gallaudet that Paris, not England, was the place to go. But perhaps she never read it. It was one near miss after another with Gallaudet and Green. What is perhaps of greatest significance in these missed connections, however, is that the Hartford group did not know about Green's call for an Anglophone reworking of de l'Épée's book to render it suitable for teaching written English and did not realize that such a reworking was needed before Americans could make use of it. Cogswell could have started on that work, perhaps in cooperation with Lydia Huntley, who was perhaps the one person in Hartford who did read French.

Even without Lydia Huntley's testimony, one could hardly imagine that Cogswell had read Green's translation of de l'Épée's book and failed to understand from the get-go that the Braidwoods were jealously secretive about their "art." Had he read Green's preface, Cogswell would never have let Gallaudet waste many months in London and Edinburgh spending the money of Hartford donors while waiting for the Braidwoods to come through. Yet that is just what he did. So, despite Gallaudet's 1818 claim that he read Cogswell's copy of de l'Épée's book early in his acquaintance with Alice, all other evidence suggests that Green's translation of de l'Épée and all of Green's, de l'Épée's, and Sicard's other works were essentially unknown to both him and Cogswell. Gallaudet would play catch-up on the language challenge after the school had already opened and he at last got his hands on Green's 1801 translation — many weeks *after* the Asylum's first day of class: Gallaudet's personal copy is dated in Cogswell's hand July 1, 1817.

Before continuing with Gallaudet as he valiantly sets forth to master the "art" of deaf education in England, we must discard any simplified dichotomy between "oral" and "manual" modes of instruction, a perceived either-or that is in reality but a misleading shorthand for the competing ideas of how classroom communication should be conducted. Purely oral instruction did exist at this time — in Prussia. There, pupils were trained in speech production and lipreading, taught academic subjects by speech they could not hear, and made to recite in artificially acquired vocalization. Such an approach was not taken anywhere in the UK during Gallaudet's day. As for purely manual instruction *in a natural signed language,* which is how we understand manual instruction today, that method was practiced nowhere in the world in the early years of the nineteenth century. The Paris school taught in manually encoded French, constructed by de l'Épée and Sicard from the natural sign lexemes they acquired from deaf Parisians, plus gestures they invented for French tenses, person, mode, number, gender, and so forth.

Neither Francis Green nor Gallaudet viewed the Braidwood-Épée divide in terms of oral vs. manual. For both, the difference between deaf education in the United Kingdom and France was that the Braidwoods claimed a secret "art" that included speech training, while the Abbés de l'Épée and Sicard were happy to show any interested party the artificial code, gigantic chalk boards, and seat-of-the-pants techniques with which they conducted their lessons.[13] It's worth noting here, too, that one did not have to be an educated person like the French abbés or Gallaudet, or even a hearing person, to figure out how it could be done. Charlotte Elizabeth Phelan (1790–1846), an Englishwoman who had become deaf at age ten, took deaf Irish children off the street near Kilkenny and educated them in her home. "The teacher must first learn of his pupil, by observing what signs he makes use to express different ideas," she wrote. Just as hearing toddlers learn English "by catching a word here and there" rather than by studying a book of English grammar, "any person" may instruct a deaf child by watching for opportunities to introduce English equivalents. Gallaudet would surely have liked and admired "Charlotte Elizabeth," as she signed her many publications, for she was a fanatic anti-Catholic who took those deaf Irish children into her home largely in order to convert them. However, she did not commence this work until after she'd left her husband in in 1819, when Gallaudet was already operating his school in Hartford.[14]

It's nevertheless true that the Braidwoods taught all their students to speak, with success ranging from nil to passable, while the French abbés regarded it as largely a waste of time. Taking the longer view available to the twentieth century and considering the two approaches in the context of the history of ideas, Jules Paul Seigel argues convincingly that French deaf education conducted in silence was a natural excrescence of Enlightenment philosophy, or, as he says, "*l'esprit philosophique*," whereas in Great Britain, deaf education was inhibited by "religious zealotry" and "political conservatism." In both countries, deaf education was initially in these years conducted by the clergy, but whereas de l'Épée and Sicard were concerned "for human and moral progress, for individual apprehension, of truth, for improvement through science and empiricism," the Braidwoods and the

Anglican ministers who used their methods were "more concerned with dogma and the achievement of spiritual salvation." Seigel doesn't mention deaf education in America, but it's clear that Connecticut was a lot more like Great Britain than it was like France and that deaf education might well have suffered the same inhibition in New England as it did in London had Gallaudet made different choices. That he chose as he did is due in part to Sicard's willingness, and the Braidwoods' unwillingness, to train other teachers. But there are other factors, too, that tilted Gallaudet's thinking about deaf education. One of these factors is his reading of the Scottish Common Sense philosophers, who had brought *l'esprit philosophique* to Great Britain and were speculating about deaf education themselves, as we shall see.[15]

How much of all this Cogswell grasped probably amounted to nothing at all, and he set out to reinvent the wheel by duplicating Green's efforts, though with somewhat different aims. For one thing, since the Revolution, during which time the Loyalist Green was sending his son to Edinburgh for his education, Americans had become suspicious of foreign schooling. That Cogswell never seriously considered sending Alice abroad probably had less to do with his attachment to the little girl and more to do with worries that "an attachment to a foreign government, or rather a want of attachment to our <u>own</u>, is the natural effect of a residence abroad during the period of youth," or so said Noah Webster.[16]

And whereas Green had aimed to establish a *free* school, Cogswell had no such idea. Indeed, what he wanted for Alice seems to have been a social environment of her peers, deaf children of respectable professional- and mercantile-class Calvinists who were well enough off to be able to pay tuition. However, though he did want to keep out the riffraff, he was canny enough to seek state subsidies. Although there was no precedent in the United States for state or federal financing for schools of any sort, Cogswell fully expected taxpayers to subsidize their expenses in the name of benevolence, simply because the pupils were deaf. Harvey Prindle Peet, a Yale man who was trained at the Hartford Asylum and went on to head the New York Institution for the Instruction of the Deaf and Dumb, is simply fictionalizing this story when he says, in his 1852 tribute to Gallaudet, that the reason for establishing the school as "a boarding-school of the better class" was to ensure first-rate teachers, who would produce results that would cement the school's reputation and encourage state subsidies for the "indigent."[17] That was never the plan, as we see in the tragic story of the deafblind Julia Brace, who is introduced in this chapter.

Unaware, then, that he was following in Green's footsteps, Cogswell started with a request that would involve the state in his cause: a census of deaf residents. The way to go about getting this count in Connecticut, as it was for Green in Massachusetts, was through the established church, which supported clergy proportionate to population through each state. Green, whose Tory history suggests he was an Episcopalian, had to post his appeal to the Massachusetts clergy in a newspaper, which may account for the dramatic undercount he got, but Cogswell had only to mention his request to the Rev. Mr. Abel Flint of the South Church of Hartford, who happened to be secretary of the General Association, the statewide society of Congregational clergy. The Rev. Flint told Cogswell that he would have the report by the next annual association meeting, in June 1812.[18]

Cogswell already knew five other deaf Connecticut residents, because they were among the thirteen children of a lawyer in nearby Hebron: Sylvester Gilbert (1755–1846), a Dartmouth alumnus serving both in the Connecticut General Assembly and as a judge. Gilbert and Cogswell collaborated on the request for a census and on getting publicity about the effort into the papers. Gilbert's children were quite a bit older than Alice, and only the youngest of them, Mary, who was twenty-one in 1817 when the school was opened, was able to attend. (The other four presumably were already married, as age was no barrier to enrollment and marriage was the only circumstance other than inability to pay that kept a deaf person from enrolling.)[19]

In June, the results of the pastors' census of deaf residents came in: there were eighty-four deaf residents in Connecticut, leading Cogswell to figure two thousand deaf people in the United States. Like Green's figures, Cogswell's were serious undercounts, but both men were satisfied with what they took to be high numbers. Two weeks later, Congress declared war on Great Britain. The historian Phyllis Valentine writes that Cogswell "was requested to join his regiment, [in] New London,"[20] and he probably did so; in any case, his efforts to establish a school were in abeyance until 1815, when the war was over and Gallaudet, having sat out the fighting at Andover, was living with his exceedingly tolerant parents.

A very large number of letters, diary entries, and news releases from the next few years are extant — people seemed to realize that something historic was happening, so they clipped and filed. Examining these primary sources in some detail repays the effort, because what we find is very far from the simple tale of benevolent cooperation among Christian do-gooders that one is accustomed to find in works of Deaf history.

We know that Gallaudet was speculating about deaf education and his possible future in this field while he was still a student at Andover, perhaps as early as the date of the clergy's census results in his first year. He was certainly working on Cogswell's behalf as early as New Year's Day, 1815.[21] Whenever Cogswell brought Gallaudet into his plans for a Hartford deaf school, we are on firm ground with the date of April 13, 1815, when six wealthy Hartford men joined Cogswell to discuss sending someone abroad to study deaf education.[22] The disastrous Hartford Convention of the previous winter had left the Federalists in widespread disrepute. Cogswell's friend Theodore Dwight had been the convention's secretary, the Rev. Mr. Strong had opened the proceedings with prayer, and Chauncey Goodrich, Gallaudet's old law mentor, had been one of the seven delegates sent by the state of Connecticut. These men had hoped to effect constitutional changes that would protect the financial interests of Northern shipping magnates hurt by the war, but unfortunately for them, their resolutions were drowned in mass euphoria when news of Andrew Jackson's thrilling victory in the Battle of New Orleans in January reached the North. The war was over, America had won (or so they thought), but the Federalists had lost. It was time for Hartford Federalists to refocus on new avenues to power.[23]

The six men called to the April 13th meeting were, like Cogswell, staunch Federalists and evangelical Calvinists, but unlike Cogswell, exceedingly wealthy. Gallaudet would not have been invited, since he would have had nothing to contribute, at this point, to Cogswell's purpose of stroking the group for donations. P. W. and Jane Gallaudet, with the younger children, would leave Hartford for New York City in the first week of May, after which Gallaudet would lodge with the Cogswells, but at the date of the meeting Gallaudet was living at home.[24] The six men who did attend were carefully chosen for their fund-raising potential.

Daniel Wadsworth and his brother-in-law Nathaniel Terry had inherited their fortunes from Jeremiah Wadsworth, Daniel's father and Terry's father-in-law. The two men lived in adjacent mansions on Prospect Street, behind the old Wadsworth house on Main were the widow Wadsworth and Daniel's two unmarried sisters still lived, and where Alice Cogswell would soon be attending Lydia Huntley's school.[25] The widow Wadsworth was a daughter of Jonathan Trumbull Jr., governor of Connecticut from 1797 to his death in 1809, as well as a niece of the painter John Trumbull and a sister-in-law of Professor Benjamin Silliman of Yale College. As for Nathaniel Terry, he would go into politics and would serve both in the U.S. House of Representatives and as mayor of Hartford.

The brothers-in-law Wadsworth and Terry were associated with a third man at the meeting, John Caldwell, whose money came from the West Indies trade and who was in insurance as well as banking. The three together "practically monopolized" banking in Hartford.[26] The other three participants in the meeting were Ward Woodbridge, Daniel Buck, and Henry Hudson. Woodbridge, nearly as rich as Wadsworth, was a merchant and stockbroker, the owner of a cotton mill in Massachusetts, and an agent of a packet line that ran between New Haven and New York. He had founded a Hartford bank, where Buck and Hudson, as well as Terry, were directors. Daniel Buck was an importer and merchant who dealt in "Georgia cotton," "St. Croix Sugar," "St. Croix and New England Rum," and "Cuba Molasses," all slave-labor products, and he had founded a Hartford insurance company, the one today known as The Hartford. Henry Hudson was the son of Barzillai Hudson, Mrs. Cogswell's stepfather and one of the two co-owners of the *Courant;* Hudson worked for the publishers and booksellers Hudson and Goodwin, as well as serving as a director for Buck's insurance company and on the Hartford City Council. Dr. Cogswell chose these six men as representatives of all the sources of wealth in Hartford — insurance, banking, West Indies trade, and shipping — and of all the sources of power, including political office, the press, and intermarriage. For the finishing touch on this select group, he invited the Rev. Dr. Nathan Strong to provide the necessary religious endorsement.[27]

"As a result of the meeting," Cogswell descendant Grace Cogswell Root writes, Cogswell "and Ward Woodbridge were appointed a committee to collect the funds and so stirred did Hartford become overnight that in one day [actually, eighteen days] enough was subscribed — $2,133."[28] The "Original Subscription for the Deaf and Dumb, May 1st, 1815" shows that those "stirred" to donate amounted to sixty-five people, including fourteen who gave $100 each. Because so many of the donors have the same surnames as the original six men (Terry, Wadsworth, Hudson, Buck) or the surnames of their known business associates and affines (a Trumbull, four Goodwins, etc.), the large number of donors is a bit misleading, and we would better regard these people not as evidence of any citywide outpouring of philanthropy but as the relatives and business partners of the six men at the April meeting, which is precisely how Cogswell expected this phase of the fund-raising to work. He knew that were he simply to ask the general public for donations, the very notion of educating the deaf would be dismissed as "an absurd and useless waste of money," as it was in New Haven where Cogswell did not have the bundlers, so to speak, that he had in Hartford.[29] The May 1st list of subscribers states that the money is "for the purpose of defraying the expenses of the Revd. Thos. H. Gallaudet to Europe, that he may acquire the art of instructing the Deaf & Dumb in an Institution to be established in the Town of Hartford."[30] Notice the word "art."

Between the April 13th organizational meeting and the May 1st meeting at which the subscription list was drawn up naming Gallaudet the person undertaking the research trip, he was shilly-shallying. Already on February 1st, he had written to Professor Jeremiah Day at Yale College asking for help in locating a substitute to make the exploratory trip to Europe.[31] The day before Cogswell's April 13th meeting, Day finally responded, telling Gallaudet that he couldn't help him: "I shall be gratified to find that your reluctance to become yourself the principal agent has diminished. At the same time, I should hesitate strongly to urge anyone to undertake the business because it is of such a peculiar nature, that I think it ought to be entered upon voluntarily, and not by constraint."[32] Receiving this letter from Day so late in the game would have dashed Gallaudet's hope for an honorable exit from the charge Cogswell wanted to impose on him. He accepted the charge on April 20 and began a diary of the trip entitled, rather grandly, "A Journal of Some Occurrences in my Life which Have a Relation to the Instruction of the Deaf and Dumb." Written into a seven-by-nine-inch leather notebook with a sewn spine, it seems to have been kept for Cogswell's donors.[33]

Two additional letters that arrived during these same key days and that may also have affected his decision to accept Cogswell's charge together suggest that deaf education had become something of a fad at Andover. One letter from a classmate told Gallaudet that an "old friend" is on his way to England and Paris to study deaf education and wanted to meet.[34] The other from another classmate said that "the deaf and dumb girl I carried you to see makes very considerable progress."[35] Why all this interest among Andover students? Though none of them say so outright, it can only be that all these young men, trained as they were to become missionaries to the heathen, had realized that deaf Americans were heathens who lived at their very doorstep. Indeed, everyone involved with the school during its founding years would speak of it as a mission.

Given this interest among young evangelical Congregationalists, why did Cogswell select Gallaudet, of all people, as his missionary and the public face of his school? Cogswell would have known Gallaudet's propensity to bail out when the going got tough (or boring) or when he became depressed, and he knew, too, that Gallaudet had no abilities in French or German or any experience teaching children, and that he struck no one as especially bright. Finally, he would have known of Gallaudet's determination after Andover to keep himself free of commitment, "to preach only occasionally as my strength will permit, to journey at frequent intervals, and to decline being settled."[36]

On the plus side, however, Gallaudet came from a respectable family, was politically and doctrinally solid, punctual — he went so far as to assert it "neither just nor Christian for an individual to delay the business of a Board or any other meeting, merely for his private convenience" — and, at twenty-seven, old enough to have sown his wild oats — the drinking party at Yale, the dance in Hartford — and thus could be counted on not to get himself involved in any risqué escapades in Europe. In short, he led a "correct life."[37] And he was entirely unemployed, without commitments or prospects of income, which circumstance would have made him nearly unique among young men otherwise suitable for Cogswell's purpose. In fact, he would undertake the trip without pay. The money raised on the May 1st subscription list would underwrite only his expenses: his fare across the Atlantic, his lodging, and his meals. Gallaudet had to ask permission, by letters sent across the Atlantic, even to buy books on deaf education, and in Paris in the late winter of 1816, he would be reduced to begging Cogswell for an "allowance of anything in the way of compensation for my services."[38]

Gallaudet attended the May 1st meeting at which the donations were tallied, and then on May 5th he took Cogswell to Glastonbury to visit one of his own pet projects, eight-year-old Julia Brace, a girl who had lost both her hearing and her sight four years earlier.[39] We would like to think that Gallaudet felt compassion for a family so poor that Julia went without shoes even in winter, but, as Phyllis Valentine suggests, the visit was likely prompted not by charity but by Gallaudet's reading of the Scottish Common Sense philosopher Dugald Stewart, who had written about a deafblind Scottish boy as proof, he thought, of his theory about innate ideas.[40] Indeed, Gallaudet was more interested in what Julia could do for Christian doctrine than in what Christian charity for one's neighbor could do for Julia. Nevertheless, Gallaudet genuinely wanted to convince Cogswell that Julia should be educated with Alice and other children of paying parents.

Also during these few weeks, he "penned [an] address to the benevolent of our own country, in behalf of the object of his mission."[41] The address is flat enough, confined to just the facts, but it includes an interesting statement of the rationale for educating deaf children. Setting aside the consolation that education would provide the parents and the "enjoyment and usefulness" it would provide deaf people, "the one single consideration of their having immortal souls, which may, by learning the glad news of salvation, become interested in that Saviour who died for all men, is sufficient." It's not clear that he actually delivered this address, and it was perhaps drafted merely as a press release.

During these same weeks, the Connecticut Asylum at Hartford for the Education and Instruction of the Deaf and Dumb was incorporated by the General Association of Connecticut, the executive branch of the state-established Congregational Church, which meant that its actions had legal status in the state. Not surprisingly, the original donors sought to lock in their control with what Valentine calls a "complicated" system for selecting directors. Incorporation by the state church was their way to protect the new school from the few Democratic-Republicans who had recently won elective office and to hedge against the prospect of state disestablishment, which would indeed come in 1818.[42]

By the 10th, Gallaudet was on his way to New York to take a ship for England. It is not clear why London was chosen as Gallaudet's destination in Europe: Napoleon's return from exile in February would have ruled out Paris for the nonce, but Paris was probably always seen by the directors as Plan B due to its repellent Catholicism and, of course, the language barrier. While poor weather delayed the departure of Gallaudet's ship, the *Mexico*, for two weeks, he lodged with his parents, now settled in New York.[43] Gallaudet wrote to Alice from New York, telling her that "I hope when I come back, to teach you much about the Bible, about God, and Christ, and the world where we shall all be after we die."[44] He also wrote to Cogswell, transcribing a letter written by his brother James about a school for the deaf in

London that he had visited in March. James, Gallaudet told Cogswell, was employed by "a very respectable Portuguese Compting house" in London and had this to say about the school:

> [T]here are about 260 scholars and they conduct themselves remarkably well. One of the ushers called up one of the scholars to him and desired us to ask him some questions. Mr. Ralston [a person who accompanied James] then asked him how long he had attended this school; he watched the motions of his lips, while he was asking the question, and then immediately answered, "3 years and 2 months." We put a great many questions to him which he answered very distinctly. His usher then handed him a Bible and desired him to read; he took it and read a number of verses audibly and with great correctness, and this Boy was once quite dumb and is now totally deaf. There was one young gentleman, a Scotchman, about 19 years old, of great property and very respectable family. He has been at the institution about 12 years; he can understand any thing you say to him, and answer any questions; he corresponds by letter with his friends in Scotland. The usher told, that that morning he had taken up the newspaper and after reading a paragraph respecting Buonaparte, remarked that as long as Buonaparte lived there would not be Peace, because he delighted in War and shedding the blood of man.[45]

Gallaudet makes no comment to Cogswell on this excerpt from his brother's letter, so we don't know what he thought of the credulity James exhibited in allowing the school to choose the pupil they would permit to be questioned or accepting as fact the usher's assertions about pupils' hearing status, previous speaking ability, or political ideas. Ushers were assistant teachers, professionals who had a stake in the reputation of the school. Gallaudet likely took James's account at face value.

He also told Cogswell in this letter from New York about a young deaf man named John H. Eddy, whom he met at a dinner party. "At Dr. Hosack's [?] table, I met Thomas Eddy, <u>a friend</u>, of this city, with his son John H. Eddy who has been deaf for 18 years, and conversed principally with his fingers, using nearly our alphabet, so that he and I were acquainted at once. Thos. Eddy entered into my project (and so did Dr. Hosack) with all the ardor of an enthusiast. He went with me to Jno. Murray, brother of Lindley, and to another <u>friend</u>, and among them all I shall receive a packet of the very first value to <u>friends</u> of respectability in Liverpool and London."

The "packet of the very first value" would be letters of introduction, without which a "respectable" gentleman could not presume to approach a stranger. The word "friend" certainly does not signify a Quaker — Gallaudet could not have been associating with anyone from this denomination — and the underlining seems to suggest that these friends are his own coreligionists. His description of John Eddy conversing during dinner with the finger alphabet suggests that the young man was deafened after he had acquired the English language in early childhood, but Gallaudet gives no indication that he recognizes this crucial distinction. The alphabet described as "nearly our alphabet" would have been the current British finger alphabet, which the American Old Alphabet closely resembles. These two stories — James's visit to the deaf school and Gallaudet's dinner with John Eddy — show that the understanding he has of deaf people is still as superficial and credulous as it was in 1807 when he met the "respectable" farmer of Saratoga.

In a subsequent letter written the morning before he boarded the *Mexico,* he told Cogswell that a Mr. Wilkes, a bank cashier, "has an English work of considerable size, in the instruction of the deaf and dumb, which possibly you might borrow." Neither title nor author are mentioned, but the book had something to do with teaching speech: Gallaudet goes on to say, "It might enable you to carry on Alice's education during my absence to advantage. I do think she might occasionally receive from you lessons in speaking much to her improvement."[46] This passage gives the impression that Gallaudet and Cogswell had agreed that Alice should be trained to speak, but there is nothing further in the record to confirm these plans.

In addition to meeting people who knew something about deaf education and collecting his many letters of introduction, Gallaudet had to make arrangements for access to cash while abroad, a challenging undertaking at this date complicated by the directors having left him shockingly short. He "purchased a bill on an undoubted house in Liverpool," he told Ward Woodbridge in a letter from New York, but, he continued, "In case of <u>emergency</u> I shall draw on my father, trusting that he can be furnished with funds for this purpose." Gallaudet follows this with the perhaps too subtle mention that when they are all in heaven, "we shall drink deep at the pure fountain of benevolence, without any mixture of that selfishness which now adulterates all our christian enjoyments," then lost his nerve and backtracked in a postscript, assuring Woodbridge that if money is tight, he, Gallaudet, can raise enough in New York to continue. Gallaudet's relationship with his Hartford sponsors looks like a real tightrope act.[47]

It was probably around this time that Cogswell (or possibly Woodbridge or Gilbert) submitted a piece to the quarterly *Literary and Philosophical Repertory* on the proposed school, soliciting funds. It outlines the purposes of the school: "To instil [*sic*] valuable knowledge into these desolate, and often, gloomy understandings. . . . To impart to them the means of learning their own degeneracy; their deplorable condition by nature; to point them to the saviour of sinners; to make known his requirements, and urge to a compliance with them; to promote their felicity in the present life; and finally to be instrumental in leading them up to heaven."[48]

Nothing is said about reading, writing, or arithmetic. Gallaudet is described as "distinguished by the correctness of his deportment and the accuracy of his scholarship, . . . an acceptable and apparently, an uncommonly pious preacher of the gospel." It sounds like damning with faint praise, but surely it was not so intended: whoever wrote this piece simply mentioned the character traits regarded as important to the enterprise. As for fund-raising, the *Repertory* article says that Gallaudet will be staying in Europe (not England) for two or three years and that the money raised in Hartford was insufficient to keep him there that long. A similar piece, minus most of the purple rhetoric, appeared in the *Connecticut Mirror* and was reprinted in the *Courant* on May 24.

Daniel Wadsworth, in New York on a visit with his sister Mrs. Terry and her children, saw Gallaudet off on the 25th. As we follow him on his historical trip, we picture him as the strangers he would meet would have seen him, "a person of very diminutive stature, with a smooth, placid physiognomy — irradiated, however, by a remarkably large, expressive eye, rolling at you over his spectacles."[49] Or at least that's how he struck Samuel Goodrich. A Hartford matron recalled Gallaudet as "rather short and slender, but with an erectness of carriage, and a somewhat precise observance of the usages of refined society, which gave him an unfailing dignity of appearance. A certain quaintness of manner and expression was an irresistible charm about him."[50]

Just how "diminutive" was he in the context of his time? At five feet six and a half inches, he was a half inch taller than Aaron Burr, who had been known in college by the affectionate nickname "Little Burr," and more than two inches taller than James Madison, referred to by political enemies as "Little Jemmy." Gallaudet was not remarkably deficient in height, then, although all these men were perceived as smaller than the average and were dwarfed by contemporaries Washington, Jefferson, Monroe, and Jackson —

even "His Rotundity" John Adams was taller. His "certain quaintness of manner," however, combined with his shortish stature gave the impression of a wispy or even elfin man. "Mr. Gallaudet's address was peculiar and cannot be described," claimed his friend William A. Alcott. "There was a liveliness of manner, an earnestness, a lighting up of the countenance and the eye that arrested and secured attention."[51] In Alcott's description, Gallaudet looks a lot like a very thin version of Clement Clarke Moore's St. Nick. That he wore his spectacles on the street (or deck) and at the table would have been remarkable in itself in this day, when eyeglasses were employed for little else but reading.

He spent his first ocean voyage mostly seasick and otherwise writing letters. One of his fellow passengers, a Mr. Otis, seemed to him "quite the gentleman," but another passenger of considerably greater interest to us seems to have made no impression at all. This was Washington Irving, on his way to England on behalf of his family's business. Just four years older than Gallaudet and with a similar mercantile family background and literary ambitions, Irving's worldview had nevertheless virtually nothing in common with Gallaudet's. In fact, Gallaudet most likely had no idea who Irving was, for though the Jonathan Oldstyle essays and Diedrich Knickerbocker's *History of New York* had created a splash in the first years of the century, the New York *Morning Chronicle* that published Irving's work was a Democratic-Republican paper and the Irvings were Episcopalians, so there was virtually no cultural interface between Irving's world and Gallaudet's. Irving had been as indifferent to his studies as Gallaudet was punctilious, and he had not attended college. Unlike Gallaudet, too, Irving had stuck with his law studies and been admitted to the bar. While Gallaudet sat out the War of 1812 playing battledore, Irving had enlisted and had served on the Great Lakes. We can almost see what's coming when Gallaudet says in a letter written just hours before he embarked that "I even think they [the other passengers] will have no objections to my acting occasionally as their chaplain." Irving may not have made a public objection, but he certainly would not have sat still for two hours or more a week of Gallaudet's monotone soteriological discourse. If the two young men engaged in conversation at all, each would quickly have been aware that the other was not his sort.[52]

The passage across the Atlantic was remarkably easy, despite being lengthened by a detour south to "avoid the islands of ice," but Gallaudet nevertheless was seasick "the longest so of any one on board." He felt none of the expected improvement in health and his time "passed somewhat tediously," for he was unable to enjoy either reading or conversation despite all the "grandeur" and "sublimity" of the sea. He seems to have had an allergic reaction to something onboard — in the cargo? — experiencing "a most profuse discharge of phlegm from my head and lungs, resembling my old catarrhal affection on shore." He nevertheless found the energy to compose a trite three-stanza hymn that he said was sung on the crossing: "Guide us, O thou great Jehovah, / Wanderers oer the mighty deep," and so on.[53] In a letter to Cogswell written onboard, he asked Alice to find St. George's Channel (between Ireland and Wales) on a map, and he drew her a picture of a lighthouse he observed off the Irish coast on Tuskar Rock.[54] The next day, June 25, they docked in Liverpool.

It was a Sunday, so Gallaudet went to church, "delighted to do this after having spent so long a time on board." He found the sermon by Mr. Raffles rather more "impassioned" than he was accustomed to, and, seemingly homesick and disoriented, he asked Cogswell to write him about "the religious state of Hartford."[55]

He arrived in London on July 5 and wrote Ward Woodbridge on the 10th about his overland trip from Liverpool, filling a long letter with praises of the "extreme neatness" of the countryside and a minute description of the sermon he heard in Leicester, down to the preacher's height and manner of gesturing, all of which gained Gallaudet's admiration, "though" this Mr. Hall was a Baptist.[56] Woodbridge was a layman, of course, but the letter suggests that he shared Gallaudet's interest in "eloquence of the desk," and it is in small matters like this that we see why Woodbridge and his associates regarded Gallaudet as trustworthy. Curiously, Gallaudet entirely omitted mention of having stopped en route at the deaf school outside of Birmingham under the direction of Thomas Braidwood, and what impressions he may have had of the school or its pupils went unrecorded — perhaps the school did not allow him into the classrooms.[57]

He also wrote to Wadsworth from London. That letter is lost, but Wadsworth's reply indicates that it included accounts of Gallaudet's "disappointments," his "ill health, and consequent low spirits," as well as "the Poverty and vice which are to be met with in great Britain [sic]." On this last point, Wadsworth tells him that this is true of all countries of Europe, and that the cause is overpopulation abetted by misguided benevolence that aims to alleviate poverty without promoting "industry" among the poor. The blame-the-victim view articulated by Wadsworth here was held by everyone in the Wadsworth-Terry-Woodbridge-Hudson social set, and it explains, in part, their reluctance to subsidize tuition for poor families. This strange letter concludes with similar remarks on the failure of charity and on the religious privileges of Americans.[58]

It is in these early days in London that Gallaudet must have mailed a letter of introduction to Hannah More, who was then seventy-five years old and living near Bristol. More and Gallaudet would come to think very highly of one another, and a comparison of their social and religious views is instructive. More's father had been a Presbyterian, and she was associated earlier in life with political and cultural reactionaries such as Samuel Johnson and Edmund Burke, so in that sense she shared a great deal with the Yale establishment. But she also associated with more progressive Christian reformers such as William Wilberforce and Zachary Macaulay. In partnership with her sister Martha, she had set up twelve schools for poor children that taught reading and the Bible, but not writing, because More did not regard the ability to write as proper for the lower classes. The notion of writing as a strictly upper-class pursuit was widespread in England, turning up in novels such as Maria Edgeworth's *Belinda,* where Clarence Hervey raises a girl to be a perfect wife by not teaching her to write. Another contemporary novel, Elizabeth Gaskell's *My Lady Ludlow,* illustrated the dangers of literacy alone in its story of a servant who, fatally, could read a message during the French Revolution. When the More sisters were attacked as Methodists and Jacobins for teaching the poor even to read, they responded that literacy was necessary for them to be hired servants.[59] But worse than all this, from a present-day perspective, is More's view that the purpose of education was to break the child's will and to instill acceptance of his lowly station in life. Such was the state of progressive schooling in England.

Gallaudet never opposed reading or writing for the lower classes, and by the time of his arrival in London More had turned her attention to writing religious tracts, Francophobic pamphlets, and praises of the English gentry, all of which would be highly attractive to Gallaudet. More and Gallaudet never actually met, though she gave him a letter of introduction to Zachary Macaulay, along with two copies of her *Essay on Saint Paul.* Gallaudet would dedicate his first published book to her, she would donate £10 to the Asylum, and Gallaudet would hang her portrait in the school's library, which was financed by her donation.[60] More's friend Zachary Macaulay would marshal all the forces of the *Christian Observer,* of which he was the editor, to promote Gallaudet's efforts in deaf education. Just a couple of years later, Macaulay would be writing to Gallaudet about his activism against the slave trade — "it's not to be endured" — but he probably did not raise this topic when Gallaudet met him in London.[61]

Gallaudet's first letter to Cogswell from London was written on July 11, the day after he attended an exhibition by the Abbé Sicard of the deaf teachers Jean Massieu and Laurent Clerc and their pupil Goddard. Their presence in London was entirely fortuitous: when Napoleon returned to Paris from his exile in March, Sicard, a monarchist who had never made any secret of his opposition to the emperor, took these three deaf men, whom he could exhibit to paying audiences, and fled to London. Gallaudet's attendance at one of these exhibitions was an event of such moment for American Deaf history that it is remarkable how unmotivated it was and how little impression it made on him at the time. His letter to Cogswell began, instead, with a complaint of "such an inflammation in my eyes that I have not ventured to read or write at all," and went on to relate that he had delivered his many letters of introduction (which were from Nathan Strong, a couple of state governors, President Ashbel Green of Princeton College, William Wilberforce, and many others) to the Rev. John Townsend at the charity school for deaf children in London's East End. Townsend's doctrinal beliefs lined up perfectly with those of the directors, and the school's head-master, Thomas Watson, just happened to be a nephew of the Braidwood family. Gallaudet was fully expecting a favorable response regarding teacher training within a few days, but in the meantime Townsend had taken him to see Sicard. It was Townsend's imprimatur that enabled Gallaudet to ac-quiesce to the meeting; it's not at all likely that Gallaudet would otherwise have made any effort to attend Sicard's exhibition.

In relating the story to Cogswell, Gallaudet sounds not exactly impressed but rather starstruck. The exhibition was attended by the bishop of Lon-don and "several of the nobility," including the duchess of Wellington, he gushed. Massieu and Clerc, whom Gallaudet failed to understand were teachers and took to be Sicard's adult pupils, responded to questions "<u>in french</u>," "with chalk on two large blackboards." Gallaudet was amazed by the blackboards — he would remain a staunch blackboard activist for the rest of his life. About the exhibition itself, he related two sample questions and answers in English, which someone in the audience must have translated for him, but that's about it. Since he had no French, needing an interpreter even to introduce himself to Sicard, he could have had little idea of what he had just seen, his blackboard epiphany notwithstanding.[62]

Fortunately for us, Massieu and Clerc prepared a bilingual facing-page edition of questions and answers from the London exhibitions. Many concern philosophical interests of the day: "What Difference is there between the Mind and Matter?" and "What Difference is there between Mind and Intellect?" Massieu's answers are poetic — "*Authority* is the head; *power* is the arm" and sometimes make little sense — "Hope is the flower of happiness" — while Clerc's are more concrete — "*Hope* is the expectation of a happy event." Responding to requests to define thunder or to explain the difference between noise and sound, the matter-of-fact Clerc says he is deaf, and "I do not, therefore, exactly know what it is." On some questions, however, we see a spark in Clerc's answers that Massieu's do not convey. Massieu defines "man" as "the only being endowed with reason," but Clerc's definition is "the master-piece of God, who created him after his own image." One wonders if Gallaudet saw — and understood — the answers to the question, "Do the Deaf and Dumb think themselves unhappy?" Both men replied that one cannot miss what one has never had, and both added that "la parole par des signes" is "une grand consolation."[63]

The questions suggest that the true object of the audience was to "stump the deaf," and one questioner succeeded in doing just that with a trick question, asked in French: "Quelle Différence y a-t-il entre un Brouillon de Papier et un Brouillon de Société?" In English, "What is the difference between a rough draft and a meddler?" makes no sense at all, but in French it's a bit of word play dependent upon familiarity with two French idioms that incorporate the same word. Massieu and Clerc, it turned out, were familiar with one, *brouillon de papier,* "a rough draft," but not the other, *brouillon de société,* "a meddler." They reasoned, logically but incorrectly, that a *brouillon de société* was an uncouth person, just as a rough draft is an unpolished text.

At this point, Sicard intervened, and the audience was treated to a live, impromptu lesson of what the abbé called *l'analyse, cette marche admirable* — his teaching method of leading pupils from the known to the unknown using reason rather than memorization. Adroitly getting Massieu and Clerc back on track, Sicard began by asking the meaning of the verb *maçonner,* "to build," then the meaning of *maçonnerie,* "masonry." Having thus recalled to them the affixes with which the French language creates new words, he proceeds to *brouiller*, "to disorder," then to *brouillerie,* and this time, the two deaf men get the definition right: a *brouillon de société* is someone who disorders what others are putting in order: a meddler.[64] Gallaudet may have witnessed this very lesson, or he may have witnessed another similar impromptu lesson. To the Londoners present who knew French, the trick question unlocked Sicard's method. But Gallaudet would not be able to grasp any of this until he'd boned up on the language and traveled to Paris himself, a full year later.

Instead, he was still chasing what he thought was the "art" of deaf education, which he understood as a sort of key in the possession of a select group of initiates. Contemporary usage of the word includes Maria Edgeworth on the "art" by which lawyers raise money — "It might have been the black art, for any thing I know to the contrary" — the American playwright Susanna Rowson on the "art" of seducing women, or, conversely, of tricking men into marriage; and Thomas Carlyle, translating Goethe, on the "art" of manipulating the strings of a marionette.[65] An "art" is a skill that can be taught and learned, such as double-entry bookkeeping, but perhaps with implications of both sleight of hand and, perhaps, an intention to deceive. This is not to say that Gallaudet ever imagined, at this early date, that the oral approach to deaf education involved deception, but he did seem to see it as something like the art of operating a marionette: it seems miraculous that the puppet can dance, until you know how it's done. In the Goethe novel that Carlyle translated, Wilhelm Meister's beloved takes up one of Wilhelm's marionettes and "soon got the art of turning him deftly on his wire; she made him bow, and repeat declarations of love," which sounds a lot like the way oral training was conducted with deaf children. By 1823, Gallaudet would be denouncing the notion that deaf education was an art, telling the American public that "The instructors of the deaf and dumb are no magicians, and what they accomplish is done in the way of slow, gradual, patient, and laborious effort." And by 1867, we find the advocate of oral education, Samuel Gridley Howe, turning the tables by accusing advocates of sign language of posing "as men possessing an art which nobody else understands."[66]

Letters and journal entries written throughout the remainder of the summer in London tell the story of Gallaudet chasing Townsend and other members of the school's committee around London, trying to nail down an agreement by which he would be instructed in their art. But when he visited classrooms and vocational workshops, he made nothing beyond the vaguest of comments on what he saw, such as "several of these unfortunates . . . engaged in shoe making, tayloring [*sic*], and printing"; the pupils "appeared to be industriously employed under the care of his several assistants"; and the like. When he gets a chance to chat with some pupils, he asks the one question, of all others, to which the children must have had a prepared answer: "What do you think of the Son of God, Jesus Christ?" Gallaudet deems one pupil's answer to be lacking a conjunction, and tells the boy so. With a second pupil, an Irish boy interested in America, Gallaudet permits *him* to ask all the questions.[67] Thus did he waste an opportunity to learn to what extent the pupils were capable of thinking for themselves. But of course he had missed the preliminary lesson of Sicard, who most definitely did teach pupils to think.

Gallaudet's negotiations with Townsend and Watson show him claiming again and again that he could commit to only six weeks or two months, but not longer — even though the newspapers back home were told he would be gone for two or three years — and that he was not authorized to bring an assistant back to Connecticut with him, which, however, was true. Any suggestion from Watson that either more time or a trained assistant would be necessary was brushed aside. Gallaudet's July 26th journal entry shows the two men talking completely past one another. Watson told Gallaudet that the customary length of time for learning to teach deaf children was four or five years, and that the training that qualifies one is "not so much from any private instructions or lectures of his own, as from taking charge of an uninstructed pupil and conducting him regularly through the several stages of his improvement."

Watson was right: in the present century, it is understood that to become competent to teach deaf students requires *more* than four or five years of classroom experience, in addition to language training and tutoring. At Gallaudet University, during my own tenure on the faculty there, many departments stopped hiring "new signers," no matter how academically qualified or enthusiastic, because it wasn't considered humanly possible to gain minimal competence by the time such a person was up for tenure in her seventh year. But in Gallaudet's uninformed view, Watson's "personal feelings and biases would lead him to give as much importance as possible to his profession and to make it appear that a considerable length of time and patience was requisite for the acquisition of his art."[68] He would be disabused a few years later when he was faced with training teachers for the Hartford school, and in 1821 he would write that "no one should undertake the education of the Deaf and Dumb, who has not been trained to it by a long and intimate acquaintance with them."[69]

The bizarre dialogue with Watson is explicable only when we understand that Gallaudet is still under the misapprehension that deaf education is an "art" that he will be able to practice back home if someone in London will simply show him how it's done. Watson may well have had a mercenary motivation and, in his negotiations with Gallaudet, may have prioritized the Braidwood monopoly over the good of deaf Americans, but on the basic facts Watson was telling Gallaudet the truth. Over the following two weeks, the two continued to go round and round: on August 1, Gallaudet claimed that he, and he alone, was qualified to know when he had the skills to teach the deaf; on the 10th, he wanted Watson to give him a trial period and judge his skills at the end of it; on the 11th, Watson offered him a one-month trial period, but Gallaudet haughtily spurned it — after consulting with three local clergymen who told him he could do better in Edinburgh. On the 12th, he complained that Watson's plan "would very much retard my progress in the art, for after having made myself fully acquainted with one stage of the process I must still wait for the pupil before I could advance to the succeeding stage." On the 15th, he finally got around to asking Watson what he would be teaching, and when he learned it was penmanship, he exploded.[70] And he was outraged by the salary offer of £35 a year during training, "toiling for [Watson] from morning till night with only one-half day's recreation in the week allowed me !!! Think, my dear sir," he tells Cogswell, "what a wound my feelings have received."[71] One of the directors of Watson's school finally lost his temper and told Gallaudet that since he would not take professional direction, he might as well "make experiments upon the deaf mutes in the Asylum in America as well as here."[72] It is Massieu, Clerc, and Sicard we have to thank that that did not happen.

Aside from the anxiety that Gallaudet's ignorance was causing him at the London deaf school, he seems to have been aghast at London in general. For example, the expense and magnificence of St. Paul's Cathedral horrified him to the extent that Wadsworth had to cool him off in a letter by noting that its building employed many workmen and fed many families.[73] Gallaudet sounds at times as though he were in hysterics during his time in London.

He was also terribly anxious over not having received any letters from Cogswell. His irritation is clear in his phrasing in an August 15th letter: "My Dear Sir: . . . I expected to have been made acquainted, before this time, with the progress of the concern in which we are mutually and so deeply interested." And although he had accepted the job without remuneration, he was starting to chafe at that: "As I have devoted myself to the deaf and dumb . . . with no stipulation with regard to my future support, trusting for this to the ordering of events by a kind Providence, . . . I might now be indulged with something more than the mere paying of my expenses."[74] This is an extraordinary tone to take with one's employer.

In the same letter to Cogswell, Gallaudet mentioned Julia Brace, the deafblind girl in Glastonbury whom they had visited that spring. "You may think it chimerical, but I do believe she might be taught many words and perhaps to read, by having raised letters, in relief, as it were, which she might feel. This is the way the blind are taught at Amsterdam. . . . They are now learning to *read the Bible* with their fingers."

In closing, he expressed, perhaps for the first time, his feelings toward the deaf: "I long to see Hartford once more and to be in the midst of my deaf and dumb children." His pupils would turn out to include adults, a circumstance he may not have expected, but similar passages in other letters show that he regarded all deaf people as children: "I long to be in the midst of my deaf and dumb children — for such I mean to consider them."[75] Of course, paternalism was not regarded as an inappropriate attitude toward deaf and disabled people in the nineteenth century. Clerc would refer, in 1818, to the death of de l'Épée as having "removed that excellent father from his grateful children," and Gallaudet was universally praised for "his paternal interest in the cause of deaf-mute education."[76]

Back in Hartford, Alice Cogswell was writing him letters under the direction of her teacher, Lydia Huntley. On July 6, Alice drafted the following: "My Dear Sir: I am very glad. few days. I you go long, ship to wave. God keep away. — must. Forgot. I was not, Morning and Evening Pray is God keeps Alice yes. Hartford," and she finishes with a Bible verse. Miss Huntley corrected this letter for her after determining her meaning through sign language, and had her recopy the corrected letter.

Alice wrote again on August 14: "You letter come to paper — and Alice this morning." It is a terrible loss to Deaf history that Gallaudet never recorded his thoughts on these letters, beyond the brief comment he wrote on the envelope of the second one, "Interesting and valuable from Alice Cogswell."[77] From all surviving evidence, however, Gallaudet believed that a key to correcting Alice's "word salad" could be his for six weeks of training. He wrote to her on August 15, telling her about the question he asked the deaf boy, "What do you think of Jesus Christ?" and he urged on her the importance of penmanship — "Learn to write beautifully" — and of lip-reading — "Look at persons' lips when they speak, and try to see if you can't understand some words that they speak. Get Mary and Elizabeth to speak some words to you, such as chair, table, door, water, fire, run, walk, etc. They must speak very slowly, and you must try to remember how their lips move."[78]

Poor Alice! Even if one grants that learning to lip-read these words is a good idea, this certainly isn't the way to go about it. It seems Gallaudet never had the opportunity to sit in on a lip-reading lesson, where he would have learned that a normal rate of speaking and the use of phrases rather than single words was how this was done. Again, the letters of this summer reveal a man who is so sure he's right that he never dreams of having to check the facts.

Gallaudet left London in a smack down the Thames and north along the coast to Leith, where he arrived after a three-day, four-hundred-mile trip. He delivered various letters of introduction, including one to Robert Kinniburgh, the head of the deaf school in Edinburgh, whom he found friendly and polite, someone who "teaches his scholars to know who God is, and who Christ is. And he teaches them that they are all sinners."[79] But Kinniburgh was under a bond to the Braidwoods for £1,000 not to provide any teacher training to anyone for seven years, so, having learned nothing from his dealings with the Braidwoods (via Watson) in London, Gallaudet wrote to Thomas Braidwood asking for a waiver. When that was declined, he contemplated sweetening the deal by "making Mr. Braidwood an offer that may tempt him to give up the bond,"[80] but the directors nixed that idea. He then made the desperate argument in various public venues that the bond was invalid with regard to Americans, which induced the Braidwoods to accuse him of "obtuseness of understanding" and having a "defective moral system."[81]

This second round of negotiations with the Braidwoods had the same result as the first, and it needn't be traced in detail. Gallaudet continued to complain in letters to Cogswell that "if after having devoted myself to this object simply on the condition at present of having my expenses defrayed, I am left in the lurch . . . I shall be extremely disappointed." In the midst of this petulance, he lets drop a remark on "laboring to procure acquaintance among persons of influence here who may be able to assist me." [82] Back in Hartford, a Yale degree alone was enough to establish his social bona fides, but once across the Atlantic he discovered very quickly that there was no Yale privilege, and procuring acquaintance among persons of influence involved "labor" that he hadn't planned on.

In contrast to London, where Gallaudet felt overwhelmed by the city, its residents, and St. Paul's Cathedral, Edinburgh was in his eyes "the Athens of the world." He bought a "complete set" of Sicard's books in French and hired a tutor, a Mr. Barré, to assist him in reading through them.[83] Eager to meet some of the city's philosophers as he was, he did not seek out its even more celebrated poet. Walter Scott, whose novel *Waverly* had come out the previous year, was quite open to visiting Americans, had Gallaudet been interested. When Washington Irving paid Scott a visit two years earlier to present him with a copy of *Knickerbocker's History of New York*, Scott had greeted him at the gates to his estate, on foot and amidst the baying of his dogs.[84] Some of the best work of these two writers — *Ivanhoe* and "Rip Van Winkle" — would appear in 1819 when Gallaudet was getting his Hartford deaf school underway.

But had Gallaudet read any Scott, he would have been appalled by his views of Presbyterians. In the 1819 *Bride of Lammermoor*, the Presbyterian characters are social snobs who thwart the noble Ravenswood, while in the 1814 *Waverley*, the Presbyterians are comically ridiculed as hypocrites and fanatics who denounce those of other religious persuasion as having drunk from the cup of the fornication of the "muckle harlot" of the Book of Revelation. In one memorable scene, the (Catholic) highlander Donald Bean Lean disguises himself as a Presbyterian peddler and infiltrates the armed guard that is carrying Waverly to prison, ingratiating himself by "groan[ing] with great regularity" about the "puir blinded popish" practices of "heathenish dancing and dicing upon the Sabbath." Needless to say, none of this would have been amusing in contemporary Connecticut, and Scott's treatment of Presbyterians put him simply beyond the pale for Gallaudet and most of his compeers.[85]

Another writer whom Gallaudet did not bother to look up is not as well known today as is Scott but was just as famous in Edinburgh at this date: Susan Ferrier (1782–1854), whose 1818 novel *Marriage* was then under revision. Gallaudet would have approved of Ferrier's heroine, Mary Douglas, who "had scarcely ever read a novel in her life," and *Marriage*'s disparagement of women who attend salons to "prate" about Byron's 1813 *Giaour*. But Ferrier and her characters share a thorough familiarity with contemporary belles lettres and have complicated relationships with books, a nuanced stance on literature Gallaudet would not have been able to grasp.

Unlike Susan Ferrier, the Scottish Common Sense philosophers were straightforward enough to appeal to Gallaudet. Common Sense philosophy had emerged as a reaction to the empiricism and skepticism of Bishop Berkeley, David Hume, and others who had argued that we are not endowed with any ideas at all at our births; everything we know, or think we know, derives from (perhaps faulty) sensory perception. This point — the reliability, and possible unreliability, of information delivered by our senses and processed by our minds — was a central problem of the Enlightenment,[86] addressed by writers such as Oliver Goldsmith, whose vicar substantially personifies it, and Samuel Johnson, who less subtly thought he was disproving the theory of Bishop Berkeley by kicking a stone and crying, "I refute it thus!" Faced with the uncertainty Hume had introduced, the Scots responded much as Dr. Johnson did by developing what they regarded as common sense principles: that the material world is real, that our sensory perceptions and our intuitions about it are correct, and that this is so because — begging the question here — we are innately endowed with correct ideas and intuitions by our Creator.

The Common Sense philosophers, like the Connecticut Congregationalist clergy, were motivated by the threat that Hume posed for Christian doctrine. As they very rightly saw it, Hume had provided the world of the Enlightenment with "a model of intellectual enquiry in which disagreement and questioning are welcome, exploration of new and possibly mistaken ideas is encouraged, and a tentative tone dominates throughout."[87] One aim of Scottish Common Sense philosophers and the Connecticut clergy alike was, therefore, to make Hume's intellectual inquiry appear foolish.

At Yale, President Dwight told his students that "the common sense of mankind" was concordant with reason; neither God nor nature holds any surprise, and there's no need to think about this any further.[88] At Andover, Leonard Woods, the professor of Church History, assigned passages from Common Sense philosopher Thomas Reid,[89] presumably, since Reid had not written on the subject Woods was supposed to be teaching, for the same reason Dwight did — to choke off inquiry. And so, at a time when Hume's thought was creating "an explosion of intellectual activity" in Germany and elsewhere, the New England clergy's adroit deployment of the Scotsman Reid and his acolyte Dugald Steward ensured that "torpor" was the mood of American intellectual life.[90] That Gallaudet reminisced in a letter to an Andover classmate that "you and I have often *Dugaldized* together"[91] shows us just how savory Steward's thin gruel appeared to New England divinity students of the day. It's no exaggeration to say that Common Sense "undergirded [Gallaudet's] thinking" throughout his life.[92]

The precepts of Common Sense philosophy, as stultifying as they were to American philosophy, proved liberating for the deaf. If a moral sense were indeed innate and moral truths indeed self-evident, as Common Sense would have it, then morality was independent of the acquisition of language, and people born deaf were indeed moral agents like anyone else. It was the right conclusion for the wrong reason, and it's hard to see how deaf education could ever have gotten its start in Connecticut without this fortunate fault.

Also of immense importance for deaf education was Stewart's endorsement of sign language. Phyllis Valentine has argued persuasively that it was Stewart's imprimatur that convinced Gallaudet of sign language's superior efficacy: "It was Dugald Stewart," she wrote, "who made Thomas Gallaudet an advocate of manualism. It was Stewart who persuaded the Connecticut clergyman to abandon his original plan of combining both articulation and sign language in teaching American students. All this took place in Edinburgh, many weeks before Thomas Gallaudet turned his attention toward Paris and its school for the deaf."[93] Gallaudet may not have been quite so certain as Valentine takes him to have been, but it's safe to say that, at a minimum, Stewart's dim view of speech training had a profound effect.

Gallaudet knew the 1812 version of Stewart's disquisition on the deafblind boy James Mitchell even before he arrived in Edinburgh, and from this work alone he could have derived his later disapproval of oral training, which Stewart called "astonish[ing] the vulgar by the sudden conversion of a dumb child into a speaking *automaton*." Speech training, Stewart wrote, is an "art" that ranks "only a little higher than the art of training starlings and parrots."[94] Clearly, however, Gallaudet had not really taken in Stewart's denigration of oralism prior to the winter he spent in Edinburgh, when he perhaps first read Stewart's *Elements of the Philosophy of the Human Mind,* the second part of which, published in 1814, defined "natural language" as "certain expressions of the countenance, certain gestures of the body, and certain tones of the voice." Here Stewart discussed Roman pantomime, the signed language of the Plains Indians, and the pupils of the Braidwood family, who, Stewart claimed, were to be seen using identical sets of signs when they first enter the school.[95] In a further section of *Elements* that was not composed until 1827, Stewart would argue for the intellectual equality of the sexes, taking as examples the novels of Madame de Staël and the nonfiction of the novelist Maria Edgeworth,[96] but Gallaudet, who would have been horrified, was not likely to have been aware of these ideas.

Professor Silliman had told him that "in all your travels you will not find [Dugald Stewart's] superior,"[97] but he hardly needed to be prompted to seek Stewart out and had prepared to meet the great man with a report on Julia Brace.[98] In light of what actually happened to poor Julia, it's worthwhile to consider what Gallaudet hoped for her at this point. He told Woodbridge,

> The philosophers here, and Dugald Stewart at their head, take a deep interest in Julia Brace, the little deaf, dumb and blind girl, and . . . I ask [Cogswell] as a peculiar favor, that every attention be shown her, which can tend to prepare her to become my protégé on my return. I wish an experiment to be fairly tried with her, either by Dr. C[ogswell] or her mother, or some kind person who will be faithful in attending to it. Let some letters be made, either of wood, or iron, or clay, about half an inch in height, so that their shape can be easily perceived by the touch. With these letters, placed in a proper order, spell the names of some objects with which she used to be most familiar before her blindness, and which she knew the names of in her spelling book.[99]

Later, in London on his way to Paris at the end of February or beginning of March 1816, he thought of Julia again and asked Cogswell to send him a medical diagnosis he could show Stewart and others. He also reminded Cogswell of his hope that he

> or some other person, will do what can be done to instruct this little unfortunate, by attempting to teach her the names of objects by a *tangible alphabet*. If she likes, I am resolved to have her under my immediate care. This is one of the only two cases of the kind known in the world; and while James Mitchell has attracted, and continues to attract the attention of the first philosophers in Europe, it would be a disgrace to our country, to

its philosophical character, and to its character for benevolence, to suffer
an unhappy female, whose situation is, if possible, more interesting than
Mitchell's, to grow up unheeded and neglected.[100]

And yet that is exactly what would happen. By the time a tuition waiver
was put in place for Julia in 1825 — through the efforts of Mrs. Sigourney,
not Principal Gallaudet or Director Cogswell — Julia was eighteen, long
past the language-acquisition threshold, and she would merely vegetate at
the school until her sister took her away in 1860.[101]

That November in Edinburgh, Gallaudet decided to attend the lectures
of Stewart's replacement at the university, Thomas Brown, who was lectur-
ing on the topic of the philosophy of the mind — "with which in reference
to my intended pursuit I ought to be thoroughly acquainted."[102] Although
not widely known today, Thomas Brown (1778–1820) was "one of the most
influential and widely read British philosophers of the first half of the
nineteenth century."[103] His lectures at the University of Edinburgh for the
ten years before his untimely death in 1820 were much talked about, not
only for their substance but for Brown's peculiar prose style and personal
affect. Some thought his prose to rank with that of Shakespeare, Milton,
Homer, and Walter Scott; others said that counting Brown among such
company was like praising a group that included "the organ, the harp, the
trumpet, the violin, and the sewing machine." In Gallaudet's much milder
view, "Dr. Brown has a great deal of the most luxuriant imagery in his
writing; almost too much for a metaphysician, and abundance of classical
allusion and quotations." Others remarked on "a manner so affected and
so odd, that there is no describing it."

Thomas Carlyle, who had abandoned his divinity studies in Edinburgh
in 1814 and would shortly be translating Goethe, called Thomas Brown the
"immaculate Dr. Brown" and even "Miss Brown," describing him as "a really
pure, high, if rather shrill and wire-drawing kind of a man." Gallaudet may
have been among those who, *contra* Carlyle, were fascinated with Brown's
manner, or he may simply have been interested enough in Brown's ideas,
as Carlyle was not, to disregard the man's effeminacy. Gallaudet's oblique
nod to Brown's sexuality is his mention that Brown, who was thirty-eight
at the time, was "unmarried, and his family is made up of his mother and
sisters." In either case, Gallaudet was able to borrow books from Brown's
library of works on deaf education, as well as Stewart's copy of a book by

George Dalgarno — was it *The Art of Signs: The Deaf and Dumb Man's Tutor*? He didn't note down the title.

Brown's ideas were first aired in a book he had written in 1798, when he was but eighteen, which was a response to Erasmus Darwin's 1794–1796 *Zoönomia*. Here, Brown argued against Darwin's controversial views on the material existence of the life force, which Darwin had called "the spirit of animation." (Percy Bysshe Shelley, writing the preface to his wife's novel *Frankenstein,* claimed that according the "Dr. Darwin," the creation of the living creature in a dorm room was "not of impossible occurrence," indicating that the Shelleys were among the many who did not accept Brown's criticism.) Later, Brown would expand on his ideas in his study of causation, which he viewed as merely "invariable antecedence." Similarly, in the case of the lectures Gallaudet attended and which were later published, Brown argued that psychological faculties (understanding, memory, and so on) were nothing but shorthand for mental processes. Brown appeared to be uninterested in or indifferent to religious belief, and he was criticized for his "essentially pagan" system during his lifetime and in the decades following posthumous publication of his work. Today he is regarded as not a Common Sense philosopher at all, but rather a follower of Hume and a forerunner of John Stuart Mill's positivism, which holds that truth is accessible only through the senses, not via revelation or inspiration. What the pious graduate of Andover Theological Seminary would have made of all this in 1815–1816 would be hard to say if we hadn't Gallaudet's own testimony to an Andover classmate:

> He differs from all his predecessors in his views of the human mind. He thinks the Scotch metaphysicians have made too many divisions of the powers and faculties of the mind, and that the French have aimed at too great simplicity. He pursues a middle course. In general, I like his nomenclatures. It is somewhat new. Of the essence of the mind we know nothing. We only know its states and phenomena. These may be divided into internal and external affections. The latter includes all that we usually call sensations. It embraces those traits of mind whose existence and modifications depend on external objects. The former includes all the mental phenomena, and is divided into intellectual states of mind and emotions.[104]

As is clear from these remarks, Gallaudet understood that Stewart's replacement Brown was not Dugaldizing at all. In any case, all this was pretty heady stuff relative to what Gallaudet had learned in New England seminar rooms, where Dwight was still teaching Yale seniors in 1814 that there was "no truth in the position, that the mind is a part of the body, or that they are parts of the same thing. . . . As mind has no parts, it cannot be divided: and in this respect it is essentially different from matter."[105] Gallaudet spoke with Brown outside of the lecture hall on at least one occasion, because, as he told Alice, he showed Brown an uncorrected story she had written for Miss Huntley ("little boy — Name man Peter Colt. very much curls little boy — hair white Oh . . . "), and Brown had professed himself glad to see that she could write so well — or so Gallaudet told Alice.[106]

During the fall of 1815 and the following winter, while Gallaudet was discussing Julia Brace with Dugald Stewart and attending Brown's lectures, he was also getting to know a pupil of Kinniburgh's named Joseph Turner. In his September 30th entry in his "Journal of Some Occurrences," Gallaudet transcribed a story Turner had written in July, "about the approaching harvest": "the harvest is somewhat green now," Joseph wrote in run-on sentences, "and it will be yellow and ripe in the end of August and a farmer will collect the people and send them to cut corn, wheat and barley with their sharp sickles and they will be reapers." Gallaudet, in his simplicity at this date, made no mention of whether this essay had been corrected by a teacher or was uncorrected and straight from Joseph's pen. The grammar is correct, though not remarkably idiomatic, and the story seems to have been copied into Gallaudet's "Journal" as an example of good work by a deaf teenager.

An entry at the end of October transcribed a letter Joseph wrote to Gallaudet, clearly in answer to the same question Gallaudet had posed to a pupil of Watson's in London: "What do you think of the Son of God, Jesus Christ?" Joseph's answer begins, "Dear Sir, I will tell you what I think about Jesus Christ the only Son of God who is in heaven above. I think Jesus Christ is the only Son of God and is the saviour of sinners and was very good and kind to the sinners." At the end of December, Gallaudet made a third transcription of Joseph's writing: asked to define the word "repent," the boy wrote, quoting Luke 13:3, "To repent is to be sorry for sins. Except ye repent, ye shall all likewise perish." At an exhibition in February, Turner told the audience that "Believe is to give credit to," that "He who loves God and believes the gospel is a Christian," that "Eternal is everlasting — God is eternal — the world will not be eternal but have an end," and so forth.[107]

With all these examples, as with the first, Gallaudet provides no context, giving the impression that he regarded these as good answers. The answers are indeed good if one's goals in teaching are hypercorrect grammar and rote memorization of Bible verses. Gallaudet is still a very long way from adopting de l'Épée's goal of teaching pupils to *think*. We can compare, here, Gallaudet's remarks to Cogswell that same autumn, to the effect that what pleases him most is not Alice's improved English but rather her memorization of the Fourth Psalm, which he takes to be evidence of her improved "regard for . . . the truth of religion."[108] Alice's English was in fact improving, however, if her letter to her cousins that same month was uncorrected, as it seems to be. "Rev Thomas H. Gallaudet all gone and .1. year come back in school deaf and dumb me go school." Not grammatical, but her meaning is clear.[109]

Despite his excitement in observing Joseph Turner, chatting with Dugald Stewart, and attending Thomas Brown's lectures, Gallaudet seems to have been just as depressed as he was in London — in fact, he was starting to sound a lot like he did in the winter of 1810–1811 when he rode across the Alleghenies alone with his thoughts. In October, he told Cogswell, "My health is but so, so, no great improvement to it from my voyage and travels."[110]

He was dismayed by the difficulty he saw in teaching deaf children: "The business of instructing the deaf and dumb is a very gradual one. . . . I find that at both the London and Edinburgh schools four years is the least time in which pupils can make even such progress as to render them interesting."[111] By December, he was writing in his "Journal" that Providence was thwarting his project because of his sins, and it is the deaf and dumb who are injured. "Can I make them any recompense? With God's blessing it shall be in devoting myself more faithfully to their relief. I long to be surrounded by them in my native land; to be their instructor, their guide, their friend, their father."[112]

Today, no deaf person would be willing to serve as the means for a hearing teacher to work out his salvation. At this date, however, perhaps the deaf were grateful for instruction however it was motivated. Whatever the case, this is not a prescription for a healthy pupil/teacher relationship, and we will watch Gallaudet's faulty notion of his dream role as father of the deaf unspool over the following decade and a half in Hartford. It's as if Gallaudet began his work in deaf education with the same idea that inspired Victor Frankenstein to create life: "A new species would bless me as its creator and source; many happy and excellent natures would owe their being to me. No father could claim the gratitude of his child so completely as I should deserve theirs."[113] Luckily for the deaf, Gallaudet's project worked out much better than Frankenstein's.

That same month, Alice wrote from Hartford about the Theodore Dwight family's move to Albany, a hundred-mile journey that, for reasons unexplained, Dwight made on foot. She told Gallaudet about the birth of a new cousin, playing "hide and go seek," having a toothache and the tooth being pulled by her father, and Miss Huntley's visit to her parents in Norwich for Thanksgiving, ending with thanks to Gallaudet for the book he sent her. Whether Gallaudet received this letter in London or had it forwarded to him later, it must have made him homesick for the simple life of friends and family.[114]

On February 12, Gallaudet left Edinburgh for London, stopping off in Cambridge where "an acquaintance" gave him an original letter of Samuel Johnson.[115] In London, Gallaudet met Zachery Macaulay, as Hannah More had urged him to do, and struck up a lifetime friendship. Macaulay was the editor of the *Christian Observer,* the vehicle of the Clapham Sect of evangelical Anglicans who formed a network around William Wilberforce and urged the reform of prisons as well as abolition of the slave trade (and later, of slavery itself). Gallaudet seems to have submitted for publication in the *Christian Observer* an essay on one of his lifelong hobby horses, emulation, because Macaulay would inform him in April that it would soon appear.[116] Under Macaulay's editorship, the *Observer* regularly publicized and never questioned Gallaudet's plans for the deaf school in Connecticut. (It would not be until the time of Macaulay's successor, Samuel Charles Wilks, that the *Observer* would suggest that the language of instruction Gallaudet instituted at the American Asylum was in any way controversial.)[117]

It was also during this week in London that John Quincy Adams, then serving with the U.S. Legation, gave Gallaudet a letter of introduction to David Baillie Warden in Paris. Warden was the author and translator of studies as varied as *The Frame of the Material World Manifest, That There Must Be a God,* and *An Enquiry Concerning the Intellectual and Moral Faculties and Literature of Negroes,* and Gallaudet looked him up.[118] Despite such positive contacts and prospects, Gallaudet wrote to Ward Woodbridge from London on March 4 that "this 'seeing the world' is a very pretty thing in prospect, but the world soon sickens to the taste. For what do we see in it? A complicated mass of wretchedness and sin."[119] He left for Paris the very next day.

FIVE

GALLAUDET ARRIVED IN PARIS on March 9, a Saturday, with a letter of introduction from Zachery Macaulay to the Abbé Sicard. He had already met Sicard in London, of course, and Sicard had already invited him to visit the Paris school, so the letter was just to satisfy Gallaudet's compulsive persnicketiness — he even went so far as to have lined up Mr. Warden to escort him to the school so that he did not appear, improperly, alone.

A young lady from Presbyterian Edinburgh whom he had recently met on the channel crossing told a friend that "on many subjects . . . our opinions were very different" because, as she saw it, he had set up "a much higher, much purer standard, of opinion, than I could, living in the world so much." The young lady's assessment is generous, but clear: Gallaudet's remarks to strangers on boats revealed a set of ethical standards incommensurate with "living in the world," even the genteel world of this young lady who lived with her widowed mother. With Gallaudet's standards, she said, "I should be miserable, because I should be constantly forced to act, in opposition to my principles."[1] If her observations are just, they would go a long way toward explaining Gallaudet's chronic misery in life. Unattainably rigid standards added to the obvious obsessive behavior he was exhibiting at this time look like a recipe for madness. Two days after his escorted visit to Sicard, he had himself in a dither about whether the contacts "who have great influence" with Sicard will actually provide enough clout to secure the Abbé's cooperation.[2] And he was still begging an expense account from Cogswell, although it seems that the Hartford committee had already granted his request to buy books "consistent with a strict regard to propriety."

On Saturday the 16th, Gallaudet attended a lecture given by Sicard at which Jean Massieu was exhibited. No mention is made of Laurent Clerc, who may or may not have been there. By Monday the 18th, Sicard had drawn up a weekly schedule of instruction for Gallaudet, "and here at length I may consider my work as beginning." On April 8, he began daily private language lessons under Massieu. It is not until May 20 that Gallaudet's journal abruptly mentions Clerc: "In a conversation which I had with Clerc this day he proposed going to America with me as an assistant if the Abbé Sicard would give his consent. I think of addressing the Abbé on the subject."[3] And on the 21st, he did exactly that. What caused the shilly-shallying Gallaudet to resolve to carry a deaf Catholic assistant back with him to Hartford when he was never authorized to bring any assistant at all? The answer lies partly in how Gallaudet saw the Paris school staff.

Roche-Ambroise Sicard (1742–1822) had been born in the West Indies. As an abbé, he had completed theological studies but was not ordained and thus, as an unordained cleric, occupied the same position in society as did Gallaudet. As well, Sicard was a Jansenist who actually shared many of Gallaudet's Calvinist precepts, for Jansenism, a seventeenth-century movement within the French church, was essentially Calvinist in its doctrines concerning original sin, human depravity, predestination, grace, salvation, and the importance for every Christian of reading the Bible. Although Jansenism was officially defeated in the early eighteenth century, many of its tenets lived on among educated French Catholics: in Stendahl's 1830 *The Red and the Black,* for example, Julien Sorel's mentor the abbé Pirard is a Jansenist. French Jansenists and Connecticut Congregationalists found a common enemy in the Society of Jesus: as Connecticut avidly fitted the Jesuits into its conspiracy theories, French Jansenists and Jesuits were locked into mutual accusations of heresy. Sicard would have welcomed Gallaudet to his school as a brother, and Gallaudet would have felt at home.[4]

Jean Massieu (1772–1846) was born deaf into a poor family with six deaf children. Naturally, the family put the deaf children to work without any attempt at schooling, and Jean was the family's shepherd. Massieu later described his village childhood as a time when he was treated "like a dog."[5] At age thirteen, he had the great good luck to be noticed by a kind stranger and sent to the deaf school in Bordeaux, where the abbé Sicard was then teaching. The rest is history. But for Massieu, the rescue seems to have come too late, for while he had the learning to tutor Gallaudet and was regarded as a genius by his colleague Clerc, he remained childlike in many ways: he habitually wore three or four watches, stuffed his pockets with books and blackboard chalk, dressed "after the fashion of Louis XIV," believed he would die young because he had always been so healthy, and refused to eat eggs. Genius or no, Massieu's puerile eccentricities made him seem harmless to Gallaudet.[6]

Such would not have been the case with Louis-Pierre Paulmier, a hearing instructor who, Gallaudet later asserted, had also tutored him in "the language of signs." Gallaudet found Paulmier's manners odd, and later in Hartford he told Edmund Booth a story about what happened when he asked what was owing for his lessons. As Gallaudet related it to Booth, Paulmier replied, "'Nothing, only let me kiss you.' And, said Mr. Gallaudet, 'I consented, and Paulmier put his arms around my neck and shoulders and kissed me,' concluding the story with a cheerful laugh."[7] We're glad to see that Gallaudet could laugh about it years later, but we can imagine the shock to his frigid Yankee manners, and the story gives us some insight into Gallaudet's unease in Paris.

As for Clerc, here a lifelong friendship bloomed. Born in December of 1785 and thus just two years older than Gallaudet, he grew up deaf in a family of notaries east of Lyon. His parents believed he was deafened from a fall into the fireplace, but he seems to have doubted that, and rightly so: families with no history of deaf members are always quick to blame an accident or illness that occurred around the time that the child failed to begin to talk, and Clerc was probably born deaf. As with Massieu, there was no attempt to educate him, and he passed his childhood helping his mother with the livestock. Clerc's father, however, was much better educated than Massieu's and arranged for the twelve-year-old to attend the deaf school in Paris, where Massieu became his first teacher. By 1806, Clerc was a teacher himself. Unlike nearly all other deaf people in this period, Clerc had little to say, initially, about his religious beliefs before, or after, his schooling, suggesting perhaps that religion was a nonissue for him. His nonchalant attitude toward Catholicism when Gallaudet first met him might have suggested that he was open to Calvinist salvation. And at about five feet eight inches, he wasn't that much taller than his new little American friend. Whatever it was about Clerc, Gallaudet trusted his expertise as he had never trusted the Braidwoods, despite the fact that Clerc was telling him pretty much the same thing Watson had.

So Sicard, Massieu, and Clerc were men Gallaudet could work with. And he probably felt easier in a school that segregated the sexes — he seems never to have so much as seen any of the female pupils. He was clearly getting comfortable in French and, as for the sign language he was learning, well, that was French, too, not a natural sign language at all but an artificial code for *written* French invented by Charles Michel de l'Épée. And although de l'Épée had given lessons in articulation when he deemed it worthwhile for a particular pupil, Sicard had discontinued the practice, considering oral training "almost always very *painful, harsh, discordant,* and *comparatively useless.*"[8]

The Paris school described its pedagogy as proceeding "from the *known* to the *unknown,*" and we have seen a brief example of the method in the book Massieu and Clerc had published about their London exhibitions. A more complex example might be how teaching the French copula led to recognition of the soul. Natural signed languages, like Russian in the present tense, do not employ any copula at all, so the copula's meaning and function were entirely mysterious for deaf pupils learning French. Sicard would first teach his pupils to understand that a quality, such as the color "black," could be detached from a black object, such as "hat," so that a black hat was designated by two signs. To unite the quality with the object, pupils were taught to write a line thus: "hat — black." Once they got that, Sicard introduced the copula, and pupils were taught how to choose the proper form of the verb to produce a sentence like "The hat is black." Pupils were now on their way to abstract nouns such as "blackness" and on to "beauty" and "heat." And once they were given to understand that the human will was an action that cannot be seen, the way was paved toward an understanding of the soul and "the most sublime truths of religion."[9] Or so Clerc summarized the method. It's a pity we don't have more such detailed examples.

The language of classroom instruction, "methodical signs" or sign-encoded French, was an artifact of de l'Épée, who for all that he was the beloved father of deaf education in France had had remarkably low expectations for his pupils. In a 1783 letter to Sicard, he wrote, "Do not hope that your pupils can ever express their ideas by writing. Let it suffice that they translate our language into theirs, as we ourselves translate foreign languages, without being able to think or to express ourselves in those languages."[10]

De l'Épée's goal was to teach written French, period, and he regarded dictation from sign-encoded French as the test of educational achievement. The code signified French grammatical particles and affixes with invented morphemes that were drawn from the hand shapes and motions found in the natural language of the Parisian deaf community. For example, for the masculine and feminine articles *le* and *la*, de l'Épée referenced a man's hat brim to stand for *le* and a woman's bonnet string to signify *la*. These two signs were carried to the United States by Gallaudet and Clerc, where they are still to be found in American Sign Language to mean *male* and *female, boy* and *girl, man* and *woman*. De l'Épée also altered natural sign morphemes to incorporate the initial letter of the French equivalent. For example, a common natural sign for *physician* is to put the fingertips of the right hand on the pulse at the left wrist. De l'Épée altered that sign to make the fingers of the right hand form the letter *m* for *médecin,* "physician."

Likewise, the natural sign for *seek* (*chercher*) incorporated the letter *c,* and the natural sign for *with* (*avec*) was made with the letter *a.* All three of these signs incorporating initials of the French equivalent are still current in ASL, and most American signers are blissfully unaware of that.

Harlan Lane provides an example of how a line from Racine — "To the smallest of the birds, He gives their crumbs" — would be rendered with forty-eight signs in de l'Épée's code: *gives* alone required five signs; those for verb, present, third person, singular, and finally the meaning, *give.*[11] Methodical signs were described by a godson of Sicard, Roch-Ambroise Bébian, a hearing man who was living at Sicard's school when Gallaudet visited in 1816, as "a kind of syllabic spelling of French words in gestures instead of the direct translation of thought and its living image." For example, the French word meaning "to comprehend" was rendered with the signs *take* (Latin *prehendo*) and *with* (*cum*), thus giving the word's etymology but not its meaning.[12] Sicard, Bébian wrote, completed and perfected de l'Épée's program, adding compound tenses of verbs until the system bulked to the size described by Harlan Lane, forty-eight signs for one short sentence.

Gallaudet, unlike Bébian, seems to have bought into the system uncritically. We see him asking Massieu or Clerc, in a conversation scribbled on a paper café tablecloth, for demonstrations and worrying about the differences between French and English grammar. The French copula in the first-person singular is written out in all tenses on this tablecloth fragment, each construction followed by symbols as though Clerc or perhaps Massieu were demonstrating the methodical signs for the tenses as Gallaudet made notes. In French, Gallaudet exclaims, "But we do not have the same tenses of the verb as you, and although sign language is universal for purposes of the expression of ideas, however it is difficult to apply that language to English grammar." The French sentences he wrote on this tablecloth, it's important to note, are not at all idiomatic, but rather calques of English. For example, he wrote "Je craigne que j'ai arrivé tard," translating each English word of the meaning he has in mind — "I'm afraid I have arrived late" — and thus producing not the French sentence *Je crains que je sois arrivé tard* but rather an ungrammatical string of words — which Clerc (probably not Massieu) appears nevertheless to have understood. This evidence that Gallaudet saw translation between French and English as simple word substitution is important for our understanding how he could have been taken in by methodical signs for so long.[13]

Gallaudet also found a safe place in Paris outside of the school as temporary pastor of the Chapel of the Oratoire, the English-language Protestant church in Paris. According to Nathan Chang, the sermons Gallaudet gave in this church adhered to Edwardsean Calvinism, including the doctrines of salvation by divine grace alone, the absolute sovereignty of God, and the mystery of how free will might be understood in such a doctrinal system — just as these doctrines were preached by Dr. Strong at the Center Church back home.[14] Gallaudet's sermons, collected and published in London through the intercession of Zachery Macaulay, treated of Christian fellowship, the Lord's Supper, repentance, consolation, petitioning God and searching Scripture, the doctrine of Divine Influence, and the like, all of which the reviewer for the *Christian Observer* (probably Macaulay) found doctrinally sound, observing, too, that Gallaudet's sermons "invest[ed] christianity with an amiable and dignified character." It was Gallaudet's first book, and he dedicated it to Hannah More.[15] That this church meant more to him than a reader today would guess is suggested by the fact that Gallaudet's sole poem written in Europe concerned a "conversation with a young Englishman in the crowd, for a few minutes," whom he identified as a child of God: "Stranger! I read it in thine eye, / And in thy accents meek and mild, / And in thy words of charity, / That God has chosen thee his child."[16]

Outside of the safe havens of Sicard's school and the Chapel of the Oratoire, however, Gallaudet was again depressed and downright fearful during his first few weeks in Paris. "I am in a Hotel meublé as it is called, that is furnished. I hire my room of the landlady; procure my breakfast from the porter who brings it to me, after purchasing and cooking the articles that I need; have my room cleaned and bed made by his wife, and dine and sup at a restaurateur in the neighborhood. My lodgings are in the Fauxbourgs [*sic*] St. Germain near the Abbaye. — It is a lonely way of life. I am quite sick of it."

His hotel was right across the street from where Sartre would sit more than a century later in the café Les Deux Magots, perhaps writing *Melancholia,* the working title of the existentialist manifesto *La Nausée*. It must have been a depressing spot! But Gallaudet was neither inclined nor equipped to sit in a café contemplating the Abyss, and in a letter to Dr. Cogswell in March, he imagined his sponsor thinking, mistakenly,

> what a delightful excursion I must be making, and what a rich feast of novelty I must have continually spread before me. It is far otherwise.

Public amusements I have abstained from entirely and the temptation to forget divine things, is so great when one once begins, even for a day or two, to make a <u>business</u> of seeing what is to be seen, that I declare to you, with my present feelings, were it not that I thought my usefulness might be diminished by my returning home ignorant of what all travellers speak of, I would not put myself out of the way to see one of the wonders of this wonderful city. — It is hard I know to hit the middle course; but it is always safest to keep as far as possible from the world and its influences. The precepts of our Saviour were very explicit on this subject. . . . Ah! how this poor heathen people want the bible and the sabbath.[17]

He had been in Paris five whole days. Professor Benjamin Silliman urged him to get out and about: "Should your time and health permit, I should be much gratified by hearing from you while in Paris — If you get time to step into the lecture rooms, cabinets and laboratories of the physical science, I should be gratified to learn from you the present state of those subjects in France."[18] Needless to say, Gallaudet did nothing of the sort, and in any case he had left Paris by the time this letter arrived. As odd as Gallaudet's attitude seems, Noah Webster's response to Paris was similar. He went to consult the Royal Library but left a month earlier than planned because he was horrified that Paris theaters were open on the Sabbath.[19]

Within a month, Gallaudet had moved from his hated hotel to "two very snug rooms in the house of a French lady whose whole family consists of herself, daughter and servant," a twenty-minute walk to Sicard's school. This letter to Cogswell provides a glimpse of Gallaudet learning methodical signs and is well worth quoting at length:

Each day at ½ past ten I attend one of the classes in the institution and continue with it till ½ past twelve. At present I attend the class under <u>Massieu's</u> care. It consists of 15 or 16 lads. He is teaching them the names of objects, and qualities, both mental and bodily and their <u>relations</u>; — the divisions of time, of the earth, of the water etc. etc. etc. together with short phrases — by signs. All this is very improving to me. I take my seat by him, imitate all his pantomimes, and watch the manner in which his pupils catch his ideas. He has a long wand in his hand to point with. — the room is surrounded with black boards on which the boys write with chalk — a part are actively employed, while others form a corps of observers. I have often thought how you would smile to see me making all sorts of gestures and faces. But I am more convinced of the utility of this language of pantomime to a <u>certain extent</u>. This very morning Massieu dictated 8 or ten French verbs to me by signs which I had never seen before and I knew their meaning at once and wrote down the verbs. — at 3'oclock [*sic*] I go to Massieu's chamber and receive a private lesson till 5 for which I pay him about 15 dolls p month. — I have already learned the signs of most of the Tenses of the verbs in all their moods and in all their varieties. — most of the articles which are numerous in the modern French Grammar, of many adjectives, pronouns and prepositions. — Dont be alarmed at this system of signs I shall learn and practice just as much of it as I think best. My present opinion is that a <u>great deal</u> of it is truly valuable and will very much accelerate the progress of my scholars — During the rest of the day, I read and talk French, revise my lesson in my own chamber and read on the general subject of instructing the deaf and dumb.[20]

It's clear in this letter that he was worried Cogswell would not approve. Further remarks here reiterate his opinion of Paris: "From religious privileges and domestic and social enjoyment I am almost entirely cutt [*sic*] off and what is the gaiety of Paris to me. As a Philadelphian and I hope as a Christian I despise it." The comfort of Hartford and his friends there "outweigh all the pomp and splendor, and gaiety, and novelty, and science of this proudest of European cities. I do thank God that a sight of the world has taught me more of it's [*sic*] vanity." One short month later, Gallaudet had solved both his difficulties — the time required to learn methodical signs and classroom techniques and the horror with which he was surrounded in heathen Paris — when an American friend urged him to take passage on a ship soon to sail for the United States and "Mr. Clerc, of his own accord, offered to go with me." He asked for Sicard's blessing to take one of the school's best teachers, endured a hug and kiss from Paulmier, shook the dust of Paris off his feet, and was gone.[21]

When the precise tipping point might have occurred is nowhere told; the critical moment when Gallaudet suddenly understood that deaf education was not an "art" at all but a matter of a *shared language*. This critical moment is elided in both Gallaudet's and Clerc's narratives. Whether Gallaudet asked Clerc to return with him as his assistant (as Clerc remembered) or Clerc proposed the idea (as Gallaudet told Sicard and as he later represented the story to Cogswell),[22] the epiphany, so momentous to the history of

Deaf Americans, slipped under everyone's radar. All we can say for sure is that something clicked for Gallaudet that May in the happy comfort of his friendships with Sicard and Clerc, enabling him to see that the spirit of the school in which they labored was what he must duplicate in Connecticut.

Before setting out, though, punctilious Gallaudet drew on his legal studies of many years previous to write out a formal contract that engaged Clerc to reside in Hartford for three years, to teach six hours a day on Mondays through Fridays and three hours on Saturdays, with six weeks of vacation annually, to travel with Gallaudet and assist at all public lectures, and to refrain from undertaking any lectures or other connections with any other establishment, though he could give private lessons in his room on his own time. Clerc was "not to be called upon to teach anything contrary to the Roman Catholic religion which he professes, and in which faith he desires to live and die."

Gallaudet was to pay all traveling expenses, including laundry, to provide room and board at no cost in Hartford, and pay a salary of 2,500 francs per annum and return fare to France at the expiration of the three years.[23] He must have had good reason to fear that Cogswell and the other directors would not be happy, because he left Paris with Clerc without telling them even that Clerc was with him, let alone the details of the contract.

Once safely out of Paris and on the road to Le Havre, Gallaudet plucked up his courage to tell Cogswell what he had done. This letter is an exemplary text of rhetorical techniques for breaking unwelcome news:

My dear Sir,

Tomorrow I expect to sail from this port in the Mary Augusta, Capt Hale, for New York in company with Mr. S. V. S. Wilder, Mr. Upson's particular friend, and a Mr. Clerc whom perhaps you may have heard of or seen his name mentioned in some of the papers. He is a Frenchman, born near Lyon, and ever since one year of age has laboured under the same difficulty with Alice. The Abbé Sicard has had him under his care for these 15 years past during 8 of which he had charge of one of the classes in the institution. He is the identical Clerc, who with Massieu made such a figure among the nobility in London last summer. He goes with me somewhat in the character of an assistant in our intended establishment and as I do not like to have any thing uncertain when it can be made sure, after having obtained the Abbé's consent, I have entered into actual stipulations with

Mr. Clerc by which he is bound to remain with me for 3 years for a certain sum, which I will not mention at present, but which if the good faith, my fellow citizens, do not choose to pay — I will quite take him off their hands. — But I am ironical when I ought to be serious. — Yes — my dear friend — Providence has most kindly provided for my speedy and successful return by furnishing me with the most accomplished pupil of the Abbé Sicard and one, too, who is not the less recommended by the probity and sweetness of his character, so far as I have been able to ascertain it, than by his rare talents. He already understands a good deal of English. We shall work hard together in the passage in order that he may acquire more and a few months in America will quite make him master of it. The train of events which has thus led to my very unexpected departure I have not the time to tell you. — I should have written you before but the affair was not <u>entirely</u> finished till within a few days past, and I did not like to write while there was any fear of disappointment — [24]

Declining to name the promised salary may not have been such a brilliant maneuver, though, and we can well imagine Cogswell being stunned by his young friend's audacity in legally binding the donors to an unspecified expense that they had not approved. Gallaudet sent this letter by the Manchester Packet, which was expected to arrive in New York long before the passenger ship in which they were about to embark, the *Mary Augusta*. As it turned out, they caught up with the packet just west of Nova Scotia, and Cogswell would have received the letter at most only a day or so before Gallaudet debarked with Clerc in New York.[25]

The year 1816 was the Year Without a Summer: the most powerful volcanic eruption ever recorded had killed tens of thousands in Indonesia the year previous, and volcanic ash was now causing temperatures to plunge all across the Northern Hemisphere. The Year Without a Summer is remembered today chiefly in connection with the cold, rainy weather that kept Mary Godwin, Percy Bysshe Shelley, and Lord Byron indoors telling German ghost stories instead of tramping around the Alps as planned, and also in the strange skies of English landscape paintings made that year by John Constable and J. M. W. Turner. In Hartford, a "dry fog" dimmed the sunlight so severely that one could look directly at the sun with naked eye. There was frost every month. In May, snow fell in Albany and river ice was observed all summer as far south as Wilkes-Barre, Pennsylvania. Everywhere crops failed, and the price of corn and oats in Connecticut increased more than thirteenfold. The outmigration Connecticut had always suffered was increased, as farmers pulled up stakes and headed to the Western Reserve.[26] During the summer crossing, however, neither Gallaudet nor Clerc noticed anything unusual, although the voyage did take somewhat longer than expected.

Popular Deaf history paints a happy picture of "Thomas" and "Laurent," as Harlan Lane's magisterial history of deaf education has taught us they called each other, with Laurent learning English from Thomas and Thomas learning French sign language from Laurent. In their own diaries and letters, however, they were still "Mr. Gallaudet" — or, rather "M. Gallaudet" until Clerc grew more at home in English — and "Mr. Clerc," and so they would remain. As for Gallaudet's putative shipboard studies, he was so indisposed with seasickness — as Clerc said, he often "paid a tribute to Neptune" — that he couldn't have done much of anything, and besides, he was still disgusted by gesticulation: of French orators, he said that "[h]e would wish that they did not shake the head, nor hand, nor arm so much: in a word, he would seem to wish that they would stand like statues." Clerc nevertheless tried to teach him "the method of signs for abstract ideas" when he was well enough to attend to a lesson.[27]

Clerc, in contrast, worked hard on his English during the voyage: "He has not been sick a single day," Gallaudet said, "and has been the most industrious man on board, always at his books or writing."[28] As Gallaudet had so clearly explained to Cogswell in the letter from Le Havre, Clerc was no beginner with the language. His onboard "Diary" is clearly the practice book of the intermediate student he was. However, in the letter sent from the New York harbor, Gallaudet told Cogswell, "You will be astonished at the progress which [Clerc] has already made in English, principally during our voyage," and appended a brief postscript by Clerc as if to illustrate his progress. Unfortunately, Cogswell, who was primed to believe that Gallaudet was returning with some kind of a deaf wonder, assumed that Clerc's postscript was "written only 60 day [*sic*] after he commenced learning the English language,"[29] and he repeated his mistake to newspapers. The misunderstanding was unfortunate because it established the expectation, in the public mind, that deaf Connecticut children could do as Clerc had done, learn English from zero to fluency in sixty days. When that didn't happen, the school had to scramble to explain why not. Clerc's "Diary" is fascinating in its luxuriant similes and descriptions that tend to circle around somehow to Jesus, which was, of course, the topic particularly approved by the friend who was correcting his work. Reading it today astonishes one with the effort this deaf man put into acquiring a second written language. Yet for all his hard work, Clerc clearly wasn't driven by the Protestant ethic as Gallaudet was, and the diary is full of remarks having to do with Gallaudet waking him up from what seem almost continuous naps.

Clerc's story of Gallaudet's reunion with his family in New York on August 9 is classic. "I anticipated much pleasure in witnessing his joy at again seeing his parents, brother and sisters, after so long an absence; but I must acknowledge that I was rather disappointed; for I did not see any greater demonstration of welcome on both sides than the mere shaking of hands."[30] That's a description not only of chilly Connecticut manners but also, although Clerc doesn't mention it, of a mourning family, for Gallaudet's youngest sibling, five-year-old Wallace, had died just a few days before the *Mary Augusta* arrived in New York.[31]

Clerc's memories of the city feature his dismay at how fast people walked and how alike they all looked. He found New York a city without elegance, taste, amusement, or the sublime. But he was delighted to meet the family of a Columbia professor, Nathaniel F. Moore, at P. W.'s house. Moore's father conversed happily with Clerc by writing on a slate, and his sister, or perhaps daughter, did so as well, but in French, which pleased Clerc no end. The professor himself, however, showed his ignorance — and bad manners — by using the opportunity solely to try to figure out "how abstract ideas are communicated to the deaf and dumb."[32] Almost two hundred years later, I myself was asked that question in a job interview. Clerc was clearly better prepared for this question than I was — he had already been hired, while I never got called back. He was probably just as outraged, however. Later in life, he hinted at his irritation in the story of a Parisian lady whose ignorance about abstractions led her to declare that "there was no means of making the deaf and dumb acquainted with the rules of grammar, much less with the laws of syntax." Even as an old man, a deaf acquaintance said, Clerc had to steel himself to take ignorant, bigoted, insulting questions for the sake of convincing people to open their wallets. One of his pupils in Paris, Ferdinand Berthier, complained specifically about the persistence of the idea that abstract concepts can be conveyed only through speech: "I have yet to come across a single hearing person who in a discussion of this topic (and what hearing person can resist the itch to get in a word on it?) did not from the beginning throw these big words [abstract nouns] in my face," and Clerc presumably felt the same way.[33]

Because the question of whether deaf people could learn abstract concepts held a bizarre fascination for the hearing in the early nineteenth century, it's worth pausing to consider what Gallaudet himself had to say on the subject when he was asked this question at a public lecture in Cincinnati in 1835. According to the reporter, who seems to have been working from notes made at the lecture, Gallaudet started by stating, correctly, that deaf children learn abstract concepts the same way hearing children do: "There is no state of mind, no intellectual act, however subtle and evanescent; no feeling or emotion however delicate, which has not a corresponding action in the muscular system. This Mr. G. exemplified in the case of many thoughts, feelings, and mental operations; and then showed that it was by these physical accompaniments that [all] children were taught what name to apply to those acts of their minds and movements of their hearts, of which they themselves were previously conscious."[34]

But he quickly segued into an explication of how abstract concepts *were signed.* "The mute," he said, "at once analyses the idea, and thus gets a thorough knowledge of its elements. When e.g. the mute wishes to express virtue, he rapidly gives you the sign of power, mind, overcome, evil, i.e. *the power of the mind to overcome evil.* The mute must, in every such case, use analytical expressions, and therefore his ideas here are generally far more clear, distinct, and definite, than those of other learners." Needless to say, no deaf person signs "virtue" like this today, at least not outside of Sunday school classes.

While Clerc was fielding impertinent questions about abstract concepts and, in the process, inspiring "general admiration" in New York, Gallaudet was again "in a state of very great debility and with hardly resolution enough to put my pen to the papers." He had earlier mentioned the heat in New York — this in the Year Without a Summer! — as the cause of his lassitude, but the symptoms he mentioned look more like depression.[35] Leaving New York for Hartford, he stopped briefly in New Haven to visit President Dwight and give Clerc a tour of the Yale campus. Dwight had been ill since the summer of the previous year with what Silliman called "a chronic affection of the bladder" — prostate cancer — but by the summer of

1816 he had recovered enough to "hear his classes recite" and, presumably, to enjoy seeing Gallaudet again and meeting his interesting new friend.[36] The two arrived in Hartford on August 22, getting out of the coach directly in front of the Cogswell residence. Alice was in school at Miss Huntley's, but she was sent for and, according to Clerc, had a lovely chat with him.

Alice, we know from a letter she had written in April, had been worrying about her soul. Gallaudet had written to her in March, "do you learn now any verses in the bible and any hymns or psalms. And do you often think about God? — Do you pray to him to make you good, and to make you ready to go to Heaven when you die?"[37] One wonders to what extent he was gratified to learn that all this was making her "very much afraid. I am feeling bad, very bad. I am weeping very many feeling bad — very sorry. . . . I think so very wicked, God made me Deaf and Dumb. Perhaps me very bad I hear not me Perhaps blind and Deaf and Dumb. I hope not. . . . I dont know reading Holy Bible. I am very sorry books all very many Best me think reading Best Holy bible I wish and very want read I know and did not I am very sorry."[38] She is all of ten years old.

As for Julia Brace, the other little girl Gallaudet was hoping soon to father, there is no record of Gallaudet taking Clerc to visit her. Alice had earlier written about having been to visit Julia, probably with Miss Huntley, who took an active interest in the deafblind child. Alice had found Julia "very poor she live in very little house very cold, she no frock me very much sorry, have yes me give one new frock her very much glad she for Winter."[39] Clearly, Cogswell was taking no interest in this poor child. The day after their arrival in Hartford, Gallaudet took Clerc to a meeting of the directors to introduce him.

By the beginning of September, Gallaudet, Clerc, and Cogswell were off to Boston by overland coach, armed with the requisite letters of introduction from Governor John Cotton Smith, "to pick their pockets *genteelly*," as Cogswell put it. As phrased in a press release, the purpose of the trip was "to solicit the appropriation of Funds by the affluent, to educate gratuitously the Deaf and Dumb children of persons who are indigents — belonging to [Massachusetts] and other States — in the Institution which has been organized, in Connecticut — where funds have already been realized, or made certain, sufficient to complete all the Buildings necessary for it."[40]

This news release was very far from the truth — there was no money for buildings, and educating the children of the indigent any time soon was not then under consideration. The prospectus for the Asylum, signed by Cogswell and Wadsworth and published as a broadside on March 21, clearly stated that "it is with deep regret, that they are under the necessity of pleading the *poverty* of the Asylum, at its very outset, as an obstacle in the way of receiving charity scholars, excepting from those *few towns* which have contributed to its resources."[41]

Newspapers in the 1810s had no reporters to speak of and customarily printed articles precisely as submitted by the parties involved; if this press release indeed came directly from Cogswell, it's hard to understand his intentions. The announcement goes on to explain that all money raised outside Connecticut would "be devoted exclusively to the extension of the blessings of the Institution beyond the State."

In a study of Gallaudet's rhetorical strategies, James Fernandes describes a "consistent pattern" in his fund-raising tours: first, publicity announcements (such as the one summarized above) placed in newspapers and on handbills; then private meetings with the state's governor, the city's mayor, the state legislature, and other influential people. This accomplished, Gallaudet would hold a public demonstration in which he and Clerc (or, later, George Loring) were introduced by a leading local resident, and Gallaudet would read an address composed by Clerc that always included a thumbnail biography, a rundown of statistics on deaf Americans, and emotional appeals. Clerc exhibited an uncanny ability to tailor these appeals to his audience: when addressing men or a "promiscuous" audience, he appealed to nationalism; when addressing ladies, he appealed to the heart — "I look into your eyes, and by your eyes, I can judge the bottom of your heart. I feel it is good, tender, and sensible."[42] Questions from the audience given in writing were answered on a chalkboard, and, as we have seen from the London exhibits, it was in this segment that the meeting could began to resemble a freak show. As Cogswell put it, "Clerc is doing wonders — he makes them all stare."[43] Finally, a committee of prominent locals would set up a subscription drive with a strongly proestablishment message appealing to the "patrician class rather than the masses."[44] These subscription texts were penned by Gallaudet and typically referenced the healthful and central location of Hartford, the allegation that any funds collected would be used for pupils from indigent families, and patriotism. Of European schools, Gallaudet would write, "Princes are their patrons," while in the United States, patrons are "all who feel for the honor of their country."[45] A recent historical study of American charity drives credits Gallaudet as the first to "consolidate" and "mobilize" a tour of this kind, but of course he had learned it all from Sicard.[46]

Their next stop was New Haven, where the governor and both houses of the legislature were meeting, to request that the state subsidize their new school. How exactly they explained their request for public financing for a school that would remain under private control would be interesting to know. The prospectus published in March had stated that the (expected) state donation would be directed either to "a *fund* for the relief of the indigent" or "as the exigencies of the Asylum might require," but the funding bill that resulted, granting the school $5,000, specified that it was "to be laid out for the relief, education, instruction and support of the indigent deaf and dumb persons belonging to this state." Cogswell was infuriated at the small sum and wrote to his wife, "nothing short of an immediate revelation would touch the hearts of the obdurate democrats and ignorant and selfish federalists — the house, in the abundance of their liberality granted $5000."[47] The directors, on the other hand, seem to have been more worried about the language of the bill specifying the purpose to which this donation was to be used, and they set about devising a spin: was the money actually to be earmarked for direct support of charity pupils, or could it be spent however the directors wished? What they wanted to do with donations from both wealthy philanthropists and state taxpayers was not waive tuition for poor families but rather build a campus. The nuisance language of the appropriation bill would just have to be creatively interpreted.[48]

Cogswell hoped that New York would be more generous, but he worried about a group of wealthy New Yorkers who were planning a school to be headed by a different deaf Frenchman, a Mr. Gard of Bourdeaux. With Gallaudet and Clerc in tow, Cogswell hurried on to New York City in a "Steam boat," a novel mode of transport for Cogswell, who marveled that they arrived "without the slightest accident." Cogswell had planned to buttonhole each of the dozen wealthy New York donors, but when the decision about whether to open their own school or send their children to Hartford was postponed, Cogswell, Gallaudet, and Clerc hastened up the Hudson to urge Governor DeWitt Clinton to pledge New York taxpayer support of the Hartford school.

Clerc was a sensation in Albany, where the *Albany Daily Advertiser* printed his address to the legislature in full.[49] Clerc, speaking for Gallaudet

and the directors, described the school as a kind of internal mission —
"They send missionaries to Africa and Asia to convert the Idolatrous to
the true Religion. . . . Do foreigners merit rather your preference than
your own countrymen?" — and kept his focus largely on the superiority
of one, and only one, large school in Hartford that would serve the entire
area. He mentioned as rationales the expense — one big school is cheaper
than many small schools — and, for perhaps the first time in this country,
the matter of "*Uniformity* in the signs of thought, the language of the deaf
and dumb." He also deployed one of Gallaudet's hobby horses by citing
Hartford's "distance from the largest cities which often attract youth by
various objects and corrupt their manners." However, his main argument for
a single large school was something Gallaudet would never have approved:
"There will be great emulation among [the pupils], and they will become
better instructed." Gallaudet read this address aloud to the legislature,
suppressing his own deeply held views — perhaps with great difficulty,
perhaps with no qualms at all — for the sake of funding. The questions
from the audience that were printed in the Albany newspaper may have
surprised all three men, for they largely concerned not the idea of a New
York school but rather religious matters. When asked "What idea had you
of God, before you were taught by the Abbe [*sic*] Sicard?" Clerc gave an
unrehearsed answer: "I do not recollect what idea I had of God. I think I
never had some." Henceforth, he would have an approved answer at hand
that would drive home the notion of deaf children as heathens.

Gallaudet preached at the Second Presbyterian Church in Albany and
then on the following Sunday at the Two-Steeple Dutch Reformed Church,
where he delivered "a genuine Connecticut sermon, 'in doctrine pure,'" that
included a passage from the English poet William Cowper (1731–1800).
Cogswell observed that Gallaudet was "certainly a beautiful little Cowper,
and he resembles him [in] more respects than one." What exactly Cogswell
meant by that remark is unclear. Cowper was admired for his hymns, his
translations of Homer, and his activism against the slave trade, but there
was no parallel with Gallaudet in these areas. Cogswell would have known
that Cowper was institutionalized for depression after several unsuccessful
suicide attempts, made under the conviction that God had doomed him
to eternal damnation and wanted him to start his sentence in hell immediately, and perhaps it was Cowper's melancholy and fears concerning his
soul that reminded Cogswell of Gallaudet. Whatever passage from Cowper

Gallaudet was quoting in his sermon, "the Legislature are impressed with a high idea of him as a Scholar, a Divine," and they raised $1,882. Cogswell went home to Hartford and the other two proceeded to Philadelphia.[50]

Fund-raising did not go well in Philadelphia, and Gallaudet was so disappointed that he wouldn't even summarize it for Cogswell, referring him, instead, to a Mrs. Ellsworth, who "can inform you of what transpired there." Apparently, many Philadelphians wished to establish their own school for the deaf, and the leading citizens on whom the Hartford forces had counted to bundle subscriptions stopped accepting money while the controversy played out. One of these men, Charles Chauncey, wrote to Gallaudet in January about what he called "the narrow minded views and selfish feelings" of Philadelphians. It's interesting to notice this kind of language cropping up again when the Hartford plans are thwarted by people who might be considered allies in their support for deaf education. People who support deaf education but decline to be dictated to by Gallaudet and his Hartford handlers are deemed selfish.[51]

Gallaudet and Clerc left Philadelphia in mid-December and headed for Burlington, New Jersey, where their pitch for subscriptions was better received. Gallaudet reported to Cogswell that "Good father Boudinot wrote his name in our red book with 500$ against it." Boudinot then desired them to visit "the ex-king of Spain, Jos. Bounaparte," who lived in Bordentown — but he was away from home, so Clerc wrote him a letter enclosing a subscription paper.[52]

Who were these men? The "ex-king of Spain" Joseph Bonaparte was a brother of Napoleon, whose installation on the Spanish throne provoked the Peninsular War. Joseph had managed to flee the country in 1813, taking with him the royal family's jewelry, as well as much of their collection of paintings by masters such as Velázquez, Raphael, and Leonardo, which he cut out of their frames. The paintings he abandoned in the mud at the Battle of Vitoria, but the jewelry provided him with a living in New Jersey. Gallaudet's tone in writing about Joseph Bonaparte suggests, unsurprisingly, a negative attitude toward the man, but Clerc, in contrast, had no evident qualms buttonholing him. As for "good father Boudinot," Elias Boudinot (1740–1821), a minor founding father, was a staunch Presbyterian with some Huguenot ancestry who had served in the Continental Army, the Second Continental Congress (one year as its president), the U.S. House of Representatives, and as director of the U.S. Mint. He later became a major donor to the Foreign Missions School for Indians in Canterbury, Connecticut and founded both the American Bible Society and the American Society for Meliorating the Condition of Jews, the aims of which were to relocate Jewish converts to Christianity to a reservation: he donated four thousand acres in northwestern Pennsylvania, now partly flooded by the Kinzua Dam, for this purpose. The new deaf school was a charity after Boudinot's own heart, and he bought himself a lifetime vice presidency on its Board of Directors. Gallaudet clearly revered him.

From New Jersey, Gallaudet and Clerc continued to New York City to await the nail-biting decision on whether a deaf school would indeed be established there. It was probably upon their arrival in New York that Gallaudet learned of the death of Timothy Dwight on January 11. Nathan Strong, the Gallaudets' pastor at the Center Church of Hartford, had died on December 25 — not Christmas in Calvinist Hartford, but an ordinary Wednesday in Connecticut. Gallaudet must have felt much as a man feels at the death of his father — and there he was, just on the cusp of making both Strong and Dwight proud of him. As for the New York school, Cogswell saw the vote in favor of it as a setback. The deciding factor seems to have been that such a large number of deaf people — forty-seven — were counted in the city, but the report also refers to evidence of the efficacy of deaf education gleaned not only from the "Mr. Gard of Bordeaux" but also from Gallaudet's old nemesis Watson of London and, ironically, from Laurent Clerc, with whom the committee conversed "exchanging sentiments by writing on a slate." Cogswell was so angry, he would do everything in his power to undermine this school, and though Gallaudet's first thought had been the more schools the better, he soon came around to Cogswell's desire for a monopoly, telling an Ohio man as late as 1819 that other parts of the country have to be patient "and let us get fairly under way."[53]

Back in Hartford, the directors had hit their first major bump in the road toward the opening of the school in April: their difficulty in finding a suitable married couple to hire as "superintendent," a combination physical-plant director, dean of students, and matron, the head of what Gallaudet would call the "domestic department." Out of ideas, they invited the pastors of all the churches in the city to meet for prayer on the question in February. It was not until the beginning of April that the Rev. and Mrs. A. O. Stansbury were hired for the job. Gallaudet gave Stansbury a pep talk, addressing him as "my Christian brother" and urging him to "a sense of responsibility to God and of devotion to the cause of Jesus Christ."[54] And as the school approached its opening, Gallaudet was still suffering "considerable indisposition," probably constipation.

A letter from a stranger asking after Julia Brace arrived around this time. Julia had not been admitted to the school because her parents could not pay, and now a Boston man, Redford Webster, was inquiring about her. A Mr. Loring, probably the father of George Loring, one of the Asylum's original seven pupils, had told Redford Webster that Gallaudet has "knowledge of such a person, but by reasons of [his] engagements in establishing the Institution for the education of the Deaf and Dumb, had no time to attend to any other subject." A Professor Dewar of Edinburgh, the letter continued, was seeking accounts of deafblind persons, and Webster was sending a friend to see Gallaudet for this reason, bringing a pamphlet of Dewar's with him. We don't know if Gallaudet got such a visit or whether he knew anything about Dewar — certainly he had been discussing deafblind people with Dugald Stewart in Edinburgh without mentioning any Dewar. Whatever came of this, Gallaudet kept the letter and filed it with Julia Brace's name on the heading, but nothing was done for Julia herself.[55]

The Connecticut Asylum for the Education and Instruction of Deaf and Dumb Persons opened on April 15, 1817, a Tuesday, in the City Hotel on the corner of Main and Gold Streets, right across Gold from the Center Church and directly across Main from the present Wadsworth Atheneum. It had been built just the previous year by Daniel Wadsworth, who added it onto an old boarding house, and it would later, after its reversion to a hotel, host Lafayette and Charles Dickens.[56] The school apparently occupied the old part of the building, which would have been comfortable quarters. The Rev. Mr. Stansbury wrote to his brother describing the view of the Connecticut River from the second floor and of the school garden, where lettuce, radishes, beets, beans, corn, cucumbers, and cabbages grew in a twenty-five-by-forty-five-foot plot.[57]

By the following Sunday, when Gallaudet would preach a sermon at the Center Church on the opening of the school, there were seven pupils, and by June 1st there were twenty-one. We can imagine Gallaudet's struggles to keep up, just like any other new signer who finds himself in front of the class. The Stansburys, in contrast, never learned to sign at all. Clerc must truly have been holding the little school together. In addition to Alice Cogswell, there was George Loring, aged nine, from Boston, who would soon become the main attraction at Galaudet's fund-raising exhibitions; twelve-year-old Wilson Whiton, also from Massachusetts, who traveled to Hartford with Loring and would later be a teacher at the Asylum; thirty-one-year-old Abigail Dillingham; fifty-year-old John Brewster, the itinerant painter of portraits who had once painted Dr. Cogswell's father; twenty-one-year-old Mary Gilbert, the one child of Sylvester Gilbert of Hebron who was able to attend; fourteen-year-old Levi S. Backus, also from Hebron; twenty-four-year-old Eliza C. Boardman of Whitesborough, New York; and Parnell and Sophia Fowler of Guilford, Connecticut, aged twenty-nine and nineteen. (The name "Parnell," sometimes spelled "Parnel," is the feminine form of "Peter," and though unusual today it was fairly popular at the time in the New England.)

None of these pupils was exactly unmolded clay, let alone a mind locked in a prison house, as Gallaudet would say in his first sermon for the school. Abigail Dillingham had a deaf sister, Nancy, and fourteen other deaf relatives; Mary Gilbert, of course, had four older deaf siblings and an activist father; Eliza Boardman had a deaf brother; Parnell and Sophia Fowler had each other as well as a deaf cousin who lived right across the road. Details about the family backgrounds of George Loring and Wilson Whiton are lacking, but the many members of the extended Loring family were prominent in Boston, the two boys knew each other, and the fact that both became teachers at the school suggests that they arrived well prepared for the curriculum. As for Levi Backus, although he would cause much trouble for Gallaudet with his rebellious behavior, he knew the deaf Gilberts and must also have been well prepared for school, as is evident from his later career as a teacher at the school for the deaf in Canajoharie, New York, and as a printer and editor.[58] All these pupils and their parents were persons of Gallaudet and Cogswell's social class who could afford the hefty annual tuition of $200, along with traveling expenses to Hartford.[59] We can imagine Gallaudet in over his head with these lively adolescents and young adults. Not only were most of them no longer children, but they all seem to have been active social agents, managing their own time and friendships. And the number of pupils at the Asylum rapidly increased, to a total of thirty-one by the end of 1817.

Gallaudet's sermon that Sunday in the Center Church began with a tribute to Strong, who had not yet been replaced, and took as its text Isaiah 35: 5–6, which Gallaudet, and indeed all Protestants of the day, interpreted as a prophecy of the Millennium: "Then the eyes of the blind shall be opened, and the ears of the deaf shall be unstopped. Then shall the lame man leap as an hart, and the tongue of the dumb sing: for in the wilderness shall waters break out, and streams in the desert."

It's easy to see why Isaiah was so popular among nineteenth-century Christians expecting the Millennium, with its hopeful predictions of new beginnings, a charismatic savior, and an Edward Hicks style Peaceable Kingdom on earth. The Asylum would always be run, during Gallaudet's lifetime, as "one link in that golden chain of universal good-will, which will eventually embrace and bind together the whole family of man."[60] The sermon proceeded by listing the benefits of deaf education as Gallaudet conceived them. First, it was an "important aid to many researches of the philanthropist, the philosopher, and the divine"; the "very singular condition in which the minds of the deaf and dumb are placed . . . may furnish opportunities for observation and experiment," and throw much light on those "*original truths*" with which our minds are endowed, "the *original notions* of right and wrong," the conscience, the innate knowledge of God. Here we see the signal importance for the establishment of deaf education of the belief that, contra Hume, we are born with innate morality and ideas about the world. Three decades later, Gallaudet would (tacitly) admit that this was not so: "[Of] all of the mutes that came under my instruction, from the old man [referring to Brewster] to the child of 10 years [Alice], I never found one who had the least notion of a God, the immortality of the soul, future accountability, or of any of the other great truths of morality and religion. Their dispositions and characters I have noticed to be often selfish, passionate, rude, untractable [*sic*]."[61]

Gallaudet was very seriously depressed during the school's first few months, as we know from his poem, "Written during a season of great despondency, May 1817." It begins, "While long the path of distant years / I stretch an aching eye, / Thorny to me each step appears / Of Sad futurity." The sense of hopelessness and dread is overpowering. An undated and untitled poem beginning "Mirth, thou dost cost me much" was also written around this time.[62] Despite its stated topic, the poem is about pain and is made all the more dour by being written in unrhymed iambic pentameter, an unusual choice for Gallaudet. The horror of his emotional state depicted here shows how he has worked himself into a position in which he must actively avoid being happy.

Mirth, thou dost cost me much;
For when I weave thy chaplet round my brow,
Full of gay flowers and blithesome buds of joy,
Yielding a momentary fragrance, — soon
My temples feel their thorns keen piercing; — soon
The thorns <u>alone</u> remain, the flowers so gay
Quick wither, and the buds that promise made,
Deceitful, of perpetual blossoming,
Mock, as they droop their dying heads, the hand
That was so idle as to gather them.
<u>The thorns alone remain</u>, a painful crown
Unlike the one of cruel mockery,
Which he once meekly bore — the Man of sorrows.

But the crown thou weavest, Mirth, hath thorns
That pierce the soul and make the conscience bleed.

This is a terrible burden of guilt he thought he had to bear.

The pupils, meanwhile, spent their days tightly scheduled. Out of bed, dressed, and attending worship every morning before breakfast at seven o'clock, they studied until nine, attended classes until noon, dined and enjoyed a bit a free time, endured an hour of writing instruction under the Rev. Mr. Stansbury, who could not communicate with them and must have taught merely by having pupils copy his work — as we saw in Watson's school, pupils were taught penmanship before they were able to read what they were writing — and sat for another three hours of classes from three to six o'clock.[63] A signal event of the Asylum's first year was a visit from President James Monroe, who had been elected in 1816 in a landslide — despite having lost Connecticut. When it was announced that he would tour the state, Hartford civic leaders gritted their teeth and escorted him into the city with the governor's Horse Guards, determined to treat the duly elected president with "Toleration" unless or until his conduct contradicted his profession to uphold the Constitution. After reviewing the troops and meeting the city's clergy, the president "afterwards visited the Asylum for the Deaf and Dumb, where he witnessed with apparent satisfaction the progress of the pupils, under the instruction of Messrs. Gallaudet and Clerc, and put to Professor Clerc several questions, to which he replied in writing with his usual promptness and facility."[64]

From Samuel Griswold Goodrich, aka Peter Parley, we have the amusing story that Monroe was so hesitant to frame a question for Clerc that everyone present was mortified until he came up with, "Ask him how — old he is."[65] Monroe could hardly have been as bashful and tongue-tied as Goodrich makes him out to be, however: in 1806, he had conducted a deaf Virginia boy, St. George Tucker Randolph, to London, lodged him in his own home there, and temporarily enrolled him in one of the Braidwood schools while negotiating for the boy's enrollment at Paris, which Monroe considered far superior. When St. George transferred to Paris, he studied with Clerc. So Monroe would have known who Clerc was and would have been pleased to meet him in Hartford.[66] In any case, the old-fashioned tricorne hat that our last Revolutionary-era president wore on his visit to the Asylum originated the ASL sign for "president."

During the summer of 1817, long before the school acquired its own chapel, Clerc began taking a few pupils to the Episcopal church every week, where they could follow along with the printed liturgy, while Gallaudet conducted the rest of them to the Center Church, where they were placed in two groups according to sex and apparently expected to sit in silence without a clue as to what was taking place.

The Stansburys were supposed to have been escorting the pupils to church but "absolutely declined sitting with them,"[67] and when Gallaudet lodged a complaint in September, they retaliated with a complaint against Clerc. Considering how inexperienced Congregational Connecticut was with outsiders who were not fully conversant with its prevailing social mores, the only surprise here is that it took five months for the first complaint to be made. The Stansburys attested that Clerc was in the shocking habit of sitting in the school's sitting room without Mrs. Stansbury's permission, and there conversing with pupils, including the young ladies. Gallaudet countered that to deprive Clerc and the pupils, "[s]hut out as they are from the usual sources of enjoyment," of the chance to converse "would almost be cruel." And besides, the pupils were at school specifically to "acquire language, and his language of signs is the foundation of all their improvement."[68] It's not as though Gallaudet were unaware that in Connecticut, girls were not to be left alone with men; his argument here assumes a childlike sexual innocence in deaf people that obviates the need for rules requiring chaperones — which is ironic considering that within just a few years, Clerc would marry one of these young ladies, and so would Gallaudet.

However this debacle was resolved, Gallaudet had made a serious enemy in the Rev. Mr. Stansbury. In a letter to his brother that month, Stansbury claimed that God had assisted him in "disappoint[ing] the machinations of a malignant enemy" — that is, Gallaudet — and avers that he has "the character of Jesuit. I am now on my guard."[69] Stanbury's use of the word "Jesuit" was common at this period to mean "a dissembling person; a prevaricator" without religious connotations, but people of dissenting religions seem to have been called Jesuits often enough, as in John Adams's remark on "some Jesuits, who call themselves Quakers."[70] That both Gallaudet and Stansbury were ministers of the gospel in the established Congregational Church of Connecticut makes this language the more astonishing, however. Stansbury must truly have hated Gallaudet. Gallaudet, for his part, began at this point to make every effort to get the Stansburys out of his school.

Also this first autumn, several impostors claiming to be either a "deaf and dumb pupil" of the Asylum or, alternately, Gallaudet's brother Edward, were collecting cash from "the humane and the charitable" in Greenfield and Portsmouth, New Hampshire.[71]

That winter, the Center Church called Gallaudet's Andover classmate Joel Hawes as its pastor. Hawes was salaried at $1,200 a year and ordained on March 4, 1818, though there was some concern about his being an Emmonsite, one who believed that sin was a free-will exercise and that regeneration required active participation by the believer, both doctrines anathema to the Calvinists of Hartford. But the Center Church was getting soft in some areas by this date, having already begun, in 1815, to heat the meeting house during the winter.[72]

Gallaudet hired a third teacher, William Channing Woodbridge, who had studied theology at Princeton after graduating from Yale. Woodbridge was initially hesitant to take the job because he had made his mother a deathbed promise to "be an apostolic Preacher," to which Clerc responded, in his written interview of Woodbridge, that the deaf in the United States are just as much "idolaters" as are the residents of Africa and Asia. Woodbridge wrote, "You are a good lawyer for the deaf and dumb," and he joined the school in December.[73] Thus ended the first year of Gallaudet's ministry to the deaf.

IT'S TEMPTING TO LINGER over the pupils, a remarkable assembly of deaf people from around New England who founded American Sign Language and Deaf culture as they lived and studied together and formed marriages and lifelong friendships. Looking over their writing samples today, what seems most remarkable is that so many of them accomplished so much, for they all entered the classroom without fluency in a native language of any sort and were all long past the natural age for acquiring one. No one connected with the Asylum at the time had any notion that language acquisition was age dependent, and Gallaudet actually recommended *raising* the minimum age from nine to twelve, reasoning that pupils would be more mature and easier to instruct.[1] But older pupils were less capable of learning not only language but even how to sit still at a desk to decipher and form the tiny alphabetical characters they had to learn.

The Asylum did not teach sign language. Believing that it was universal and both semantically and grammatically transparent, Gallaudet expected new pupils to pick it up quickly from classmates, as indeed they did. A large number of deaf people using a well-developed (but unfortunately undocumented) sign language were living on Martha's Vineyard, but only five Vineyard children, all from Chilmark, attended school at the Asylum under Gallaudet and these were not enrolled until the years 1826 to 1830, by which time American Sign Language would have been well on its way to taking the form it held through its first hundred years.[2] Gallaudet very quickly became a proficient signer in this language-immersion situation and, oddly enough considering his Calvinist reserve, seems to have been something of a born actor. Edmund Booth, a pupil who went on to become a newspaper editor in Iowa, remembered him as "by nature inclined to the dramatic in representation of and in depicting the grand and sublime in nature. Occasionally he would take a text [for his Sunday sermons at the school] on the starry heavens, and in the language of signs describe and illustrate their illimitable depths and draw therefrom ideas of the vastness and almighty presence and power of God."[3] Alice put it more bluntly: "Two years ago you cannot understand and make signs when you went to France, I am very glad that now you can make signs, you must thank God for you know signs."[4]

Pupil proficiency in English was, inevitably, a disappointment, for Gallaudet and Cogswell had begun the school under the assumption that every deaf person was an embryonic multilingual like Laurent Clerc. Extant pupil exercises show extraordinarily high expectations. A lengthy word list in manuscript looks like it was designed for present-day SAT preparation:

Perspicuity

Visible	Invisible
Discoverable	Undiscoverable
Discernible	Indiscernible
Plain	Undiscerned
Perspicuous	Imperspicuous
Manifest	Undescried

A list of adjectives headed "Brilliancy" is thirty-one words long and includes "Lightsome," "Beamy," "Illuminative," "Fulgent," "Effulgent," "Refulgent." One unknown pupil created pages of correct, contrasting sentences using, for example, the verbs "to comprise" and "to consist" and page after page of sentences illustrating the correct usages of "so as," "such as," and "as to" and the difference between "not at all" and "not the least." Unidiomatic phrases are corrected: "What is a physician? He is a man who visits the sick persons." Some of the vocabulary to be defined is religious — "saviour," "spirit," "heaven," and so on — but our unknown pupil also gave a religious cast to definitions of everyday words such as "happiness: The body will die, but the soul will live forever in happiness or misery." Alice Cogswell's notebook shows attention to similar-looking words, like "crowd" and "crown," "conscious" and "conscience," "constrain" and "construct" — "Who constructed the signs? The Abbe De'l'Epee [sic]." Like her unknown classmate, Alice sometimes provided catechism-like sentence samples for ordinary words: "God conveys the knowledge of Christ to me in the bible" and "Samuel crowned David king over all the jews."[5]

Original compositions of greater length and wider topic show unidiomatic constructions jarringly juxtaposed with idiomatic sentences. Eliza Boardman started a letter, "My Dear Madam, How long you well?" but continued to describe, with acceptable grammar, a two-mile walk that she took with some classmates and "Mr. Clerc," who, though Eliza does not yet know it, will shortly propose. In another letter, she told her correspondent that "I am very glad to my shoes from," but in a third letter, this to her mother, she began, "I have received your kind letter of Nov. 27." This mix of "word salad" strings ("I am very glad to my shoes from") and fluent sentences ("I have received your kind letter") suggests that the pupils were memorizing set phrases and learning where and when to deploy them, but they were unable to put together a grammatical sentence on a novel topic like new shoes.

If parents were expecting miracles, these letters must have resulted in many a worried discussion with the principal. Actually, the pupils were doing very well. Considering that they had aged out of the language acquisition threshold (Eliza was twenty-four when she enrolled) before they had any opportunity at all to acquire a language with a natural grammar, either signed or spoken, they knew that the way to ensure correctness was to stick with what they'd memorized. But exercises in the correct usage of "so as" and "such as," "imperspicuous" and "undescried" were pretty quickly abandoned.[6]

A letter Sophia Fowler wrote home in December gives an accurate picture of the level of the more advanced pupils who were grouped in the class Gallaudet taught: "I improve some the world. Mr. Clerc is very good and Mr. Gallaudet is very good with I talk my fingers. I think of you, you will soon forget me. I never forget. I love very much, your friends I am often at church. Mr. Gallaudet and Mr. Clerc are very well. all the Deaf and Dumb are very well, I like Hartford very much, I love our friends some, I wish you soon write to me, I wish to see here. Perhaps will you to come Hartford? 29 pupils are in the Asylum. Miss Dillingham and Miss Alice Cogswell and Mr. Backus and Mr. Loring are in my class, my sister and I love to your family."[7]

Of the pupils Sophia names, George Loring, Levi Backus, and Alice Cogswell would become more fluent with time — they were still children in 1817 — but Sophia had turned nineteen shortly before enrolling, and her English would never improve much beyond this level. Gallaudet would marry her in 1821, and his loving letters to his dear wife would always be written as though for a beginning reader. Edward Miner Gallaudet later boasted about a letter from his father to his mother in 1818 that used 219 different words, but the sentence structure is strictly first-grade level.[8] Gallaudet covered up the problem the best he could by letting failed (mostly older) pupils drift quietly back home — Parnell Fowler, for example, left in 1819 to make her home with a brother — and by trumpeting the successes of those few who did well. But he despaired. Many years later, a man who taught at the Kentucky School for the Deaf remembered the signal importance for him of Gallaudet's candor in this matter: only a few pupils "do even moderately well," he remembered Gallaudet telling him, and most acquire "almost next to nothing." Were it not for the example of George Loring, Gallaudet had said, he "should have felt that [his] success in instructing mutes was small."[9]

There was virtually no other academic content during these early years beyond English literacy and evangelical Protestantism. In the *Second Report of the Directors* in May of 1818, Gallaudet claimed that he had given some "simple lessons . . . in astronomy and geography," along with "occasional descriptions" of the world's "diversified population, with its varieties of climate, manners, customs, and Government. Still, correct orthography, the meaning of words, and their combination into phrases and sentences, have been the objects of instruction to which the attention of the teachers has been, and must, for some considerable time to come, yet be, principally, directed."[10]

However, in all these extant collections of pupil writing samples, there is only one instance of any topic beyond "God and Christ," school and social events, and this is in bad-boy Levi Backus's sample letter to Jean Massieu: "Which do you like best the king of France or the Emperor N. Bonaparte?" Levi naively asked him.[11] At least this pupil was aware of the world outside of Hartford church society, though it's doubtful that Gallaudet appreciated Levi's curiosity. Nevertheless, Gallaudet's pupils appreciated his clarity. Many years later, one of them remembered his "clear and perspicuous signs, aptness at illustration and versatility and readiness of mental resources, and . . . conspicuous simplicity and force of argument."[12]

Gallaudet was worried about Clerc's impending return to France when his three-year contract ended and how new teachers could be trained without him, for, as Gallaudet explained to the directors in June, teachers had to acquire a vocabulary of twenty to thirty thousand signs, which Clerc alone could teach and which "cannot be reduced to writing."[13] In addition to Woodbridge, he had hired Lewis Weld and Isaac Orr, but it wasn't easy to interest the sort of men Gallaudet wanted. School teaching was regarded as a low-pay, low-status occupation, suitable only as temporary work for young men before they decided on a career. Teachers of the deaf were not paid any more than any other schoolteachers, and yet the job required such intensive training that it could be undertaken only with a view to a lifetime career.[14] And men whose families had put them through Yale deemed a career as a schoolteacher to be a poor return on their investment.

One of the men Gallaudet approached in the spring of 1818, Thomas Perkins, was advised by his father not to accept the job offer on the grounds that he would find the work "extremely irksome."[15] Whether Weld and Orr took the job Gallaudet offered because, like Woodbridge, they were more interested in missionary work than Perkins was, or because they had few if any other prospects, is not clear. But the imminent departure of Clerc, who was sticking with his plan to return to Paris permanently in the spring of 1819, brought Gallaudet's worries about the new teachers into sharp relief.[16]

When the directors floated a plan to address the staff shortage by bringing new teachers from France, Gallaudet's nerves were so attenuated that his reaction was well-nigh hysterical. Putting strange Catholics into contact with the pupils, he claimed, would be "the touch of death" to their souls. For all that he supported Clerc at every turn, his anti-Catholicism was intact. Perhaps the directors' suggestion that one of these French teachers should be female was a significant cause of his overreaction — Gallaudet hired no women as teachers beyond the token employment of Abigail Dillingham.[17]

Teacher training for the deaf classroom is of its nature always extensive and intensive (and expensive), but additional challenges for Gallaudet were created by the school's use of the so-called methodical signs, the gestural encoding system for the spoken language that Gallaudet and Clerc brought from Paris and struggled to adapt for use with English. It was the huge number of signs that this encoding system required for dictating even the simplest English declarative sentence that increased the number of signs teachers had to know to the twenty- to thirty-thousand figure Gallaudet gave the directors. The switch from this sign-encoded English to a natural sign language (proto-ASL) for teaching written English would be implemented quietly after Gallaudet left the school — and after the system was decisively abandoned by the New York school. But the testimony of F. A. P. Barnard, a late-deafened man hired the year Gallaudet quit (and who later went on to serve as president of Columbia College), assures us that English was taught with methodical signs during Gallaudet's day. It had been obvious to Francis Green that while the system worked for what linguists today call synthetic languages like French, it was of little use for an analytic language like English; it took Clerc, however, more than fifteen years to realize that. Gallaudet perhaps never did come to understand that teaching English with methodical signs was a fool's errand.[18]

The pupils ridiculed the system. John R. Burnet (1808–1874), a deaf poet and later a teacher at the New York school, described the "principle of repugnance . . . which opposes this attempt to make a language of one set of elements conform in syntax to a language of a totally diverse set of elements." Would anyone, Burnet asked, endorse the proposal that Latin be taught to American schoolboys using English words and invented suffixes arranged in Latin word order?[19] One would suppose that at least one or two of the Yale men Gallaudet hired came to a similar conclusion, but, of course, methodical signs were the key to the dazzling dictation exercises exhibited to potential donors and state legislators.

One solution to Gallaudet's hiring difficulties was to resort to his former pupils, who made cheerful, effective teachers without the language training required of the Yale men. The directors took gross advantage of these young deaf men by paying them only a quarter of the already low salary paid to the Yale alumni. George Loring, Wilson Whiton, and, later, Edmund Booth earned only $250 a year, not nearly enough to live on. Gallaudet argued for higher wages, but the directors' view of the matter was that Booth, for example, "had been educated on charity [so] he should be glad to offer some of his services gratis."[20] What's perhaps worse, the hearing instructors, joined by Clerc, declared themselves "the Faculty" and denied their second-class deaf colleagues any say in curricular or disciplinary matters. To give just one egregious example, all the letters that pupils wrote were censored by their instructors, but "the Faculty" denied that right to the deaf instructors. (Gallaudet's position on this matter was that the principal had oversight of all censoring of all letters of all pupils. What the deaf instructors' views may have been is nowhere recorded.)[21] It's not surprising that Edmund Booth soon went west to make a life on the frontier, and George Loring, who was independently wealthy, simply returned to private life after a time, though William Whiton stayed on at starvation wages.

Another challenge, but one that took Gallaudet completely by surprise, was pupil disciplinary infractions. Discipline should have been under the purview of the supervisor, Stansbury, who was not only not up to the job but in April 1818 was taken off Gallaudet's hands when the New York Institution hired him, of all people, as principal. At the Asylum, the Stansburys were succeeded by the Whittleseys — Samuel, another Congregational minister, and Abigail, a sister of Samuel Goodrich, aka Peter Parley, whose memories of Hartford personalities have been mentioned before. The Whittleseys would do no better than the Stansburys, however, and would actually create even more trouble for Gallaudet, for while Stansbury had called him a Jesuit, Whittlesey would call for his firing.

The insubordination of some of the older male pupils may have been amplified by families keeping tractable deaf boys home to work on the farm and sending only their problem children. Ancestors of my own, according to family lore, were roundly criticized for sending their teenaged son to the deaf school in Philadelphia instead of keeping him home for the heavy lifting on their Appalachian farm, and I've often wondered if Uncle Charlie had made trouble for his parents. That he was the only member of the immigrant generation to acquire English literacy suggests that his parents were not exactly keen on education — why didn't they send their hearing children to school? — but rather simply wanted him out of their hair for few years.[22]

In any case, the average age of Asylum pupils at admission was eighteen, and Gallaudet was rapidly to discover that his paternalism "was not always an effective approach to students who considered themselves adults."[23] In one incident, he later recalled, he pulled a misbehaving boy out of church, tied him hand and foot to a chair, and prayed aloud that God have mercy on him until the boy began to cry. A story dating from the years when Gallaudet's oldest son was a small boy living with his parents at the Asylum concerns a male pupil rushing at Gallaudet with a knife. When Gallaudet "bared his bosom and bade the boy strike," the story goes, the boy, in shock, dropped the knife. This story reminds us of Bronson Alcott, who disciplined his pupils by giving them the rod and bidding them strike him. Alcott's daughter Louisa reported the technique to be effective, but there's no margin for error when the pupil has a knife.[24]

In December, "the Faculty" — which included Whittlesey in addition to Gallaudet, Clerc, Woodridge, Orr, and Weld — addressed the case of Otis Waters, who had been admitted at age twenty-seven and had been treating his teacher "with insult." Waters was to be given one last chance to apologize before his family was informed they would have to come and pick him up. Apparently he did apologize, because two months later, in February 1819, the faculty were faced not only with Waters's continued disrespect but also with the similar "improper conduct" of Levi Backus, James Barnes, who was admitted at age twelve, and three men who had been admitted as adults. Barnes and Backus were still boys, and their fathers were to be informed. Waters was dismissed, but all the others stayed on at the school for a few more years, then married — three married deaf women who had also been pupils, so whatever their behavior was, it obviously was not unattractive to their classmates — and supported themselves as farmers or mechanics or, in Backus's case, teaching and editing a newspaper in Canajoharie, New York. In 1818, though, these pupils were confounding the faculty.[25]

Gallaudet had some concrete ideas on how to address pupil misbehavior. In an August 1818 letter to the directors, he proposed, firstly, an upper age limit for admission of twenty or twenty-five, to "enable the instruction to be bestowed upon such as would most rapidly improve." Secondly, he wanted to require for admission a familiarity with the manual alphabet, penmanship, and the English names of some objects, and he proposed making up a packet of woodcuts, the alphabets, and rules for families considering admission. Gallaudet, who called this "begetting habits of attention and study," correctly understood that entering pupils had to arrive with the ability to sit still and the hand-eye coordination and fine motor skills needed for literacy. These were matters ordinarily attended to by mothers, but Gallaudet realized that mothers of deaf children needed support. He warned the directors that a day of reckoning was soon to arrive at which the majority of the present pupils "shall be found to have made but a slow progress."[26]

The Whittleseys, whose job it should have been to oversee all those adult men who could not sit quietly through the school day, followed the Stansburys in not learning to sign and thus likewise could not communicate with the pupils they were supposed to superintend. An 1821 memorandum concerning insubordination charges against Levi Backus records the boy's defense: "If you show me many words I do not understand actively. If Mr. Gallaudet comes here and talks with you, you will ask him to tell me, and I shall make signs and Mr. G. will speak to you — because I cannot write by writings."

Troubles for the school caused by ineffectively superintended adolescent boys and young men became worse and worse as "male pupils have occasionally, if not frequently, been to some of the cellar-shops in Town and purchased liquors and cakes, for which they have paid their own money" — behavior "altogether inadmissible." And although Whittlesey's order that dormitory windows remain closed overnight was "distinctly known to them," they "broke an iron hasp of considerable strength, put on with a padlock by the Committee, and broke open the window"![27]

By September 1823, the directors' committee to investigate pupil misbehavior called for the termination of the Whittleseys due to "apprehensions for their personal safety" and, at the same time, took Whittlesey's recommendation that Gallaudet be terminated as well. The report held the Whittleseys responsible for conversations between male and female pupils "in an indecent and altogether improper manner, which if not immediately put a stop to, may lead to the most disgraceful and most deplorable consequences," but the principal and instructors were blamed for setting the tone of disrespect toward this inept couple and for "gross neglect" in failing to "censure" the guilty pupils. Gallaudet's ten-point reply observed that "if respect, love, and obedience cannot be gained by the personal influence and authority of a superior, it avails but little to endeavor to enforce them by the directions of others," but this had little effect and his job was saved only by a 10-10 tie vote.[28]

By this time, Gallaudet had already hired a steward, Harvey Prindle Peet, a new Yale graduate who was planning a career as a missionary, so when the Whittleseys were let go in 1823, Peet, joined by a matron, Martha Dudley, was ready to take over. Peet would be hired away from the Asylum in 1830 by the New York Institution, but Dudley would stay on for many years and was especially important in caring for the language-less woman that Julia Brace had become when she was finally admitted to the school. Years later, the widowed Mrs. Whittlesey would publish Gallaudet's essays on family life in her *Mother's Magazine,* so there was clearly no bad blood between those two actors, perhaps because she blamed her husband for the trouble at the Asylum.

So pupil achievement was disappointing, the behavior of the young men confounding, the trust of the directors in their principal weak, and Gallaudet had to keep all this information from the donating public. As for the primary mission of the school — evangelization — one pupil, and only one, had "publicly professed herself to be his disciple" at the Center Church by the end of 1818. Sophia Fowler's "conversion narrative," the first made by a deaf person in Connecticut, was given in the old Puritan style as she was "repeatedly examined" by the Rev. Joel Hawes and the deacons before making her profession before the entire congregation. For a deaf girl from Guilford, baring her soul to hundreds of hearing people must have been a frightening experience, even with her teacher Mr. Gallaudet acting as interpreter, as he must have. Miss Fowler's profession was regarded as so astonishing that it was written up in the *Boston Recorder* under the headline "Deaf and Dumb."[29] The event opened the gates of heaven to her — and cleared the way for Gallaudet's courtship. By the following October, the new Mrs. Clerc, née Eliza Boardman, would be telling her husband that the Hartford ladies were abuzz over Gallaudet's visits to Miss Fowler.[30]

If Gallaudet hoped that Sophia's conversion was the first of many, he was bitterly disappointed. Not even Alice Cogswell took such a step. Mass conversions among the deaf had always been regarded not only as the school's primary purpose but also as its primary justification for using sign language. Gallaudet taught his pupils the meaning of "good" and "evil," the terrors of doomsday that impenitent sinners would face, and the Holy Spirit's ability to cleanse the heart of the "lonely heathen of a Christian land" who knew not that he possessed an "immortal principle . . . which will exist for ever beyond the grave." Sign language, Gallaudet asserted, "will *the soonest* enable the teacher to make the interesting subjects of his care acquainted with the consoling doctrines of the pardon of sin through the blood of Jesus Christ."[31] If Gallaudet was correct about his methodology, his pupils should have been flocking to profess their belief.

He certainly pushed them hard, sometimes so hard as to seem cruel by today's standards. In the fall of 1829, he wrote a letter to a twelve-year-old pupil who was dying of tuberculosis: "My Dear Phebe, I am sorry to hear that you are very sick. Perhaps you may die. God is good. He has made you sick." He signs off cheerily, "I send my love to Frances. Your affectionate friend, Thomas H. Gallaudet."[32]

He had family worries, too. His mother died sometime in 1818 at age fifty-three, and P. W.'s Christian bookstore in New York was in the red almost from the start. The shop issued reprints of British books, which were not covered under copyright law in the United States — mostly religious works for children but also Gallaudet's *Discourses on Various Points* — and contracted with the New-York Religious Tract Society, which also issued British reprints. Despite these arrangements to reprint and sell what would today be called pirated editions, the business was sued by people to whom it owed money, and P. W., as he wrote in his will, "was obliged to make an assignment of my stock for the benefit of my creditors."[33]

In addition to business woes, P. W. was ill with "inflammation of the lungs with fever" and planning a move back to Philadelphia. When Gallaudet visited in September of 1820, he found Ann and another sister nursing their father and "look[ing] feeble," Ann coughing up blood. The sisters had started a school, but it was not a success.[34] Gallaudet may have made a small loan at this point — his father would die owing him money — but there wasn't much more he could do.[35] His brother William Edgar, the only other of the Gallaudet family to have been educated at Yale, died in New York very suddenly in April 1821, aged twenty-four.[36]

For Gallaudet, the stress created by the dire straits of his family and the realization that most of his pupils would neither become fluent in English nor devote themselves to Christ was compounded by the constant need to spin all of the Asylum's disappointments for the donating public. He sank into his wonted depression. In January of 1818, when Clerc had been out of town for ten days, Gallaudet wrote,

> I have of late begun to ponder a good deal on the difficulty of my continu-
> ing to be principal of such an establishment as this with which I am now
> connected will probably be. — Most gladly would I have as my superior
> here and as the head of the Asylum some one of acknowledged piety and
> talents and of more character than myself. . . . Oh! raise me from this
> bodily and intellectual and religious lethargy which has now so long pros-
> trated all the energies and deadened the affections of my soul!"[37]

Edmund Booth, the pupil who later edited a newspaper in Iowa, put his finger on the trouble: "He was not born to command but to persuade, and yet to be always in the right. . . . What he lacked was will power."

Booth went on to comment on Gallaudet's habitual dour expression: "his aspect was not always the pleasant smile as shown in the photographs. It was usually easy gravity or thorough earnestness."[38] Booth was being kind, but his comments suggest to us that Gallaudet's chronic depression was always with him in his years as principal, an underlay to every encounter, ready to prostrate him when something like Clerc's leaving him alone with the school for ten days allowed his demons to come rushing back. Indeed, all the pupils were very well aware of his trouble. In a September 1818 collection of pupils' assigned letters to Gallaudet, we read version after version of "You are often sick"; in stark contrast are their remarks on Clerc's "ruddy" good health.[39]

A contributing cause of Gallaudet's depression this year was surely the expectation among Connecticut Congregationalists that the Millennium would be delayed by the disestablishment of the state church at the 1818 constitutional convention, a move that all the Hartford delegates had op-posed. But though Congregationalists had at first regarded disestablishment as the "triumph of Satan," the church quickly recovered. The era in which the church had been the sole source of community entertainment, social

life, and intellectual activity was now past, and churches were already di-
versifying with lending libraries, lyceum lectures, and magazines. Revivals
brought huge increases in church membership, and the clergy found fresh
avenues to power through control of new reform societies that aimed, by
and large, to mold society into a rigid hierarchy that would govern every
aspect of the lives of state residents. Whereas previously a pastor's ability
to inhibit overindulgence in alcohol was limited to excoriating individual
drunkards in his congregation, a temperance society could create widespread public odium for drunkenness as a sin that had to be eliminated
before the Millennium could be ushered in. And whereas the Rev. Mr.
Abel Flint of the South Church of Hartford, for example, had previously
controlled the religious education of the children of his congregation, as
president of the new Sunday School Society he controlled the education
of five hundred children whose parents were members of other churches
or of none at all.[40] The Asylum was understood to operate in much the
same manner as these reform societies: one or two ministers (Gallaudet,
Stansbury, Whittlesey) with the organizational backing of civic leaders
(the bankers) would evangelize all the deaf in New England. So, while the
church lost some political power and legitimacy, it more than compensated
by control of reform societies.[41]

In fact, the new constitution did not bring the changes to the state that
the Democratic-Republicans expected. Connecticut was still extremely
conservative, its school system out of date, in-migration next to nil, and
the state legislature still undemocratically represented townships regardless
of population, thus putting small towns and rural areas in control. Newly
elected Democratic-Republican legislators did expand the franchise (to
white men regardless of property ownership, while eliminating it for black
men), but they cut taxes, cut poor relief, reduced the number of judges,
ended appropriations for common schools, and continued the bans on
theater — a "rope dancer" who performed in Hartford in 1825 was fined
$60 and court costs, and actors in a play staged in a shack behind a tavern
were arrested while the play was in progress. And the religious situation
continued "unfavorable to polite letters," in stark contrast to Massachusetts,
where the flowering of Unitarianism ushered in a literary renaissance.[42]

Gallaudet blamed the deaf for his depression, or, more precisely, the difficulties of teaching them. Writing to a Glasgow correspondent in 1818, he
referred to the "very feeble state of my health" due to "my novel employ-

ment."[43] But at the same time, he resisted practical measures that could have improved his "feeble state." A month previous to this complaint, Gallaudet, accompanied by ten-year-old George Loring, had traveled to Saratoga, where fashionable people took the waters. We might think that the chronically constipated Gallaudet was there for the water cure — to "astonish the bowels" as his soon-to-be antagonist Samuel Gridley Howe put it[44] — but we would be wrong: he was there to solicit subscriptions to the Asylum from the wealthy businessmen to be found at the spa in the heat of August.

Loring "contributed not a little . . . to the celebrity of the Institution," Gallaudet reported, which must have relieved his fears that fund-raising would suffer when the celebrated Laurent Clerc returned to France as expected.[45] In a letter to Cogswell written in Saratoga, he actually stated that he was still seriously constipated, "my usual indisposition, attended most of to day with much pain," but was being very careful *not* to drink the water and to restrain young Loring from doing so.[46] The little that did cross his lips seems to have done the job, however, for by the end of the month he was able to report rather graphically from Ballston, the nearby site of another mineral spring resort, "My complaint which troubled me so much the last winter is entirely removed."[47]

It was at some point during the Asylum's first three years that Gallaudet became known in Hartford as a regular user of opium. Whether the incident described by Emily Baldwin in her 1820 letter to a friend (quoted in chapter 3) shamed him into a clean break with opium, or whether his use was so habitual as to have created an addiction he could not break, are questions that can't be answered by extant evidence. We know from a passage in his "Petition of the Battledores" that he regarded opium use as blamable. In this poem, he uses the British rhetorician James Ogilvie's habit to shame him. Battledore, he says,

> Answers the purpose of laudanum,
> To drive dun fog from pericranium,
> As Ogilvie from 'cross the ocean
> Was wont to take an opiate portion,
> To clean his brain and warm his fancy
> For oratoric necromancy.

Ogilvie (1775–1820), an associate of both Thomas Jefferson and Washington Irving, had admitted to laudanum addiction after a satirical attack on him in 1809,[48] and Gallaudet had fun in this poem insinuating that the righteous students at Andover played wholesome battledore instead of resorting to drugs. So one wonders to what extent the public scandal of his own opium use some seven years later must have humiliated him in his own eyes.

Somehow in the midst of all this constipation and depression, getting high and hiring teachers, Gallaudet found the time and energy to write his first textbook: *A Scriptural Catechism, Designed Principally for the Deaf and Dumb in the American Asylum.* This book exists today only in the editions of 1829 and later, but the copyright page declares Gallaudet the owner as of December 17, 1818: the book must have been used at the school in manuscript for its first eleven years. *A Scriptural Catechism* begins with the watchmaker argument of William Paley that Gallaudet had used as a Yale undergraduate. "Who made this watch? . . . Who made you?" Despite its title, it is not really a catechism, a list of fundamental beliefs, but rather a list of Bible names: "Who was Cain? Lot? Balaam? Jesus Christ? John the Son of Zebedee?" It was not until the 1848 edition that subsequent teachers at the school added questions that required thought or even knowledge of doctrine, such as "How do you know that the bible is the word of God?"

The year 1819 brought momentous events to the little world of the Asylum. In May, Laurent Clerc married Eliza Boardman, thus assuring his continued residence in the United States. In June, an anonymous donor bought a $100 lifetime Directorship for Gallaudet, which gave him more input into Asylum policy than he had had as the hired principal.[49] The school moved into a bigger house on Prospect Street, where the entire faculty continued to live cheek by jowl with the growing number of pupils. There must have been questions raised already at this early date about why speech training was not offered, because in the school's 1819 report, Gallaudet gave over almost two pages of his eleven-page narrative explaining why not — and citing Dugald Stewart's remarks on starlings and parrots.[50]

The year also brought momentous events to the new nation that would affect the Asylum in ways no one could have guessed. The Panic of 1819 was a nationwide financial crisis caused, in part, by unrestrained speculation in land and the resultant spate of bankruptcies among wealthy New England speculators, which constituted the Asylum's donor class. One of the unexpected effects of this crisis was an abrupt reversal of attitudes toward the poor. Philanthropy came to be understood as actually causing poverty; the formerly benevolent now began to express antipathy toward those they had worked to relieve.[51] This shift in attitude proved instrumental in cementing Asylum policy against tuition assistance.

The other consequential event for the nation was the Missouri Compromise, which Monroe would sign into law in 1820 and which allowed for the spread of slavery into new states beyond the Mississippi south of the 36° 30' parallel, and also into the state of Missouri which was north of that line. The deal was no compromise: the South conceded nothing at all because the big money in slave labor plantations came from crops that grew only south of parallel 36° 30', and, because the law recognized states' rights to legitimize slavery, it was "*a wrongful concession of principle,*" as Abraham Lincoln characterized it.[52] Of course, not all Northerners were antislavery and some supported the Missouri Compromise, but still, there was widespread outrage in Connecticut when its U.S. senator, James Lanman, voted with the South. He was burned in effigy, and the *Courant* published letter after letter calling Lanman's vote a "derogation of principle" and accusing him of "degrad[ing] our national character."[53] Many correctly predicted that the clash of the states over enslaved labor forces had only just begun, and that the North would become ever more complicit in it. Probably no one connected with the Asylum dreamed at this date that its financial foundation would very soon be established on exactly this kind of complicity.

But the introduction of overt complicity with slavery was in fact the result of the March 3, 1819, Act of Congress granting the Asylum "a township of land, or a tract of land equal thereto, . . . in any of the unlocated lands of the United States to which the Indian title has been extinguished."[54] This grant was the result of the trip Clerc had made to Washington City the previous year that had left Gallaudet all alone at the school with his depression, and it was apparently Gallaudet's own "brain-child."[55] The land to which the Asylum received title had been part of Georgia's vast and troublesome western frontier, occupied by Indian tribes that held treaties with the federal government. Georgia's attempts to sell off this land in 1789 and 1795 had been illegal on the face of it, and were, in addition, tainted with corruption. But in 1802, the Democratic-Republican administration of Thomas Jefferson bought this vast territory from Georgia, settled all land claims deriving from previous fraudulent sales, and extinguished all Indian claims, driving the Indians off their land. In 1817, the western half was admitted to the Union as the state of Mississippi, and in 1819 the eastern half was admitted as Alabama.

The grant of tracts of this land was made with the understanding that it would be sold and its proceeds would support the school's operating expenses. To realize the cash, the Asylum hired an agent to locate the lands, procure patents, and to sell lots for, they hoped, no less than five dollars an acre, issuing mortgages as necessary, all for a commission of 2.5 percent. Their choice for this job was William Ely, a Yale graduate who had made his fortune in trade and retired at age fifty-two in Hartford. It should have been easy: cotton planters were eager to establish larger plantations on this newly unencumbered land, and New England needed to keep its new textile mills supplied with the planters' product. If anyone in Hartford worried about their beloved deaf school selling prime cotton land for slave-labor plantations, they left no evidence of those worries, certainly not in any newspaper. Gallaudet and the directors would have seen this as a straightforward land sale; where the buyers got their workers was their business.

Just a couple of weeks after the grant was made, Ely was already running into complications and found that he would have to remain in Alabama "a longer time than he expected, at considerable inconvenience to his private affairs and hazard to his health." For one thing, the land was not one township but rather was located in at least two parcels, one of which is now within the city of Birmingham in central Alabama, while the other was along the Tennessee River in the northeastern corner of the state. Ely established headquarters on what he regarded as the worthless land in the center of the state and called it Elyton. He traveled to collect payments but was worried for his safety, harassed, in his view, by the "barbarous" yeoman farmers who couldn't afford to buy but were interested in renting. He never went out unarmed or without his two bodyguards, and he kept cash proceeds and documents locked up in an iron chest inside a locked trunk in Tuscaloosa. He may not have expected that buyers would pay in cotton, but they did, and Ely had to arrange shipments to New York and sale in that city, which he found "very tedious and troublesome" but undertook in order to maximize income for the school.

The land on the Tennessee River proved very difficult to sell as the price of cotton dropped, and the timber on it, which contributed to its value, was purloined by neighboring planters who sent their slaves to cut it, then professed ignorance at what the slaves had done. Ely also had trouble collecting the baled cotton due as payments. In one report to the directors, he explained that his assistant John Boardman "has been constrained to make collections by legal process, and in some instances has had his Execution levied on Slaves. . . . Other debts are in suit, and the Executions, when obtained will be levied on more slaves." He said that none of the slaves had been sold as of the date of this letter, May 14, 1829, and our documentation disappears at this point, but of course the directors, through their agent Ely, would have had to sell all the slaves they acquired in lieu of mortgage payments due them.[56]

What Gallaudet thought of this business — selling land to wealthy planters for large slave-labor camps and then confiscating their slaves when they defaulted on their mortgages — we don't know, since he seems never to have mentioned the details of the Alabama land in writing. He was, however, a director of the Asylum as well as its principal, and as such he was aware of every detail in every report that Ely and Boardman sent from Alabama. The directors had acted immediately to purchase an extensive and picturesque campus on a hilltop just outside of the city and then to erect buildings on it, assuming "considerable debt" in expectation of the proceeds of the land sale. "To cancel this [debt], however, and to meet the future current expenses of the establishment, the Directors look forward with encouragement to the avails of the lands, which were granted by the liberality of Congress to the Asylum." In other words, Ely had to get the cash in hand so the directors could pay off the debt they incurred for their new campus.[57]

The school's entanglement with slavery has yet to be investigated or even admitted. But the correspondence archived at the school makes its active complicity inarguable. Could Gallaudet, or Cogswell, or anyone else associated with the school have reasonably been expected to speak up, to say, no, we can't be taking possession of and then selling enslaved human beings to collect debts? When in 1838, the Rev. Thomas Mulledy, president of Georgetown University, arranged to sell 272 slaves from the college's Maryland plantations to cotton planters in the Deep South in order to pay off debt, the reaction was swift. The head of the Jesuits' international branch declared, "It would be better to suffer financial disaster than suffer the loss of our souls with the sale of the slaves." Father Mulledy was reassigned, and Pope Gregory XVI barred Catholics from trafficking in slaves the following year, "no matter what pretext or excuse."[58]

The Georgetown episode shows both that American schools were quite capable of slave trading when it was a case of their bottom line and that some people involved could and did vocally disapprove. Apparently, however, no one in Hartford — not Gallaudet, not Cogswell, not Clerc, Weld, Wadsworth — voiced any public disapproval. The Asylum would still be involved in lawsuits against delinquent mortgage holders at least as late as 1836. When the debt for the new campus was paid off, the school would be left with a $300,000 endowment, "a noble fund" in the words of Gallaudet's biographer Heman Humphrey.[59]

During the years in which the directors were pursuing payment from delinquent planters, the Asylum was vigorously defending its policy of "erecting buildings as speedily as possible" and deferring all charitable aid to poor deaf children by claiming that their policy was the "most favorable to the general interest of the deaf and dumb in our country. If, while pursuing such measures, the Directors have not had it in their power to afford charitable aid to very deserving individuals, they have hoped that an enlightened public would candidly consider the reason for this, and duly appreciate the benefit of that course of proceeding."[60]

And yet at the same time that it was claiming not to be able to subsidize poor pupils, it was reducing tuition for the wealthy and middle class: of the total cost per pupil of $140 a year, families paid $100 and the endowment paid the remaining $40.[61] Gallaudet may have felt conflicted when he drafted this report for the directors to sign. Or he may not: there is no suggestion that he lodged a protest, and all the evidence suggests that none of this — not the school's enrichment from slavery or its failure to serve the least of his brethren — ever entered his mind. If we look at a sermon he delivered to the Hartford Evangelical Tract Society the previous winter, for example, we see him considering First Corinthians 1:27–28, in which Paul teaches that God often chooses "obscure, unpromising, and apparently insignificant instruments for the accomplishment of His vast and incomprehensible designs." Based on this passage, he urged his audience to "think of the thousands in your country who are debarred, either by poverty or ignorance, from many of the sources of religious knowledge and improvement which you enjoy."[62] But the people he had in mind were not the enslaved laborers in Alabama or even the impoverished deaf in New England, but rather the undereducated white residents whom he wished to provide with religious tracts.

The Asylum moved to its new campus in the spring of 1821. Now Gallaudet had a chapel in which he could lead prayer and deliver sermons in sign language, with a large blackboard to write the Bible verse under discussion along with the sermon's bullet points.[63] The Clercs were given the former Sigourney home adjacent to the campus, which Charles and Lydia Sigourney had had to leave when Charles lost his fortune in the 1819 Panic. Gallaudet, though not yet married, was given the "Mansion House." His "Discourse Delivered at the Dedication" was notable for its focus on the school as a missionary enterprise. Asserting that the Asylum was "the gate to heaven for these poor lambs of the flock," he declared that Alice Cogswell had been purposely deafened by God, "afflicted, as it were, by Providence, for the very purpose of turning her calamity into the source of blessings upon her fellow sufferers." The "Discourse" then took an unexpected turn to the rampant misbehavior among the pupils. Success in education, he said, "depends upon the docility of the pupil," and that it is precisely "the influence of the religion of Jesus Christ" that "purifies and hallows all the affections of the heart." Successfully evangelized children will keep their dorm windows closed, he seems to be saying here. He would surely have been thinking of Sophia Fowler, who had made her profession of religion two years previous and was presumably a model of docility, because at the time of the dedicatory speech, he would already have determined to marry her in August.[64]

T. H. and Sophia Gallaudet settled into the Mansion House just as Laurent and Eliza Clerc, with their new baby, Elizabeth, left for Philadelphia, where Clerc would serve as acting principal of the Pennsylvania Institution for the Deaf and Dumb. This school had gotten its start on an entirely different model than that of the Asylum. David Seixas, an artisan and tradesman and a member of the small Jewish community in Philadelphia, started out much as Charles-Michel de l'Épée and Charlotte Elizabeth Phelan had done, taking the deaf children of impoverished families into his home, where he fed, clothed, and attempted to instruct them at his own expense.

In 1820, the wealthy Philadelphians whom Gallaudet and Clerc had courted took over Seixas's school, naming Episcopal bishop William White as president but allowing Seixas to continue as principal. Seixas spent the summer of 1821 at the Hartford Asylum learning their methods and returned to Philadelphia a firm supporter of sign language. That September, however, the board informed Seixas that pupils had registered complaints of unwanted touching, and he was dismissed. Anti-Semitism was surely in play to some extent, for efforts to hasten the Millennium by converting Jews were underway among the same donor class that supported deaf schools. The American Society for Meliorating the Condition of the Jews, which, as

Thomas Hopkins Gallaudet, by Philip Hewins, ca. 1834. Hewins came to Hartford in 1834 and painted scripture narratives for the Center Church, of which Gallaudet was a member. This is the only portrait Gallaudet ever sat for. Courtesy of the American School for the Deaf.

Peter Wallace Gallaudet, Gallaudet's father, a commission merchant in Philadelphia and Hartford who later ran a Christian bookstore in New York. Unknown artist, undated. Courtesy of the Gallaudet University Archives.

Have there been any supernatural appearances since the
days of the Apostles?.

Affirmative.—

So prevalent had been the belief of supernatural appear
ances among all nations & in all ages, and so numerous & respectable
have been its advo

Gallaudet

sapere aude

Gallaudet signed his name to a notebook recording the "correct" answers to
debate questions posed by his professor, Timothy Dwight, at Yale College in
1804 or 1805. The Latin epigram embedded in the signature, "sapere aude," "Dare
to use your own reason!" is a quotation from Immanuel Kant that became the
Enlightenment motto. Library of Congress.

Timothy Dwight, president of Yale College, was Gallaudet's mentor and role model. John Trumbull, 1817. Yale University Art Gallery.

Mason Fitch Cogswell was a neighbor of the Gallaudets in Hartford who was inspired by his deaf daughter, Alice, to initiate planning for the school for the deaf. By Ralph Earl, ca. 1778. Museum of Fine Arts, Houston.

Lydia Huntley Sigourney was a teacher in Hartford who incorporated Alice Cogswell into her class and taught her to read. John Trumbull, 1838. Courtesy of the Wadsworth Atheneum Museum of Art, Hartford, Connecticut.

Laurent Clerc (Deaf), who taught French Sign Language to Gallaudet in Paris and later taught at the American Asylum in Hartford. Charles Willson Peale, 1819. Courtesy of the American School for the Deaf.

Eliza Boardman Clerc (Deaf), posing with her right hand forming the initial of her name, E, and holding her daughter Elizabeth Clerc. Eliza was one of the earliest pupils at the American Asylum and married her teacher, Laurent Clerc. Charles Willson Peale, 1819. Courtesy of the American School for the Deaf.

Catharine Esther Beecher founded the Hartford Female Academy.
Unknown artist, ca. 1830s. Courtesy of the Harriet Beecher Stowe Center,
Hartford, Connecticut.

Sophia Fowler Gallaudet (Deaf) was one of the earliest pupils
at the Asylum and married her teacher, Thomas Hopkins Gallaudet.
Unknown daguerreotypist, ca. 1842. Courtesy of the Gallaudet
University Archives.

we have seen, was founded by Asylum donor Elias Boudinot, not only had a reservation in western Pennsylvania upon which converts would be settled but was sending out Hebrew translations of the New Testament — in the bizarre belief that Jews spoke Hebrew. Needless to say, there were no converts, but this was the atmosphere in which Seixas's school was appropriated.[65]

Clerc was brought to Philadelphia, then, as a temporary replacement for the disgraced Seixas. During the seven months the Clercs were resident, they had their portraits painted by Charles Willson Peale, Eliza with the baby on her lap and her free hand forming the letter E, the initial she and the little girl shared. The Pennsylvania institution's directors soon found a permanent replacement in Hartford's Lewis Weld, and the Clercs returned to Hartford.

The Gallaudets' first child, Thomas — no middle name, for he was the namesake of Thomas Gallaudet, P. W.'s father — was born nine months after his parents' wedding, the second native user of American Sign Language after little Elizabeth Clerc, and his sister Sophie came along in 1824. The children grew up at the Asylum, playing with the pupils boarding there, who gave little Thomas his name sign, "rubbing down the back of the neck with the right hand," because of his long blond curls.[66]

In 1823, Catharine Beecher opened the Hartford Female Seminary with a genuine high school curriculum, and Gallaudet's old Yale acquaintance James Fenimore Cooper saw the publication of his new book *The Pioneers,* which established in the popular mind both the endearing character of the lone frontiersman with his rifle and hound and the racial anxiety that would characterize frontier settlements and American concepts of its Manifest Destiny. In 1824, Congregationalists were shocked by the opening of a Universalist church near the Old State House; Lafayette visited Hartford; Dr. Cogswell pioneered the surgical ligature of the carotid artery (inadvertently killing the patient);[67] and Alice Cogswell completed the program at the Asylum and left the school.

P. W. Gallaudet had moved to Philadelphia after his wife's death, but in 1824 he moved again, this time to Washington City with one of his sons, James, both in dire need of work. In a very pathetic letter to John Quincy Adams, then serving as secretary of state under President Monroe, P. W. solicited "employment in writing, either for myself or my son or both, by filling any Clerkships that may become vacant to which we might be adequate, or by doing at the offices or at our house any extra writing." James was then thirty years old; P. W. sixty-eight.[68] Adams was elected to the presidency that year, inspiring hope in conservative and antislavery New England that the country would be restored to a more traditional social order.

In 1825, the Unitarians broke away from the Congregationalists to establish their denomination in Boston. In 1826, another baby boy was born to the Gallaudets, Peter Wallace, always called Wallace in the family, as his grandfather was. The so-called Colored Congregational got its own meeting house, a "Federal-style stone and brick church" at the corner of Market and Talcott Streets.[69] Hartford's African American Congregationalists had previously established their own congregation in the basement of the Center Church with the services of a volunteer white minister, Horatio Nelson Brinsmade, a Yale alumnus hired by Gallaudet who taught at the Asylum from 1823 to 1831.

As for Gallaudet, he was focused on fund-raising. His "Sermon on the Duty and Advantages of Affording Instruction to the Deaf and Dumb" was composed for use on a tour of northeastern state legislatures with George Loring and two other boys. The "deaf and dumb sermon," as he called it, began with a lengthy explanation of the deaf as heathens like "the Hindoo, the African, and the Savage," except that, contrary to the cases of these other kinds of heathens, "kind Providence" had protected the deaf with their very deafness against "the contagion of bad example." Gallaudet explained the duty to convey the doctrines of revealed religion to deaf countrymen and also, he added for his out-of-state audiences who presumably had some secular as well as religious concerns, to provide them with the means "of gaining a livelihood by their own personal exertions."[70]

The blackboards he needed for his fund-raising exhibits were such an oddity that at a church in Montpelier, Vermont, "a piece of board, being ordered to be fastened to the pulpit, was covered with black paint," according to one of the pupils on the tour.[71] Tuition at the Asylum had been lowered to $115 with some of the income from the endowment, but the directors warned that any other mode of "dispensing gratuitous aid . . . would result in the complete destruction of [the school's] continued and extensive sphere of usefulness." Mr. Peet was called to account for some improvements he had made in "clothing and mending for poor pupils," which the directors deemed subject to their discretion alone.[72]

The Alabama land grant was regarded as such a blessing to the Asylum that in February 1828, Gallaudet made an overland trip to Washington

City "to promote the passing of a bill in Congress, granting portions of the public lands to several such Institutions in the country."[73] The requisite exhibition was conducted by Lewis Weld, the new head of the Pennsylvania institution, with three of his pupils, but Gallaudet was on hand to lend a note of celebrity and demonstrate that he was able to converse with Weld's pupils without having previously met them. President Adams learned of the exhibition while on his morning walk and decided to stop by. It's interesting to observe that Adams clearly understood what the vast majority of the public assuredly did not, that the sign language and the finger alphabet were two very different things:

> Their language of gesticulation is twofold: one consists of spelling words, each letter of the alphabet being marked by the sign of a distinct collocation of the fingers; the other is by motion of the arms and hands, and of the whole body, and by significant expressions of the countenance; it is altogether pantomimic. By spelling the letters[,] they read and write, and thus they identify words. But it is through the pantomime only that they understand the meaning of their discourse, and two of them in writing a sentence occasionally used different words. Their writing is, in this respect, a translation of the discourse delivered by gesticulation, and different translators use different words to convey the same thought.

Adams's summary also shows that congressmen and senators were playing the usual game of stump the deaf. John C. Calhoun asked Weld's three pupils to distinguish between power and right, a loaded question that had Adams fuming for days, although the pupils "did not suspect what was running in Mr. Calhoun's head when he put the questions." Andrew Stevenson, the Jacksonian Speaker of the House, seems not to have understood how the game was played, however, and asked the pupils of the "greatest example of true glory," a thing they could not do because the prompt was far too open ended for the kind of basic responses to a limited set of prompts that they had been trained to. Adams, too, asked a question without a cue: could the pupils identify the figure above the clock? They could not. (It was the Muse of History.) When Adams asked Gallaudet if he could make the pupils understand the difference between "irrefragable" and "incontrovertible," Gallaudet made a game attempt to deflect what must have been a gathering mood of doubt by saying that "he could not immediately discern the distinction between them himself." Adams's diary entry on the exhibition provides a useful comparison with the scrubbed accounts available from the Asylum, its employees, and its news releases. Gallaudet told a friend that many congressmen would have liked to help the new deaf schools but thought it was "contrary to the Constitution."[74]

That May, the Connecticut General Assembly resolved to pay the tuition and expenses of fifteen deaf state residents "who or whose parents are indigent."[75] A month later, however, Cyrus Swan, a member of the assembly who seems to have been lobbying for the Asylum, told Seth Terry that he didn't think the grant would get through the State Senate. As Swan explained it, "this would be a very popular measure were it not for the almost universal opinion that prevails, that the Institution, though professedly a benevolent one, is not disposed to adapt its means to the circumstances of the needy."[76] And it is no wonder. As the Asylum was making these efforts with the state legislature, Seth Terry, styling himself "Atty. to the Asylum," was writing to the father of a pupil, Andrew McKinney of New York City, who had enrolled the previous year at age sixteen: "The committee will permit you to return your Son into the Asylum for the D&D . . . on payment of $57.50 and a good and sufficient Bond being lodged with the Treasurer for the payment of the like sum so long as he shall remain annually, in advance," for, Terry told the father, "the surety to your bond of last year is known here, and is <u>known to be a Bankrupt</u>." Perhaps it was Gallaudet himself who drafted that letter for Terry to sign; a year and a half later, he complained that "the correspondence of the Asylum, more especially that which relates to . . . the peculiar circumstances of the pupils as connected with their accounts with the Treasurer, has occupied no inconsiderable portion of my time."[77]

Also that spring, Lewis Weld returned to Hartford to marry Mary Austen Cogswell, Dr. Cogswell's oldest daughter. Gallaudet composed "A Marriage Hymn" especially for the occasion, but it was so purely conventional as to say nothing whatever about Lewis and Mary.[78] That same month, the Asylum's *Annual Report* was printed with an engraving of Sicard by Edward Gallaudet as frontispiece. Sophia was making long visits with her brothers in Guildford, presumably as the only form of birth control available to her, and that fall she had taken four-year-old Thomas with her, leaving the others at home in Hartford under her sister Parnell's care. And Andrew Jackson was winning the presidency in a landslide. In January 1829, he visited Hartford, which naturally had voted for Adams, with U.S. senator Martin Van Buren.[79]

Gallaudet had already begun to ask for relief from teaching duties and was warning the directors that he could not continue otherwise. As he put it later, "My present daily confinement, and the peculiar effect of making signs upon my health, is what I <u>cannot</u> much longer sustain."[80] How this was understood by the directors — who knew, of course, that he was married to a deaf woman and must therefore be signing all the time at home — is not clear, but they took him at his word and in June canvassed the other teachers about the possibility of releasing Gallaudet from the classroom. Clerc, perhaps surprisingly, was wholly unsympathetic: Sicard taught at his school until he was sixty, Clerc observed, and Gallaudet was only forty. Clerc thought that the principal should be kept on in his present duties with an increased salary.[81]

On January 11, 1830, Gallaudet wrote a sixteen-page memo to the directors stating his demands and providing rationales — or rationalizations. The demands were release from teaching a regular class and the provision of free time in which to add to his income by writing books. The "or else" was that he would resign. But for all its simple message, it's an oddly unfocused missive, swinging between descriptions of his heavy and varied workload, which truly looks both exhausting and exasperating, and the kind of depressive rants he had earlier called his hypochondriacal wailings, blaming the "incroachments [*sic*] upon the constitution and bodily health" on "the employment of making signs daily for twelve years." That all this amounted to a textbook case of teacher burnout is clear from Gallaudet's description of his duties: "to plod on in the same round of elementary instruction to 12 or 15 infantile minds for 12 years, with no hope of being released from it." In March, he made it plain to his faculty that he desired to devote no more time to the school than was usual for "Professors in our Colleges and theological Institutions." He was also asserting the veto power over his faculty that he believed college presidents had.[82]

To regard the Asylum, which essentially taught little more than basic English, as a kind of college or theological seminary seems a stretch today, but the instructors took Gallaudet seriously, and one of them, William Turner, consulted Professor Denison Olmstead concerning "the principles of a Faculty Government" at Yale College. Olmstead replied that the president of Yale College never used his veto power over the faculty, which Gallaudet, when he was informed of Olmstead's answer, found so outrageous that he caught the next stage to New Haven to have it out with the professor.[83]

Memos between Gallaudet and his hearing instructors, Yale men all, in the last week of March focused on whether the principal was to select all books, approve all exercises, and visit all classes, as Gallaudet claimed, or whether these duties were to be undertaken only with regard to the deaf instructors, as the hearing men, joined by Clerc, maintained. (The designation "deaf" was encoded in this correspondence as "those who were pupils.") What the view of the deaf instructors may have been, again, never appears.[84]

So what did Gallaudet want? Release from teaching duties? Shorter hours? A higher salary? Autocratic control over the classrooms of the Yale men he himself had recruited? Simple respect? The new teachers interrupted his classes many times a day to ask him how to sign this or that, and it's easy to see how this could be insupportable.[85] But the instructors and directors alike must have been just as confused as we are by his shifting demands. The directors had released him from teaching the previous spring, and the faculty repeatedly averred that they would "cheerfully" accept whatever powers the directors chose to invest in the principal, but still Gallaudet would not be satisfied. His April 7th letter to the directors cites the faculty's accommodating statements as evidence that continuing to work with them would be "a constant series of anxieties."

In a thirty-page letter apparently written around the same time, Gallaudet narrated the history of each iteration of the regulations and transcribed three letters he had solicited from four Yale professors on their support for presidential veto power, as well as on their view that "the pursuit of general literature and science" was a normal part of their duties and the reason they devoted no more than three hours a day to their students.[86] Gallaudet claimed that his "acquaintance" with "Intellectual Philosophy, Language and the means of acquiring it, Grammar universal and particular, and the Education of children and youth" and his view of the importance of "the enlargement of his own mind" was not shared by the faculty. He concluded that "regard to the gradations of office . . . is not less the dictate of wisdom, than the evidence of a genuine magnanimity of soul," and supported his views with quotations from St. Paul's Epistle to the Romans: "all members have not the same office." In an April 19th letter, he petulantly referenced the faculty's "implied incapacity" to support his desire for dictatorial powers, quoting their reference to themselves as "Gentlemen of a liberal education, and under the influence of a proper self-respect," as though, somehow, Gallaudet thought they weren't.[87]

Gallaudet's belief in the "gradations of office" in a rigid hierarchy with himself at the pinnacle — an organizational model he had first observed as an undergraduate at Dwight's Yale — was so deeply seated that he was flabbergasted when the other Yale men on the faculty regarded themselves as his moral and intellectual equals. Could this really have been the reason for his resignation, that he could not work with anyone who had any "self-respect"? In truth, Gallaudet probably had no idea exactly why he wanted to resign and was floundering for rationales as his adversaries/colleagues acquiesced to one after another of his demands. Then, after the directors revised the bylaws so as to give the principal precisely the autocratic powers Gallaudet demanded, and after one last trip to exhibit four pupils to the state legislature in New Haven, he resigned.

NOW WHAT? He had a wife and five children, but no home — he had to quit the house on Asylum property — and his erstwhile protégé Lewis Weld held the dream job at the Asylum that he had negotiated for himself. His fourteen years as a fund-raiser for the Asylum had made him famous, and attractive offers had been pouring in for a couple of years already. He seems to have had his pick: to serve as principal of a high school in New York, a high school to be established in Monticello, Virginia, a female academy in Norwich, the new Massachusetts Normal School, the Oneida Institute, and an infant school in Boston; to teach at the new teachers' seminary at Andover; to head the Lane Seminary in Cincinnati or take a professorship there; to run both a school and a magazine for "the education of the free colored population" in New Jersey. He had already served on a committee to establish an infant school in Hartford that he could have headed, but that apparently went nowhere.[1]

Like many another student of Timothy Dwight, Gallaudet had been imbued with his mentor's disapproval of emulation, his focus on instilling self-control, and his notion that education was a process not of stuffing a young person with information but rather teaching him how to think and learn. Gallaudet sometimes looks like a gadfly hopping from one opportunity to another, but he, like Henry Barnard and William Channing Woodbridge, was an idealist in search of a situation in which he could effect his ideals. And so he dithered.[2]

One offer to which he gave serious consideration was to head the new Boston school for the blind. According to Edward Miner Gallaudet, he was the Boston organizers' first choice, and Heman Humphrey reports that they offered him the fantastic sum of $2,400 a year. But an offer to a teacher of the deaf to teach the blind is rather like the proffer of a braille menu to a deaf restaurant patron — communicative strategies of the deaf and the blind are mutually exclusive. Gallaudet nevertheless made a trip to Boston in the fall of 1830, but he kept the promoters dangling for the better part of a year before they gave up and hired Samuel Gridley Howe.[3]

Also in the fall of 1830, Gallaudet attended a "convention of gentlemen engaged in education and literary pursuits" — to design the curriculum of the soon-to-be-established New York University. The Rev. James M. Mathews, who would later be named chancellor, had invited Gallaudet's input, and several weeks prior to the convention Gallaudet was giving Mathews tips on how to run it. When Albert Gallatin, then nearly seventy and a private citizen living in New York, addressed the convention with a proposal that the new university offer an English track — a degree that did not require Latin and Greek — Gallaudet backed him up, calling it an experiment. He must have been surprised when a certain Dr. Lieber responded that such a program was already in place at an experimental institution in Paris, the Ecole Polytechnic. Of course, Gallaudet knew nothing about the Ecole Polytechnic because he had spent his time in Paris avoiding the city and its institutions. When the planners later decided to offer a program for the preparation of common-school teachers, they appointed Gallaudet to the Chair of Pedagogy. One still finds sources alleging that Gallaudet was an NYU professor, but the fact is that he put the planners off for months before finally declining the formal offer, which came without salary. He pleaded (no surprise) his health.[4]

One other prospect interested Gallaudet enough to make an investigative trip. In 1829, he had seriously pursued an offer then on the drawing board in Princeton to take charge of a "Seminary of the Experimental kind" that would "embrace infant learning, connected with a more extended system for youth." In this case, it was he who seems to have initiated correspondence with the planners, in April 1829, and he made the trip there in May.[5] That Princeton was the heart of Presbyterian America surely had much to do with his interest — the locations of the other two offers that most attracted him, Boston and New York, were in contrast dens of doctrinal heterodoxy, the first full of Unitarians and the second rife with Episcopalians. The Princeton plans, however, came to nothing, and how much interest the school's planners may have had in Gallaudet is doubtful.

Gallaudet's support of and involvement with "female education" has been alleged by biographers since his death, but all the evidence suggests that his support was merely notional and lukewarm. The ideas were certainly out there, and Gallaudet must have known what the arguments were. Emma Willard had written about the improvements needed in female education as early as 1819, and Catharine Beecher had opened her Female Academy in Hartford in 1823, at the urging of Gallaudet's pastor, Joel Hawes. Hawes, Daniel Wadsworth, and the ubiquitous Seth Terry served as Catharine Beecher's trustees, but not Gallaudet.

When he was asked to give an address at the dedication ceremony of Miss Beecher's new school building, it would have been a good opportunity to lay out the obvious analogy that girls, like deaf children, were handicapped by low expectations and poorly conceived educational goals, but they could succeed academically with more years of schooling, trained teachers, appropriate textbooks, and instruction in thinking rather than memorization.[6] He did give the address, but didn't suggest anything like that. Instead, he listed defects in all schools of the day — boys' schools, girls' schools, deaf schools, private schools, common schools, even Miss Beecher's school and, though he doesn't say so, the American Asylum: overemphasis on memorization, insufficient cultivation of the English language, no attention to the various operations of the mind as described by Edinburgh philosophers, and a lack of practical applications such as how to use arithmetic — for a girl, that would be "when she goes a shopping [and] cannot tell how much the articles which she has bought come to, without a pencil and paper." Throughout the address, Gallaudet made repeated disclaimers about his views on a woman's place: "Women cannot plead at the bar, or preach in the pulpit, or thunder in the senate house," he said, approvingly. "In the retirement of her own family, in the circle of her friends and acquaintances," she can accomplish a great deal of good and "solace many a season of a husband's weariness or sickness." If Gallaudet had any interest at all in female education, he doesn't betray it in this address.[7]

Likewise, Gallaudet's 1838–1839 essays in the *Connecticut Common School Journal* on "Female Teachers in the Common Schools" take as their premise that because young men have "so many other avenues open . . . to the accumulation of property, and . . . attaining of distinction," the public must turn to "the other sex for aid in this emergency." He observes that few families are willing to pay tuition for a daughter to train as a teacher, so he proposes that young women board with "respectable families" in which they could earn their keep by doing housework.[8]

As for the Hartford Female Seminary, by 1832 Catharine Beecher's frustration with Hartford had reached the point at which she decided to resign, and Gallaudet agreed to serve as interim principal, only until a new man could be hired later that year. Barnard's memorial tribute to Gallaudet spins this tenuous connection into a claim that Gallaudet taught composition and moral philosophy to "females," but Edward Miner Gallaudet, in his biography of his father, is more honest in referring to Gallaudet's connection with the seminary as "for some months, to an emergency."[9] The two Hartford educational reformers Catharine Beecher and Thomas Hopkins Gallaudet never worked together.[10]

"Whether Mr. Gallaudet had distinctly marked out for himself any particular course of life and labor when he left the Asylum, does not appear," Heman Humphrey diplomatically states.[11] His excuses for turning down one offer after another suggest that he had in fact no plan. After all, when a man repeatedly considers an offer for some months or even years and then declines by claiming ill health, why then, one wonders, had he considered it at all?

Something did happen in 1830, however, that may well have contributed to his desire to stay in Hartford: Dr. Cogswell, who was nearly seventy, had died in early December, and by the end of the month Alice Cogswell, too, was dead. She was twenty-five years old, and, like all her classmates except Sophia Gallaudet, had never undertaken to profess religion. Her death was shocking and immediately obscured with multiple layers of sentimental gauze. Lydia Sigourney may have originated the now-accepted story that Alice died of grief over the death of her father, but, of course, healthy young people don't just drop dead of grief in twenty days, as Alice did. Had she had a chronic condition such as tuberculosis, which killed so many of her classmates, it might be barely conceivable that grief pushed her over the edge, but everyone who knew Alice and commented on her death declared that she had been in blooming health until she fell into "a state of almost constant delirium" two days after her father died.[12]

That leaves suicide with an agent such as arsenic, which can take more than three weeks to cause multiple organ failure. In fact, a young lady of Alice's social circle, Sarah Ann Colt, had killed herself just this way during the previous year. Sarah Ann's family had been close to the Cogswells for decades, and one of Alice's earliest attempts at storytelling—in heavily Sign-inflected English—had to do with Sarah Ann's relative, Peter Colt, who as a boy had had his beautiful curly hair shorn for a preacher who wanted to have a wig made of it.[13] Sarah Ann was the first of two children of Christopher Colt who would commit suicide, and the incident so puzzled Alice that she wrote about why "such a sweet young lady" would have prepared for herself "the poison of Arsenic, which she unresistingly swallowed up." Alice's conclusion: "The way of divine Providence might have directed her to do what I above mentioned" so that she could join her mother and sisters in Heaven.[14]

Granted that Alice knew how one could commit suicide with arsenic and that she regarded such a step as perhaps a part of "divine Providence," would she would have wanted to take her life? Nearly all of her writing after 1824, the year she left the Asylum, is lost — quite possibly deliberately destroyed — so we can only guess. Alice's father had been a colossal, and colossally controlling, presence in her life. He had never allowed her to live at the school, as Gallaudet and Clerc repeatedly said was essential, so while Alice's classmates were shocking the directors by flirting with one another — and while the Gallaudet and Clerc kids romped around campus as native signers teased by the older deaf boys — Alice was at home every evening with her hearing family. While her classmates married and began their own families or left Hartford for jobs and her sisters and brother did the same, she was left behind. Gallaudet's son Thomas remembers Alice visiting his mother regularly, but that seems to have been about the extent of her social contact. Why she never married may very well have been that her father never let a deaf boy get near her. He was his daughter's whole life. When he died, what did she have?[15]

Of course, this is speculation, but had something like it happened everyone connected with the Asylum, including not only Gallaudet but also Alice's brother-in-law Lewis Weld, would have understood instantly that it had to be covered up. Private donations and state legislative allocations would dry up if the school's poster child turned out to be a suicide. A letter from Gallaudet to one of the NYU planners written three days before Alice died describes her father's death and her delirium as reasons for postponing any decision about his career path.[16] Was he needed in the little Asylum community to help the school get past what could have been a ruinous public relations fiasco? Quickly, Lydia Sigourney wrote a poem about Alice in heaven with her father — and able to hear — and the community's damage control was underway.[17]

Having turned down all job offers, Gallaudet cleared his desk to write. But he had already given up on the dream of becoming a poet; poems he had placed in local newspapers in the mid-1820s were embarrassments, even by the clunky retro standards of Connecticut. "A Hymn," which appeared in the *Record and Telegraph* in January 1824, has a jog-trot meter that might have come off better sung than read: "Wandering far from Thee and Heaven / Through the world's deceitful maze, / To its sinful folk is given, / All my earliest, brightest days." "The Widow," published that December in the *Mirror,* takes as its speaker a bereaved woman who clasps her dead husband's "manly form" and macabrely fancies that "his lips were warm." "On a Sleeping Infant" appeared in the *Connecticut Observer* the next month, featuring bizarre similes such as "Upon its mother's breast; / As on a bed of roses," and "Thy balmy lips breathe sweeter / Than Araby's perfumes." "Lines Written in Affliction," dated November 1825 in manuscript and published in the *Connecticut Observer,* is an unsettling depressive poem about the sorrows of life and the speaker's realization that he must submit to God, who "sees it best, for thee to bear, / Sometimes, the chastening of his rod." The sentiments are conventional, the prosody undistinguished, and it's anyone's guess why Gallaudet would have wanted to see something like this in print.[18] Gallaudet's poetry of this period demonstrates that the English Romantic poets Byron, Shelley, and Keats, all of whom had flourished and met with untimely deaths by the mid-1820s, were entirely unknown to him, as was the American Romantic Edgar Allan Poe. Gallaudet's verse was passé, but the society he lived in was so deliberately isolated from the Anglophone literary world that he had no idea what the new models were.

And so he returned to the children's books he had already begun to write. Textbook publishing was still a new frontier in 1830, but Hartford already had more than thirty publishing houses looking to turn a profit in this new field. Gallaudet's friend Theodore Dwight Jr. tried to encourage him: "I thought you had enlisted for the <u>during</u> (as they used to say in the Revolutionary War) under the banner of Education. . . . Now that you have been relieved from the manual labor so long required of you, I have fancied that you were pursuing your plans with double zeal. . . . You must not dream of deserting that standard of which we have considered you the bearer."[19]

Gallaudet' first textbook, *An Elementary Book for the Use of the Deaf and Dumb, in the Connecticut Asylum* (1817), had been little more than a very long list of common words in semantic groupings — body parts, common objects, food, weather, and so on — followed by sentences that seem intended to be copied — "my head aches," "this apple is good." It seems intended as a reference book rather than a textbook. *A Scriptural Catechism, Designed Principally for the Deaf and Dumb in the American Asylum* (1818) was, as we have seen, slightly more ambitious.

The Child's Picture Defining and Reading Book also dates to Gallaudet's years as principal at the Asylum: the 1830 edition stated that it was "originally designed for the use of some of the younger classes" but was now offered for "the education of children and youth who can *hear* and *speak*." Gallaudet's preface called the book an experiment in teaching words with reference to "some sensible object, or visible occurrence or transaction," or, because most "sensible objects" are not present in the classroom, "the language of pictures, being founded in Nature, and thus a Universal Language." The first part of the book consists of pictures with word labels: a line drawing of a cradle is labeled "Cradle. small. I rock. / He is sleeping in the cradle." Sample questions for the teacher to ask his pupils are provided on another page: "What other things are small? Who rocks a cradle? How does a person rock it? Why is it rocked? What other things can your rock? Who sleeps in a cradle? When did you sleep in a cradle? On what other things can you sleep? Of what is a cradle made? Who makes a cradle?"[20]

The second part of the book is a collection of texts that explain the accompanying pictures. A picture of a woodcutter returning home with a bundle of sticks is explained by the text, "This old man is carrying a bundle of small sticks on his back. . . . He is smoking a pipe. He has a black hat on his head. His axe is under his right arm. . . . He looks old and he walks slowly along. He worked hard all day, and is very tired," and so on. Each of these texts ends with a Christian admonition, in this case, "He will read in the Bible, and he will pray to God with them [his family] before they go to bed. Little boys and girls should pray to God every evening before they go to bed, and every morning when they rise." Most of the texts are stories from the Old Testament, like this one: "These two men are Cain and Abel. They were the sons of Adam and Eve. They were brothers. Cain, who has a club in his right hand, was a very wicked man. He did not love and obey God," and so forth, ending with the admonition, "If you wish God to love you, you must be good, and love and obey God like Abel."[21] It's not clear to what extent this book was revised from the version Gallaudet had developed for the Asylum. It was later reprinted by the American Board of Commissioners for Foreign Missions in 1835 in Ojibwe, and a fourth edition in 1839 was designed especially for use in American infant schools.

And with that, we see the difficulty of assembling the children's books that Gallaudet authored. He kept no records of his publications. Books were used in manuscript and were reprinted with or without permission. There were translations and redesigns for different readerships, in which he may or may not have been involved. The discussion here is therefore merely illustrative of the kind of books he produced after he left the Asylum. Those he had written as principal represent the two genres that would occupy him for the next decade and more: religious instruction and elementary reading. Gallaudet intended all of his children's books in both these genres to be used in both the classroom and the home.

Well into the early nineteenth century, reading continued to be taught by syllable lists developed in the eighteenth century. As Elizabeth Gaskell's character Lady Ludlow put it, this was "teaching us our a b, ab — b a, ba." Dilworth's speller, *A New Guide to the English Tongue* (1740), was published in the United States by Benjamin Franklin in 1747 and taught Americans from Noah Webster to Abraham Lincoln how to read. Webster reworked Dilworth to make it more interesting to children, but his "Blue-Backed Speller"[22] was still just a syllable list. Theodore Dwight Jr., in a letter to Gallaudet, analyzed the failings of Webster's system, which he found to be no system at all. He realized, as Webster did not, that if you are going to teach little children to pronounce and spell at the same time, then foreign words needed to be flagged, and sound shifts that are regular in English needed to be explained (e.g., that the letter *s* in "provision" is pronounced as "zh" ought to be explained as a rule of English orthography and phonology, not an exception).[23] Obviously, however, no matter how a phonetic system of instruction like this was tweaked, it would be meaningless to deaf children.

The Asylum used whole-word instruction, presumably adapted from the Paris school. Charlotte Elizabeth Phelan, too, had hit on the whole-word method independently. Explaining that she proceeded "without regarding the general plan of previously teaching the alphabet," she began by forming words with letters she had cut out of cards, and she taught the finger-spelled word at the same time.[24] Outside of deaf education, one place where whole-word reading was in use was Edinburgh. It's no wonder, then, that Gallaudet was sold on the whole-word method.[25] He was the first to bring it to the American public with his *Mother's Primer*.

In his 1830 "Methods of Teaching to Read," published in the maiden issue of William C. Woodbridge's *American Annals of Education,* Gallaudet said that his experiment with whole-word instruction had been continuing for seven years — with his own children as the guinea pigs, though he didn't say so here. As he explained it, he would write a different simple word on each of three cards and teach the child to recognize each word on sight. The next day he would add a fourth card and each subsequent day another until the child had fifty cards and could recognize each of the fifty words. At that point, he would begin teaching the alphabetic characters by, for example, covering up all the letters in the word "horse" except the *h,* telling the child its name, and asking the child to find another letter *h* in another word in his pile of cards. This point is important, because critics of whole-word reading, then and now, elide the fact that the alphabet is indeed taught — just postponed until after the child gets a sense of how much fun it is to read.[26]

The Mother's Primer was brought out in 1836, we assume: no first editions have survived and even second editions are scarce today. The first page has line drawings of a boy and girl, labeled with the names "frank" and "jane" (all lowercase). "Directions to the Teacher" are in small print at the bottom of the page: "Say to the child, pointing to the first picture, 'What is that? Do you know his name? I wonder if he has a name. Suppose we call him *Frank.* O there is his name, right under him,' pointing to the *whole word,* Frank, but not to the letters. *Nothing is yet to be said about letters.*"

Subsequent words are *dog, cat, bee, hive, sheep, lamb, ox, yoke, quail, swan, mule,* and *zebra,* at which point the child is to be taught the letters *d, o,* and *g.* We eventually learn that the dog's name is Spot, which suggests that our twentieth-century whole-word friends Dick, Jane, Sally, Spot, and Puff are direct descendants of Frank, Jane, Spot, and Jane's unnamed cat. (The adventures of Dick and family, however, are purely secular, quite unlike those of Frank and Jane, who "loved to go to church.... Do you love to go to church?") Later lessons introduce phonetic values of alphabetic characters in rhyme charts: "hide, tide, ride, side, wide" and "daw, law, paw, saw, draw," *daw* being a kind of crow, not a nonsense syllable: there are no nonsense syllables. Capital letters are introduced only in one of the last lessons.[27]

The Mother's Primer garnered quite a lot of attention, unsurprisingly. Some educators gave it their unqualified approval, and a few produced imitations, not always giving credit where it was due. Oddly, the most enthusiastic supporters of Gallaudet's whole-word approach were to be found in Unitarian Boston: Cyrus Peirce, who would within a few years be president of the first American normal school in Lexington; Josiah Bumstead, whose *My First School Book* (1838) adopted Gallaudet's method; Mary Tyler Peabody, whose best-selling *Primer of Reading and Drawing* (1841) did the same; and Horace Mann, who would marry Peabody in 1843, and who, as Massachusetts secretary of education, had the biggest megaphone of all.

The Boston primary schools adopted *The Mother's Primer,* and by Mann's *First Report* in 1838, after only one year's trial, he could state that the whole-word instruction was no longer new or theoretical. Like Gallaudet, Peirce, Bumstead, Peabody, and the Englishman Henry Dunn, whose *Principles of*

Teaching Gallaudet would adapt for the American market, Mann observed that alphabetic characters were difficult for little children to recognize and tiresome for them to learn because they are devoid of any human mental associations, a "senseless table of a, b, c." The alphabet as a whole was capricious, Mann asserted, and a "stiff and lifeless column" with letter names that did not coordinate with the sounds they signify in any given word. In any case, he concluded, English spelling is not "phonic" and the "power" of an individual letter — that is, the phoneme it signifies in any given word — was a thing devoid of meaning, so starting children off with the alphabet and its "powers" was a sure-fire way to induce repugnance, and a lifelong dislike of school.[28]

But many educators registered their opposition to whole-word instruction. In 1844, thirty-one Boston schoolteachers published a 144-page response to Mann's *Seventh Annual Report,* correctly noting that whole-word instruction turns alphabetic reading into ideographic reading (as though there were something wrong with that), but completely missing the fact that both the alphabetic characters and their phonetic values were in fact taught in *The Mother's Primer* as well as in the methods of all Gallaudet's imitators. "A person might read Chinese, without knowing a single sound of the language," they write, "and we confess ourselves not a little surprised" that Mann, who was on record as deeming Chinese "an unscientific language," should be urging that English be taught like Chinese. But, of course, he had urged no such thing.[29]

Back and forth over 1844 and 1845 flew the learned mischaracterizations of the schoolmasters and the arrogant indignation of Mann, hitting rock bottom with an attack on whole-word reading instruction by one Samuel S. Greene solely on the ground that it was developed for the deaf. Greene pretended to have been shocked by the "striking resemblance" between Mann's whole-word method of reading instruction and the methods observed by a Boston man visiting the Asylum, as though the origin of the method had ever been a secret — Gallaudet admits his inspiration outright in his preface to *The Mother's Primer*. Counting on his readers' bias against the deaf, just as all parties had been counting on reader bias against Chinese, Greene self-righteously averred that "none shall go before me in commiserating the condition of the deaf and dumb" but proclaimed his "protest against treating all children as though they were deaf and dumb. On the same principle, and with about as good reason, might one urge the general adoption of a book prepared with raised letters for the blind."[30]

Remarks attacking whole-word reading on the grounds of its association with the deaf can still be found in our day. In 1973, Samuel L. Blumenfeld wrote of the detective work he undertook to discover the "missing link" in the evolution of whole-word instruction. His discovery that the "source of the sight-vocabulary method" was T. H. Gallaudet, a teacher of the deaf, is presented as a tainting disclosure, and Blumenfeld preposterously accused Gallaudet of not understanding that hearing children already know the words they are being taught to read. More recently, Geraldine E. Rodgers so mischaracterized *The Mother's Primer* as to claim, falsely, that it "breaks words into pieces" and calls its approach "the 'guessing' technique": deaf people, she explains, require "constant repetition of sight words, a controlled vocabulary, and context guessing!" [Exclamation point is in original.] Even the novelist John Updike entered the lists against whole-word reading in a 1976 newspaper essay, accepting without question Blumenfeld's contention that it "has been taught our children as if they were deaf or Chinese." At least Updike admits that phonics didn't work for his children, either. All these objections suggest that something about whole-word instruction touches a nerve, triggers a conspiracy theory, and sends opponents into bigoted invective.[31]

We have no record of Gallaudet himself being on the receiving end of any of this, but perhaps only because he did not hold a prominent public position as Mann did. Yet something happened to cause him to change his mind, for in 1840 he and coauthor Horace Hooker brought out *A Practical Spelling-Book with Reading Lessons* like this:

> Lesson I: ba be bi bo bu by
> da de di do du dy
> fa fe fi fo fu fy
> ha he hi ho hu hy.

After ten such lessons, we finally get some words:

> Lesson XI: babe he kite rope mule
> plate here lime home tube
> cage me fire hole tune

By Lesson XVI, we are starting on sentences:

James has a top.

His kite is at home.

Jane has a bag.

He gave me a pen.

The fox is in the hole.

A Practical Spelling-Book was followed by a second book with Hooker in the same vein, *The School and Family Dictionary.* What might have induced Gallaudet to abandon the whole-word method he had innovated and to turn out such conventional drivel, he never said, nor did anyone else at the time seem to have commented on his about-face. Gallaudet himself took some pains to suppress his earlier efforts in whole-word reading, reporting to an Andover classmate planning a reunion in 1845 that the books he authored were *Book on the Soul, Scripture Biography*, and the two books with Hooker. Perhaps it was a case of feeling damned by Unitarian praise.[32]

Gallaudet was a truly seminal figure in reading education, at least until his 1844 defection, but in the storybooks he wrote for children he was a follower, aiming to imitate what was already selling well. The notion of a book, other than a primer, written specifically for children had appeared in England as early as the mid-eighteenth century, but, we have the sense from Gallaudet's defensiveness on the subject, male authors were still twitted for writing for children. In an 1830 article in the *American Annals of Education,* though, he turned the tables on detractors by claiming that addressing children is simply too difficult for most people, because their sense of self-importance gets in their way.[33]

From the beginning, children's books avoided irony and all figurative language that might suggest that words could have more than one meaning. They taught moral values — deferring gratification, being industrious — using stark black-and-white, either-or terms, and they excluded any hint of adventure that might inflame the imagination or inspire hopes that could not be realized.[34] Gallaudet followed established precedent on all of these points. As for format, many children's books were written as dialogues between a child and a parent or teacher, with the child's part always controlled by the parent figure who allowed questions but steered them in catechistic fashion. Maria Edgeworth was an early practitioner of such dialogue books for children, and Gallaudet was one of the many and various who followed her lead. Dorothea Dix, another reformer whose cultural assumptions were virtually identical to Gallaudet's, wrote dialogue books for children on Bible stories, diligence, geography, and weather, but so did the Anglican actress and playwright from Philadelphia, Susanna Haswell Rowson.[35]

What Gallaudet uniquely brought to the practice of writing for children is his extraordinary auctorial voice, which those who knew him claimed was only the shadow of his remarkable manner with children in the flesh. A Hartford woman said that children, who had instinctual understanding of the genuine, spotted it immediately in Gallaudet. His manner had a "magic influence," she said, in opening a child's heart to receive "'the good seed' of serious admonition" that was never fully captured in his books. Horace Hooker declared that Gallaudet "excelled almost any one . . . in gaining the good-will of children, winning their confidence by his kind and benevolent manner, and fastening their attention by the simplicity and pertinence of his instruction." Hooker explained that Gallaudet's years at the Asylum taught him how "to take a complex idea to pieces and exhibit and illustrate its several parts, . . . making an abstruse subject intelligible and interesting for the young." On the downside of that remarkable voice, Henry Barnard believed that Gallaudet's "power as a preacher was weakened by his habit of simplifying his thoughts, and extending his illustrations for the deaf and dumb and for children," although, he admitted, the style was perfectly suited for preaching to prisoners and the insane.[36] Aside from that snarky reference to incarcerated persons, Barnard probably gets it right; in any case, Gallaudet's tone for children was so startlingly different from that of other writers that any reader, after experiencing Gallaudet's prose style, can easily spot in others the false notes and pandering.

Perhaps the first effort Gallaudet made after his retirement from the Asylum was a three-volume collection of Bible stories for children, adapted from an English edition for the American Sunday School Union. *The Story of Isaac, or, The First Part of a Conversation between Mary and Her Mother* was brought out in 1832 and was followed by *Jacob and His Sons, or, the Second Part* and *Simple Scripture Biographies, or the Third Part,* which covered stories from Moses and the Pharaoh all the way through to the birth of Christ. The three volumes were circulated by the Sunday School Union until 1848, when the second volume was removed upon the complaint of a Southern slaveholder who found one of the passages "discourteous." The objectionable passage, which was in the story of Joseph being sold into slavery by his brothers, seems unremarkable today:

What is a slave, mother? asked Mary; is it a servant?

What is a slave, mother? asked Mary; is it a servant?

Yes, replied her mother, slaves are servants, for they work for their masters, and wait on them; but they are not hired servants, but are bought and sold like beasts, and have nothing, but what their master chooses to give them. They are obliged to work very hard, and sometimes their masters use them cruelly, beat them, and starve them and kill them; for they have nobody to help them. Sometimes they are chained together and driven about like beasts.[37]

The "objection made by our Southern friends," as the Sunday School Union termed the complainants, concerned the phrase "kill them; for they have nobody to help them." The complaint alleged that no state has any such law on its books, and, what's more, the fact that "more lives have been taken by slaves than by masters" showed that the laws "avail more for the slave than the free man." The effrontery of this assertion and the Sunday School Union's craven acquiescence to it are shocking today. But Gallaudet acquiesced to it as well. He didn't write it, he said: he just let it stand as it had appeared in the British original.[38] The Congregational church in Farmington, about ten miles west of Hartford, protested the Sunday School Union's withdrawal of the book on the grounds that Gallaudet was not by any means an abolitionist but rather "a strong and leading colonizationist — long, and we believe still, an officer of a colonization society."[39] As we shall see when we take up his activities on behalf of the so-called colonization efforts, he was indeed proud of his unwavering anti-abolition record. This affair with the Sunday School Union was the sole instance of his running afoul of the interest of the slave states, but he hadn't written the passage in the first place and had already omitted the *Conversations between Mary and her Mother* from the list of books he gave Andover in 1845. Gallaudet was hardly alone among children's book authors in avoiding the issue of slavery. Dorothea Dix mentioned it but once, and then it was to blame "the natural indolence of the negroes" for giving white people the idea of enslaving them.[40]

Other efforts by Gallaudet on books for the religious instruction of children were brought out by commercial publishers, at least at first. *The Child's Book on the Soul: Part First* and *Part Second* (1831) was Gallaudet's first new effort in his retirement, his first children's book not originally intended for deaf children — and his first attempt to bring Thomas Brown's theories of the mind to bear on Divine Revelation. It would prove to be his best seller.[41] In his preface addressing the parents and teachers who were intended to read this book to children, Gallaudet explains the importance of learning to distinguish among sensations, emotions, mental states, and operations of the mind. All we know of God, he wrote, is *"derived from what we know of the emotions, states, and operations of our own spirits. Without these elements, all that Revelation proposes to teach us of God, would be wholly unintelligible."*[42] The book is a series of dialogues between an apparently very well-to-do widow, Mrs. Stanhope, and her five-year-old son Robert, who live "in a small white house near the church." The house has a library with a large collection of books, and in the back is a "beautiful garden." Mrs. Stanhope has a "pretty watch" that features prominently in the dialogues, as do a younger child named Eliza and a dog named Tray. That they have servants is clear from Mrs. Stanhope's activities, which include nothing beyond sewing, walking in the garden, presiding over tea, and homeschooling her children. Robert is preternaturally ingenuous:

R. Mother, what do you call these two little things that go round and round, and tell us what o'clock it is.

M. They are called *hands*.

R. That is strange, mother; I was going to call them so, and to tell you, that the little wheels inside make them go, just as *something inside of Eliza makes her hands go.*

The Child's Book on the Soul went through several editions, some by the Tract Society, and it was translated into French, German, "modern Greek," "Greco-Turkish," "Armeno-Turkish" (these two languages for Christian communities in the Ottoman Empire), "Siamese," Chinese, and "the language of the Sandwich Islands." Gallaudet was still tinkering with it in 1843 when he floated the idea of a revised edition to the publisher George Merriam.[43]

Following on the success of *The Child's Book on the Soul,* Gallaudet wrote *The Child's Book on Repentance, Designed, Also, for Older Persons* (1834), which was a collection of fireside chats about sin, and *The Youth's Book on Natural Theology,* which appeared sometime in the 1840s. In *Natural Theology,* Mother leads Robert to understand that every feature of the natural world is specially designed for specific uses. Chicken claws, for example, are exactly right for scratching for food and for roosting. And the fact that we can see stars that are "5,000,000,000,000 miles away" demonstrates God's "infinite power and wisdom; and his great goodness, too, in doing it all for the convenience and comfort of man."[44] Robert, now "a few years older," has by now learned a thing or two outside the home:

R. I can do one thing with my fingers, that I have never told you about.
M. What is that?
R. I can make the alphabet that the deaf and dumb use. A little boy taught it to me last Saturday afternoon. Here is an engraving of it, which he gave me.
M. That is another way, in which the hand shows the skill and goodness of God.[45]

An engraving of the finger alphabet is included. Both *Repentance* and *Natural Theology* seem to have been brought out originally by the Tract Society. The title of the latter was changed to *The Class Book of Natural Theology for the Use of Schools,* and under both titles it was translated into Tamil, Marathi, "Hawaiian" — a certain Sheldon Dibble translated it as a missionary there — and perhaps other languages. Neither of these sold nearly as well as *Book on the Soul,* but the Tract Society paid over a thousand dollars for rights to both and a few other books in August 1834 and continued to pay 10 percent on receipts, which the following year amounted to $458. William Alcott thought them just as excellent as *Soul.*[46]

Meanwhile, Gallaudet was continuing to mine the rich vein of Bible stories with a series of Scripture Biographies for the Young for the American Tract Society. He completed seven volumes: 1, Adam to Jacob; 2, Joseph; 3 and 4, Moses; 5, Joshua and the Judges; 6, Ruth and Samuel, including the life of Saul; 7, David and Solomon, including Saul and Rehoboam. After his death, the series was extended by Horace Hooker, beginning with the 1853 publication of volume 8, Jeroboam to Ahaz. In the prefaces to his seven volumes, Gallaudet explained to parents his views on what sorts of books children should read. In *The History of Joseph,* for example, he makes the case for parents that children ought to acquire the habit of reading attentively:

If they read none but story books, intended almost entirely to entertain them; or if they read so many of these books as to dislike to read those of a more serious and instructive kind — *then there is very great danger of their acquiring a strong dislike to the reading of the Bible. . . .* Let parents and teachers beware — lest, by indulging children too much in the perusal of mere books of amusement, they acquire such a fondness for fiction, that it will be difficult for them to read any thing that demands patient and continued attention, and tends to produce serious thought and feeling.

Addressing his young readers, he warns *them* against fiction, too: "Your mind will become enfeebled . . . you will sink down into indolence and inefficiency . . . the Bible, the best of all books, the word of God, the record of divine truth, will seem to you dull and tedious." Why he would want to suggest this view of the Bible to a beginning reader is unclear.[47]

The Tract Society also brought out Gallaudet's "histories" of Old Testament characters. These included *The Child's Book of Bible Stories, with Practical Illustrations and Remarks on the Fall* (1834), a personal favorite of mine that cleverly explains each step in Adam and Eve's Fall by offering analogies to tales of children who disobey their parents. Others in the series are *The History of Jonah, for Children and Youth* (1833), *The History of Joseph* (1834), and *the History of Josiah* (1837). Gallaudet's prefaces sometimes include the same sort of remarks about the dangers of fiction. In *The History of Jonah,* for example, he repeats verbatim the paragraph from *The History of Joseph* beginning, "Let parents and teachers beware," adding that fiction "is training them up, in too many instances, to a loose, desultory, luxurious, and disconnected kind of reading, which will render to them, in maturer life, all our *standard works of religious truth,* by which the souls of English and American Christians, of earlier days, were nurtured to deep thought and a vigorous faith — insipid, irksome, revolting."[48]

ALTHOUGH GALLAUDET NEVER RETURNED to teaching school, he maintained direct involvement in educational reforms through advocacy. School reform in Connecticut during the 1820s and 1830s was premised on the Counter-Enlightenment view that the purpose of public education was the production of God-fearing citizens. In the previous century, patriotism had been seen as the main purpose of schooling, with New Englanders such as Samuel Knox, whose prize-winning essay declared that schools were to impress children with "the benefits of that happy constitution under which they live and of the enormity of their being corrupted in their right of suffrage," and Noah Webster, who counted U.S. history and American

principles of liberty among the values that schools must teach. By the 1820s,
however, American history, the principles of liberty, "that happy constitution,"
and voting rights were no longer so much as mentioned in the educational
ideals expressed by Gallaudet, Henry Barnard, or William C. Woodbridge. As
Gallaudet put it, education was to prepare the child for "a higher and nobler
condition of being beyond the grave," period.[49]

As for Connecticut's Standing Order, the preservation of the social hier-
archies that were threatened by mass literacy remained front and center. As
the ruling class had observed in the previous century, newly literate youth of
the working class could, and did, read Paine's *Rights of Man* — if their schools
failed to inculcate acceptance of their divinely ordained lot in life, that is.
Such arguments were often framed in near-hysterical rhetoric, as illustrated
by Elizabeth Gaskell's character Lady Ludlow, who believed that mass literacy
would lead to "the terrible scenes of the French Revolution acted over again
in England." In Lady Ludlow's view, which Gaskell satirizes, and in Gallaudet's, which was his sincere belief, the working class has "duties to which they
are called by God; of submission to those placed in authority over them; of
contentment with that state of life to which it has pleased God to call them."
By the end of Gaskell's *My Lady Ludlow,* the poacher's son has become the
new parson and Lady Ludlow is serving tea to the wife of a Baptist baker and
a young lady born out of wedlock — a happy ending in our view, but one that
would have befuddled 1820s Connecticut.

It was the precept of Maria Edgeworth, not of Elizabeth Gaskell, that perfectly articulated Connecticut's desire to inculcate passive acquiescence to
existing social injustices and the right of the upper classes to make decisions
for everyone else. Public education came to be seen as an arm of the state and
a substitute, to some extent, for the disestablishment of the church. Books like
Gallaudet's written as catechistic pseudo-dialogues were expressly designed to
form the child's moral habits and assist the internalization of submission to
authority, producing a citizen who could read but was unlikely to reason for
himself. Of course, keeping books expensive would help to limit the access of
working-class readers as well, and the later clamor among slaveholders against
the inexpensive newspapers put out by abolitionists was adumbrated decades
earlier by people such as Elias Boudinot, anti-Semite and Asylum donor, who
deplored the sale price of Paine's *Age of Reason* that put it within the reach
of servants.[50]

Gallaudet's forays into public education began while he was still running the

Asylum and was focused on innovations in the physical schoolroom and teaching aids. In 1828, along with the principals of the Hartford Grammar School and the Hartford Female Academy (the latter was not Catharine Beecher but rather a certain John Brace), Gallaudet offered a prize of $25 "for the best design for new, adjustable schoolroom seats." In 1830, the *American Journal of Education* published a letter he had written in answer to an inquiry about "black tablets" — blackboards. The *Journal* editor prefaced Gallaudet's letter with comments about the difficulty of obtaining large slabs of slate and instructions for preparing a substitute "from lime and plaster of Paris colored with lamp black." We recall Gallaudet's expedient, during one of his fund-raising tours, of a board painted black. The advantage of the composite over such a painted board, the editor wrote, was that "the trace of the chalk can be removed by a dry cloth, or a brush made of sheepskin with the wool upon it," as could be done with real slate. Gallaudet's interest in blackboard technology dates from contact with Sicard and extended to the chemical level, as we see in an 1817 letter he wrote to Professor Silliman asking for advice about chalk dust and the possibly of black chalk on a white board. It's sobering today to see the effort that Gallaudet and a handful of others had to invest in perfecting the technology and getting schoolteachers to understand how to use a blackboard and how to erase it.[51]

He was also, during these years, beginning to look at training for teachers in common schools, inspired no doubt by his difficulties in training new teachers at the Asylum. His first mention of a normal school was in an 1824 letter to the man with whom he and Clerc had sailed to New York, S. V. S. Wilder.[52] The following year, he wrote a series of essays in the *Connecticut Observer* that were collected and published in book form the same year in Boston as *Plan of a Seminary*. Here, Gallaudet argued that the best way to educate children in common schools ought be determined by a professionalized teaching corps, which could be created by specialized training for teachers. His ideas are now taken for granted, but they were surprising in 1825: a library of "theoretical and practical" works, students who aim to make a career of teaching, and a model school, which he believed would prove a "most delightful and interesting spectacle" to quicken the curiosity of the public.

The seminary itself would investigate various approaches to discipline, to imparting Divine Truth to pupils, and to writing for children. He makes analogies with apprenticeships for trades, a gardener's care for his plants, and on the money spent by tract, missionary, and Bible societies on adults, who were far less amenable to instruction than children. His remarks in the eighth installment on the importance of language for salvation are interesting: disclaiming any intention to minimize the Calvinist doctrine of God's supernatural power to confer grace on an individual, he argued that we are nevertheless bound to cooperate with God by conveying divine truth to the unconverted, and that "*[t]his truth must be conveyed in language.*" The fourteenth and final installment addressed costs with an argument that embarrassingly dates the whole thing, but shows Gallaudet at his most authentic. Taking as given that eight years is necessary for a good basic education, he claims that seminary training for teachers would enable them to provide that basic education in only five years, resulting in "an immense saving to the state," which would have to pay for only five years of education per child. These savings would extend to school expenses like wood (for heat), and parents would be able to send their children out to work for wages during those saved three years. Sadly, his pandering failed to have the intended effect on the state legislature, which would not pay for a normal school for another twenty-five years.[53]

Connecticut's unwillingness to fund any aspect of public education derived in part from a suspicion of "pecuniary aid" from the state, with which "comes a claim to control or dictate; and their influence may generally be expected to be of an irreligious or _unreligious_ character." In part, too, it derived from a historical happenstance that should have worked out better than it did: the establishment of a school fund from the proceeds of the sale of state land in Connecticut's Western Reserve. Unfortunately, the proceeds of this sale were to be distributed not directly to townships but rather to the established clergy, each of whom could, if he wished, establish a common school in the town in which he was settled, or he could use the money as his own. Not all of the clergy decided on a school, but local governments that had previously funded a common school nevertheless withdrew their funds from it, on the grounds that the money should be coming from the Western Reserve via the church. Parents likewise believed that the school their children attended was the sole responsibility of the school fund. As a result, public schooling in Connecticut ranged from nonexistent to deplorable.[54]

In 1827, Gallaudet, along with his friends Horace Hooker, the Rev. Thomas Robbins, Chauncey A. Goodrich (a son of Yale professor Elizur

Goodrich), the Rev. Mr. Joel Hawes, and Asylum director Ward Wood-bridge, founded the Society for the Improvement of the Common Schools. One of the few things, perhaps the only thing, to come of this society was a teachers' convention in Hartford held in November 1830. Gallaudet was in charge of arrangements, Heman Humphrey gave the introductory lecture, Noah Webster reported on his etymological research, and William A. Alcott spoke on "The Location, Structure, and Ventilation of School-houses." The *Courant,* which may well have been printing a press release from Gallaudet, commented that one topic was not discussed but should have been: how reading was currently taught as pronunciation without understanding. There is no evidence of any further activity by this society, and it appears to have been reorganized as the Hartford Association for the Improvement of Common Schools in 1839, with Gallaudet as one of four vice presidents.[55]

Meanwhile, the clergy and other leading citizens continued to blame parents for everything that was wrong with the schools, and Gallaudet joined in the general clamor. When the New York Public School Society asked him in 1833 to write a simply worded pamphlet for the working-class parents thought to be responsible for failed schooling, he conceived his readerships to be so dim-witted as to be unable to understand their children's long-term interests. His pamphlet, *Common Schools, Common Blessings,* asks parents whose children are not in school, "how can they ever expect to *rise in the world,* to acquire property, and to gain respectability and influence?" Young people who have received basic schooling can be assured of "having good treatment and respect," and will earn "*ten, twenty, fifty, or a hundred times* as much as they do now" and thus will be able to take care of "you" in old age. Schooling is to be had at no expense to you, he pointed out, and your son will cost you less in clothing because there will be less wear and tear on it in the classroom. As for girls, illiterate girls "will never be respected" and "*will stand a very poor chance of getting husbands that are at all worth having,*" because educated men want a wives who can read and write letters. Besides, a man's "respectability is increased by the respectability of his wife." Not only that, but public schools teach girls "*plain and fine needle work*" without charge to parents. A twentieth-century editor of *American Writings on Popular Education* who did not know the identity of the author of this anonymously published pamphlet and who could thus speak freely without worrying about besmirching an education icon, said of this pamphlet that "it appeals to parents to send their children to school mainly for reasons of personal profit and individual success; but it does so in terms that indicate a lurking social bias — didactic, paternalistic, and even elitist — on the part of its sponsor." Appeals to ordinary working people would not succeed until they were framed in egalitarian terms, a thing that Gallaudet could never do. Perhaps he would more appropriately have accepted an offer from Theodore Dwight Jr. that year to coauthor a book on "Fathers at Home."[56]

Similar efforts to locate school failures in working-class families are seen in his 1839 essays on the "habit of attention," which needs to be developed in the children who attend common schools.

> When listening to instruction, or reciting a lesson, or performing a task, [children] should not be permitted to indulge in lazy, lounging postures of body, unmeaning expressions of countenance, faint and languid tones of voice, and vacillating or heartless looks of the eye. These will all inevitably re-act on the mind, and produce there a listless and fickle attention. On the contrary . . . teach them to sit and stand erect; to plant the foot firmly on the floor when they come to recite; to brace up the body; to look to the teacher; to fasten the eye upon him; to catch clearly and immediately the words that he utters; and to speak . . . in an animated, prompt, cheerful, and distinct manner.[57]

Try it yourself, Gallaudet advised, and "the result will furnish additional proof of the mighty influence that the body has both over the mind and the heart." If the pupils in common schools would only sit and stand like middle-class children, they would be able to learn, he seems to have supposed. In a series of articles appearing in the *Connecticut Common School Journal* around the same time, Gallaudet encouraged working-class parents to speak of the school and its teacher with respect, take the initiative to become personally acquainted with "him (or the young lady, as the case may be)," and recognize the teacher as the presiding authority. Presumably, respectful deference from parents and good posture from children would go a long way toward turning education around in the state. To be fair, Gallaudet's support for pupil posture in common schools, like his support for battledore at Andover twenty-five years previous, was an expression of his belief in "the vast importance of physical culture," a belief that continued to inspire him to the end of his life when he would advocate battledore for mental patients at the Hartford Retreat.[58]

Henry Barnard, in contrast, was approaching school inadequacy by seeking to arm himself with research data. The son of a trader who sold New England livestock to slave-labor sugar plantations in the West Indies and bought West Indian molasses for New England rum distilleries, Barnard was a state legislator in 1838 when he introduced a bill establishing the Board of Commissioners of Common Schools; when it passed unanimously, Barnard saw to it that Gallaudet was named secretary. The duties of this position were personal inspection of schools, preparation of an annual report, editing of the board's journal, and the usual public relations and meetings. The salary must have been embarrassingly low because, according to Barnard, "individuals" offered to top it up by one-third if Gallaudet would accept the position. Gallaudet declined "because of the apathy as to the importance of this cause," he was supposed to have said. "To break up this apathy, requires more of youthful strength and enthusiasm than can be found in an invalid and a man of fifty years of age." Barnard took the job himself, but brought Gallaudet along on a tour of every county in Connecticut to speak with teachers, volunteer societies, and, of course, clergymen, who were still nominally running the schools. Barnard's proposal for a state normal school to train teachers for the common schools was defeated in the legislature, but he did succeed in launching the *Connecticut Common School Journal,* which, despite erratic publication, was an invaluable contribution to public education in Connecticut for the fifteen years it was in existence, and Barnard's reports published therein were widely reprinted, even in Europe.[59]

As a money-saving measure, Connecticut abolished its Board of Commissioners in 1842. The *Connecticut Common School Journal,* all the workshops and conventions, and even Henry Barnard, who decamped to Rhode Island, disappeared with it. Gallaudet did live to see the opening of Connecticut's own normal school in 1850, and he might have been aware that its students had formed a "Gallaudet Society," but one year later at the school's first semiannual examination and exhibition, the members of the Gallaudet Society would be wearing black mourning armbands.

GALLAUDET'S CAREER as a writer of religious books for children and his volunteer efforts in public education would seem to have taken a great deal of time, but everyone who knew him commented rather on how much time he spent with his family. Catherine (Caty) was born in 1831, a fourth daughter he named Alice Cogswell in 1833, and Edward Miner, who seems to have been the family's "bonus baby," in 1837.

Gallaudet established a small family school with a hired teacher for his own children and some of the neighbors'; a family friend gave them a piano, which they never could have afforded otherwise. Little Alice was crushed when a chance remark from her mother brought home to her the fact that her mother could not hear the music. No one seems to have remarked at the time that Gallaudet was not following through on his courtship promise to Sophia to continue *her* education — that point was later made by a deaf professor at Gallaudet College and friend of Edward Miner's in Sophia's obituary. At some point, Gallaudet gave up on the home school, and his oldest daughter Sophie was set to teaching "Eddy" (always called "Ned" outside of the family) his Latin. In the family's pew at the Center Church twice every Sunday — these were still the big box pews with half-walls that were owned by the prominent families that could afford them — Gallaudet set his children on footstools with appropriate pious reading material so that they would not develop habits of "mental inattention" or learn to dread church. There is no record of how Mrs. Gallaudet handled these long sermons, for they were certainly not interpreted either by Gallaudet or anyone else. Perhaps he summarized them for her later. At least one friend of Gallaudet's, William A. Alcott, thought that his marked attention to his children was due to the deprivations they suffered by having a deaf mother, a remark that demonstrates how very little the public — even people who knew Sophia and her children personally — were able to grasp the idea of mothering in sign language. The entire family, in turn, learned how to handle Father's depression. As his oldest son, Thomas, said many years later, "on such occasions he rarely spoke, and the other members of his family generally knew when he had the 'blues,' and they let nature take its course."[1]

The children were frequently ill with the usual childhood illnesses: "At one time," he told a correspondent, "five of my children were all under the daily care of a physician." On at least two occasions, there was serious cause for concern. In 1830, when Sophie came down with pneumonia, Gallaudet told her "that God had made her sick, and asked her if she thought God was good — she said 'yes.'" He was pleased with the assurance that Sophie was "numbered among the lambs of his flock" and that he therefore need not fear her death. The following year, Thomas came down with scarlet fever while he was with his mother at her brother's home in Guilford, where Sophia had gone to give birth. This time, Gallaudet was more seriously alarmed, and he took time out from his other obligations to travel to his son's bedside. Sophia named the new baby Rachel after her mother and had the infant baptized under that name in Guilford, but the baptismal certificate shows "Rachel" crossed out and "Catherine" inserted, which Gallaudet must have had done when he arrived in Guilford to visit his presumably dying son. His veto of his wife's entirely unexceptionable preference to name the baby after her mother tells us, perhaps, all we need to know about how decisions were made in this family. Gallaudet himself had a bout of scarlet fever around the same time as young Thomas and an attack of pneumonia in the first months of 1832 that, he told a correspondent, "brought me to the borders of the grave." The 1832 worldwide cholera epidemic spared Hartford, however, and Gallaudet was able to make "an excursion of more than four hundred miles, through the western parts of Connecticut and Massachusetts, to Boston" and home that year. "My ride has been of service to my health," he explained.[2]

Gallaudet believed that the family was a "minor theocracy," in which "the parent is, as it were, *in the place of God, to the child*" — and "parent" here means "father." Children raised with "the necessity and the duty of yielding" to the "parent" are prepared to understand that God "bring[s] into complete subjection, the wills of all the beings whom He has formed." Thus he prefaced an American edition of Thomas Babington's *A Practical View of Christian Education*. Babington, like Hannah More and Zachary Macaulay (who named a son for Babington), was a member of the evangelical Clapham sect, and thus Babington's views met with Gallaudet's complete approval — as augmented on a few points, that is. In his preface to the American edition, Gallaudet emphasized that religious instruction by parents "*Can never be adequately supplied in any other way*"; that Sabbath schools were dangerous in their tendency to delude parents into neglecting their duties in this area; that continual reference to a child's duties to God must be worked into academic instruction during a child's entire schooling; that teachers must be screened not only for morality but also for true piety; that the authority of parents and teachers must be subordinate to the authority of God; and that the child must be "brought into a state of uniform subordination and obedience." The preface is a good example of Gallaudet's deployment of Timothy Dwight's ideas, his paranoid style, and his diction, as we read of the forces of "Infidelity and Atheism" making plans, delivering lectures, and publishing books to spread "the contamination of this deadly poison," dissolve marriage, break up the family circle, and so forth. We begin to see here why Gallaudet did not send his children outside the home to attend school. Like Dwight before him, he regarded it as the father's duty to exert total control of his children's very thoughts.[3]

Gallaudet surely would not have permitted little Sophie to attend a circus in 1835 if he had been in town. Since he was out west at the time on a scheme to thwart the Roman Catholic Church from taking over Missouri (more on this to follow), Sophie got to see leopards, lions, tigers, hyenas, an ostrich, parrots and macaws, a polar bear, camel, "rhinocerous," zebra, gnu, buffalo, and two elephants, as she enthusiastically told her Uncle Nelson Fowler. Gallaudet wasn't always a killjoy, however. When other leading citizens promoted "the cause of moral reform among the youth of our city," Gallaudet thought they were too hard on innocent amusements and gave an address to that effect.[4]

This address was expanded into a book that was planned as the first in a series, *The Every-Day Christian,* but proved to be the only installment. It opens with "General Principles" stating Gallaudet's Panglossian view of the material world in which a person's duties are a part of "the vast moral machinery" wielded by God for his own ends. Temperance is defined as abstention not only from inebriating drink but also from "luxurious dainties" and "the use of a vile and filthy weed." On "the family state," which is the main topic of this volume, Gallaudet elaborates on his notions that the "political order rests for its support on the *moral order,*" which can be learned only in childhood within the family environment. Again channeling Dwight, Gallaudet declares that morality is learned only from the father, who must be clear that it is "*his right* to govern, and *the duty* of the rest to obey." To this end, the father has a duty to spend time with his family. As for the mother, "the very idea" that she would leave the house or at any moment give less that her very best effort "is revolting." Families should be together every evening, studying "arithmetic, geography, and history," or examining "tasteful and improving prints." Children should not leave the home at all in the evening unless accompanied by their parents; volunteer organizations should excuse fathers from evening meetings. Young men away from home working as apprentices or clerks should be lodged in the homes of their employers and treated like family, but where this is not possible, "municipal regulations" might be needed.[5]

Gallaudet had more to say on the "family state" two years later in *The American Annals of Education.* Here he rephrased his argument that good citizenship is not the result of laws and fear of punishment for breaking them but rather the habits developed in a childhood spent in the bosom of a godly family. Habits like subordination to parents and teachers, industrious employment, observance of the Sabbath, and the like produce "*self control under the influence of an enlightened conscience*" and "firm [support] of a *rightful civil government.*"[6]

Gallaudet returned to the matter of apprentices in *Starting in Life,* which seems not to have been published until after his death. This book addresses the young man who has left home to work, rather than the paterfamilias who employs him, and advises plenty of reading (but no "trashy tales"), a careful choice of companions, resistance to peer pressure, determination to do one's best, cheerful obedience, honesty, temperance, Sabbath observance, and so forth. A supplement entitled "Going Apprentice," said to have been taken from one of Gallaudet's letters, more specifically describes how to establish one's character as steady, faithful, and moral on the very first day on the job and warns young men never to enjoy any jokes about religion or to countenance any profanation of the Sabbath merely to avoid sneers. All good advice, but it is couched in the same sort of unctuous patronizing that spoiled his *Common Schools, Common Blessings:* "Perhaps your lot has been cast among that class which comprises most of our Sunday-school teachers, and which is known as 'the WORKING class': therefore, for you to live you must work, and we do not suppose that you wish to live without [working]. If you do, as it is a wish not likely to be realized, the sooner you give it up the better."

This from a man who did his best to stay as unemployed as possible. As his friend William A. Alcott put it, Gallaudet turned down paid work and "contrived, by means of the sales of the books which he had written to keep his head above water. He sometime preached, but it was, in general, for the merest pittance." But then, Gallaudet did not regard himself as a member of "the WORKING class" and would never have dreamed that his advice might have applied to himself. It's interesting that he explicitly classified teachers here as members of the working class, shedding some light on why he argued, a few years previous, for a release for classroom teaching and the perquisites and respect granted the president of Yale College.[7]

The lyceum movement, which was conceived as continuing education for the general (male) public, proved to be a good outlet for Gallaudet's ideas on the family. The Goodrich Association, established in Hartford in February 1832, was a forum for lectures by its membership. Named for Gallaudet's erstwhile law mentor Chauncey Goodrich and aimed at moral and intellectual but nonsectarian improvement, the organization featured Gallaudet as one of its earliest speakers and Lewis Weld as a founding vice president. Gallaudet's Goodrich lecture "On the Principle of Association, as Giving Dignity to the Christian Character" was published in a collection of three Goodrich lectures, the other two by Joel Hawes and Horace Hooker. "On the Principle of Association" begins with some philosophical window dressing about the mental associations of ideas and emotions but soon gives this up to proceed in pure sermon style, quoting from 1 Corinthians 15 and from the poets William Cowper and James Beattie (who made a name for himself among evangelicals by his supposed refutation of Hume), to demonstrate that Christian faith alone "sheds a new and cheering light upon the tomb, and robs death of its sting, and the grave of its victory." Descriptions of nature by Virgil or Byron, he continues, cannot compare "with those of the Word of the God of Nature." A commonplace activity like eating takes on a "richer zest" in the knowledge that the body is "the dwelling place of the immortal soul," and the endearments of the family circle are enriched by the assurance that "the tenderest sympathies, and purest love . . . stretch into eternity." The lecture is baggy, its structure uncertain, as though he were not sure who his audience would be and what they would expect.[8]

Gallaudet was also active in the American Lyceum Association, which would later become the American School Society. In 1838 he served as president pro tem in the absence of "General Terry" at a meeting that featured a letter from William C. Woodbridge on two "singular Sicilian arithmeticians." The lyceum movement was an upper-class endeavor; for the working class, there were mechanics' societies. Joel Hawes sponsored a course of lectures, including one by Gallaudet for the Hartford Mechanics Society in 1829. The society had a library of seven hundred volumes and $1,000 to buy more. What would seem to be a wasteful duplication of efforts in these class-segregated societies was dictated by Hartford's unbreachable caste system.[9]

Gallaudet substituted at the Asylum from time to time but stayed unaccountably silent as controversy over sign language instruction developed among the self-styled experts who were shaping and controlling the many new of deaf schools around the country. The one exception to this silence was a private letter he wrote to Horace Mann with regard to Mann's *Seventh Annual Report,* the same report that had kicked up such a fuss among the Boston schoolmasters about whole-word reading instruction. Mann and his friend Samuel Gridley Howe had taken a dual honeymoon tour of Dutch and Prussian schools, the latter especially enjoying a buzz among New England educators. No one among the two couples spoke Dutch or German, and the two men were easily tricked at the deaf schools they visited. Mann fell for the assertion that the deaf could be taught to speak and understand speech so reliably that they could be restored to society "substantially in all cases." "I have had abundant proof," he claimed: "though an entire stranger, and speaking a foreign language, I have been able to hold some slight conversation with deaf and dumb pupils."[10]

The Boston schoolmasters who objected to Mann's support for whole-word reading made space in their first complaint to explain that his claim regarding oral training was unfounded. Mann, they averred, was "laboring under the disadvantages of having no practical acquaintance with deaf mute instruction, and, perhaps, not even acquainted with the history and extensive literature of the science." The American Asylum also responded, by sending Principal Weld to tour Swiss and German schools accompanied by two professors from the Paris school for the deaf. Weld and his colleagues correctly observed that the illusion of uniform success in the oral schools was created by expelling most of the pupils "on the score of their being unable to speak." The Asylum wisely decided to introduce "articulation" only for hard-of-hearing and late-deafened pupils, these being surely the only successes in the Prussian schools.[11]

Gallaudet's letter to Mann, written about a week after Weld's departure for Europe, is couched in mild language but begins by telling Mann that he doesn't know what he's talking about. Education, Gallaudet lectures Mann, includes the pupils'

> intellectual and moral training; their government, by moral influence; the imparting to them of moral religious, and other knowledge; their participating, understandingly, in the social and public devotional exer-

cises of the Institution; the furnishing of their minds with the ideas, the facts, and that amount of knowledge, which are necessary to prepare them to understand a vast number of the *words* which must be taught them; their becoming acquainted with our social and civil institutions; with arithmetic, grammar, geography, and history; with the history, simple doctrines, and the precepts of the Bible; with their duties to God, to their fellow-men, and themselves; and their acquiring a trade, or some means of gaining a livelihood; and especially their being taught to *write* the English language correctly, and to *read books intelligently.*

To teach all this, the instructor must use a language known to the pupil. After citing "Degeraldo" (presumably Dalgarno) and Dugald Stewart, he signed off with an invitation to visit Hartford. It does not seem to have occurred to Gallaudet what Mann's real motivation was, but a former pupil named William Willard nailed it in a letter to his old teacher that summer: "Do you not think that the extravagant conclusions of advocates of exclusive oral instruction are . . . gotten up as an argument to withdraw a portion of the patronage from the existing institutions (the American Asylum in particular) and set up other enterprises the kind for local or individual effect and aggrandizement?"[12]

Gallaudet's private letter to Mann was published only after his death. But in 1847, he finally broke his public silence with an essay, "On the Natural Language of Signs," published in the maiden number of *American Annals of the Deaf and Dumb.* It opens with a picture of a deaf toddler inventing a sign language and teaching it to his parents and siblings. We can imagine how shocking this picture would have been to the reading public of the day, and that is perhaps why Gallaudet had it published in a professional journal for teachers of the deaf who knew full well that they had to learn the language from their pupils. It's a lovely picture: "The wind has been kindly tempered to the shorn lamb," was how he described the gift of signing. This is followed by an even more surprising discussion of the sign language in use among Plains Indians, as described in an 1822 report of a scientific expedition dispatched by Secretary of War John C. Calhoun. Gallaudet studied this report carefully and chose judicious examples from Plains signs that are quite similar to signs used at the Asylum.[13]

The essay continues in the next issue of the *Annals* with more surprises, as Gallaudet criticizes the "frigid, monotonous attitude, and quiescent limbs" of New England's public speakers and the restraint that everyone in the region imposes on their feelings "as if we were too fearful, or too cautious, to look, move and act as we think and feel." Attempts to stop deaf children from signing are cruel, he says here, for that deprives them of intellectual and moral development: "I would as soon think of tying the wings of the young lark that is making its first aspiring essays to fly upward and soar in the ethereal expanse." Much of the remainder of the essay puts into play recycled ideas about the need for language to convey divine revelation and about the material basis of all language and the suitability of a natural language for addressing the heart, but he ends with some of the truest remarks ever made about sign language and the hearing people who think they want to work in the Deaf community:

> For the language of natural signs is not to be learned from books. It cannot be delineated in pictures or printed on paper. It must be learned, in a great degree, from the living, looking, acting model. Some of the finest models for such a purpose are found among the originators of this language, the deaf and dumb. The peculiarities of their mind and character, and the genius of that singularly beautiful and impressive language which nature has taught them, should be the constant study of those whose beneficent calling it is to elevate them in the scale of intellectual, social and moral existence; to fit them for usefulness and respectability in this life and for happiness in that which is to come.[14]

In contrast, an *Annals* essay he wrote in 1849 is little more than descriptions of sign-mime games, in which well-known stories — Noah's ark, the sacrifice of Isaac, Washington crossing the bridge at Trenton — were enacted by facial expressions alone. One such story involves a visit to the Asylum by the artist John Trumbull during which Gallaudet portrayed, with his face alone, a scene from Roman history, presumably flabbergasting this celebrated painter of historical narratives. There is also a description of an alphabet game played with only facial expression: *A* is indicated with an expression of awe, *B* with an expression of boldness, *C* with curiosity, and so on. It's dismaying today to see how easily professional arguments for the efficacy of sign language education could slip into tales about parlor games.[15]

A now unknown number of Gallaudet's essays appeared in Abigail Goodrich Whittlesey's *Mother's Magazine,* many issues of which are no longer extant — it would be another century or more before anyone thought of archiving women's magazines. An essay "On Family Devotions" explains that *"tediousness ought to be avoided"* and reminds mothers how "irksome" it would be to attend to devotional exercises "if the thought or the language were above our comprehension." One wonders, reading this, if Gallaudet was thinking of his wife's tedium during the morning and afternoon services at the Center Church. A series of essays on "Domestic Education at the Table" instructs the mother to bring her child to the table in a high chair at ten to fifteen months of age, and if he breaks a cup, to tell him "that he must be more careful in the future." It may be inconvenient, Gallaudet wrote, but God designed the "desire for food . . . to promote the most important ends" of bringing the family together for the cultivation of "the habits of punctuality, order, and neatness; subordination to parental authority; temperance, moderation, and self-control; the kindly and generous feelings; the elements of good breeding; polite manners; the cheerful and social affections; the talent of agreeable and instructive conversations; the bonds of family attachment; the love of home and the sentiments of a devout gratitude."[16]

GALLAUDET HAD BEGUN to make heavy investments in various reform societies while he was at the Asylum, and indeed the Asylum itself was a reform society, one that aimed at getting deaf people into heaven. The professed purposes of these societies, as well as the usually unstated motivations of the individuals who joined them, are open to debate. In the mid-twentieth century, historians' emphasis was on the reformers' desire to control their social inferiors, especially, in Connecticut, after the disestablishment of the Congregational Church, and it's undeniable that some reformers were indeed motivated by what they saw as the incapacity of the poor to control themselves. This is why many reform societies seem, today, more like organized bullying with their emphasis on scolding the disadvantaged with "Thou shalt not." On the other hand, it's true to say that many reformers were genuinely motivated by Millennial hopes — which just happened to coincide with getting working-class behaviors into line with Calvinist ideas of order. Then, too, there were remnants of the post-Revolutionary hopes for an informed and self-reliant citizenry and for the reduction of "sectionalism," and there were evangelical hopes for spiritual awakening and the conviction among the Calvinist Elect that it was their duty to provide for others the means of receiving divine grace as they had. Gallaudet would have been motivated by all these hopes and fears.[17]

There were detractors of the reform movement, of course, just as there had been detractors of Timothy Dwight's Yale. Some contemporaries objected that the reform societies gave too much power to the leaders; some thought that joining a society meant substituting another's conscience for one's own; some believed that the duty to press reform on others was trumped by the beneficiary's liberty to do as he liked. In 1833, residents of a hamlet in the Hudson Valley condemned reform societies on the grounds that they tended "to establish chains of communication from one to another and ramifications, concentrations, auxiliaries and focuses of power [to] obtain an influence of dangerous tendency [and] a lust for power." All true, but none of it made a dent in the resolve of Gallaudet and his network of Hartford colleagues busily engaged in directing the various societies and auxiliaries.[18]

The American Bible Society had been founded in 1813 and the Hartford Auxiliary Bible Society in 1816. Gallaudet was the auxiliary's president during its three years of existence. The society's purpose was to put a Bible in every household, as "a guard over property and life," as well as to prevent poverty, which, the society supposed, was caused solely by "ignorance, vicious indulgences, or indolence."[19] The national society could produce a Bible for 62.5¢ by adopting the new technologies of stereotyping and power presses; the auxiliaries were formed to distribute them. The Hartford Auxiliary, however, proved strangely unable to locate poor people who didn't already have a Bible, as President Gallaudet reported in 1818. We are reminded of the bemused Hume saying that Scotland was a land of one and a half million people and three million Bibles.[20]

The Connecticut Peace Society was also short lived. The international Peace Society was founded in London in 1816: Gallaudet had been distributing its pamphlets from the beginning, and his father was an official retailer of the New York Peace Society's tracts in his Christian bookstore. Gallaudet served as the corresponding secretary of the American Peace Society for some time during the 1830s and founded a Connecticut branch in 1832. In both organizations, he focused on the enlistment of the clergy in the cause of promoting arbitration, rather than war, to settle international disputes. At the 1835 meeting of the Connecticut society, Gallaudet gave an address, and so did William Ellsworth, a law professor at Trinity College (and later governor of the state) who blamed the teaching of "heathen classics" for current wars in Europe and on the English poetry and art that pay tribute "to the butchers of our race." By 1839, Gallaudet's name disappeared from published reports, but whether he became disillusioned or just overextended is not known.[21]

Missionary societies had been the first volunteer reform associations to appear in Connecticut. The Connecticut Mission Society journal, the *Connecticut Evangelical Magazine,* began publication in 1800 with fifteen editors, including James Cogswell, the doctor's father; Jeremiah Day of Yale; the Rev. Levi Hart, a proto-abolitionist minister in Preston, Connecticut; and the Reverends Nathan Strong of the Center Church and Abel Flint of the South Church of Hartford. A national society, the American Board of Commissioners for Foreign Missions (ABCFM), was established in 1810, and in 1817 it started a school for "heathen youth" in Cornwall, in Connecticut's northwest corner. Gallaudet's involvement in mission efforts seems to have commenced in 1819 with a visit to this school, when he was said to have remarked that "it was more interesting . . . than a hundred college commencements." As he later related to a British correspondent,

> I gathered round me one evening, a dozen of the pupils, among whom were individuals of three different tribes of our American Indians, some Owhyeans [Hawaiians], and Otaheitans [Tahitians], and one Malay. I talked to them by mere signs. I was understood on all common subjects. I even succeeded in making them comprehend some questions which I proposed to them about a future state, and their souls and the Supreme Being. I ascertained the correct meaning of many of the words in the Owyhean language, by signs merely. Not long after, one of the their number, Thomas Hoopoo, who has since gone to the Sandwich Islands as a missionary, visited our asylum. He conversed with our pupils by signs, a full hour, and was well understood.

His conclusion was that a missionary who knew sign language would "have a medium of intercourse with them, *almost at once.*"[22]

The visit from Thomas Hoopoo was not followed by any serious interest among Americans preparing to be missionaries, however. But at least one of them regretted that he didn't take advantage of Gallaudet's offer: Hiram Bingham, writing in 1821 from the Sandwich Islands, where he was laboring with Thomas Hoopoo, deplored the fact that he "had only begun to learn the A.B.C. of that language" before he left and was therefore "exceedingly limited in my address," as indeed he must have been if he imagined that sign language was learned by the alphabet — but perhaps he is speaking figuratively here.[23]

Two years previous, as Bingham was setting out for the Sandwich Islands, Gallaudet had performed his wedding of a young lady who was willing to accompany him — the ABCFM required its missionaries to be married. Gallaudet's sermon on that occasion asserted his belief that while the missionary cause was "to *save souls,*" missions also were "the most powerful instrument of civilization and happiness in this life." We know how that worked out in the South Pacific, but few in the early nineteenth century recognized that the missionaries were in fact corrupting, not converting, the residents. In the 1830s and 1840s, Margaret Fuller was a rare observer who recognized the missionaries' ignorance and scorn for indigenous cultures; Herman Melville was another. But in 1821, Gallaudet didn't question Bingham's description of Hawaii as "the domain of Satan" or his self-congratulatory tone in reporting that he had brought the island nation to "a most interesting crisis."[24]

Gallaudet had asked Bingham to be on the lookout for "any deaf and dumb persons, to observe their signs, and tell [him] how far they correspond with [his]," so Bingham duly reported at some length on his interactions with a deaf Hawaiian. This man had brought Bingham firewood, stipulated how it was to be divided among the missionaries, and later offered to sell him a hog of a certain size and shape. "I was much amused by the interesting but speechless stranger," Bingham said. This very long letter goes on, somewhat surprisingly, to urge Gallaudet to leave the Asylum to preach in Hawaii, saying that he "could probably do more in 5 years than all the rest of us both in gaining a knowledge of the language and in preaching to the rulers of the people, and thus beyond calculation facilitate the progress of learning, of civilization and christianity in this land, and on your return you would doubtless be better qualified to aid foreign missionaries . . . and who can tell how much you might thus do to hasten the approaching millennium."

Bingham was hoping that "the king and some of the most important chiefs, who many never take the trouble to learn to <u>speak</u> the English Language, might be taught to read it, and write it, and transact their business with Americans, without an interpreter, and thus have access to English literature, and of course to science, which may otherwise be forever beyond their reach." To what extent Gallaudet understood how deluded Bingham was in his plan to teach the king to read is not clear. He certainly never seriously considered the job, but he did continue to press his idea of sign language for missionaries.

"The Language of Signs Auxiliary to the Christian Missionary," the essay that he had been contemplating in his 1820 letter to a British correspondent, finally appeared in the *Christian Observer* in 1826, as the third and final essay in a series on Principles of Language. In these essays, Gallaudet asserted the arbitrary nature of human languages, both spoken and in written form. Neither the sounds nor the graphic characters have any intrinsic meaning, he explained; they can convey meaning only when meanings are assigned to them and agreed to by other speakers of the language. (Gallaudet is implicitly contrasting spoken and written languages with signed languages, which he believed were purely iconic, like pictures.)

Readers interested in Gallaudet's theories of language may recognize that he is assuming as definitive the work of the English philosophers he read at Yale: Thomas Hobbes and John Locke. These men saw language as a simple encoding system for the material and mental worlds: first you see an object or feel an emotion, then you simply give it an arbitrary name. Language thus unproblematically designates objects and thought processes that have independent prior existence. German thinkers such as Wilhelm von Humboldt and Johann Gottfried Herder had already exploded these reductive notions by pointing out that language was a rule-governed system, not just a collection of words, and that many words in our lexicons were co-emergent with the ideas they seem to designate — in a sense, words can constitute ideas rather than designate them. However, their work was just beginning to be available in English, and Gallaudet's intellectual curiosity was so circumscribed that we can scarcely imagine him checking into what Herder and Humboldt were writing even if he had access to translations.[25]

So he plugged away with the reassuringly uncomplicated assumption that language designates aspects of independently existing reality, and that was all there was to it. When he considered words that designated mental processes, he therefore sought to locate some kind of material reality for the thought process in question, and he did, in the distinctive facial expression and posture that designate each mental process in the natural language of the body. He expanded this notion a few years later in three essays on the "Language of Infancy" in the *American Annals of Education:* "Long before oral language is used, the mother and the child have *a symbolical language of the countenance and tones of voice.*" Mothers, he thought, had a natural talent for letting their faces "exhibit the *internal workings of the soul.*" Without this language of infancy, he believed, "*oral language* would be of very difficult attainment, if it could be acquired at all." And in an 1838 essay for the *Mother's Magazine,* he argued that "the Spirit of God" made use of the mother's face "among other *means of grace,* to renew and save the soul."[26]

Gallaudet's recognition of the arbitrary nature of phonemes is an accepted principle of modern linguistics, as are his remarks on the importance of a caretaker's facial expression for proper language development in an infant. But he was on shakier ground with regard to the materiality of all our ideas. His notion "*that the elements of the meaning of all language must be found either in the actual presence of objects, or in their expression by symbolical signs*" was belabored at greater length in an 1830 article on the "Philosophy of Language" in the *American Annals of Education,* in which he asserted that "it is a great mistake, to suppose, that language . . . *ever conveys any new simple ideas to the mind.*" Elsewhere, his total disregard for grammar causes him to make preposterous assertions; for example, that a child who knew the meanings of *I, go,* and *door* would yet find the statement *I go to the door* "unintelligible . . . unless accompanied with the action itself of going to the door." Particularly dated in this essay is his praise for Charles Bell's *Essays on the Anatomy and Philosophy of Expression,* which argued that "*an extensive apparatus of muscles and nerves*" connected with the heart "are, also *the organs of expression,* and necessary to the development of emotions." Bell's essay provided the gruesome details of experiments he made on animals by cutting different facial nerves and observing the resultant impairments.[27]

Returning to "The Language of Signs Auxiliary to the Christian Missionary," which builds on these fallacious assumptions, we find Gallaudet's views of the languages spoken by preliterate peoples breathtakingly patronizing, as when he writes of "their own barren language" and of "the propensity of all rude nations to use signs and hieroglyphic symbols in their intercourse with each other, and in the preservations of their simple historical annals." In a newspaper account of Thomas Hoopoo, Gallaudet went on record asserting that "savages, whose language is very poor and imperfect, make up its deficiency in signs." Language chauvinism was common in Gallaudet's day, as was the assumption that sign language was always and necessarily iconic and transparent. The sign language he knew was more iconic than ASL is today, but even Bingham, who shared Gallaudet's views on the inadequacy

of the languages of preliterate peoples, knew that the sign language used at
the Asylum comprised a great many "abbreviations," as Bingham phrased
it — shifts away from the iconic toward the arbitrary.[28]

Another kind of missionary work that attracted Gallaudet's interest was
with the population of local jails and prisons. In 1829, he paid $2 for a year's
membership in Louis Dwight's Prison Discipline Society (PDS) but was
never active, though his name appeared as an honorary vice president from
1834 until some years after his death. The Prison Discipline Society aimed to
meliorate the commonly horrific conditions under which debtors, drifters,
trespassers, "lunatics," and other public nuisances were incarcerated — fel-
ons were hanged outright — and to make them pay for themselves. The
grossly disproportionate imprisonment of African Americans led the society to conclude not that racism was widespread in law enforcement or that
the unemployed poor were filching food, but rather that if black children
could not be taught to keep themselves out of trouble as adults, then they
would have to be deported.[29]

In the meantime, it was essential to urge temperance, Sunday schools,
prison chaplains, safe and healthful ventilation, and separate asylums for
the "idiotic" and "insane," and to keep inmates from communicating with
one another by giving them private cells. This last in effect meant solitary
confinement — it was not until 1843 that the PDS realized that solitary
confinement was causing mental breakdowns. A group of Hartford men
independently scheduled a series of lectures against imprisonment for debt,
held at the Rev. Hawes' chambers in 1832. Speakers in this series included
Gallaudet, Hawes, Asylum instructors Weld and Brinsmade, and the psy-
chiatrist Eli Todd from the Hartford Retreat for the Insane.[30]

In December 1837, Gallaudet began to conduct church services at the
Hartford County Jail every Sunday morning at nine o'clock. The jail had
moved to a new building in that year, but it had no authorization to spend
any of its budget on "moral and religious instruction," so Gallaudet worked
without compensation. He urged the need for daily prayer and Bible classes,
but there were no other volunteers and Gallaudet could donate only his
Sunday mornings. He continued in this volunteer service until 1844, when
he was "reluctantly obliged to discontinue on account of a chronic affection
of my throat and lungs," he reported to an Andover classmate.[31]

The American Sunday School Union was founded in 1817 and was overseen by, among others, Francis Scott Key and Bushrod Washington, two

men who also played large roles in the American Colonization Society, discussed in the next chapter. The Union was a nondenominational society that aimed to establish Sunday schools in underserved areas but also maintained a large presence in religious publishing—in 1830, Gallaudet began work on his three volumes of Bible stories for children for the Union.

The American Tract Society was founded as the New England Religious Tract Society in 1814 by Andover professors seeking to halt the spread of Unitarian ideas, and it remained in Andover until 1827. Gallaudet and Joel Hawes had both been students there when the society was established; Hawes was a founding member, Gallaudet was not. In 1816, the Hartford Evangelical Tract Society was founded by men then engaged in the establishment of the Asylum: Daniel Wadsworth, Henry Hudson, Daniel Buck, Seth Terry, Mason Fitch Cogswell, and Nathan Strong. Gallaudet joined the Tract Society in 1820 and wrote an essay for its *Fourth Report* on how God works through seemingly insignificant things (like tracts) to effect his Providence.[32] By 1832 he was helping to prepare the annual reports, and by 1833 had been elected president, an office he would continue to fill into the 1840s.

The Tract Society's stated purpose was to publish and distribute nondenominational religious literature, but in practice its tracts heavily favored the social status quo: as Gardiner Spring, writing on behalf of the society, said in 1850, the rich had a great deal of social influence because they deserved it; in the words of a detractor, the English radical William Cobbett, the society "would, if they could, make the labourer content with half starvation." The Tract Society's publications show a strong tendency to blame slaves for their plight by calling them, as the anonymous tract *The Children's Friend* did, "a very ignorant and miserable race of men in their own country; very indolent, and very wicked," which is "why the colored people in Africa let the white people come and steal them."[33] All of Gallaudet's religious books for children, excepting the three volumes of Bible stories he adapted for the Sunday School Union, were published or reprinted by the American Tract Society, and although none of his books contained racist notions of the sort articulated in the anonymous *Children's Friend,* they all presented the present social order with rich white men at the pinnacle, as God designed.

Temperance was a reform movement that generated many independent societies to address the behavioral aberration of public drunkenness. Cider was the most widely imbibed alcoholic drink, but in 1830, Americans also drank five *gallons* of distilled spirits per capita every year, mostly in the form of rum. Whereas in the eighteenth century, that Golden Age for New England Federalists, spirits had been the exclusive preserve of the gentry, now cheap rum and a corn whiskey glut caused by agricultural surplus were producing widespread drunkenness among the working class.

It was the new identification of intemperance with the lower classes that created the temperance movement among the elite. In fact, this movement was also begun at Andover, by Gallaudet's professors Stuart, Woods, and Porter, while Gallaudet was a student there. Over the next decade, temperance was picked up by the influential Boston paper the *Panoplist* (which published Gallaudet's valedictory address) and the Tract Society, which published a pamphlet widely used by the clergy for sermons on the topic. Temperance soon came to be seen as an outward sign of salvation, as well as a means of getting rich — drinking squandered capital but sobriety increased production, as Horace Mann never tired of pointing out. Jeremiah Day, Gallaudet's friend who succeeded Dwight as Yale president, was president of the state temperance society, and Asylum director Seth Terry sat on the executive committee. Gallaudet, his father P. W., and his brother Edward were all vociferous abstainers. Gallaudet himself believed in banning liquor throughout Connecticut by state law. Hartford also had three chapters of the working-class Washington Temperance Society by 1841 — one was for women and one for youths — which were not religious at all but rather focused on individual alcoholics. The elite were embarrassed by working-class men speaking in public and by the lack of prayer at their meetings and turned on them, accusing them of irreligion.[34]

The temperance movement's chief alliance, odd as it seems today, was with the anti-abolition wing of the antislavery movement. Lyman Beecher made the analogy specific in 1827:

> We have heard of the horrors of the middle passage — the transportation
> of slaves — the chains — the darkness — the stench — the mortality and
> living madness of woe — and it is dreadful. But bring together the victims
> of intemperance, and crowd them into one vast lazar-house and sights
> of woe quite as appalling would meet your eyes. Yes, in this nation there
> is a middle passage of slavery, and darkness, and chains, and disease, and
> death. But it is a middle passage, not from Africa to America, but from

time to eternity, and not of slaves whom death will release from suffering, but of those whose sufferings at death do but just begin.[35]

The following year, Heman Humphrey ratcheted it up a notch by claiming that intemperance was worse than slavery not only for the soul but in the here-and-now: "However cruel and debasing and portentous African servitude may be, beyond the Potomac, there exists, even in New-England, a far sorer bondage, from which the slaves of the South are happily free." He compared the number of deaths from each cause: while deaths of kidnapped Africans during the middle passage amounted to three or four thousand a year, with eight to ten thousand additional deaths in the first year of slavery, the number of Americans who die each year from strong drink was thirty-six thousand. Not only that, but every slave has a "clear conscience," while the drunkard "suffers more every day and every night than he would under the lash of the most cruel driver." And unlike slaves, drunkards imperil the Republic when they cast votes and win public office. Frederick Douglass and other abolitionists complained about the analogy between intemperance and slavery, but African Americans' views didn't mean anything to Beecher, Humphrey, and their ilk. Temperance was one cause in which Gallaudet never became personally active, but he supported it in a variety of his writings and he maintained warm personal and professional contacts with Beecher, Humphrey, and others who went on record with these views.[36]

Campaigns against intemperance frequently veered into anti-immigrant, anti-Catholic action, and here Gallaudet did become involved. The downfall of the Papacy was widely thought to be a major step in the coming of the Millennium, and there was at least one society, the Christian Alliance, that aimed to bring this about by establishing schools and newspapers and distributing Bibles, tracts, and an Italian translation of Merle d'Aubigné's *History of the Reformation in Europe.* Lyman Beecher was president of this society; Hartford's Horace Bushnell was on the board, as was Gallaudet's friend Theodore Dwight Jr., a journalist in New York; Leonard Bacon was a featured speaker. But even this group had nativist elements, arguing for its cause not only on Millennial grounds but also as a means to stop immigration from Catholic countries. All they needed, they thought, was money to pay an English-to-Italian translator for the Merle d'Aubigné book and the pope would be toppled.[37]

The nativist element in anti-Catholic rhetoric is usually front and center, as we can see in a series of articles in the *New-York Observer* in 1834,
penned by "Brutus" — Jedidiah Morse's son Samuel. Samuel F. B. Morse's
conspiracy theory, in some respects an update of the Illuminati theory, had
it that Prince Metternich, chancellor of the Austrian Empire and *"greatest
enemy of the human race,"* was carrying on a surreptitious attack on the
United States by means of Jesuit priests, who were, in turn, undermining
the integrity of our elections by getting immigrants to the polls and "invei-
gling our children" into Catholic schools.[38] Lyman Beecher took up the cry,
alleging further that (unnamed) European countries were paying the fares of
paupers to emigrate to the United States, where they filled our prisons and
poorhouses, "quadrupling our taxation" and skewing our election results
with "alien votes." Beecher believed that Catholic schools were funded by
European monarchs and that wealthy Europeans were suspiciously converting their money to dollars and buying land in the United States.[39]

In August 1834, Beecher was in Boston giving sermons to this effect,
where he got the congregation so riled up over irresponsible rumors that a
nun was being held prisoner in Charlestown's Ursuline Convent that they
formed a mob and burned the convent down. The nuns and sixty girls who
were pupils there ran out the back door while city fire engines stood by
and watched the blaze. Thirteen people were arrested, twelve were acquitted, one pardoned, the mother superior blamed, and the whole thing was
chalked up to a snare set by "Popery."[40]

The impetus for the Charlestown riot was unique; the many other anti-
Catholic riots that occurred in these years had to do more with the role of
the King James Bible in public schools. The upper-class Protestants who
had a lock on public schooling regarded this translation as nonsectarian
and made it a part of every child's school day. When Catholic parents complained, they were accused of being tools of a nefarious papist plot. Not all
Protestants felt this way, and in fact many of the pupils at the Charlestown
Ursuline convent were the daughters of Unitarians who found the sisters
far less objectionable than the Congregationalists controlling the public
schools. Still, anti-Catholic hysteria was pervasive, and it spiraled into a
"morbid obsession" with bizarre allegations that Catholics were suppressing
savings banks, imposing costly religious holidays, and supporting priests
whose vows were so outrageous that they could not "with any regard to
decency, be fully stated" — that was Beecher's son Edward, referring to

priestly celibacy. Virulent anti-Catholic works from abroad were published and widely distributed in the United States, including those by writers as disparate as Charlotte Elizabeth Phelan, the deaf teacher of the deaf in Ireland, and John Scudder, a medical missionary in Ceylon. Theodore Dwight Jr. went so far as to urge that state inspectors search Catholic schools for dungeons.[41] Dwight, Beecher, Morse, the Bible Society, the Tract Society, and T. H. Gallaudet — all were motivated by the same morbid obsession with Catholic conspiracy. For the elder Beecher and for Gallaudet, German Catholic immigration to the Great Plains seemed to pose the greatest danger. In 1832, Beecher accepted an offer to head the new Lane Seminary in Cincinnati because he thought it would enable him to save the West from Rome, and sometime in the mid-1830s Gallaudet and another Hartford man, Richard Bigelow, founded a secret society called LUPO.

What we know of LUPO today comes largely from research by the United Church of Christ (UCC), the present-day church into which the Hartford Congregational churches and many other Calvinist faith communities were eventually folded. Edward Miner Gallaudet admitted in his biography that scattered references to LUPO in his father's papers meant nothing to him until an unnamed Hartford woman whose late husband had been a member told him that the acronym stood for "Look Upward, Press Onward." He mentioned eight or ten wealthy merchants of the city as his father's collaborators but suppressed their names. He clearly did not recognize that his father's notations of cash transfers to Bigelow and Seth Terry, some of them carried out by his oldest brother, Thomas, had anything to do with the secret society. UCC sources confirm that LUPO was "carried forward absolutely without attracting public attention," and, as Edward Miner Gallaudet's research confirms, Gallaudet never revealed who was paying him.[42]

E. M. Gallaudet understood correctly that it was LUPO that sent his father west in 1835 "to acquaint himself with the condition and needs of the then great North-west in religious matters." This exploratory trip took Gallaudet from Hartford in January to New Haven, New York, Philadelphia, Harrisburg, Pittsburgh, Wheeling, and Columbus, then into Kentucky and on to Indiana and Missouri, and back to Hartford in June. Along the way, he preached and gave lectures. But at the time, not even Sophia knew the purpose of the trip, telling her brother that "He wished to see the West country, and get information about education." Henry Barnard, who got a letter from Gallaudet from Cincinnati, and William A. Alcott were also led to believe that the trip concerned education, while a Cincinnati newspaper reported that Gallaudet was "a gentleman of fortune, who is travelling through the West for the purpose of viewing the country, studying its resources and history, and the manner and habits of its people." That must have been some fancy expense account LUPO gave Gallaudet if he could pass as a gentleman of fortune.[43]

As we know from other sources, Gallaudet also stopped off in Cincinnati to visit the Beechers. Lyman Beecher, whose anti-Catholic diatribe *Plea for the West* was published that year, was heading the Lane Seminary; Catharine was living with her father and planning a Western Female Institute but was frustrated in her attempts to raise money for it. Gallaudet gave a fund-raising address for her when he was in town, but by this time Cincinnati was so fed up with the abolition activism among the students at Lane Seminary that it wanted nothing further to do with any of the Beechers, even though both Lyman and Catharine, like Gallaudet, were anti-abolitionists.[44]

Gallaudet also gave an address to the Cincinnati Mechanics Institute, where admittance was free and the audience comprised mostly merchants, mechanics, and businessmen — not doctors, lawyers, or clergymen, the city's *Whig and Intelligencer* sniffed. As the newspaper characterized it, Gallaudet's address "proved" the immortality of the soul by experiments on a deaf child. Gallaudet's style was "plain, unaffectedly unassuming . . . correct, chaste, and very significant," as well as "inimitably pathetic," that last being meant as praise. He repeated the lecture on another night to give all those doctors, lawyers, and clergymen a chance to attend.[45]

LUPO is now known to have played an important role in the establishment in the United States of the German Evangelical Church — one of the Calvinist churches that later joined the UCC. Gallaudet's 1835 trip and his subsequent report on conditions in the Midwest resulted in LUPO's decision to bring two graduates of the Basel Missionary Society to the United States the following year. These two Swiss men, Joseph A. Rieger and George Wendelin Wall, arrived in New York at the end of May 1836 and continued to Hartford, where they were "lovingly" received by Gallaudet in June. They spent the summer in Hartford as guests of Bigelow, Seth Terry, and a "Mr. Ely," most likely William Ely, the Asylum's land agent in Alabama who had been selling slaves for the school during the previous decade. "The days spent at Hartford were of utmost importance, for here they were introduced to the religious and social life of America," according to a UCC website. It was in Hartford that Rieger and Wall applied for American citizenship with the help of lawyer Terry and were tutored in English by a Miss Clara Stone. The UCC website elides the anti-Catholic purpose of LUPO, claiming that Congregationalists "were worried about the religious fate of the thousands of German Protestant immigrants arriving in the Mississippi valley," but an earlier piece in an Evangelical German Church magazine reports forthrightly that LUPO's aim was "to provide the destitute German communities in the West with an adequate spiritual ministry which would protect them against the inroads of Roman Cathol-icism," and a 1957 article in the *Sunday School Times* correctly identified LUPO as "a secret society to oppose the influence of the Roman Catholics in the West and Northwest," adding that "one could wish that we had more societies like it today."[46]

What's never explained in these three church publications is why Gal-laudet and his colleague Bigelow turned to the Basel seminary, of all places, for missionaries. The German-speaking immigrants they were worried about were not all Catholic, and in fact most were Lutherans. If the goal was to suppress Catholic demographics, why not simply sponsor German Lutheran missionaries? The short answer is that the LUPO activists did not regard the doctrines of Martin Luther as theologically sound: they were seeking to convert not only the Catholics but also their fellow Protestants, the Lutherans, to their own Calvinist doctrines. The challenge for them was that John Calvin's theology had never made any inroads to speak of in German-language communities; there were therefore no German-speaking Calvinist missionaries out there to employ. So LUPO turned to a seminary in German-speaking Basel that taught the doctrines of yet another theo-logian of the Reformation, Ulrich Zwingli, whose views they regarded as sufficiently close to those of John Calvin.

The Zwinglians Wall and Rieger, supported by LUPO, settled in the wilderness a day's ride south of St. Louis, at what came to be called the Gavois Settlement. In 1838, they built a log church on a hill that they called St. Johannes, which still exists as St. Johns (no apostrophe) Evangelical United Church of Christ on the same spot. Eventually, other churches were established, the German Evangelical Synod of North America formed, the Eden Theological Seminary was founded, and the whole network eventually rolled into the UCC with other Calvinist denominations.[47]

From the perspective of the UCC, Gallaudet's secret society was hugely successful. His role in the success of the German Evangelical Church's success, however, was greater than any of the church historians knew, because he not only raised the money and planned and orchestrated the mission but also served as the straw purchaser of 320 acres of land along the Mississippi just south of what is now the Iowa state line in Lewis County. Bureau of Land Management records show this purchase as having been made on September 1, 1838, and a letter from Henry Leavitt Ellsworth, U.S. patent commissioner, to Gallaudet in October 1844 shows that the land was not regarded as Gallaudet's personal property. Ellsworth, a son of Founding Father Oliver Ellsworth, had been born near Hartford in Windsor, Connecticut, had graduated at Yale in 1810, married a daughter of Yale professor and Gallaudet friend Elizur Goodrich, and served briefly as mayor of Hartford before accepting the position in the Patent Office in Washington in 1835. (His twin brother, William, remained in the state, taught law at Trinity, and served as governor from 1838 to 1842.) So Ellsworth definitely knew Gallaudet and everyone else involved with LUPO very well. In his October 1844 letter to Gallaudet, Ellsworth asks, "Have you done anything now about your land in Missouri — who pays the taxes!" Secret societies, as Al Capone would discover, risk running afoul with the taxman, and Ellsworth, clearly in league with the LUPO activists, wanted to make sure he got the story straight. How the taxes were settled and what use the German Evangelical Synod made of the two tracts of land Gallaudet purchased are yet to be discovered.[48]

NINE

Perhaps few men in our wide-spread country have felt more deeply than Mr. Gallaudet for that long-neglected and trodden-down people, the African race. And if he did not make all the effort his friends sometimes desired and expected in their behalf; and if he did not make it in the particular manner some of them desired, of one thing we may be sure, that no man could be more kind to them, as their wants came under his daily observation, and few, with the same means, have done more for their moral and intellectual improvement.

THIS STATEMENT about Gallaudet by his friend William A. Alcott may give us pause. After all, Gallaudet was proud of his anti-abolition credentials and of his decades of volunteer activism against both abolitionist organizations and black "uplift" efforts, which he regarded as covers for agendas of racial amalgamation, federal overreach, and the violation of states' rights and property rights (of planters). So it's true that he didn't make the efforts his "friends" desired. And it's not a stretch to assume that while Gallaudet believed that deporting black people from the country would solve all the problems introduced by slavery, he was also "kind" to them. It has been observed of Roger Pearson, the anthropologist, academic journal editor, and white nationalist, that he was impeccably courteous to black delivery men at his editorial office. And so it must have been with Gallaudet.[1]

The antislavery North, as historians have been pointing out for decades now, was "largely a myth," and it was never any secret in Hartford that the West Indies trade with slave-labor sugar plantations had made the fortunes of every one of its leading citizens. If Connecticut ships were no longer transporting slaves after importation was outlawed in 1808 — itself a doubtful proposition — they were still carrying New England cod and corn to feed the enslaved workers on Caribbean plantations, and the state's manufactories were not only distilling rum from the slave-grown sugar but also making the tools to operate those plantations, a business opportunity that gained new life when Southern cotton replaced Caribbean sugar as New England's monoculture goldmine. A Hartford company located on Fulton Street sold fertilizer specifically formulated for cotton planters; the Collins Axe Works in Hartford County turned out a quarter of a million axes a year, sold by the crate for clearing land in Alabama and Mississippi for cotton planting; the American Asylum, as we have seen, built its campus and established its endowment by selling the land on which these axes and this fertilizer would be used by enslaved Americans. "From seed to cloth, Northern merchants, shippers, and financial institutions . . . controlled nearly every aspect of cotton production and trade." Abolition would have "jeopardized everything," and everyone in Hartford knew it.[2]

As for Connecticut's own enslaved population, it had in colonial times been larger than in the rest of New England's combined, but by the time the Gallaudets moved to Hartford, the state's gradual emancipation laws had freed all but the elderly, and high levels of out-migration had resulted in but a small free black population, concentrated in New Haven where there was employment. Some white residents actually "forgot" that there ever were slaves in Connecticut. Leonard Bacon, pastor of the First Church of New Haven, which was located on Temple Street in the middle of the Center Green, claimed that "slavery never existed here to any considerable extent, and for years it has been a thing unknown" — this he said at a time when slaves were being sold off the auction block in that Green under his very nose. James Mars, who regarded himself as the last slave sold in Connecticut, was prompted to write an autobiography because so many white state residents had told him "that they did not know that slavery was ever allowed in Connecticut, and some affirm that it never existed in the state." In fairness, the same phenomenon can be observed in Massachusetts: Nathaniel Hawthorne, attending the Williams College commencement in 1838, was surprised to notice "a good many blacks in the crowd" and supposed that they had emigrated from New York. For his part, Gallaudet joined in a statement issued by the Connecticut Colonization Society to the effect that "slavery was never successfully introduced into New-England."[3]

Some white residents did remember slavery but tucked it away into a romanticized past where enslavement was but a kindness to the poor heathen Africans who were too simple to care for themselves. In this view, emancipation had turned the formerly childlike slaves into free men who were "thieves, liars, profane drunkards, Sabbath-breakers, quarrelsome, idle, and prodigal . . . [who] ape those who are above them, or rather people of fashion, in a manner sufficiently ridiculous" — in the words of Yale president Timothy Dwight. Professor Benjamin Silliman had added to his income by leasing out the enslaved children he owned, but when these hard-working young people were emancipated on their twenty-fifth birthdays, he deemed them uneducable, which, if true, was certainly caused by their having spent their childhoods as rented drudges to supplement

Silliman's Yale paycheck. Upon emancipation, it was alleged, the African Americans who had cooked one's dinners, cared for one's children, and attended church with one's family every Sunday became the carriers of a moral contagion that would degrade any white person who had anything at all to do with them.[4]

Denigration of black Americans was everywhere in Gallaudet's day. Peter Parley's geography textbook taught white schoolchildren that Africans "have always been a simple people, and for many centuries it has been the practice of other nations to use them as slaves." Circus clowns performed in blackface, as did T. D. Rice, who, as Jim Crow, was a "sensation in northern theaters in the 1830s." Satirical broadsides exaggerated black people's facial features and dialect to portray their allegedly "ridiculous and pathetic efforts to assume the forms of civic participation." Newspapers and travelers' accounts described African Americans promenading on Sunday evenings dressed in poor taste and taking up civic sidewalk space. In science, it was averred that the so-called facial angle in Africans proved them to be the missing link between white men and orangutans. The 1840 census was said to have shown that Northern (free) blacks had ten times the lunacy and idiocy of Southern (enslaved) blacks. A medical journal article alleged proof that persons of mixed race were sterile, like mules. Phrenology, a pseudo-scientific fad in the 1840s, alleged the smaller cranial capacity of negroes.[5]

Clergy preached that blacks were incapable of comprehending eternal damnation and that God, who elects some individuals for salvation and others for damnation, had elected the entire African race for hell. The contrasting view that African Americans were, in the words of abolitionist William Jay, "our brethren for whom Christ died" was held by surprisingly few churchmen or pious congregants. The English novelist Elizabeth Gaskell satirized such failures by ordinary Christians to grasp Christianity's radical central message when her character Miss Galindo complains about the new parson: "Why he tries to make us all feel pitiful for the black slaves, and leaves little pictures of negroes about, with the question printed below, 'Am I not a man and a brother?' just as if I was to be hail-fellow-well-met with every negro footman." Alas that the United States had no satirists with the skills and the readership that Mrs. Gaskell had in England.[6]

Most white Americans believed that the U.S. Constitution was never intended "for people of every color," and that it actually prohibited abolition. Gallaudet in fact signed a statement asserting that "the National

Government has no control over the subject, for the right of the slave-holder to his property is guaranteed by the very compact on which the National Government rests for its existence." And in addition, it was widely understood that slaves did not even want to be freed, a view Harriet Beecher Stowe satirized in her 1859 novel *The Minister's Wooing:* when one of the characters confidently states, "I am quite sure my servants do not desire liberty, and would not take it, if it were offered," another responds, "Call them in and try it." Harriet Stowe's sister Catharine Beecher, however, much like Gallaudet, straightforwardly blamed abolitionists for giving black Americans the idea that they "ought to be treated as if they were white."[7]

Hartford never had as many black residents as New England's coastal cities. Perhaps 0.5 percent of Hartford's total population was black, compared to, for example, 10 percent of New Haven's. Yet even with this tiny demographic, the city's housing was segregated, as were listings of households in the city directory. Black people departing Hartford by stagecoach found their race marked on the coach's waybill to warn subsequent ticket buyers what sort of company they would have if they bought a ticket. Even Hartford's reform societies were segregated. Gallaudet belonged to the Hartford Co. Temperance Society, while another Congregational minister, James W. C. Pennington, was president of the all-black Connecticut State Temperance and Moral Reform Society. When Joel Hawes of the Center Church held a meeting of Hartford clergy in his home to discuss opposition to slavery, Pennington was not invited, nor was membership in the Connecticut Anti-Slavery Society or the Hartford County Anti-Slavery Society open to him.[8]

According to Craig Steven Wilder, however, Hartford's tiny black community was thriving, with its own clubs, insurance co-ops, cemeteries, and other business, and it certainly had its own schools, taught by such accomplished African Americans as Amos Beman, the Rev. and Mrs. James W. C. Pennington, the daguerreotypist Augustus Washington, and the poetess Miss Ann Plato. In all of Gallaudet's extensive activism for common schools and teacher training, neither these schools nor their teachers are so much as mentioned. When Amos Beman asked him for a letter of reference, Gallaudet wrote two sentences, describing Beman as "unexceptionable" and his own information on Beman as limited to "so far as I am informed."[9]

And, of course, black residents of Hartford, as in other cities of the Northeast, formed their own church — in response to being banished to the so-called nigger pews or black boxes of the churches in which they were members. In New Haven, the Dixwell Ave. Congregational Church was established in 1820 with a white pastor, Simeon Jocelyn, and white residents of Philadelphia had likewise contributed to the city's first black church. In contrast, Hartford's black Congregationalists met unrecognized by the Hartford North Consociation of Congregational ministers, even when they had the white Asylum teacher Horace Brinsmade as their pastor; after 1833 when the congregation had African American pastors, the consociation declined to invite them to its annual meetings. After quitting the Asylum, Gallaudet periodically "supplied the pulpit" of any Congregational church in the area that needed a substitute pastor, and he did so once at the "Colored Congregational" on Talcott Street, but his diary entry deviated from his usual practice of naming the pastor for whom he was substituting: "Off. in the colored church. Talcott S," he tersely wrote. When Pennington preached in a church in London, where he was attending an 1843 Peace Conference, he told the congregation that it was his first time preaching in a white church because no white clergyman dared to invite him to preach in Hartford. This so embarrassed the Hartford clergy when they read about it that Pennington did get a few invitations when he returned from his trip, and he was even elected moderator of the Hartford Central Association of Congregational ministers in 1848, but his name seems never to have passed Gallaudet's lips.[10]

In Hartford as elsewhere in the North, it irked middle-class whites to see their black neighbors taking on the trappings of respectability — the temperance societies, the new brick church, the schools with full-time, year-round teachers, the PhD from a European university that Pennington was granted after Yale denied him the divinity degree he had earned there. Street-corner violence was endemic: black men ventured out at night only if armed and black women only if escorted. A British visitor to Hartford in the 1830s claimed that there was no city in the United States "containing the same amount of population, where the blacks meet with more contumely and unkindness than at this place. . . . To pelt them with stones and cry out nigger! nigger! as they pass, seems to be the pastime of the place." During the 1830s, this kind of casual everyday violence erupted into riots in which white mobs attacked black businesses, churches, and homes, and those of white abolitionists as well. An abolitionist student was clubbed at commencement exercises at Amherst; an abolitionist editor was murdered at his printing press in Alton, Illinois. Dozens of people were killed, most, perhaps, inadvertently in the chaos. Unsurprisingly, Connecticut had the distinction of by far the largest number of riots per capita of any state in the Union.[11]

Exactly how many riots took place in Hartford itself is difficult to determine. In 1830, the Boston abolitionist William Lloyd Garrison lectured at the Talcott Street church in Hartford without inciting a riot. At one point during that visit, Garrison came face to face with Gallaudet, who proudly reported to the American Colonization Society that he had maintained "a perfect silence" — in other words, Gallaudet publicly cut him.[12]

In June 1831, a Hartford resident who signed himself "J. K." wrote to the abolitionist organ the *Liberator* referencing "all the riots in this place." J. K. reported that the "recent occurrence" was caused by the rape of several respectable colored girls by "a number of white profligates": "The prey was taken from the clutches of these seducers" by men of color; the rapists took "much offence, and they were determined to have their revenge." J. K. summed up the situation in Hartford: "They will not marry our colored women, nor be seen with them in the daytime; but at night they are to be found in all the corners and all the lanes of the city — the darkness of night covers all distinctions." A few months later, in October, a mob of white men stormed the Talcott St. church during worship, broke windows, and drove away the congregants, but we know of this riot only because seventy years later a Rev. Wheeler gave a sermon on the occasion of its diamond anniversary. In January 1834, a white mob attacked a man leaving the Talcott St. church, setting off three days of rioting. Over the next two years, church members were attacked at least three times, the worst case occurring in 1835 when a riot that started outside the church led to the vandalizing and looting of black homes and neighborhoods. Most such white mobs appear to have been beneath the notice of Hartford newspapers, but the *Courant* did pick up this one. On the evening of Tuesday, June 9, the paper reported, a mob of white men gathered around the Talcott St. church, first harassing passers-by and then members of the congregation when they left the church. One black man went home, got a gun loaded with shot, and discharged it into the group of whites, seriously wounding one of them. He was arrested, and the mob demolished his house. On the following evening, the mob tore down two buildings in the black neighborhood. According to the *Courant,* the sheriff was present but allegedly unable to prevent the destruction. By the third evening, "special constables" had been sworn in and the riot was over, with no white arrests.[13]

Both J. K. and the Rev. Wheeler were careful to avoid antagonizing the city's ruling class, and so they identified the rioters as "profligates" and "lewd-fellows of the lower sort" (in Wheeler's words), but several historical studies of the rioters tell us today what no one would admit at the time, not even African Americans like J. K. and Wheeler: the rioters were not in fact all working-class "lewd-fellows." Many were lawyers, politicians, bankers, merchants, and shopkeepers. Episcopalians were more prominently represented among the rioters than other religious affiliations, and many rioters were also the same leading citizens active in colonization societies. The majority of white residents did not participate in the race riots, either as rioters or planners, but these evinced "almost total lack of resistance to mobs in their communities." Abraham Lincoln blamed slavery for the riots; nearly everyone else blamed abolitionists — or African Americans. *Miriam Coffin,* an 1834 novel set on Nantucket, actually managed to blame African Americans for a riot *and* to claim that they had never lived on the island![14]

And where was the Rev. Mr. T. H. Gallaudet during all these riots? He was at home in his solidly white neighborhood ignoring the mobs while attending to the important business of sending black Americans out of the community to live in Liberia, where they would be managed by the American Colonization Society. The ACS had been founded in 1816, shortly after Gallaudet's return to Connecticut from Paris; early organizers were all slaveholders who wanted to deport free blacks, whom they regarded as threats to the plantation way of life. Soon, however, the society attracted antislavery evangelicals like Gallaudet, as well as Quakers, who believed, quixotically, that deportation would encourage slaveholders to manumit their slaves. In New Haven, Yale president Jeremiah Day took the leadership; in Hartford, the Corresponding Committee included Asylum director Seth Terry, the Rev. Joel Hawes, Dr. Cogswell, and Henry L. Ellsworth, who would be helping Gallaudet's secret society LUPO with its taxes twenty years later; at Andover, it was Leonard Bacon, who, from his seat as pastor of the First Church of New Haven, would become a strong anti-abolition voice. Gallaudet's early hire Isaac Orr became a general agent of the national society, and his biographer Heman Humphrey, president of Amherst College, helped with fund-raising.[15]

The ACS operated on a "mixture of fascism and philanthropy," muddling Christian ideals with middle-class notions of propriety. It gained adherents by constant reference to free blacks as "insolent and domineering," "useless and pernicious, if not dangerous." "Their fecundity is proverbial," the ACS repeated ad nauseam, and promised to remove from our shores the looming dangers of emancipation and intermarriage. The ACS was seen by the public as an ordinary reform society, like those that advocated temperance, Sunday school, and Bible reading, and its attitude toward free black Americans was regarded as the same as the Temperance Society's toward drunkards: both were a "threat to the order and decorum of society." But, of course, drunkards were to be reformed, not deported, and the refusal of the ACS even to consider the kind of education and uplift that would integrate African Americans into white communities made this a reform society in name only. Garrison satirically supposed that temperance advocates were to transport drunkards out of the country while assuring liquor distilleries that they had no intention of meddling with their business plan.[16]

Gallaudet was not an early member; his involvement in colonization probably did not begin until 1827, with the founding of the Connecticut Colonization Society in Hartford. Founding members included the Rev. Leonard Bacon of New Haven, Asylum director Seth Terry, Prof. Silliman, Lydia Huntley Sigourney (the only woman), and Thomas Hopkins Gallaudet. Gallaudet served as secretary and wrote some of the society's annual reports. At its annual meeting in May 1829, Gallaudet was worried about the society's finances. He presented elaborate plans for county auxiliaries to hold fund-raising drives every year on the Fourth of July, and he gave the address at the July 4th fund-raiser in Hartford that year. Gallaudet also proposed at the May meeting "that the liberated slaves should be bound to pay for their passage, and even their freedom, if necessary, after their arrival in Africa." Bacon and Gallaudet formed a two-man committee to establish a similar society in Massachusetts.[17]

Gallaudet became heavily involved in the national organization in 1828, during the affair of Abd al Rahman Ibrahima ibn Sori. Born in 1762 in Timbo (now in Guinea), this Muslim prince had studied in Timbuktu and was leading his father's army when he was ambushed and sold into slavery, eventually ending up on a Mississippi cotton plantation. There he was recognized decades later, quite incredibly, by an Irish surgeon John Cox, who had known him as a prince in Timbo. Cox's efforts to free him — the planter refused to sell, and by this time there were also a wife and nine children, all enslaved — drew the attention of the newspapers and of Charles Tappan, a Boston merchant and ACS member who arranged to purchase "Prince," or, more correctly, as his biographer tells us, Ibrahima. Tappan's brother Arthur saw a business opportunity, the ACS saw a fund-raising opportunity, and Gallaudet saw a missionary opportunity. Together, they conspired to send the sixty-six-year-old to Liberia.[18]

There was just one hitch in Gallaudet's plan to deploy Ibrahima to evangelize Africa: he was not a Christian at all. Some 20 percent of the Africans captured and sold into slavery in the United States were Muslims, though no white American seemed aware of it — a decade later, the Tappans were shocked to learn that the *Amistad* captives were "Mohammedans," too.[19] In an October 1828 letter to Ralph R. Gurley at ACS headquarters, Gallaudet asked about the prince's son, "who he says is a Baptist minister," and whether it were true that Ibrahima himself had joined a Baptist church. In this same letter, and in a preemptory tone, he instructed Gurley to get all the information about Africa that Prince had and to see to it that it was published.[20] Gallaudet had written to Ibrahima that May, shortly after he and his wife were purchased and liberated, promising an Arabic Bible and enclosing a book — probably, judging from Gallaudet's description of it, Hugo Grotius's 1627 *On the Truth of the Christian Religion,* translated into Arabic for the (British) Church Mission Society. Addressing a man who had been held in slavery by Christians for forty years, Gallaudet wrote,

> Perhaps you have met a few persons who are Christians in heart, and who imitate the example of Jesus Christ. What do you think of them? What do you think of that religion which has removed darkness from their minds, and made their hearts love God and love their fellow-men? Look at such men. Are you not glad to have them for your friends? They are the ones who wish not only to do you good in this world, but to prepare you after death (which oh, my venerable friend, can not be far distant from you and your dear wife), to be happy forever in Heaven."[21]

Ibrahima arrived in Hartford on October 1, 1828, where a fund-raising sermon at the Center Church netted $156. Gallaudet and the prince then proceeded together to fund-raisers around the state before continuing to New York, where Gallaudet joined forces with Arthur Tappan and an Episcopal priest to badger Ibrahima about his religious beliefs. Gallaudet had the feeling — correctly, as it happened — that the prince's protestations of conversion were insincere, made only with a view to securing his fare out of the country. But in his New York addresses on behalf of the prince and the ACS that month, he spoke of a converted man whom God had kept in slavery until that conversion was accomplished: "The finger of God seems to point to great results arising from his return [to Africa]. His life appears like a romance, and would be incredible if the evidence were not undeniable. We see in these events, that God's ways are not as our ways, nor His thought as our thoughts. We see why the prisoner was not to return with his Moorish disposition and his Moorish sword; that Providence continued him here, till grace had softened his heart."[22]

Gallaudet's *Statement with Regard to the Moorish Prince, Abduhl Rahhahman,* published in New York in the same month, suggests what else was contained in the unrecorded full text of the address. Here we learn that Ibrahima's owner "of whom Prince always speaks with great affection and respect, doubted whether his freedom would increase his happiness"; that the slave trade could be stopped only by "commercial intercourse" with the African interior; that "Prince" wished to assist in this effort of "introducing commerce, and civilization, and freedom, and intelligence, and Christianity, in to the heart of Africa." A note appended to the *Statement* avers that Ibrahima had been baptized "a year ago last May," with would mean May 1827, a thing that Gallaudet knew to be either untrue or, if true, invalid — but perhaps that note was added by someone else involved with publication.[23]

After Gallaudet returned to Hartford from his New York excursion with the prince, Arthur Tappan wrote about his plan to raise cash by sending Ibrahima on tour with Gallaudet, who was not only a proven fund-raiser but, as principal of the deaf school, a proven attraction for big audiences. A week later, Gallaudet wrote to Gurley from his son's sickbed, describing a doubtful recovery for six-year-old Thomas before turning to that matter of "vast importance," the prince. Gallaudet again admitted his doubts that Ibrahima was truly a Christian, but he wanted to proceed with Arthur Tappan's fund-raising plans, which now included sending African American youths to Liberia with the prince as commercial agents in the interior. The tone he took with Gurley in this letter and others is remarkable for its brusque imperiousness. Anyone reading these scoldings ("un-business-like mode," "you are all asleep") would think Gallaudet were Gurley's boss.[24]

Ibrahima and his wife were eventually carried off to Liberia in 1829, their children and grandchildren left behind in slavery. Tappan felt sure Ibrahima would die upon arrival — and he did, on July 6, 1829.[25]

Nothing daunted, Gallaudet returned to New York a few months later to address an ACS fund-raising meeting. Gallaudet's importance to the colonization effort can be deduced by the fact that on this occasion he shared the stage with ACS founder Francis Scott Key and a Captain Stockton of the U.S. Navy, which was, in a sense, working for the ACS.[26] If one expected Gallaudet to address the religious benefits of the colony, however, one would be wrong. Requesting the "cordial support of every American patriot, philanthropist, and Christian," Gallaudet plunged headlong into *the delicate and perplexing subject of slavery!*" (italics and exclamation point his), by declaring that antislavery and proslavery sentiments were both just regional prejudices. The ACS removes these regional prejudices, he said, and brings "together Patriots and Christians, from every section of our country, to have their minds enlightened and their best affections kindled." Slavery may never be "entirely removed" from the United States, but the ACS ensures that "rash and imprudent measures" — that is, any form of abolition — are avoided. Speaking as though he believed that Ibrahima were still alive, he referred to commercial advantages of friendly negotiations the prince would conduct. Coffee grows wild in the "woods," he said, and residents of the interior want to buy writing paper, handkerchiefs, and woolen caps, he bizarrely averred. "The negro fights, and sells his prisoner of war as a slave, that he may thus obtain some European article of comfort and luxury. Furnish him with this, and receive in return some one of the productions of his country," he declared, and "the slave trade will cease."[27]

The address is extremely painful to read today. There can be no doubt, however, that Gallaudet believed every word of it. A few years later, he sent one of his house servants, Elizabeth M. Thomson, and her husband to Liberia, and kept in touch with her after she moved from Monrovia to start a school in Cape Palmas, a new settlement founded by the Maryland Colonization Society. As she explained to Gallaudet, the ACS settlement of Monrovia was notoriously insalubrious, and her husband's health was poor; in fact, he presently died, and Mrs. Thomson's letters to Gallaudet became increasingly pitiful. The natives worshipped the devil, she reported, and had other "bad habits." They killed a colonist and his children over a sheep. She couldn't persuade them to observe the Sabbath. She had no financial support from the ACS or other American backers for her school. In 1841, she responded to a letter from Gallaudet asking if she "had ever seen a deaf and dumb person in this country." We don't have any of the letters he sent to her, but judging from her responses, it certainly seems fair to say that his major interests in colonization lay elsewhere than in the well-being of this Hartford woman.[28]

As for Ibrahima, as late as 1848 Gallaudet was working on an article about him and had to write to the ACS for basic information: had he taken his wife, five sons, and grandchildren with him? Or did they follow him? he asks. Clearly, Gallaudet had not troubled himself to remember that all of Ibrahima's children had remained enslaved in Mississippi and had within a few years been dispersed throughout the South in sales made by their owner's heirs. Gurley at the ACS had told him all this in 1828. Gallaudet's major interest, of course, was in learning if the prince had "abjured the Christian religion, and relapsed into Mahomedanism?" We don't know if Gallaudet got any response, or whether he ever realized what a fool's errand he'd been on.[29]

THAT A MAN WITH ACTIVE INTERESTS in public education should not have been interested in the education of African American children in Connecticut may seem perverse. However, it certainly was not uncommon for white men to support public education for poor whites and deportation for blacks. One of the founders of the ACS, Charles Fenton Mercer, for example, regarded common schools as a means to control working-class white Americans; for black Americans, deportation was his answer. The Connecticut Colonization Society asserted that educating a black child was worse than a waste of time: "you have added little or nothing to his happiness — you have unfitted him for the society and sympathies of his degraded kindred, and yet you have not procured for him and cannot procure for him any admission into the society and sympathy of white men." When the Quaker colonizationist Elliott Cresson persistently urged the ACS to support African American education, he was marginalized by the society. Gallaudet's friend Theodore Dwight Jr., who was a journalist in New York, was another naive supporter of black education who got frozen out — by Gallaudet. In 1834, Dwight started a "new Inf[an]t Sunday School of Africans," that is, African Americans, which he believed would "show that African talent and character [were] naturally equal to anybody's." His plan was to publish a book about this school without mentioning that the pupils were black and only later to "produce effect" by announcing that fact. Unfortunately for Dwight's plan, he depended on Gallaudet to arrange for the Sunday School Union to publish his book. That appears not to have happened.[30]

The ACS was prevented by its constitution from any sort of schooling or training of black Americans, so in 1829, realizing that better-educated emigrants were needed in Liberia, some colonizationists formed the African Education Society to meet that need independent of the ACS. The society promised, however, that it would provide more of a boot camp than a school: it would not simply instruct black youths for a few hours a day "and then dismiss them to dissipate, among idle and vicious companions, the slight impression made upon them," but it would take charge of them in "early childhood" and subject them to a program of "constant and untiring inroads on their wrong habits and propensities." Officers and managers included Francis Scott Key, Gerrit Smith, Leonard Bacon, Gallaudet's old Andover classmate Nathan Lord, his old Yale classmate Heman Humphrey, his hire at the Asylum Isaac Orr, and R. R. Gurley — but not Gallaudet. Gallaudet had made efforts two years earlier to enlist support for such a school but, as related by Edward Miner Gallaudet, had found nothing but resistance. One of his associates, James Milnor, told him that to attempt to educate youths who had spent their earlier years in slavery "will very rarely be practicable," and a second, Gerrit Smith (who was not yet the abolitionist he would become) wrote that he would be "very loath to undertake the education of so many irreligious blacks." By 1829, then, Gallaudet had given up on the idea. Oddly, during these very years, the Episcopal Church was running an African Mission School in Hartford, with the same goal as that of the African Education Society: to educate youth to be sent to Africa. Never referenced by Hartford Congregationalists, it met no opposition whatever in the city, thus demonstrating the extent to which Hartford was an assembly of parallel universes delineated not only by race and class but also by church.[31]

The same year that the abortive African Education Society was formed, plans got underway for a "colored academy" or "negro college" in New Haven, to be associated loosely with Yale. Arthur Tappan had bought land and pledged money for buildings, and Simeon Jocelyn, pastor of the Dixwell Avenue church, was on board. So were William Lloyd Garrison and, at the other end of the antislavery spectrum, Leonard Bacon, although Bacon dropped out when Jocelyn pushed to allow students to remain in the United States if they chose to do so. Bacon, and many others, would support only a plan than bound graduates to deportation. Unfortunately for the plan, its announcement appeared in newspapers the same day as news of Nat Turner's rebellion; some papers ran these two stories side by side. Yale professors and respectable residents of New Haven were horrified by the use of the word "college" in conjunction with "negro." The city squelched the project. Tappan and Jocelyn were chided by the *New Haven Religious Intelligencer* for a project that sought to raise black youth to the level of whites and attach them more firmly to their native land, and thus to "counteract and thwart the whole plan of colonization." Catharine Beecher scolded the planners for their unchristian behavior in choosing a location with a large number of Southern students who would be offended, and in making any announcement about it at all, which she regarded as "nois[ing] abroad" the plan. White mobs attacked Arthur Tappan's home, then a black neighborhood, and finally Simeon Jocelyn's home. Almost all reports on New Haven's response to the planned college, both pro and con, agreed that the main reason for stopping the negro college was to protect Yale, specifically Yale's cash cow of Southern alumni donors. Gallaudet said not one word on the planned college, but his silence suggests that his views did not differ much from those of Bacon and other members of his social class and religious circle, or at least they did not differ enough for him to feel obliged to speak out. He was worried about the bad press that such schemes created for the ACS, however, and suggested that Gurley begin a campaign to convince the public that the society had no objection to education but just would not support it.[32]

A second high-profile debacle for African American education in Connecticut occurred a few years later, after Prudence Crandall, a young Quaker woman running a private girls' school in Canterbury some forty miles east of Hartford, admitted a black pupil. When white parents withdrew their daughters, Miss Crandall closed her school and opened a new one exclusively for girls of color. To the horror of Catharine Beecher, she took out newspaper advertisements offering piano and drawing lessons to African American girls. The Congregational church in town closed its doors to her pupils, and the wife of the Episcopal priest threatened her. Canterbury's selectmen determined that "the *establishment or rendezvous,* falsely denominated a school, was designed by its projectors, as the *Theatre,* as the place to promulgate their disgusting doctrines of amalgamation and their pernicious sentiments of subverting the Union," and they appealed to the ACS. In 1833, Connecticut adopted a law stating that no person could set up any kind of school for instructing colored persons who are not inhabitants of Connecticut, nor harbor nor board them — and applied it retroactively. The fine was $100 per offending pupil, and Crandall was regarded as in violation. Although even the ultraconservative *Courant* came out in opposition to the law, the Connecticut Colonization Society issued not one word against it, nor did Gallaudet. Miss Crandall and one of her pupils were arrested, charged, and jailed. In the course of two trials and an appeal, which was held in Hartford, white mobs broke the school's windows and eventually burned it down. A ruling at the second trial that drew on the argument of assistant prosecutor Andrew T. Judson produced the first-ever legal statement that African Americans were not American citizens, which was later cited in the infamous 1857 Dred Scott case. Until the 1833 law was repealed in 1838, every person in Connecticut involved with educating a black child from out of the state was a criminal. And this applied to the directors and employees of the American Asylum.[33]

It comes as a shock to realize that the Asylum — run by a set of blatantly racist directors, overseen by a man who worked to remove African Americans from their native land, situated as it was in America's worst city for harassment of black residents, and during a time when all other schools in the city were rigidly segregated — nevertheless had three African American pupils during the 1820s and early 1830s until the exclusionary law went into effect. The first, Charles Hiller of Nantucket, Massachusetts, enrolled during Gallaudet's tenure, in 1825. (He was born around 1810, which gives the lie to the assertion in the novel *Miriam Coffin* that any blacks on Nantucket had come from the mainland.) How was it possible that the Asylum accepted Hiller as a pupil? We need only look at the bottom line. Cogswell and the directors believed that the school could be made to pay only if it held a monopoly in the northeast — this was the reason for the frantic efforts in 1816–1817 to sabotage the New York school and for all those tours by Gallaudet and George Loring to convince New England state legislatures to sponsor any deaf pupils they chose at the Hartford school. Massachusetts was a valuable resource for the Asylum, and it was the Massachusetts legislature that had chosen Hiller and paid his fees. To decline to accept him would have been to jeopardize what the directors hoped would be a lucrative pupil pipeline from the Boston statehouse. (Why Massachusetts, whose own schools were all segregated, would have paid for a black child to attend the Asylum is another question.) Hiller studied at the Asylum for four years, through 1828. In 1829, Reuben Jones, a Maine resident, was the second pupil of color to be admitted; in 1830, Horace Way of Massachusetts was the third.[34]

No one connected with the school ever mentioned these pupils' color, at least not in extant documents beyond their internal intake papers. They were probably all of mixed race; they may have been seated in the rear of the classroom, fed in the kitchen, and lodged with the servants. The one historian who has looked into the Asylum's black pupils has assumed that they were normally integrated, but the uniform silence of everyone associated with the school means that we simply don't know. All letters home written by pupils were passed through careful censorship by the hearing faculty, and one result of this rule was that no parent of any pupil appears ever to have received a letter mentioning any classmates of color.

By the time Hiller was admitted, the school had moved to its new campus, which was at some little remove from the city where black locals were being pelted with stones as they passed through the streets. There is no way these black or "mulatto" boys could have walked with their classmates three times a day from the old schoolhouse on Prospect Street to take their meals at the City Hotel. Also, Alice Cogswell had already left school by the time of Hiller's arrival — it is inconceivable that her father would have kept her in a classroom with a black boy. Perhaps Hiller's admission was the reason that Alice ended her education when she did. As for the so-called Black Law passed in response to Crandall's school in 1833 and in effect until 1838, Jones ended his studies in 1832, and Way in 1833. No other children of color were admitted until the 1840s, years after the law was rescinded.[35]

It should be sufficiently clear that the Asylum, at least during Gallaudet's tenure, was no happy haven of integration. Because, however, one so frequently finds assertions to the contrary, it's worth pausing a bit to examine such claims. One frequently finds it assumed by historians of the deaf that Lewis Weld, who succeeded Gallaudet as principal in 1830, was a fervid abolitionist just like his better-known brother Theodore, and that it was he who was responsible for admitting black pupils. The first to thus credit Lewis Weld was a contemporary, Edward Strutt Abdy, a British abolitionist and associate of Theodore Dwight Weld who visited Hartford in 1833. Abdy described seeing at the Asylum a "black boy, or rather a mulatto" — this would have been Horace Way — "who had been sent by the State of Massachusetts to the Asylum." Abdy assumed that Way was admitted "probably through the influence of [Lewis Weld] and at the suggestion of his brother."[36]

But there is nothing in the historical record that would support any such assumptions. For one thing, as we have seen in discussion of Gallaudet's tenure as principal, the school was run by the directors, and the principal was just another employee with no authority to set admission policy. For another, Horace Way was patently selected by the state of Massachusetts; his admission was not at the command of the Asylum at all. For yet another, Theodore Weld's letters to his brother Lewis even as late as the year of Abdy's visit make no mention at all of abolition, which suggests that the brothers did not enjoy a shared view of the cause. A letter that Theodore wrote to Lewis in 1833 was about a cholera epidemic and a fellow student who lost his faith as he lay dying.[37]

In 1837, several years after Abdy's grossly mistaken guess about the Weld brothers' agency at the Asylum, Theodore was in Hartford for an abolition meeting. As it happens, Gallaudet reported on that meeting to a colonization associate in Virginia, the planter John H. Cocke. The abolitionists, Gallaudet told Cocke,

> have lately met with a great discomfiture in this city. Mr. Birney, Mr. Weld, and Mr. Tyler, three of their most powerful and active agents were here together, in May, during the session of the Legislature, and made a strenuous effort to get a foot hold. There was one tumultuous meeting, while Mr. B. was endeavoring to deliver a lecture, in which no citizens of any weight of character were concerned, and which I deeply regret, for it is not the way to counteract their efforts with this exception, they were met with nothing but calm and dignified public sentiment, and the <u>official</u> closing of all our city and town rooms, the state house and the churches against them.... It is my decided opinion that they will not make head-way in Connecticut, and that this state will begin the reaction that within a year or two will check their career.

If Theodore Weld were gaining any "foot hold" or making any "head-way" with his brother, the principal of the American Asylum, let alone with Asylum policy, one would suppose that Gallaudet would have noticed that and would not have been crowing to his friend Cocke about the whole city being of one mind, intent on shutting Theodore Weld and his associates out.[38]

On this visit to Hartford, Theodore Weld did meet with his brother, but only to tell Lewis about his upcoming wedding with Angelina Grimké. Lewis "thanked God for blessing his younger brother with love" and told

Theodore that he was rethinking "his 'aristocratic feeling' toward . . . the role of women." Nothing was said about the abolition meeting. It's true that when Theodore Weld and Angelina Grimké were married in Philadelphia the following year, Lewis Weld attended along with African American and white abolitionist guests (who, in some cases, were women's rights activists as well), including William Lloyd Garrison, Abby Kelley, John Greenleaf Whittier, Gerrit Smith, Lewis Tappan, and Henry Stanton (who would marry Gerrit Smith's cousin Elizabeth Cady in 1840). Lewis Weld's presence in this assembly was so strongly desired by the happy couple that Angelina changed the date expressly so that he could attend. None of this demonstrates that Lewis shared his brother's views on abolition. What it does demonstrate is that Lewis did not balk at associating with abolitionists when it was a case of his own brother's wedding. But when all of Hartford was closing its doors on his brother in 1837, he either supported the anti-abolitionist mainstream or, at the least, maintained perfect silence on the matter. Either way, Gallaudet was positive that Lewis Weld's views were no different from those so smugly ascribed to all of Hartford in his letter to his planter friend General Cocke.[39]

Cocke was a fervent evangelical and a leading advocate for temperance, slave evangelization, and colonization. (Slave evangelization, by the way, was a surprisingly controversial subject; Dorothea Dix, for example, thought that enslaved persons didn't need to know the difference between right and wrong and that saving their souls would only make them wretched in life. So Cocke was indeed a liberal on this one point, supporting evangelization.) He was acquainted with Harvey Prindle Peet and Isaac Orr, both at the New York institution at the time, and Gallaudet seems to have entered into correspondence with him in 1828, when Cocke was looking to hire a pious clergyman to tutor his niece. Negotiations continued for months, Gallaudet offering to persuade the mother of a seventeen-year-old girl who looked like a good prospect and declaring that he has not "let a week pass without keeping up a correspondence on the subject." What could have made him so zealous in Cocke's affairs at a time when he was complaining of overwork at the Asylum is not explained. But he arranged for Heman Humphrey to show Cocke around Amherst in December 1829 and for director Ward Woodbridge to send Cocke three pigs and a recipe for succotash, while he himself was keeping Cocke minutely apprised of his negotiations over his Asylum position with the directors. In January

1830, when Gallaudet's retirement was still under negotiation, he wrote to Cocke about a planned high school at Monticello: "Ah! my dear Sir, often have I thought of this very situation for myself, as affording me three or four years of comparative relaxation, in the education of my own children, and the preparation of some books."[40]

Just days after this letter from Gallaudet about taking a job at the planned Monticello high school, Isaac Orr wrote Cocke about the abortive African Education Society. Cocke must have demurred about the possibility of educated black men remaining in America, because a month later Orr assured him that the society would "require pledges" from students that would oblige them to emigrate. Nevertheless, Cocke declined the society's offer of the presidency on the grounds that any push for negro education would hurt the ACS and that any education that might be provided should be undertaken only after the emigrants' arrived in Africa.[41]

In 1834, Cocke made another trip to New England and told Gallaudet about his visit to Boston, where the "good sense of New England will soon put down the mad schemes of a few enthusiasts [i.e., the abolitionists] who are at present disturbing the public mind." In 1837, Gallaudet sent Cocke a copy of an essay he had written on differing views about slavery. In trademark Gallaudet fashion, he called for discussion and reasoning.

> If any movement is ever made for the removal of slavery, it must be made
> by the slave-holding states after a full investigation of the subject, and
> the non-slave-holding states, or individuals residing in them, must not
> expect to bring about such an event, without an opportunity for such an
> investigation, commensurate with the extent and difficulty of the subject.
> They can ask to be heard on it only while exercising a truly benevolent and
> christian spirit, keeping strictly within the bounds of the constitution and
> law in all they say or do.

The essay also called for discussion of the extent to which Northern states and the federal government should compensate slaveholders — not *if* they should compensate slaveholders, but rather to what extent. In 1839, he sent Cocke a recent sermon by Horace Bushnell, pastor of the North Congregational Church in Hartford, that he described in his covering letter as influential in "arresting the program of 'the Anti-slavery Societies.'" He wished that Bushnell took more interest in colonization, but at least he belonged to "the opposers of 'the Anti-slavery Societies' here at the North, of which I am one more decidedly and fully than ever." Notice the scare quotes he uses to set off the "Anti-slavery Societies."[42]

In an 1840 letter, Gallaudet responded to Cocke's plan for a new plantation in Alabama that was intended to assist the colonization effort. This must have been an early iteration of a scheme Cocke detailed in a letter to Gallaudet five years later. The plan would enable a Virginia planter to "remove his slaves to the Cotton Country [and] realize an amount from their labour which in a term of years varying probably from seven to ten would pay the full value of the slaves to their owner and enable him to send them to Liberia." In other words, the Alabama plantation Cocke established was intended to provide a way for slaveholders in Virginia to put their unwanted slaves to hard labor clearing land and chopping and picking cotton, so as to earn for their owners not only their trans-Atlantic fare but also their full market value. They could then be shipped to Liberia at no cost and no loss to the slaveholders. This plan gives us a pretty good idea of what colonization meant to Gallaudet's friend General Cocke: it was a way to get rid of one's excess "negroes" when one replaced labor-intensive tobacco with crops like wheat that simply did not require the slave-labor forces that these planters owned and had to feed and clothe.[43]

During the twenty years the two men corresponded, the subject of education was reverted to once, when in 1831 Gallaudet sent Cocke a circular for the American Society for the Promotion of Education in Liberia, which would provide elementary education in the colony under the governance of trustees in the United States: the three Connecticut trustees would be Gallaudet, Leonard Bacon, and Willbur Fisk, president of Wesleyan University. By this date, however, any public support for the education of African Americans *in Africa* that there may at one time have been had melted away — and the African Education Society along with it.[44]

The colonization movement was never viable. Birthrates, the cost of transatlantic fare, the increased value of slaves as cotton land opened up in Alabama and Mississippi, and the widespread refusal among free African Americans to emigrate could have shown, with back-of-the-envelope arithmetic, that the ACS plan of racial cleansing by transport alone was impossible. The society was in denial not only on the math but also about the fact that they were sending "colonists" to their deaths. The extraordinarily high death rate for African American colonists in Liberia was explained by noting that they "as a class were imprudent in observing even the essentials of personal hygiene." By 1843, a total of 4,571 emigrants had departed for Liberia, but only 1,819 were still alive. As well, the ACS was in denial about the role played by rum in the colony. The truth was that colonists used it to trade with the interior for the export products the society wanted, and when Northern colonizationists like Gallaudet considered this practice wholly unacceptable, the ACS simply claimed that the 1,400 barrels of rum sold every year to the colony were for medicinal purposes. Gallaudet was a constant critic of the society, complaining repeatedly not only about the rum but also about colonization publications that blatantly admitted the purpose of the ACS to be ridding the country of free blacks in order to secure private property in slaves. He nevertheless continued to be a loyal and active member.[45]

The tipping point for the reputation and financial health of the ACS came in 1829 from a wholly unexpected quarter and took the society completely by surprise. On July 4, while Gallaudet was addressing a Hartford colonization fund-raiser, William Lloyd Garrison, another young member of the society, was speaking in a similar venue in Boston, forcefully presenting a startlingly new understanding of slavery: that the Declaration of Independence meant exactly what it said about all men being created equal and endowed by their creator with inalienable rights. From this premise, Garrison argued that a Christian's duty clearly lay in the immediate overthrow of the institution of slavery in the United States. The ACS was stunned. Garrison struck again in 1832 with *Thoughts on African Colonization,* and by 1833 the society was bleeding members, its finances in the red. Fourth of July donations dropped from $12,000 in 1832 to $4,000 in 1833. Arthur and Lewis Tappan quit over the rum issue and the riots that closed Crandall's school; Gerrit Smith quit over the society's attacks on the civil liberties of abolitionists and over a riot in Utica in which the colonizationists had been complicit. Zachary Macaulay in London denounced the ACS as "delusive" and "unchristian."[46]

Many of the defectors had come to know black people personally and thus were aware of their views on colonization. Garrison, for example, had worked on a newspaper in Baltimore with black colleagues and had lived with African Americans in a boarding house there. Arthur Tappan had been persuaded out of colonization by Philadelphian James Forten. Theodore Dwight Weld had gone into black neighborhoods in Cincinnati when he was at Beecher's Lane Seminary, teaching children to read and attending social events and church in the African American community there. He broke with Lane over this issue (and took most of the student body with him to Oberlin) and by 1837 was living in the New York home of one black family and taking his meals with another.[47]

Such personal associations provided Garrison, Tappan, Weld, and many others with insight into how deeply seated African American opposition to white-led colonization really was. As for Gallaudet, in contrast, when in 1831 the Rev. Pennington held a meeting in Hartford denouncing the ACS as "actuated by the same motives which influenced the mind of Pharaoh, when he ordered the male children of the Israelites to be destroyed," his assumption was that Pennington just needed to be calmed down and shown that his best interests lay in deportation. Newspapers cooperated in the suppression of black views by declining to report on meetings and resolutions of African Americans. Despite the cooperation of the press, however, the inability of the ACS to find willing black emigrants to fill its ships was impossible to cover up or suppress. The only remaining option, colonizationists thought, was to make African Americans keenly aware of how unwelcome they were in American communities, which is what all those riots were about. The ACS developed a bunker mentality, denouncing Garrison and supporting mob action against abolitionists.[48]

The colonizationists who stuck with the ACS and those who left the society in high-minded dudgeon were distinguished not only by whether they socialized with African Americans or not. Those loyal to the ACS were also classists who saw Garrison as an upstart from the working class, "a low-lived, ignorant, insignificant mechanic," and they doubled down on their strategy to gain endorsements from the elite that they thought would sway public opinion. They also tended to be Congregationalists and Presbyterians, while Methodists and Baptists were more likely to leave the ACS for abolitionist antislavery societies. In many cases, perhaps, the deciding factor for an antislavery man on whether he would cast his lot with the colonizationists or the abolitionists was whether or not he could accept abolition's "female orators" and Garrison's inclusion of women's rights in abolition campaigns. Like Gallaudet and most Congregationalists, the Tappans could not, but Arthur and Lewis Tappan were the rare men who left the ACS anyway and eventually formed their own all-male abolition society.[49]

There were a great many social penalties for defectors to abolition, up to and including, as we have seen, being murdered or having one's house burned down. All white abolitionists suffered a loss of reputation, but none more so than women, most of whom found themselves viciously denounced — by other women. Catharine Beecher wrote a whole book denouncing the abolitionist speaker Angelina Grimké; Dorothea Dix labeled both Grimké and Maria Weston Chapman "unfeminine and mischievous [*sic*]"; the middle-class mothers who bought Lydia Maria Child's books ceased to do so after the publication of her 1833 abolitionist *Appeal in Favor of That Class of Americans Called Africans.*[50]

But even the Rev. Joel Hawes of the Center Church took a serious risk when he came out publicly as an abolitionist. At first, word of his views leaked out slowly. In March of 1836, the Rev. Leonard Bacon of the First Church of New Haven told Hawes how sorry he was to learn that Hawes had joined the Anti-Slavery Society and asked a string of impertinent rhetorical questions: Was Hawes aware that this society sent men like Theodore Weld out on membership drives? How did Hawes propose to close his church to Weld when he himself was a society member? Was Hawes planning to shake up Connecticut churches with controversies? Did he think he was "promoting the purity of the churches"? Did he plan to excommunicate the South? Wouldn't abolition destroy the Congregational organ the *Connecticut Observer* (a favorite venue for Gallaudet)? Wouldn't abolition "Oberlinize" the state? Bacon ended his letter with a threat to bring up the question of Hawes's membership in the Anti-Slavery Society with the state's General Association. Hawes responded in June, suggesting that Bacon go ahead and see what the General Association said. As it turned out, the issue of slavery was not raised at all at this meeting — Hawes had successfully called Bacon's bluff. Later that month, Hawes followed up with Bacon in genuine Christian kindness: "May you and I, my dear brother, be found on the right side — I mean the side that will be deemed right in the millennium and before God's judgment bar . . . and will be approved by a more enlightened and christian posterity."[51]

The following year, Hawes finally deemed the time right for his maiden abolition sermon, "and struck heavy blows," as Theodore Weld, who was visiting Hartford at the time, reported to Tappan. Weld said the congregation's response to its pastor was "great wrath. If they had known he was to preach such a sermon they would have shut him out of his pulpit; and . . . if he were to come out again in the same manner a large majority of his people would insist upon his immediate dismission !! — if indeed he can escape such a visitation for his abolition sins <u>already</u> committed. His people you know are the <u>Colonizationists</u> of Connecticut par excellence. What will be the issue of the uproar is doubtful." Gallaudet was certainly present when this sermon was delivered and was certainly one of the "Colonizationists of Connecticut par excellence." In February 1838, Hawes, along with African American Hartford residents Amos Beman and James Mars, tried to attend a meeting of black and white abolitionists at the Hartford City Hall, but they were driven out by a mob. A year later, Gallaudet was tattling to Bacon about Hawes's attendance at abolition lectures in Hartford's Baptist church, adding that he was worried that any clerical support for abolition would lead slaveholders to suspend their financial support for the ACS and/or sever their connections with the church.[52]

The *Amistad* captive case that played out in Connecticut in 1839–1840 drew in many men whom Gallaudet knew from Yale, Andover, and his many reform activities — not only abolitionists like Lewis Tappan and James W. C. Pennington and the late "come-outer" Joel Hawes, all of whom worked hard on behalf of the Africans, but even orthodox colonizationists like the Rev. Leonard Bacon, who took up collections for the captives' legal fees. Yale professor George Day, who had taught for a time at the New York school for the deaf, gave English lessons to the African captives using sign language and Gallaudet's *Child's Picture Defining and Reading Book*. Actually, Day, who was working with other Yale men such as Professor Josiah Gibbs and students such as Benjamin Griswold, didn't have any copies of Gallaudet's book on hand and asked Lewis Tappan to serve as an intermediary with his request to Gallaudet for a copy of the book. It's not clear why Day thought he had to go through Tappan — but it does mean that as early as October 21, 1839, when Tappan relayed Day's request, Gallaudet knew that a contingent at Yale was trying to communicate with the Africans for the purpose of helping them gain their freedom and repatriation. As far as can be known today, Gallaudet did not offer any assistance. Another familiar name in the Amistad story was Judge Andrew Judson, who had ruled against Prudence Crandall and the citizenship of African Americans: Judson presided over the trial of the African captives on the charge of murder and, to everyone's surprise, acquitted them. The case then came to Hartford for a hearing by the circuit court, and Gallaudet would have seen the city so thronged with curious visitors that it "took on a carnival appearance."[53]

It's common to read in accounts written by amateur historians of the deaf and those for general audiences and children that Gallaudet was among those who aided the captives. Once again, however, there is no evidence to support that claim. What Gallaudet actually did when the captives came to Hartford was correctly reported in the *New York Commercial Advertiser* on September 16, 1839: he "passed some hours every day in the jail, conversing with the Africans by signs, and endeavoring to make up a vocabulary of the language."

His object on Friday was to ascertain whether they had any distinct idea of a Supreme Being, as the judge and rewarder or punisher of human actions. . . . By further questioning Mr. Gallaudet satisfied himself that *Gooly* was their name for God; and then he proceeded to inquire whether they believed that *Gooly* would punish improper actions. He made signs representing the act of stealing — that of striking, and other wrongful doings; and asked if *Gooly* would whip, or punish, for such things. This also several of the negroes answered in the affirmative; clearly showing, all the time, by their intelligent looks, and their close attention to his motions, that they not only understood but were much interested in his proceedings.

At length, however, Mr. Gallaudet, still rising in his scale of inquiries, conveyed to them the idea of murder by cutting the throat, and asked if *Gooly* would whip for this also. But the moment the negroes caught his meaning they cast down their eyes and were silent; nor could he induce one of them to resume the conversation, or indeed to hold any further communication with him. It occurred to him immediately that a suspicion had entered their minds of his being an emissary of their Spanish masters, and that he was seeking to entrap them into some confession of what took place on board the Amistad.

Fortunately, just at this time the interpreter Ferry came in, and at Mr. Gallaudet's request explained to them that he was their friend, and entertained against them no such hostile design as they suspected; and the good effect of this was quickly made apparent by their coming up in succession to shake hands with Mr. Gallaudet, and then very readily resuming the conversation.

There are no claims here that Gallaudet wished to help the Africans. His purpose for the week is clearly stated: to compile a Mende-English lexicon. Why in the world he would want to do that when everyone concerned with the case already had access to two Mende-English interpreters is not explained. Additionally, on the Friday, his purpose was to conduct an experiment on men who were as yet untouched by the Gospel message, with a view to ascertaining the existence or nonexistence of any innate ideas concerning God, which data in turn would illuminate the question of the necessity for divine revelation. He must have regarded the experiment as a failure, though, because he never mentioned these visits to the captives in the Hartford jail in any diary or extant correspondence. In truth, if his interactions with the *Amistad* captives proved anything at all, it was that these Africans did not understand his signing.[54]

A letter Gallaudet wrote to John Quincy Adams in November 1840 serves as a postscript to the dismal record of Gallaudet's involvement with the *Amistad* case. The two men had been in touch back when Gallaudet needed, or thought he needed, introductions in London and Paris, and Adams, who was U.S. minister to the Court of St. James, was able to oblige him. Since 1830, however, Adams had been serving as a congressman from Massachusetts and had, within a few years of his arrival in the House, made himself notorious by fighting the gag rule that precluded discussion of slavery. When the *Amistad* case was appealed to the U.S. Supreme Court in November 1840, Adams was asked to represent the Africans' case and was mulling over his options. This was when Gallaudet wrote to him — to ask for Adams's opinion on his new book *Practical Spelling.* Adams successfully defended the African captives in February, but there is no evidence that he ever replied to Gallaudet about his speller.[55]

Gallaudet remained an active member of the ACS for the rest of his life. When he left the Asylum in 1830, the national society and three regional branches were among the many organizations that offered him permanent positions, one of them with a salary of $1,500. Though he declined these offers, his work as a volunteer for the ACS continued unabated, and during the 1830s, as we have seen, correspondence shows him periodically concerned that the colonists were imbibing "spiritous liquors" or selling such to the Africans. Throughout his membership, however, his major focus remained on the financial bottom line, and he frequently preached around Hartford County to collect donations.[56]

As late as 1844, he claimed to be "showing conclusively, that some of the slaveholders at the South at least, in aiding the Colonization cause, are influenced by benevolent feelings towards their slaves," and in 1848 he was telling a correspondent that the society, which was in reality out of cash and virtually inactive, was "advancing" its cause in Connecticut, that the situation in Liberia was "promising," and that God had always been and always will be "Guide and protector of this great and good enterprise." Just one year before his death, he "highly recommended" a certain Henry W. Foster and his wife as emigrants to Liberia. In 1848, the ACS had its *Annual Report* placed under the cornerstone of the Washington Monument, where it still lies. In the year of Gallaudet's death, the Yale Divinity School Rhetorical Society debated the question, "Has slavery in this country been, on the whole, an evil?" The correct position was "negative."[57]

Today, Gallaudet University still occupies its original campus in northeastern Washington on Kendall Green, on land that was donated by Amos Kendall in 1857 for a school for the deaf. Gallaudet had been dead for six years by that time and had probably never met Kendall, a Massachusetts native who was a true believer in slavery as a positive good for the nation. In 1835, when Andrew Jackson appointed Kendall postmaster general, the Charleston, South Carolina, Post Office worked in league with three thousand rioters to burn abolitionist mail, along with effigies of Arthur Tappan and William Lloyd Garrison. Of course, tampering with the U.S. Mail was a federal crime, as now, but Kendall determined that the Post Office under his administration would simply decline to deliver these "most flagitious" items — except upon request of the individual addressee. President Jackson approved: "We can do nothing more than direct that these inflammatory papers be delivered to none but who will demand them as subscribers; and in every instance the Postmaster ought to take the names down, and have them exposed thro' the publik journals as subscribers to this wicked plan of exciting the negroes to insurrection and to massacre. . . . [Subscribers should be] compelled to desist, or [to] move from the country."[58]

The Northern press, which almost always condemned abolitionist tactics, nevertheless saw Kendall's response just as we see it today, a violation of the rights to a free press and, since mail is the property of the addressee, to private property was well. Other New Englanders, however, thought that Kendall was quite right, and that, as Noah Webster put it, the U.S. Post Office simply should not be available to abolitionists. In Hartford, a group of residents published an anonymous broadside against the abolitionist press, describing its mailed publications as "a high *offense* against the *principles of morality*" deriving from their "depravity of heart." Where Gallaudet came down on this question, we would have to guess.[59]

After Kendall returned to private life, he was embroiled in lawsuits stemming from his misconduct at the Post Office. Attempting to repair his finances, he bought a teenaged boy named Daniel to rent out to a Mississippi cotton planter for supplementary income. Lewis Tappan, catching wind of this, had Daniel abducted, and offered Kendall $50 for a deed of emancipation. Kendall charged theft of property and, in a racist rant, told Tappan to teach his daughters to be "proud of *kissing [Daniel's] black lips, nestling in his black arms,* and *raising up a family of wooly headed mulattoes.*"

At around the same time, Kendall bought 102 acres about two miles northeast of the Capitol for $9,000, moved his family to cheaper housing there, and turned his attention to the lucrative business of litigating telegraph patents for his anti-Catholic friend Samuel F. B. Morse. When in about 1854 an "adventurer" named Platt H. Skinner arrived in Washington with five deaf children whom he exhibited to solicit donations for a "deaf-mute" school, Kendall's finances were in better shape and his interest in the deaf had been piqued by Morse's deaf wife, Sarah. He was among many who were taken in by Skinner and made a donation. When Skinner was exposed as a scam artist, the defrauded donors went to court, and somehow the deaf orphans ended up bound to Amos Kendall. The case took a curious turn when the litigants decided to go ahead on their own with the school for the deaf, and Kendall, who had five deaf orphans on his hands, donated his home and two acres at Kendall Green for the school. He also hired a young college dropout with a deaf mother to run it. This was, of course, Edward Miner Gallaudet and his mother, Sophia. E. M. Gallaudet regarded Kendall as his "second father," and he presided over the embryonic college as an all-white institution — not only during Kendall's lifetime but for the remaining fifty-three years of his own life. In fact, Gallaudet College remained all white until 1950, when it accepted its first black student, Andrew Foster, and built segregated dormitories for the handful of African American men and women who would come after him.[60]

BY 1840, Hartford had grown to almost ten thousand residents who worked in steam-powered (coal-burning) factories making bells, watches, matches, and pewter ware and four insurance companies that sold policies nationally, including in the South where planters were quickly realizing that they could insure their enslaved field-workers and thus recoup much of the purchase price when these persons met untimely deaths, as they commonly did. Thirteen newspapers got their news from New York by daily steamboat and, after 1846, by telegraph. Yet while Hartford was thus moving with the times with regard to technology and sophisticated financial structures, the city's leading citizens still saw the world through Calvinist and xenophobic lenses. When the years-long recession following the Panic of 1837 caused bank and trading-company failures, Hartford bankers, entrepreneurs, and clergy blamed the whole debacle on sin; Hartford's middle class blamed it on immigrants. Gallaudet's own family finances, however, were in a bit better shape than they had been, thanks to a subsidized part-time position as chaplain at the Hartford Retreat for the Insane.[1]

The Retreat's campus was located just a few blocks from Washington (now Trinity) College at the south end of the city, where it is still in operation today as the Institute of Living. It had its start in 1821, when the usual group of leading citizens sought to remove the "insane" from the jails, where they had been incarcerated by exasperated public officials, and the cellars where they had been chained by their embarrassed families, and into clean, modern facilities. Gallaudet's role in this reform movement, then sweeping the nation's Northeast, was little more than that of a bystander, so the story isn't rehearsed here, but it's important to understand that the movement was bifurcated, and progress was often hampered by reformers working at cross-purposes. In essence, physicians and some lay reformers believed that "insanity" could be cured, and they aimed to do it in modern, benevolent facilities. Others believed that "insanity" was incurable and aimed merely to bring the suffers to a level of stability and inner peace in decent surroundings. The Massachusetts reformer Dorothea Dix is the salient exponent of the latter view: she believed that such an approach would suppress disruptive behavior and secure the salvation of the disturbed person's soul *without any recovery of reason.* Gallaudet never articulated this view as his own, but everything he wrote — in his "Private Journal," in letters, in public addresses — indicates that this was in fact his belief.[2]

In any case, the Hartford exploratory committee did not investigate methods of treatment, be they cures, Christian salvation, or simply behavioral control, but rather proceeded directly to "the necessary inquiries to devise ways and means for raising funds." This fund-raising was carried out by constant reference to the Asylum, then in its fifth year. A May 1821 article in the *Courant,* for example, pointed to the success of the Asylum to predict the Retreat would be equally successful, observing that "there are certainly twenty, and probably more insane persons to one that is deaf and dumb. There is not a single argument in favor of an Asylum for the last mentioned class, which will not apply with tenfold greater force, in favor of an institution for reclaiming the insane.... [T]he opportunity of affording them moral and religious instruction, it is obvious, will apply to as much greater extent . . . as the number of subjects is greater." The fact that the Asylum was a school and the Retreat was a hospital does not seem to have been understood at all — by anyone. In fact, a widow of one of the founders recalled much later that it was Gallaudet who came up with the hospital's name, "Retreat for the Insane," because the word "Asylum" had already been taken for the institution serving the deaf. The Retreat had opened in 1824 with Gallaudet listed as one of the thirty founding directors (who each paid $100 for the privilege) and Dr. Eli Todd, whom he would consult on his depression, as its superintendent. When Gallaudet took on the duties of chaplain, the hospital was under the superintendence of a mostly absent physician, Silas Fuller.[3]

Gallaudet's appointment as chaplain came about the old-fashioned way: through patronage. He had preached several Sundays at the Massachusetts State Lunatic Hospital in Worcester, and in February of 1838 he was offered a permanent full-time position there. As he always did, he mulled over the offer for months, stringing Worcester along until July, when Henry Barnard, who was then attempting to convince Gallaudet to accept the position as secretary of the Board of Commissioners of Common Schools, took it upon himself to cobble together a half-time position at Hartford's own lunatic hospital, the Retreat for the Insane, hoping that would allow Gallaudet to accept the education secretary's position as well. Because the Retreat was not willing to pay a reasonable salary (like the Asylum, it put its money into building, not payroll), Barnard took private subscriptions that doubled the offered figure to $750. As it turned out, Gallaudet took the chaplaincy but not the state position, thus nabbing a job at a subsidized salary without fulfilling the hopes of those who subsidized it for him. At the

Retreat, he did the job he was hired to do and tinkered around the edges with alleviating patient boredom, which appears to have been rather severe. But by no stretch of the imagination was he "a power behind the throne," as Edward Miner Gallaudet claimed.[4]

The hospital, like the deaf school, sought out a white, native-born, middle- and upper-class clientele, rationalizing that choice with the claim that the state declined to grant a subsidy for indigent patients — which was true in the Retreat's earliest years, but it doesn't explain why the tens of thousands of dollars raised by subscription from private citizens were not at least partially dedicated to subsidies for poor patients rather than to the cost of designing and building the picturesque campus. Just as the Asylum had done in its first decade, the Retreat used charitable donations on amenities to attract "respectable" patients, further rationalizing that homogeneous populations were the best environment in which to affect cures. The fact that only six out of thousands of patients in its first forty years were African American was explained by African Americans' alleged "constitutional cheerfulness" that made them less susceptible to mental illness. Gallaudet's planter friend General Cocke sent his son to the Retreat (where the young man died), and a clergyman who had studied under Gallaudet at Yale sent his daughter. Through the 1860s at least, the Retreat's focus was on providing an "increase of conveniences and comforts" for the wealthy. Gallaudet surely felt quite at home. One wonders, though, if he ever thought, "There but for the grace of God go I," for at least some of the paying patients were there for opium addiction and delirium tremens, and a great many were being treated for depression — if the common references to patients' typical malaise are any indication of that.[5]

The Retreat superintendent's view, and thus the institution's official position, denied that insanity came from God, but Gallaudet and many other well-educated members of the general public saw some sort of moral or divine element at work in these cases. Henry Barnard, for example, accepted that insanity was a disease "like a fever, or the gout, — that it springs from natural causes . . . not always in control of the individual," but nevertheless he defined the "natural causes" of insanity as American "freedom of thought, religion, business, and locomotion . . . uncertain employment, hazardous speculations, . . . sensual indulgences, . . . showy and fashionable styles of living." Gallaudet, for his part, unsurprisingly blamed mental illness on a faulty religious education or a willful disregard for the religious education one had received. In one telling incident, Gallaudet succeeded in convincing a patient that his derangement was caused by having neglected his prayers, only to see the patient disabused of this archaic notion by Dr. Fuller. Gallaudet had no one but his diary to tell how "I am becoming more and more convinced that a judicious physical and religious education, on the simple principles of the Gospel, with early piety, constitutes the best security against mental alienation." In his first official *Annual Report,* in 1842, he went on record with his assertion that "*religious agencies* have their proper place and proportion, as well as the medical, and what are termed the moral means of cure." The Retreat's physicians must have regarded him and his views as harmless, figuring that it wouldn't hurt the patients to get a dose of religion in addition to their medical treatment.[6]

Gallaudet's duties at the Retreat included "family prayers" every evening (the inmates served as one another's "family") and a sermon every Sunday afternoon. The Retreat chapel was constructed with entrances for the male and female patients through "separate avenues . . . connected with the male and female sides of the institution." From remarks in Gallaudet's diary, it's clear that the male and female sides of the chapel were further walled off on either side of a central aisle. And patients had to behave sedately in chapel, for Amariah Brigham, who served as superintendent in the early 1840s, "denounced evangelical enthusiasm as emotionally excessive." Such enthusiasms were not to Gallaudet's taste, either. In the 1847 *Annual Report,* he declared that any kind of emotional outbreak during chapel services resulted in removal. Gallaudet recorded an incident in his diary in which a woman walked across the central aisle and into the men's section of the chapel, causing the service to be suspended until she could be taken away. It's no surprise to find that Gallaudet's friend Thomas Robbins described the chapel "audience," inured to this kind of zero-tolerance policing, as "gloomy."[7]

In addition to his official duties, Gallaudet seems to have spent quite a bit of time mingling and chatting with the patients, taking pains to alleviate their boredom. He taught them all the finger alphabet and even organized field trips to the Asylum "or other objects of curiosity," which suggests a disturbing picture of mentally ill adults entering classrooms to gape at the deaf pupils. He enthusiastically suggested to the management that sewing and knitting parties should be got up for women, that patients play battledore inside during inclement weather, that sex-segregated reading rooms be established with appropriate newspapers and periodicals, and even that a museum of shells and minerals and a lecture series on chemistry, physics, and history be offered for patients. He certainly had his heart in the right place, and he seems to have had excellent instincts in interactions with patients. When a patient with whom he was walking on the roof of the hospital tried to jump off, he saved the day by responding, "Oh! That is easy. Anybody can do that. Let us go down and try to jump up!"[8]

For Gallaudet, the Retreat's patients were not fellow Americans who happened to be ill, but rather "a gift to him of a new family," his friend William A. Alcott observed. "Not only did he feel toward the inmates like a father, but they felt all the affection — many of them, I mean — of children." Of course, he had regarded his relations to his deaf pupils in precisely the same light. We are surprised, then, to see that the dealings he had with a Retreat patient who had also been an Asylum pupil show considerably less than fatherly love, for his only response to "McEwan" (presumably one of the brothers Ephraim and George McEwan from Stratford) was to complain that he "tittered considerably" during the Sunday service. Both of the McEwans had been supported by the state of Connecticut at the Asylum, so this man would also have been there on the state's dime, which goes some way toward accounting for Gallaudet's lack of interest in him. Despite annoyances like McEwan, Gallaudet was convinced, and made clear in his "Discourse Delivered at the Dedication of the Chapel" in 1846, that the Retreat was "under an Almighty guardianship." Rather than be discouraged by setbacks, he urged his audience to consider the vast amounts of money raised as proof positive that God has blessed the enterprise, and, presumably, Gallaudet's minor role in it.[9]

During these years, Gallaudet was also working part time for the Asylum at an hourly wage: eight hours to write an address on the dedication of a new chapel, one and a half hours consultation with Weld, $50 plus expenses of $27.20 for a ten-day trip to Providence and Boston. He charged his sons $36.50 a quarter for "services [washing and mending] and board." He got $2.87½ for performing one wedding, $1.87½ for a second, $2.37½ for a third, and $100 for marrying George Loring. He charged his associate William Channing Woodbridge 19¢ for the "expense of depositing his things in my garret." He was paid $25 for a lecture. The Gallaudet home school grew too large to be kept in the house and moved into another building under Miss Terusha Perry, and Gallaudet continued to keep his careful accounts of the school's income and expenditures: $14.62½ per term for "instruction and wood" was the charge for neighbors' children; 12½¢ was paid to "Mrs. Kent, colored woman," who perhaps cleaned the schoolroom; the teacher, Miss Perry, got $150 a year. Gallaudet maintained daily involvement in the school, making sure the children exercised out of doors every day and that the temperature was kept sufficiently low to indicate "a thoro ventilation." He had a horror of pupils dog-earring their books: "children, do you know that these curling covers are 'dog ears?' We can not have any of them in *our* books."[10]

At home, a Catherine Clark was a servant to the family who earned $1.50 a week. In 1844, Clark was replaced with an Irishwoman, Sarah Grady, whose wages he paid to her brother, although he had to agree to provide her with tea. A "deaf-mute seamstress employed by the family" was tormented by young Wallace, but if she was also paid for her work, her wages do not appear in surviving accounts, nor do we know her name. There were a great many visitors of all sorts, ranging from Sophia's deaf friends to three Chinese boys — Yung Wing, Wong Shing, and Wong Fun — who were lodged in Hartford with Asylum teacher David Bartlett. These boys had been brought to the Munson Academy in Massachusetts by the missionary Samuel Robbins Brown, for whom Gallaudet arranged a lecture at the Center Church on his Hong Kong mission. One of the boys, Yung Wing, picked up on what every deaf acquaintance saw in Sophia, remarking on her "dignified and queen-like air." Edward Miner Gallaudet, looking back on these years, recalled that it was unusual for the spare room to be empty. Parnell Fowler moved back with her sister's family but owed Gallaudet for having her shoes mended.[11]

In 1844, Gallaudet paid Dr. Greenleaf $33 "for a set of teeth," clearly for himself or possibly Sophia, since he did not debit it to any family member, as was his usual practice. A neighbor gave the family a piano and the two younger girls, Caty and Alice, started lessons. Gallaudet duly recorded his payments for tuning every few months. Son William needed a "viol-bow" one month, a "viol-string" the next month, a "violin box" and a haircut a few months later. Eddy was keeping rabbits.[12]

The Connecticut River flooded in 1841, leaving a hundred families, mostly African Americans who lived near the waterfront, bereft of their homes and belongings. Luckily, the Rev. Pennington was able to rescue his manuscript of *A Text Book of the Origin and History, etc., etc., of the Colored People,* which was published the next month. These events passed entirely below the radar of the church and school establishment of the city. Charles Dickens visited the Asylum in 1842, but as his novels were not among the those precious few Gallaudet thought could "safely and profitably form a part of the family library," he would not have arranged to meet him. P. W. died in Washington City in 1843 at the advanced age of eighty-eight, survived by only six of his thirteen children. His will presented "a bit of braintwisting, to say the least," as a nephew put it, and "his executors must have had a great deal of difficulty in finding... all the people to whom he owed money." T. H. got the family Bible, his grandfather's Book of Common Prayer, and some mahogany furniture; Catherine, who had been caring for her father, got his life insurance, bedding, bedstead, and silver spoons; the other four split their father's library and old clothes. That same year, Gallaudet turned down a $2,000 annual salary to superintend an orphanage in Philadelphia, but he must not have been able to avoid comparing his career unfavorably to those of old friends: Thomas Robbins had donated his library to the Connecticut Historical Society and was salaried as its librarian, and Laurent Clerc was honored with a master of arts from Washington College.[13]

Gallaudet's annual solo vacation of 1846 is recorded in his letters home to his children, describing tourists sites — the White Mountains, Dartmouth, the view from the top of Mt. Washington — on the way to Montreal, where he delivered a public lecture on "the deaf and dumb." When he recommenced keeping a personal diary in 1847, we find his thoughts turned to the immortal souls of his sons and daughters. In his first entry, he counted three of his daughters — twenty-three-year-old Sophie, tutoring in a family a bit west of Hartford, twenty-year-old Jane, teaching school in New York, and sixteen-year-old Caty, living at home with constant headaches, as "professors of religion." Fourteen-year-old Alice had not professed religion but he hoped she had some "germ of piety," and she did indeed join the Center Church the following year. As for Gallaudet's sons, twenty-one-year-old Wallace, in business in Massachusetts with a son of Seth Terry, eighteen-year-old William, living at home and working as bookkeeper for a wholesale iron concern, and ten-year-old Eddy had yet to profess religion. Eddy and William, their father believed, had a "germ of piety," but he didn't say that about Wallace, upon whom he was busily foisting tracts and letters urging "concerns of his soul." And what of his firstborn, Thomas, who was twenty-five when Gallaudet started his journal?[14]

Thomas broke his parents' hearts. The boy had expected to study at Yale, but his father refused to allow him out from under "home influence" and sent him to Washington College in Hartford instead. Washington College had been founded in 1823 as an Episcopal college, but the state, run by Congregationalists, made sure its charter stipulated that neither students nor professors could be subjected to any religious test. Even so, it's difficult to understand why Gallaudet would have thought that exposure to the Episcopal Church, whose "perversions to the Romish Church" greatly disturbed him, was safe for his son. It proved not safe: Thomas converted and was confirmed in the Episcopal Church before informing his horrified parents of the accomplished fact. So serious was he about his newfound faith that upon graduation in 1842, he planned to attend the General Theological Seminary in New York with several of his classmates. Gallaudet adamantly refused to allow it, insisting that Thomas teach school in Glastonbury and Meridian for a few years while engaging in rigorous private study of Calvinism, and he provided Thomas with a stack of suitable theological treatises for that purpose. He also charged the young man $1,000 for "his expenses during his four years education at Washington College," which seems vindictive.[15]

After a year of this punishment, Thomas's faith was "more firmly settled than ever." So Gallaudet made his second mistake: instead of giving his blessing to Thomas's decision to study for the priesthood, he sent him to teach at the New York Institution, where, he thought, Thomas would be under the watchful eye of orthodox Congregationalist principal Harvey Prindle Peet. Once in New York, however, Thomas outfoxed his father by clandestinely undertaking private study for the priesthood with Bishop Benjamin T. Onderdonk — and had himself rebaptized to boot, believing that his baptism at the Center Church was, in the context of his present doctrinal views, invalid. "I caused sadness to my parents," he later wrote, "for I showed my dissatisfaction with the Congregational system in which my dear parents had consecrated me as an infant to the loving service of our Heavenly Father."

As Thomas surely understood, his mentor Bishop Onderdonk was a Tractarian, a member of the Oxford Movement that aimed to bring the Anglican Church back to Rome. The movement's founder, John Henry Newman, was eventually received into the Roman Catholic Church, but in 1843 when Thomas undertook to study for the priesthood under Onderdonk, Newman was still roiling the Anglican Church and the Episcopal Church in the United States as well. The American bishops fought back, and Onderdonk found himself embroiled in controversy not only over the ordination of priests with Oxfordian leanings but also over allegations that he had behaved improperly with women in his congregation. The truth of these allegations can no longer be determined, but it's quite probable that they were concocted by his theological adversaries, rather in the manner that David Seixas was run out of his own deaf school in Philadelphia. In any case, Onderdonk was suspended from his clerical duties in 1845, leaving Thomas with his clerical training incomplete.[16]

While these matters were playing out among the leadership of the Episcopal Church, Thomas was falling in love with one of his pupils, Elizabeth Budd, an intelligent girl of a good, Episcopalian New York family. In November 1844, he wrote his father a now-lost letter that conveyed very unwelcome news, whether about his theological studies, his engagement, or both. Gallaudet responded only to say that it was "a great disappointment to us," for all the family's prayers and "monitory suggestion" had not been sufficient to ensure the salvation of Thomas's soul. He and Elizabeth were married in July 1845, with Peet as the interpreter and the groom's family conspicuously absent. The new couple moved in with the bride's parents. Thomas visited Hartford with his wife a few months later to speak at the commencement at Trinity College, and it was apparently on that trip that Thomas gave his father a note acknowledging a remaining debt of $838.00.[17]

By 1847, family relations had somehow been mended, and in his opening entry in his new journal Gallaudet was able to count Thomas, along with his three sisters, as a professor of religion and as married to an "intelligent and amiable deaf-mute." When the young couple's first child, Caroline, was born that year, Gallaudet joked on several occasions to Thomas that the baby should be named "Rose Budd Gallaudet," and Caty was permitted to be in attendance when Caroline was baptized. Soon the young family, with the baby's nurse and Elizabeth's mother and brothers, were making regular visits to Hartford, Thomas was officiating at area Episcopal churches and even at the Retreat, and Caty and Sophie were often at the Budd residence in New York. But the following year, Gallaudet was faced with a new sorrow in connection with the Budds, for Caty had fallen in love with Elizabeth's brother Bern. Gallaudet related the story to his "Private Journal" as it unfolded, replacing all names with blanks as though Caty and Bern's attachment were a family embarrassment. Beginning in December of 1848, the entries read as follows: "Sat. 23. _____ arrived. Mond. 25. A.M. Had a conversation in my study with _____ about _____. I told her she had not done right in keeping the matter concealed from me, for weeks past, but that I would endeavor kindly and judiciously."

It was Christmas Day (unacknowledged in the Gallaudet household), Caty was nearly eighteen, and her father was still living in the mythic Golden Age of Timothy Dwight, in which he had the right and the duty to be kept informed of a daughter's every thought. Subsequent entries outline his decision: Caty could visit and correspond if, and only if, Bern Budd maintained a respectable character and got a job. The worry about whether Bern could support Caty was, however, a subterfuge covering Gallaudet's real aversion to the match, which was Bern's religion. He told the young man that "I had always wished my daughters to have pious husbands, enlarging upon the topic as true religion furnishes the only s[olid?] foundation of domestic happiness and urging upon him the importance of having his heart right with God. I gave him 'Pike's Guide for Young Disciples.' I was taken by surprise in . . ."

And at that point, a half page was sealed off by E. M. Gallaudet with a note to the effect that these were family matters "of no benefit to anyone." A peek under the seal, however, reveals nothing more than a prayer for divine guidance in handling the matter of Caty. Bern Budd and Catherine Gallaudet were finally wed in 1852, one respectful full year after Gallaudet's death.

While these family dramas were playing out, Gallaudet took an unexpected step into an area he had heretofore avoided his entire life: electoral politics. One wouldn't know it from Gallaudet's paper trail, but the 1840s were bitterly contentious years for the future of slavery as an American institution. In 1840, after twelve years of Democrats Andrew Jackson and his successor Martin Van Buren in the White House, the Whig Party, which adopted generally Federalist principles, nominated William Henry Harrison, who presented himself as a frontiersman and Indian fighter rather than as the slaveholder (and father of six enslaved children) that he was; the Liberty Party, which advocated abolition, nominated James G. Birney, a colonizationist who had converted to abolition in 1833; the incumbent Van Buren stood for the Democrats. Gallaudet couldn't convince himself to vote for any of these men. The Whig Harrison won the election but died shortly after his inauguration, leaving his term to be filled by his vice president,

John Tyler. Tyler was another slaveholder who, moreover, advocated the extension of slavery into the western territories, which Harrison had not done. The 1844 election was all about the expansion of slavery and pitted Whig candidate Henry Clay, who was opposed to the annexation of Texas, against James K. Polk, who was for it, while the Liberty Party again fielded James Birney. Gallaudet again did not vote. Clay won Connecticut; Polk won nationally. President Polk annexed Texas during his first year in office and subsequently led the nation into a war of aggression against Mexico. In 1847, Liberia declared independence, though the United States did not recognize this until 1862, and the ACS, with Gallaudet fully onboard, continued with its promises and its fund-raising in complete denial of the fact that it no longer had a colony.

One can guess why an antislavery, anti-abolition man like Gallaudet was not moved to exercise his franchise during these years. He would have found Birney far too radical and the Whigs Harrison and Clay far too compromising. In 1848, however, Martin Van Buren returned to the fray, not as a Democrat but rather as the candidate of the new Free Soil Party, with a platform that proclaimed slavery to be constitutionally inviolable but calling for restrictions in the new western states. The Free Soil Party attracted a racist demographic that simply wanted to keep the West unblemished by black residents, but it was the only party in 1848 to push any kind of antislavery agenda. Democratic candidate Lewis Cass was a slave owner who had served as Jackson's secretary of war and had directed his Indian Removal policy. Cass advocated allowing slavery to spread into the western territories by having each territory vote on the question. Whig candidate Zachary Taylor was a sugar planter who owned three hundred slaves, and he was a hero of the Mexican War, but it was thought in Hartford that he was an "antislavery moderate" who would exclude slavery from the territories. No one could be sure, however, since the Whigs dispensed with a platform in 1848 and voters were left with a pig in a poke. One might have thought that Gallaudet would finally be moved to cast his vote for the Free-Soiler Van Buren, but instead, his conscience, he thought, dictated a vote for Taylor. As he told his journal, "for the first time, I was made a freeman of the State of Conn. and took the elector's oath. This morning [November 7] I voted for electors for President, such as will vote for Zachary Taylor. I hope I did this prayerfully, deliberately, and conscientiously. No one had asked me to be made a freeman, or, afterwards, to vote for any particular ticket."

Taylor died after four months in office, and it was left to his vice present, Millard Fillmore, to sign and enforce the 1850 Fugitive Slave Act. It's
unfortunate that we don't have any record of Gallaudet's later reflections,
if any, on his choice of Taylor, but his son Edward Miner, who was eleven
years old at the time, remembered proudly his own leadership of a Taylor
and Fillmore boys' club and his role in convincing his father to vote for
the ticket.[18]

Gallaudet's entries in his "Private Journal" for 1848 give a lively picture of a family and professional life jam-packed with visitors. William
almost burned down the house when he set his hat on "the pipe to dry."
Sophia spent five weeks visiting a friend in Boston. She was Gallaudet's
"counter-balance" to his "depression of spirits and despondency," and he
must have wilted when she was away.[19] Eddy and Alice started high school,
the only two of Gallaudet's children to enjoy this privilege, shortly after
Thomas Beecher took over as principal of the school. Beecher, a brother of
Catharine, had studied for the ministry and had invited Gallaudet to give
an address at the school shortly after he was installed. Wallace visited frequently but failed to respond to his father's urgent inquiries about his soul,
so Gallaudet would give him tracts to take home, at least one of which was
on dancing, which gives us some idea of why Gallaudet was worried about
him. A steady stream of Chinese and Deaf visitors dined with the family.
Daniel Wadsworth died and, although Gallaudet does not mention the fact,
bequeathed a bust of Clerc that he had commissioned to the Connecticut
Historical Society, as well as a tract of land adjacent to the Asylum to a family member.[20] A Hartford dentist committed suicide. Gallaudet's butcher
revealed himself to be a Universalist: Gallaudet gave him some tracts. A
friend of Eddy's drowned after falling through the ice while skating on the
river. Two "German Jews, who trade in Hartford," accompanied Gallaudet
to the Retreat on a Sunday, where he prayed for them to "receive Jesus as
the Messiah." A Frenchwoman who worked as a cook at the Retreat lost a
baby daughter, and Gallaudet gave her a copy of *Child's Book on the Soul*.
Joel Hawes kept Gallaudet abreast of everything William and Alice told
him about their evolving faiths. When Gallaudet was called to the deathbed
of a former Asylum pupil, he attempted to convert the dying man's fiancée.
A German missionary to the Germans of Connecticut drank tea with the
family. Aunt Parnell took some of the children to visit her brother Miner
Fowler in Guilford; another brother of Parnell and Sophia, Horatio Nelson

Fowler, visited the Gallaudet family in Hartford. No notice was taken in Hartford of the women's rights convention held that summer in Seneca Falls, New York, by veterans of the abolition movement, Lucretia Mott, Elizabeth Cady Stanton, Frederick Douglass, and others.

The following year brought more of this busy round of friends and family. The unregenerate Wallace married Margaret E. Brown in Plainfield, Massachusetts, in June. Gallaudet attended the wedding, his traveling expenses paid by a friend who gave Gallaudet a check for $100 — "May the Lord reward him," Gallaudet said, "for this token of his friendship to me and my family" — and redoubled his attempts to get the couple to read the tracts he pressed on them, sometimes at the train station as their train was pulling away. Mrs. Cogswell died in August; pallbearers included Gallaudet and Clerc. Caty's suitor Bern Budd visited more frequently, and he spent Thanksgiving with the family in Hartford. A couple of weeks after his return to New York, he wrote Caty that he had made a profession of religion and joined a church. Gallaudet was becoming worried about Sophie's health; when a diagnosis of tuberculosis was confirmed, he arranged for her to stay with an acquaintance of his in Savannah. In August, Gallaudet joined the Hartford clergy in an "immense gathering" to advocate for naval reform. Their aim was to ban both flogging and "spirit rations," meaning the provision of rum to sailors as part of their daily rations. Gallaudet addressed the assembly to tell the story of a patient at the Retreat whose insanity had some connection, in Gallaudet's mind, with his having witnessed a flogging on a whaling ship. There was no indication of awareness in Hartford that the movement to abolish flogging in the navy was led by a Jew, Uriah P. Levy.[21]

The family home on Prospect Street that Gallaudet had been renting was sold in 1849, and he decided to buy a house next door to Seth Terry, which was selling for $2,500. He had that sum in his savings account and was ready to purchase in 1850 when Terry, who was then serving as the Asylum's commissioner of its endowment fund, arranged for the school to appropriate $2,000 and present it to Gallaudet as belated compensation for this 1815–1816 trip to Europe. Other individuals, including LUPO cofounder Richard Bigelow and the younger Elizur Goodrich, donated $100 each to round off the purchase price. Gallaudet told his "Private Journal" that he saw the hand of Providence in the belated compensation for his trip. He moved his family into the new house in April, buying a new "umbrella-holder" for $2.25 and whitewashing the study and the garden fence.[22]

That same month, he attended the opening ceremony for the state Normal School in New Brittany, where he gave an address on "self-cultivation in English composition," now lost. Gallaudet gave several more lectures there over the spring and summer and was paid by the day, half day, or evening at the rate of 68¾¢ to 93¾¢, or so he recorded his remuneration in his account book. His old colleague in LUPO, the Basel seminarian Joseph Rieger, visited from Missouri in August. In September, Millard Fillmore signed the Fugitive Slave Act that would so infuriate New England. This act required local officials to arrest any person accused by anyone of being a fugitive slave and to fine any person who offered food or shelter to any alleged fugitive the outrageously large sum of $1,000. This new legal reach of the slavery interests into Northern communities was the catalyst that converted many previously uncommitted Americans to the abolition cause and brought that movement into the mainstream. Gallaudet appears to have made no mention whatever of the Fugitive Slave Act, and it's hard to say whether he saw it as constitutional — he may have. That same month, the Asylum's first-ever reunion brought nearly two hundred former pupils to Hartford, where they formed a procession, led by the governor of the state, and presented both Gallaudet and Clerc with extravagant gifts. The convocation had been planned by a New Hampshire man, former pupil Thomas Brown, who collected $600 in donations from his old classmates to purchase a silver-plated pitcher and salver set for Gallaudet and a second one for Clerc, with suitable engravings commemorating their foundational roles in these deaf people's lives. Gallaudet recorded the event as follows:

27. [September 1850] Frid. A.M. Yesterday, a silver pitcher and salver, of beautifully exquisite workmanship, with appropriate devices and inscription, the cost of the pitcher 200 dolls. and of the salver 83 dolls, were presented to me in the Centre Church, P.M. by the hands of Mr. Geo. H. Loring, one of my earliest pupils in the Asylum, in the presence of a very large assembly, appropriate addresses accompanying it as a testimonial of the gratitude and affection of many of my old pupils, between 150 and 200 of whom were present from various parts of the country, principally New England.

Lord, give me grace to view this in its true light. Let not my pride, in any degree, be inflated by it. I feel humbled before thee for my many deficiencies in duty, while laboring in the education of deaf-mutes.

At some point, he remembered the man who made it all possible and went back to squeeze another sentence in between these two paragraphs: "A similar pitcher and salver were presented to Mr. Clerc." Thomas Brown, who seems to have had as good a sense of humor as he had of generosity, asked a year later, "How does the beautiful pitcher appear? Mrs. Brown wishes me to ask if Mrs. Gallaudet has got tired of taking care of it."[23]

In November, Gallaudet recorded the appearance of "a red deposit in my urine"; lacking any further notation of other symptoms, this could have been anything from an infection to kidney stones to prostate cancer. The entry he made on his birthday, December 10, is vague in its references to three infirmities, and soon he was in bed with a bad cold, "very languid and a good deal depressed. My anxiety about the business concerns of my two sons at Holyoke, is considerable, should they be embarrassed, it would involve me to a large amount — large for me."

He had cosigned loans for them and feared they would default. In January 1851, Horace Hooker and two Asylum teachers substituted for Gallaudet at the Retreat, presumably because he was still in bed, although his letters show him cheerful. He wrote to his granddaughter Caroline about Caty's six canaries and the family cat. Sophia was obviously not at all worried about his health, for she spent nine weeks in New York and Philadelphia, only to leave again immediately to visit her sons in Holyoke. Thomas Robbins visited, as did a Yale classmate, Allen Mclean, who had become blind and who remarked on a sermon Gallaudet gave at the Retreat: "With a quieting, subdued voice he read a portion of divine truth and led in prayer. The prayer was in keeping with the differing suppliants. There was no disturbance." So at this point, Gallaudet was out of bed and back to work.[24] But his friends noticed that his health was in decline. Lifelong use of opium will have that effect: for every William S. Burroughs who lives into his eighties, there are millions of Samuel Taylor Coleridges and Jerry Garcias whose hearts give out in their fifties and sixties.

On July 12, a Saturday, he recorded in his journal that Sophia had been taken ill on the 9th and was diagnosed with dysentery on the 10th. On the day of the entry, Gallaudet himself was "seized with violent chills and obliged to retire to bed." Sophie's narrative of her father's last illness states that he had been "spending the evening with a friend" and took "wine and warm drinks" before going to bed that night. Both Sophie and Gallaudet himself were observing such delicacy in describing the symptoms that we in the twenty-first century can be forgiven for failing immediately to grasp that dysentery is the bloody diarrhea that results from a variety of infections. Treatment today consists of keeping the patient hydrated and letting the infection run its course, although antibiotics or drugs to kill the specific bacterium, virus, or parasite can be used if the patient is at risk due to age and general health, as Gallaudet was. But as we saw with the yellow fever epidemic in Philadelphia during Gallaudet's childhood, the importance of hydration was not understood, and Gallaudet's family was offering him brandy instead of water. By the 20th, Eddy had come down with the illness as well, and everyone blamed the family outbreak on the "extreme heat in the first week of July." Eddy and Sophia recovered nicely; Gallaudet continued "confined to my bed with severe sickness." What this probably means is not that the dysentery was continuing — the infection causing the diarrhea can only run its course, not turn into a chronic condition — but rather that Gallaudet was experiencing secondary complications such as colitis or kidney failure due to dehydration.

Wallace and Margaret visited, then returned to Holyoke with Jane; Thomas came from New York and returned home; Jane returned to Hartford from Holyoke; Wallace and Margaret made another visit. At the end of August, Gallaudet dictated a letter for Thomas to take to the convention of American Instructors of the Deaf and Dumb, which was to meet in Hartford, regretting that his health prevented him from attending. This time, the old familiar excuse was the truth.[25]

It's not clear how many servants were in the home at this time and who exactly was caring of the invalid, and it's difficult to imagine what it would take to care for a bedridden man with bloody diarrhea in a house with no water closet or running water of any sort. Sophia's narrative reports a semirecovery for a few weeks before "the disease returned owing as we feared from eating too freely of an orange," upon which Gallaudet returned to bed and stayed there for the last six weeks of his life. Sophia recounted how "he talked to us by signs. During all his sickness as his mind wandered in his dreams he expressed his ideas by that language." She wrote of weather continuing "excessively hot," with "the thermometer between ninety and ninety eight. Father felt the heat very much we were obliged to fan him continually day and night," and they gave him brandy by the spoonful. A few days before his death, his youngest son later recounted, Western Reserve College conferred on him an honorary LLD. Gallaudet must have been pleased: back in the 1830s, the college had earned the congratulations of the American Colonization Society for dismissing two of its professors and thus stopping "the plot to make Western Reserve a seminary for training abolitionists." Edward Miner remembered his father saying, "It has come just in time not to be too late." Eddy was then sent to Holyoke to fetch his two brothers, leaving Sophia, Sophie, Caty, and Alice in attendance when Gallaudet murmured, "I must go to sleep," and he died at two o'clock in the afternoon of Wednesday, September 10, Sophie fanning him.[26]

When Thomas and Jane arrived the next day, Thursday, the body was carefully packed in ice and a "committee of gentlemen" formed to make funeral arrangements, Thomas recounted. On Friday, they laid the body in a coffin in the parlor. By dinnertime, however, "it was evident that we must each one speedily prepare for the funeral" — the ice packing proved insufficient proof against the ninety-degree weather, and the stench was noticeable during dinner. The Center Church was closed for remodeling, so the funeral was held in the South Church. Harvey Prindle Peet, who came from New York, and Clerc made "addresses to deaf-mutes." Edward Miner remembered it as remarkable that the parish priest of Hartford's one Catholic Church attended. The family returned home that evening to "recount the pleasing providential incidents which had occurred within the last year or two of father's life, among which were . . . being settled in his own house, the deaf-mute presentation festival and the receiving of the degree of LL.D."[27]

The next month, thirty "prominent residents" met in the Center Church to discuss the need for public recognition of Gallaudet's life. Only two of the Asylum's founding directors were still living — Ward Woodbridge and Daniel Buck — but Seth Terry and two members of the Asylum's faculty, William W. Turner and Luzerne Rae, were among the thirty. The usual planning committee was formed with three lawyers, one physician, and the governor of Connecticut, and it recruited Henry Barnard to conduct the memorial service in January. These memorial services were not at all uncommon. Barnard led a similar but more star-studded affair for the Hartford industrialist Samuel Colt, while the Democrats Washington Irving, Daniel Webster, and William Cullen Bryant did the same for Gallaudet's old Yale acquaintance James Fenimore Cooper, who died four days after he did. The personalities mustered for Gallaudet — doctors, lawyers, and state governor — were therefore minimal insofar as such things typically went. The proceeds from the memorial volume were to be donated to the "deaf and dumb widow," and her entries in Gallaudet's account book show how badly she needed the money: George Loring's wife gave her almost $300, $100 came from anonymous friends, and $26 came from boarding a nephew. At least she owned her home outright.[28]

During the fall of Gallaudet's death, Harriet Beecher Stowe had been writing a forty-week serial about enslaved persons in Kentucky named Uncle Tom, Aunt Chloe, and George and Eliza Harris. The day after Gallaudet died, the episode appearing in print had Tom rescuing Little Eva from drowning. The serial was brought out in book form the following March. Also in 1852, Thomas Gallaudet established St. Ann's Church for Deaf Mutes in New York, and Caty Gallaudet married her Episcopalian sweetheart.

The first recorded instance of simultaneous interpreting occurred at the unveiling of the Gallaudet Monument on the Asylum's grounds in 1854. Henry Barnard found it so novel as to require an explanation: "Then commenced a somewhat peculiar exhibition. While Mr. [John] Carlin addressed his deaf-mute audience, in graceful and graphic signs, Prof. I. L. Peet, of the New York Institution, simultaneously read the same address to those who had 'ears to hear.' With but one oration, there were two audiences and two orators, both proceeding side by side, at the same time, in the same place, without the least mutual hindrance of interference."[29]

Edward Miner spent the first three years following his father's death working in a bank before enrolling at Trinity College. In 1857, the year the Dred Scott decision was handed down, Amos Kendall offered him the superintendency of the Columbia Institution for the Deaf and Dumb and the Blind on Kendall Green in Washington City, so he left Trinity without a degree and took his mother to Washington with him. Two years later, Trinity gave E. M. an honorary MA. In 1864, President Lincoln would sign the Kendall Green school's authorization to grant college degrees; in 1885 it would be renamed Gallaudet College for its president's father. In 1880, Gallaudet's sons Thomas and Edward Miner attended the Second International Conference on Education of the Deaf in Milan, which passed a resolution banning sign language in schools. The "language of signs" was soon eclipsed everywhere except on the campus of Gallaudet College and, ironically, in segregated schools for black deaf children in the South. In 1913, an elderly but still erect Edward Miner Gallaudet was filmed by the

National Association of the Deaf signing "Lorna Doone" for its archival *Preservation of the Sign Language.* The Asylum, renamed the American School for the Deaf, moved to West Hartford in 1920 after selling its Asylum Avenue campus to the Hartford insurance company.[30]

The temperance crusade was won in 1920, lost again in 1933. The American Tract Society and American Bible Society are still operating. The Congregational Church united with the Evangelical and Reformed Churches in 1957 to form the United Church of Christ. Four of the five Congregational churches in Hartford during Gallaudet's lifetime are still standing and conducting worship; a stained glass window in the Center Church honoring Gallaudet was sponsored by his prodigal son Wallace, a Wall Street banker. The Fifth, or Colored, Congregational on Talcott Street, is long gone, its site now a parking garage. The American Colonization Society was finally dissolved — in 1964. In 1960, Gallaudet College professor William Stokoe published *Sign Language Structure,* a linguistic study positing the shocking thesis that American Sign Language was indeed a language. At the same time, state residential schools for the deaf were beginning to close, as states saved money by shunting deaf children into local schools with more or less capable interpreters. The American School for the Deaf in West Hartford is one of the few left standing.[31]

Abbreviations

Notes

ACSP: American Colonization Society Papers, Library of Congress, Washington, D.C.

ASD: American School for the Deaf Museum.

CFP: Cocke Family Papers, Special Collections, University of Virginia Library.

CHS: Connecticut Historical Society Library.

EMGP: Edward Miner Gallaudet Papers, Gallaudet University Archives.

GFP: Gallaudet Family Papers, Gallaudet University Archives.

GP LoC: Thomas Hopkins and Edward Miner Gallaudet Papers, Library of Congress.

GUA: Gallaudet University Archives.

HBP CHS: Henry Barnard Papers, Connecticut Historical Society, Hartford.

HBP Trty: Henry Barnard Papers, Watkinson Library, Trinity College, Hartford.

Hills: Hills Library, Andover-Newton Theological Seminary, Newton, Massachusetts.

JLKP: James Luce Kingsley Papers, Sterling Library Manuscripts and Archives, Yale University.

LoC: Library of Congress, Washington, D.C.

MFCP: Mason Fitch Cogswell Papers, Beinecke Library, Yale.

MFCFP: Mason Fitch Cogswell Family Papers, Sterling Library, Manuscripts and Archives, Yale University.

SMSS: Small Manuscripts Collection, Gallaudet University Archives.

Stg: Sterling Library, Yale University.

Stg MSSA: Sterling Library Manuscripts and Archives, Yale University.

THG: Thomas Hopkins Gallaudet.

Preface

1. Paddy Ladd, *Understanding Deaf Culture*, p. 88.

2. See, for example, Harvey Prindle Peet, "Tribute to the Memory," p. 74.

3. See his Dedication to Colt's widow in his *Armsmear: The Home, the Arm and the Armory of Samuel Colt: A Memorial* (New York: Alvord, printer, 1866).

4. Joseph Harrington's "Thomas Hopkins Gallaudet" in the *Christian Examiner* states that profits went to Sophia, the "deaf and dumb widow." Luzerne Rae's review of *Tribute to Rev. Thomas H. Gallaudet* in the 1852 *American Annals of the Deaf and Dumb* remarks on the value of the appendices on p. 193. For the hopes of Gallaudet's children, see Edith Nye MacMullen, p. 186.

ONE Philadelphia to Hartford

1. Gallaudet's passport, GP LoC. His report of his weight is in an 1846 letter to his son William, reproduced in Heman Humphrey, *The Life and Labors of the Rev. T. H. Gallaudet, LL.D.* (hereafter, *Life*), pp. 322–323.

2. Name signs are the designations of single individuals. The two Gallaudet sons who lived their entire lives in Deaf communities have their own unrelated name signs, but Gallaudet University, being the namesake of T. H. Gallaudet, takes his name sign. THG to Thomas Gallaudet, 1849 Feb 2, transcribed in Humphrey, *Life*, pp. 331–332.

3. Calvinism and Federalism are discussed in chapter 2.

4. Wayne Franklin, *James Fenimore Cooper,* discusses Cooper's time in Albany on pp. 41–46.

5. On the Hartford Grammar School as teacher training for Yale tutors, see John Fulton, ed., *Memoirs of Frederick A. P. Barnard,* p. 41.

6. Eric R. Schlereth, *An Age of Infidels,* pp. 4–5; Henry F. May, *The Enlightenment in America,* p. 231.

7. The riots are discussed in Schlereth, pp. 31–40. Records of the Second Presbyterian Church of Philadelphia are held by the Presbyterian Historical Society, Philadelphia.

8. Mathew Carey, *A Short Account of the Malignant Fever,* p. 13.

9. The address appears on a classified ad in *The Pennsylvania Packet and Daily Advertiser,* 1787 Oct 2, p. 4.

10. Charles Brockden Brown, *Ormond,* chapter 4.

11. Both quotations are from Brown, *Arthur Mervyn,* part one, chapter 15.

12. Brown, part one, chapter 18.

13. Brown, part one, chapter 15.

14. THG to James L. Kingsley, 1810 Dec 3, JLKP.

15. According to Billy G. Smith, *Ship of Death,* p. 237. Full-scale outbreaks of yellow fever in New York City continued even later, the last one occurring in 1822, described by Wayne Franklin, *James Fenimore Cooper,* pp. 358–359.

16. Brown, *Ormond,* chapter 7.

17. "A Record of the Hopkins Family," and P. W. Gallaudet to THG, undated, GP LoC.

18. Peter Wallace Gallaudet's account books, CHS. The harpsichord is advertised in the *Pennsylvania Packet and Daily Advertiser,* 1787 Oct 2, p. 4. P. W.'s obituary in the *National Intelligencer,* 1843 May 19, is quoted by Eric P. Newman, "The Continental Dollar of 1776 Meets Its Maker," p. 923.

19. Lydia H. Sigourney, *Letters of Life,* p. 202. Jane Hopkins's antecedents are to be found in Lucas Barnes Barbour, *Families of Early Hartford,* and in William L. Porter to THG 1848 Jul 14, GP LoC. She sometimes appears in genealogies as "Jennet," a diminutive of "Jane" that today is spelled "Janet" or "Jeanette."

20. George Leon Walker, *History of the First Church,* pp. 352, 460–463; Gretchen Townsend Buggeln, "Elegance and Sensibility," pp. 430–435. Pews were sold to raise money for the church; those who could not afford a pew made shift to seat themselves in the rear or in balconies, or to stand, out of sight.

21. William A. Alcott, *Tall Oaks from Little Acorns,* p. 264.

22. For one of the more legible instances, see Peter Wallace Gallaudet Diaries, 1820 Dec 27, CHS.

23. Family history here follows the paternal line because this line of descent was what Gallaudet himself valued and preserved in his miscellaneous papers.

24. Nathan Chang, "The Legacy of Jonathan Edwards," pp. 45–47.

25. Peter Lewis De St. Croix to THG, 1825 Dec 31, GP LoC. Leah married Tory, and they lived in Nova Scotia after the Revolution. Of their five children, one became a physician with the British army.

26. Wayne Franklin, p. 145, for example, tells of Etienne deLancy, the Huguenot an-

cestor of Mrs. James Fenimore Cooper who moved to New York and joined the Anglican Church.

27. In an undated note from Peter Wallace Gallaudet to THG in GP LoC, P. W. tells of his Aunt Leah's "strong mind," saying that she and her Tory husband De St. Croix were "of the Episcopal Church" and that "she was a professor of Religion"—that is, one who has made a public profession of faith. About his own father, Thomas, he says nothing.

28. Some sources give this name as Peter Elihu, a mistake that seems to go back to Humphrey, *Life,* p. 17.

29. For Connecticut Congregational churches regarding themselves as Presbyterian rather than Congregationalist, see Walker, *History of the First Church,* pp. 358–359. A 1799 pronouncement from the Congregationalist Association to which the two Hartford churches belonged states that the "confession of faith, heads of agreement, and articles of church discipline, adopted at the earliest period of the Settlement of this State, is not Congregational, but contains the essentials of the church of Scotland, or Presbyterian Church in America," quoted in Walker, p. 358.

30. The Breton name means "powerful, having authority" and is a fairly common family name in Brittany. Le Gonidec, *Dictionnaire breton-français,* 1850 (St.-Brieuc: L. Prud'homme, 1847).

31. Robert Munro Erwin to Leonard M. Elstad, 1959 Apr 6, EMGP. Although we don't have independent corroboration of Erwin's evidence for this synagogue, there would have been no conceivable reason in 1959 for a Protestant to invent Jewish ancestry.

32. Claude Toczé and Annie Lambert, *Les Juifs en Bretagne,* pp. 22–24.

33. Nathaniel Hawthorne, *The House of the Seven Gables,* chapter 11.

34. Gallaudet, *Every-Day Christian,* p. 50. The discussion of diet is drawn largely from Lydia Maria Child's 1838 *American Frugal Housewife* and Amelia Simmons's 1796 *American Cookery.* See also Sarah F. McMahon, "A Comfortable Subsistence" and "'All Things in Their Proper Season.'"

35. Richard J. Purcell, *Connecticut in Transition,* p. 69.

36. On the country jail, see Daniel Sterner, *Vanished Downtown Hartford,* p. 57.

37. On agricultural exports, see Anne Farrow, Joel Lang, and Jenifer Frank, *Complicity,* p. 49; on manufactured goods for sale, see J. Eugene Smith, *One Hundred Years,* p. 39–40; on Jew Street, see Morris Silverman, *Hartford Jews* and the *Oxford English Dictionary,* sv "Jew."

38. On the Center Green auction block, see Hilary Moss, "'Cast Down on Every Side,'" p. 151.

39. On holidays, see John R. Bodo, *The Protestant Clergy,* p. 37; for Gallaudet's silence on Christmas, "Diary of Thomas Hopkins Gallaudet," GP LoC.

40. Joseph Coleman Hart, *Miriam Coffin, or, The Whale-Fishermen,* vol. 2, chapter 4. On the theater in Hartford, see J. Eugene Smith, *One Hundred,* pp. 109–110 and 129, and Jarvis Morse, *A Neglected Period of Connecticut's History,* p. 75. For a Calvinist theocracy, Connecticut was actually slow to ban theater. Glasgow had no theaters when James Boswell attended the university in that city not long before the date we are now considering, and Presbyterian mobs there had destroyed an ordinary building where a play had been staged and another where an actress was booked to appear.

41. Quotation from Leslie Fiedler, *Love and Death in the American Novel,* pp. 44 and 32.

42. Quotation from Ann Douglas, *The Feminization of American Culture*, p. 114.

43. THG, Rvw. of *James Montjoy* by A. S. Roe, *Hartford Courant*, 1850 Feb 4, p. 2.

44. Democracy as "hostile to good government" is a quotation from Samuel Griswold Goodrich's *Recollections of a Lifetime*, vol. 1, p. 117. For a discussion of the Wits, see Henry F. May, *Enlightenment*, pp. 260, 187–188, 233.

45. Richard Alsop to Mason Fitch Cogswell, 1793 Jan 16, CHS.

46. Quotations are from Richard Alsop's 1807 collection of most of these pieces, *The Echo, with Other Poems*.

47. THG to James L. Kingsley, 1810 Dec 3, JLKP. Robert Hopkins was the first modern critic to present a thoroughly ironic reading of the novel in his 1967 *The True Genius of Oliver Goldsmith: A Georgian Study*. Goethe was a contemporary reader who understood the irony directed at the vicar, quoted in George E. Haggerty, "Satire and Sentiment in *The Vicar of Wakefield*," p. 26.

48. Sally Sayward Wood, *Julia and the Illuminated Baron*, chapter 8.

49. *Mansfield Park*, chapter 25.

50. "On Chess," GP LoC.

51. From "A Reverie," an undated manuscript found among his papers but now lost, printed in Humphrey, *Life*, p. 19.

TWO **An American Theocracy**

1. See Eric Schlereth, *An Age of Infidels*, pp. 44–45 and 100–102, for discussion of established churches and disestablishment in some states.

2. Anson Phelps Stokes and Leo Pfeffer, *Church and State*, p. 23.

3. Strong's description of a revival he conducted as "calm" is quoted by Henry F. May, *Enlightenment*, p. 318, from a letter Strong wrote to Jedidiah Morse in 1799. See May, pp. 322–324, and Winthrop S. Hudson, *The Great Tradition*, pp. 68–69, for more discussion of the Second Great Awakening.

4. Timothy Dwight, "Discourse on Some Events of the Past Century," p. 33.

5. Richard J. Purcell, *Connecticut in Transition*, is still a good introduction to state government in this period.

6. Theodore Dwight, "An Oration Spoken at Hartford."

7. Richard Hofstadter, "The Paranoid Style in American Politics," gives the Bavarian Illuminati conspiracy theory as his first example. On the pervasive fear, see May, *Enlightenment*, pp. 358–359.

8. Samuel Griswold Goodrich, *Recollections*, vol. 2, pp. 116–118. Goodrich tells other tales about Strong in these pages, as does George L. Walker, *History of the First Church*, pp. 343–344n10 and 360–362.

9. Nathan Strong, "Political Instruction from the Prophecies of God's World—A Sermon," p. 27.

10. William Brown, "An Oration Spoken at Hartford."

11. See James Roger Sharp, *American Politics in the Early Republic*, passim, and Samuel F. May, *Enlightenment*, p. 254, for more discussion.

12. John Allen, a Connecticut congressman, quoted in James Roger Sharp, *American Politics in the Early Republic,* p. 179.

13. Quoted by Leon Howard, *The Connecticut Wits,* p. 399.

14. Quoted by Constance Mayfield Rourke, *Trumpets of Jubilee,* p. 20.

15. See Larry E. Tice, *American Counter-Revolution,* pp. 356–357.

16. Timothy Dwight, "Duty of Americans," pp. 12, 14, 26. The Illuminati conspiracy was not strictly news when Dwight went public with it on the Fourth of July, because two months earlier it had been posited as fact, and explained in a bit more detail, in a sermon given by Jedidiah Morse in Charlestown, Massachusetts (see "A Sermon, Delivered at the New North Church"), and in June by David Tappan, Hollis Professor of Divinity at Harvard, in an address to seniors (see Tappan, "A Discourse"). Much has been written about Robert Welsh's theories involving the Illuminati. See, for example, Sean Wilentz, "Confounding Fathers."

17. Mary Shelley, *Frankenstein,* chapter 3.

18. For historical facts on the Illuminati, see Stauffer, *The Bavarian Illuminati in America,* pp. 142–187.

19. Bishop's writings on Haiti are reprinted in Tim Matthewson, "Abraham Bishop, 'The Rights of Black Men,' and the American Reaction to the Haitian Revolution." See John R. Fitzmier, *New England's Moral Legislator,* pp. 65–66, for discussion of how marriage patterns bound and strengthened the Standing Order. See Matthewson on the backlash against the Haitian slave revolt.

20. Abraham Bishop, *Proofs of a Conspiracy,* p. 20.

21. On admission requirements, see Fitzmier, *New England's Moral Legislator,* p. 56. Franklin, *James Fenimore Cooper,* p. 47, adds a Latin prose composition, citing *The Laws of Yale College.* Noah Webster's assessment is in his 1790 "On the Education of Youth in America," reprinted in Frederick Rudolph, ed., *Essays on Education,* pp. 441–477. On Latin having been replaced by English, see Theodore Dwight Jr., *President Dwight's Decisions,* p. 205, and Larry E. Tice, *American Counter-Revolution,* p. 130.

22. On the costs of Yale and location of classrooms, see Franklin Bowditch Dexter, "Student Life at Yale College." On "defaced and dirty" rooms, see Charles Beecher, ed., *The Autobiography of Lyman Beecher,* vol. 1, p. 39. On P. W. Gallaudet's ability to cover costs, see Alcott, *Tall Oaks,* p. 266.

23. Purcell, *Connecticut in Transition,* p. 203. For Silliman, see Fitzmier, pp. 55–56.

24. Quotation is from Dorothy Ann Lipson, *Freemasonry in Federalist Connecticut,* pp. 84–85.

25. Dwight's views are stated in Theodore Dwight Jr., *President Dwight's Decisions,* p. 221.

26. Dexter, "Student Life at Yale College." Gallaudet's involvement with Brothers in Unity is mentioned by Anson Phelps Stokes, *Memorials of Eminent Yale Men,* pp. 228–230.

27. The text is from an excerpt published in Kettell, *Specimens of American Poetry,* vol. 1, pp. 237–246. Dwight's poems scan well and rhyme true if read with a cockney accent, the closest present-day approximation to the standard-elite New England accent of the early republic.

28. Humphrey, *Life,* pp. 22–23.

29. Goodrich, *Recollections,* vol. 2, pp. 126–127.

30. Discussed in Fitzmier, *New England's Moral Legislator,* pp. 44–45.

31. Although a rubric in large lettering "Disputes / Senior Year/ Yale College," suggests that those that come before it were written for a tutor or for his debating club, Brothers in Unity, while those that come after were written for Dwight, in fact all the questions are known to have been those recycled by Dwight every year, and all the arguments recorded are known to comport with Dwight's views. This could not have been the case if the positions were Gallaudet's, because Dwight assigned students to positions randomly. Gallaudet must have copied them out after the dispute had taken place in Dwight's seminar, or as cribs for class discussion, perhaps with the help of a tutor or friendly senior who knew what Dwight would say. The disputes are in GP LoC. James Fernandes, "The Gate to Heaven," p. 57, notes that all answers are consistent with Gallaudet's views as an adult; Chang, "Legacy of Jonathan Edwards," pp. 66–67, observes of one dispute, "The striking similarities between Dwight and Gallaudet's arguments were unlikely to have been coincidental; it looked as though Gallaudet took his theological arguments right out of Dwight's pages," and, further, that "Gallaudet also adopted Dwight's antagonistic tone."

32. On Dwight's student amanuenses, see Leon Howard, *The Connecticut Wits,* pp. 344 and 372.

33. Dwight gives his position in Theodore Dwight Jr., *President Dwight's Decisions,* pp. 319, and Timothy Dwight, "The Folly, Guilt, and Mischiefs of Duelling," pp. 24–25.

34. Dwight's detailed objections to plays are in Theodore Dwight Jr., *President Dwight's Decisions,* pp. 175 and 177.

35. The story is told in "An Incident," *New York Commercial Advertiser,* 1839 Sep 16, and discussed in chapter 9.

36. Dwight quoted in Theodore Dwight Jr. *President Dwight's Decisions,* pp. 220, 223–224, 229. For discussion of a national university, see May, *Enlightenment in America,* p. 312, and Kathleen McCarthy, *American Creed,* pp. 124–125. The belief that cities are improper locations for colleges was held by Noah Webster ("On the Education of Youth in America," reprinted in Rudolph, *Essays on Education,* p. 54) and authors of textbooks later associated with Gallaudet, including Jedidiah Morse's *American Universal Geography* and F. A. P. Barnard's *An Analytic Grammar with Symbolic Illustration.*

37. Bishop, *Proofs of a Conspiracy,* p. 30.

38. Theodore Dwight Jr., *President Dwight's Decisions,* p. 287.

39. Brian Kilmeade and Don Yaeger, *Thomas Jefferson and the Tripoli Pirates,* p. 37.

40. Andrew Burstein, *The Original Knickerbocker,* pp. 41–42.

41. To the Editor of the *Federal Gazette,* 1790 Mar 23. Rpt. in Jared Sparks, ed., *The Works of Benjamin Franklin,* vol. 2.

42. Chang, "Legacy of Jonathan Edwards," p. 79.

43. Franklin, *James Fenimore Cooper,* p. 47. The following narration of Cooper's adventures at Yale is indebted to Franklin, pp. 47–60.

44. "Line Written after Dreaming on Some Wedding Cake" and "A Pastoral," GP LoC. The poem from the Brothers in Unity address is given in E. M. Gallaudet, *Life,* p. 22.

45. For the assertion that THG was "Latin Salutatorian," see Isaac Lewis Peet, "Thomas Hopkins Gallaudet, An Oration on the Centennial Anniversary of His Birth, Delivered in Faneuil Hall, Boston Dec. 10, 1887," *American Annals of the Deaf* 33.1 (1888): 43–54,

assertion on p. 45. The manuscript of the oration is held by the Stg MSSA. The spelling of the possessive "its" as "it's" was common at the time.

46. For discussion of luxury as a threat, see May, *Enlightenment in America,* p. 259, 182.

47. Purcell, *Connecticut in Transition,* p. 191; Leon Howard, *The Connecticut Wits,* p. 343.

48. Qtd. by Franklin, *James Fenimore Cooper,* pp. 59–60.

THREE Drifting

1. A different Chauncey Goodrich, his nephew, would become Noah Webster's son-in-law and take over the editing of the dictionary after Webster's death.

2. Thomas Robbins, *Diary,* 1807 Jul 26, vol. 1, p. 330, tells of an overnight trip that Gallaudet, nineteen, and Elizur Goodrich, forty-six, made to a Norfolk clergyman. Dwight's biographer, John R. Fitzmier, *New England's Moral Legislator,* p. 56, says that Dwight, too, regularly used his influence to place his graduates.

3. THG to Langdon et al. (Portsmouth Church), 1814 Jul 7, GFP.

4. The theory that Gallaudet suffered from allergies or asthma was proposed by James Fernandes, "The Gate to Heaven," p. 49.

5. THG to Henry M. Wait, [no date], Phi Beta Kappa Papers, Stg MSSA. This collection includes two refusals to the fraternity in response, specifically, to their request for a poem.

6. THG to Henry Barnard, 1838 May 21, HBP Trty.

7. THG to James L. Kingsley 1811 Feb 22, JLKP.

8. THG to [?], 1818 Jan 25, GP LoC; Laurent Clerc to Mason Fitch Cogswell, 1818 May 7, MFCP; THG to directors, 1818 April, ASD; THG to Joshua Lacey Wilson, 1819 Jun 19, American Memory Collection, LoC.

9. Oxford English Dictionary, sv "hypochondria." Douglas, *Feminization of American Culture,* discusses depression among the clergy passim; for example, Lyman Beecher's case on p. 25.

10. THG to Eli Todd, 1828 Feb 12, HBP CHS.

11. THG to Eli Todd, 1828 Feb 12, HBP CHS.

12. Emily P. Baldwin to Eliza Fitch, 1820 Apr 3, Baldwin Family Papers, Stg MSSA.

13. See Edward Shorter, *Before Prozac,* pp. 15–16.

14. GP LoC.

15. GP LoC.

16. The study of English belles-lettres for aesthetic value was not established in American colleges until much later in the century. Nathan Chang, in his fifth chapter, and Phyllis Valentine, in "American Asylum for the Deaf: A First Experiment in Education, 1817–1880," pp. 69–109, have demonstrated Gallaudet's thorough familiarity with the Scottish Common Sense philosophers, whose works would surely have been studied in Yale's "English" curriculum. Gallaudet's later meetings in Edinburgh with Dugald Stewart and Thomas Brown are discussed in the next chapter.

17. The undated narrative was found on a loose paper after Gallaudet's death and published in the *American Annals of the Deaf and Dumb* 10.4 (1858 Oct): p. 249.

18. *Yale Bulletin & Calendar* 2007 Nov 30.

19. The *Courant* is quoted in Purcell, *Connecticut in Transition,* p. 177.

20. "On the Use of Ambition" and "Rival Roses," GP LoC.

21. That Gallaudet was arguing against Smith was noticed by Chang, "Legacy of Jonathan Edwards," pp. 86–87. On the American reception of *The Wealth of Nations,* see May, *Enlightenment,* p. 349. On Calvinist objections, see Charles Taylor, *A Secular Age,* p. 229.

22. Gallaudet's quotation of "Take the instant way . . ." is from III.iii, 159–166. Though we do not have his source edition for these lines, the spelling error must be his own.

23. Franklin Bowditch Dexter, *Biographical Notices of Graduates of Yale College,* vol. 6, pp. 169, 290.

24. THG to Samuel J. Hitchcock, [no date]. Franklin Bowditch Dexter Papers, Stg MSSA.

25. E. M. Gallaudet, *Life,* p. 29.

26. E. M. Gallaudet, *Life,* pp. 29–30.

27. On the Rev. Strong's distillery business, see George Leon Walker, *History of the First Church,* pp. 342–344.

28. On dancing, see John Demos, *Heathen School,* p. 68. Despite the spread of temperance, the Hartford area supported twenty distilleries as late as 1815: Richard D. Birdsall, "Second Great Awakening," p. 361.

29. TULIP: Total depravity, Unconditional election, Limited atonement, Irresistible grace, and Perseverance of the saints.

30. E. M. Gallaudet, *Life,* p. 31; THG to James L. Kingsley, 1811 Feb 22, JLKP.

31. E. M. Gallaudet, *Life,* p. 37; Chang, "Legacy of Jonathan Edwards," pp. 101–102.

32. THG to James L. Kingsley, 1811 Feb 2 and 22, JLKP.

33. On Louis Dwight, see William Jenks, "Memoir of Rev. Louis Dwight."

34. THG to Kingsley, 1811 Feb 22, JLKP. Untitled journal, entry for 1811 March 24, GP LoC. Barnard, *Tribute to Gallaudet,* p. 11.

35. THG to James L. Kingsley, 1810 Dec 3, JLKP.

36. THG to James L. Kingsley, 1811 Feb 2, JLKP.

37. GFP.

38. Gallaudet's remarks on his health in his trip journal are in the December 4 and 6 entries, GP LoC. Remarks on his mood are in the 1811 Feb 2 letter to Kingsley; those on his constipation in the 1811 Feb 22 letter, JLKP.

39. [?] to [THG], 1811 May 10, GP LoC.

40. Barnard, *Tribute to Gallaudet,* p. 11; Humphrey, *Life,* p. 24; E. M. Gallaudet, *Life,* p. 38. THG to James L. Kingsley, 1811 Feb 22, JLKP.

41. Barnard, p. 11, and Humphrey, p. 24, put Gallaudet's profession of faith before his enrollment in the seminary, which seems logical but is inaccurate. E. M. Gallaudet, p. 39, gets the sequence right. Gallaudet's guilt at taking more than his fair share of his parents' resources is in THG to Kingsley, 1811 Feb 22, JLKP. The quotation regarding tuition and expenses is from Timothy Dwight, "A Sermon Preached at the Opening of the Theological Institution in Andover," p. 10.

42. "A Sermon Preached at the Opening of the Theological Institution in Andover," quotations from pp. 26–27.

43. Susan J. Montgomery and Roger G. Reed, *Phillips Academy.* Claude M. Fuess, *An*

Old New England School, provides a good overview of how the horror at Unitarianism convinced the various factions of conservative Calvinists to collaborate on the seminary. The planned five professorships are stated in Dwight's "Sermon," p. 11. On the oath, see Douglas, *Feminization,* p. 146. Jedidiah Morse's comments on Unitarians are cited in May, *Enlightenment,* p. 351. See Hugh Davis, *Leonard Bacon,* pp. 33–34, for the professors' conservative social views. Davis provides excellent discussion of Andover and insights into a slightly younger contemporary whose education and whose social and political views were virtually identical to Gallaudet's.

44. *Annual Reports to Directors,* Andover Theological Seminary, for 1812, 1813, and 1814, Hills.

45. Leon Howard, *The Connecticut Wits,* pp. 388–389, 391. For discussion of the Connecticut clergy's opposition to the war, see May, *Enlightenment,* p. 317.

46. Society of Inquiry, Constitution and Earliest Records, Hills. The information on regular meetings and on the need for a London correspondent is from Society of Inquiry to L. M. The letter seeking a Boston agent is C[alvin] Colton, E[benezer] Kellogg, and J[oel] Hawes to [Samuel] Armstrong, 1814 Jun 27. See also Leonard Woods, *Memoirs of American Missionaries.* A discussion of the scarcity of specie can be found in Purcell, *Connecticut in Transition,* p. 71.

47. GP LoC.

48. The valedictory address was published in the *Panoplist and Missionary Magazine* 10.10 (1814 Oct): 449–455. The quotations in this sentence are a hodgepodge of biblical verses, from Isaiah, Psalms, Proverbs, and I Peter, suggesting further that it was written by a committee of students. The phrase "garments rolled in blood" seems to have occurred to more than one writer opposed to the War of 1812, turning up, for example, in David Osgood's 1812 "A Solemn Protest," quoted in Peter Manseau, *One Nation,* p. 207.

49. License to Preach the Gospel, GP LoC.

50. Gallaudet's claim is made in THG to B. B. Edwards, 1845 Jul 28, transcribed in Humphrey, *Life,* pp. 369–373. On Perkins, see www.whfirstchurch.org/about/who/history, accessed February 14, 2017.

51. Christopher T. Leffler and Puneet S. Braich, "The First Cataract Surgeons." Cataract surgery created a sensation in the United States in the 1780s. Charles Brockden Brown, for example, in chapter 17 of *Ormond,* depicts cataract surgery by an unnamed European surgeon on a reluctant Philadelphia patient in 1784 as miraculous.

52. The quotation is from Lydia H. Sigourney, *Letters of Life,* pp. 201–202. For a discussion of her school in Mrs. Wadsworth's home and of her association with Alice, as well as for the foundation of the following discussion about the Cogswells' preparation of Alice for schooling, see Edna Edith Sayers and Diana Moore, eds., *Mrs. Sigourney of Hartford,* pp. 19–36.

53. See Ruth C. Loew, C. T. Akamatsu, and Mary Lanaville, "A Two-Handed Manual Alphabet," for a detailed discussion of the Old Alphabet. It was still used by some elderly Deaf Americans into the twentieth century. The 1776 publication in the *Pennsylvania Magazine* is stated in Lucius H. Woodruff, "Primary Instruction of the Deaf and Dumb," *American Annals of the Deaf and Dumb* 1 (1848), p. 11. The 1793 observer was William Thornton, "Cadmus," p. 315. Cogswell to Harriet Cogswell, 1815 Sep 2, CFP.

54. Alcott, *Tall Oaks,* p. 268.

55. Barnard, *Tribute,* p. 12; Humphrey, *Life,* pp. 25–26, 29; E. M. Gallaudet, *Life,* pp. 47–48.

56. Lewis Weld, "The American Asylum," in Barnard's *Tribute,* p. 132.

57. Edward Miner Gallaudet, "The Influence of the Huguenot Spirit on Philanthropic Work in America," EMGP.

58. Paddy Ladd, *Understanding Deaf Culture,* p. 88.

59. Gallaudet's story is in J. M. Wainwright, "Institution at Harford," p. 128.

60. Charlotte Elizabeth [Phelan], "The Happy Mute," p. 7.

61. George H. Loring, "Address to Laurent Clerc," p. 146.

FOUR Reinventing the Wheel

1. Brewster's life and work is the topic of Harlan Lane's *A Deaf Artist in Early America.* See also Edna Edith Sayers and Diana Moore, "Lydia Huntley Sigourney and the Beginnings of American Deaf Education," pp. 377–378. On de l'Épée's familiarity with a finger alphabet, see Francis Green, "Extracts from the Institution des Sourds," *American Annals of the Deaf and Dumb* 8 (1856), p. 12; on finger alphabets being used as amusement, see Lois Bragg, "Visual-Kinetic Communication."

2. Barnard, *Tribute,* p. 13. I am indebted to a personal communication from Phyllis Valentine that Cogswell had no French. Harlan Lane, *When the Mind Hears,* p. 182, also concludes that Cogswell had no book by Sicard but supposes that he had Francis Green's translation of de l'Épée's *Method of Educating the Deaf and Dumb.* Gallaudet's own statement is in J. M. Wainwright, "Institution at Hartford," p. 128.

3. Benjamin Rush, "Thoughts upon Female Education," 1787. Reprinted in Rudolph, *Essays on Education,* p. 35.

4. [Green, trans.], "Preface of the Translator," *The Method of Educating the Deaf and Dumb,* p. xix. This discussion of Francis Green is dependent on Alexander Graham Bell, "Historical Notes," vol. 2: pp. 42–69, 119–126.

5. [Green], *Vox Occulis Subjecta,* p. vii, and quoted in Bell, "Historical Notes," vol. 2: p. 47.

6. Quoted in Bell, "Historical Notes," vol. 2: p. 51.

7. [Green, trans.], "Preface of the Translator," *Method of Educating the Deaf and Dumb,* p. xv.

8. [Green, trans.], "Preface," pp. xx–xxi.

9. These figures are for people who were born or became deaf as young children; they do not include people who lost their hearing as adults. An 1832 review of the annual reports of three deaf schools was still providing a severe undercount, asserting that the U.S. rate was .05 percent: "Instruction of the Deaf and Dumb," *American Annals of Education* 2.1 (1832 Jan): p. 25.

10. Lengthy extracts from Green's *Palladium* letters were reprinted in the *American Annals of the Deaf and Dumb* 8 (1855): 8–29. The quotation is from p. 9; the mythic narrative of de l'Épée and the twin sisters is recounted on p. 12.

11. From Lydia Sigourney, *Letters to My Pupils,* excerpted in Sayers and Moore, eds., *Mrs. Sigourney of Hartford,* pp. 68–69.

12. THG to Jedidiah Morse, 1815 Apr. 25, Jedidiah Morse Papers, Manuscript Division,

New York Public Library; transcribed in Jean Taylor Kimball Wilson, "Account of the
Gallaudet Family."

13. See Phyllis Valentine, "American Asylum for the Deaf," pp. 63–65 for more discussion.

14. Charlotte Elizabeth [Phelan], "The Happy Mute," pp. 22 and 10.

15. Jules Paul Seigel, "The Enlightenment and the Evolution of a Language," pp. 96, 98.

16. Noah Webster, "On the Education of Youth in America," in Rudolph, *Essays on Education,* p. 73.

17. H. P. Peet, "Tribute to the Memory of the Late Thomas H. Gallaudet," *American Annals of the Deaf and Dumb* 4.2 (1852), quotation on pp. 71–72.

18. The census of deaf residents in Connecticut is discussed in Lane, *When the Mind Hears,* pp. 182–183. Relevant letters are reprinted in Bell, "Historical Notes," vol. 3, pp. 131–134.

19. Bell reprints many relevant letters and provides additional information on the Gilberts in "Historical Notes," vol. 3, pp. 131–140. An 1816 July 18 letter on pp. 138–139 shows that the Gilbert children were friends of Alice's.

20. Valentine, "American Asylum for the Deaf," p. 21.

21. See [Nathan] Lord to THG, 1815 March [no day], GP LoC, and Eliphalet Kimball to Mason Fitch Cogswell, [1815] Jan 4, MFCP. This letter is dated by Kimball 1814, but on that date in 1814, Cogswell was not yet engaged in fund-raising and Gallaudet was not yet "the Rev. Mr. Gallaudet." I thank Phyllis Valentine for her assessment of the date Kimball wrote on this letter.

22. A Cogswell descendant, Grace Cogswell Root, mistakenly gives the year as 1813, not 1815. Root, *Father and Daughter,* p. 67.

23. See Theodore Dwight, *History of the Hartford Convention.* Richard Buel, *America on the Brink,* pp. 221–228, is a good recent assessment.

24. See THG to Jedidiah Morse, 1815 Apr 25, transcribed in Wilson, "Account of the Gallaudet Family," in which Gallaudet writes, "I shall make it my home at Doctr. Mason F. Coggswell's, for my father's family removes to New York next week."

25. On the Wadsworth and Terry residences, see Sterner, *Vanished Downtown Hartford,* pp. 100–101. Daniel Wadsworth would tear down his parents' house in 1844 to build the Wadsworth Athenaeum: he collected art, patronized artists, and dabbled in it himself.

26. James King Morse, *Jedidiah Morse,* p. 18.

27. See Valentine, *American Asylum for the Deaf,* pp. 23–24 for profiles of these six. On Buck's merchandise, see his advertisement in the *Hartford Courant* 1820 May 26.

28. The "one day" claim is first made by Barnard in *Tribute,* p. 14, and is repeated by nearly every subsequent biographer.

29. The quotation is from Phyllis Valentine, "American Asylum for the Deaf," p. 111, referring to views in New Haven that same month.

30. "Original Subscription" is reprinted in Bell, "Historical Notes," vol. 3, pp. 329–331.

31. THG to Jeremiah Day, 1815 Feb 1, CFP. Quoted in Fernandes, "Gate to Heaven," p. 65, where the date is mistakenly given as 1814.

32. Jeremiah Day to THG, 1815 Apr 12. GP LoC.

33. THG, "A Journal of Some Occurrences." GP LoC.

34. Nathan Lord to THG, 1815 Apr 18, transcribed in E. M. Gallaudet, *Life,* pp. 52–53.

35. Ebenezer Kellogg to THG, quoted in E. M. Gallaudet, *Life,* p. 53. E. M. Gallaudet says that his father received it the same day he received the letter from Nathan Lord concerning George Hall's trip, that is, April 20.

36. THG to Langdon et al., 1814 July 7. GP LoC.

37. Barnard, *Life,* p. 12. The quotation on Gallaudet's punctuality is from Horace Hooker's entry on Gallaudet in *Annals of the American Pulpit,* p. 614.

38. THG to [Mason Fitch Cogswell], 1816 Mar 14. GP LoC.

39. E. M. Gallaudet, *Life,* p. 56.

40. Valentine, "American Asylum for the Deaf," pp. 79–80.

41. Barnard, *Tribute,* p. 14. Barnard transcribes the address, pp. 14–17. The following quotation is from p. 16. The address was published in the *Mirror* on May 22, the *Courant* on May 24, and the *Connecticut Herald* on May 30.

42. [Job Williams], "Brief History," p. 12. Valentine, "American Asylum," 125–28.

43. E. M. Gallaudet states that his grandparents were in New York by the time his father arrived to take ship: *Life,* p. 56.

44. THG to Alice Cogswell, 1815 May 14. Transcribed in Humphrey, *Life,* pp. 30–31.

45. THG to Mason Fitch Cogswell, 1815 May 19, GP LoC.

46. THG to Mason Fitch Cogswell, 1815 May 25, GP LoC.

47. THG to Ward Woodbridge, 1815 May 23; Woodbridge replied 1815 July 6. Both in GP LoC.

48. "American Asylum for the Deaf and Dumb," *Literary and Philosophical Repertory* 2 (1815): 291–293.

49. Goodrich, *Recollections,* vol. 1, p. 126.

50. Mrs. G. M. Sykes, "Reminiscences," p. 44.

51. Alcott, *Tall Oaks,* p. 298.

52. On Wadsworth's goodbye in the New York harbor, see Daniel Wadsworth to THG, 1815 Oct 20, GP LoC. The quotations are from THG to Mason Fitch Cogswell, 1815 May 25, GP LoC.

53. GP LoC.

54. THG to Mason Fitch Cogswell, 1815 Jun 24. GP LoC.

55. THG to Mason Fitch Cogswell, 1815 Jun 26. GP LoC.

56. THG to Ward Woodbridge, 1815 July 10. Transcribed in Humphrey, *Life,* pp. 31–33.

57. He mentions this visit to the Birmingham school in his contribution to Wainwright's "Institution at Hartford," p. 129, as well as in a "Journal" entry for July 21, GP LoC.

58. Daniel Wadsworth to THG, 1815 Oct 20, GP LoC, and transcribed in Humphrey, *Life,* pp. 56–58.

59. See Alan Richardson, *Literature, Education, and Romanticism,* pp. 14, 85, and 120 for a discussion of the Mores' school.

60. Hannah More to THG, 1818 Apr 28, and Zachary Macaulay to THG, 1818 Nov 7, transcribed in E. M. Gallaudet, *Life,* pp. 104–06 and 106–10.

61. Zachary Macaulay to THG, 1818 Nov 7, transcribed in E. M. Gallaudet, *Life,* pp. 106–110.

62. THG to Mason Fitch Cogswell, 1815 July 11; THG's "Journal of Some Occurrences," entry for July 8, GP LoC. This story is recounted in Laurent Clerc's "Autobiography" and is

summarized in "Gallaudet and Clerc: Interesting Autobiographical Statements," *Hartford Daily Courant,* 1869 Jul 21, p. 2.

63. Jean Massieu and Laurent Clerc, *A Collection of the Most Remarkable Definitions and Answers,* pp. 17, 19, 35, 37, 41, 53, 90–93.

64. Massieu and Clerc, pp. 64–71. Clerc explained this example at the Second Convention of American Instructors of the Deaf and Dumb in 1851: "Some Hints to the Teachers of the Deaf and Dumb," *Proceedings* (Hartford: Case, Tiffany, 1851), pp. 64–75.

65. Edgeworth, *Belinda,* Book 1, chapter 3; Rowson, *Charlotte Temple,* chapter 4, 27, 28; Carlyle, trans., *Wilhelm Meister,* Book 2, chapter 3.

66. *Seventh Annual Report of the Directors of the American Asylum* (1823), p. 8; Howe is quoted in R. A. R. Edwards, *Words Made Flesh,* p. 196.

67. "Journal of Some Occurrences," 1815 July 26, GP LoC.

68. "Journal of Some Occurrences," 1815 Aug 12, GP LoC.

69. *Fifth Report of the Directors of the American Asylum* (1821), p. 4.

70. This and the preceding quotation are from "Journal of Some Occurrences," GP LoC.

71. THG to Mason Fitch Cogswell, 1815 Aug 15, transcribed in E. M. Gallaudet, *Life,* pp. 60–76.

72. "Journal of Some Occurrences," 1816 Aug 16, GP LoC.

73. Daniel Wadsworth to THG, 1815 Oct 20, GP LoC.

74. Transcribed in E. M. Gallaudet, *Life,* pp. 60–76.

75. THG to Mason Fitch Cogswell, 1816 Jan 11, transcribed in Humphrey, *Life,* pp. 48–49.

76. Clerc, "An Address . . . Read by His Request"; H. P. Peet, "Tribute," *American Annals of the Deaf and Dumb* 4.2 (1852): p. 73.

77. Alice Cogswell to THG, 1815 July 6 and 1815 Aug 14, GP LoC.

78. THG to Alice Cogswell, 1815 Aug 15, transcribed in Humphrey, *Life,* pp. 41–43.

79. THG to Alice Cogswell, 1816 Jan 22. GP LoC.

80. THG to Mason Fitch Cogswell, 1815 Oct 10, SMSS.

81. E. M. Gallaudet, *Life,* p. 86.

82. THG to Mason Fitch Cogswell, excerpted without a date in Humphrey, *Life,* pp. 51–52.

83. The "Journal" entry for November 10 states that he was reading Sicard in French in order to facilitate communication when he gets to Paris. That he had instruction from a Mr. Barré is found in THG to Mason Fitch Cogswell, 1816 Feb 21, GP LoC.

84. Burstein, *The Original Knickerbocker,* pp. 94, 116.

85. Walter Scott, *The Bride of Lammermoor,* chapter 33; *Waverley,* chapter 36.

86. See May, *Enlightenment,* p. 294, for discussion.

87. Samuel Fleischacker, "The Impact on America," p. 332.

88. Theodore Dwight Jr., *President Dwight's Decisions,* pp. 346–347.

89. See Chang, "Legacy of Jonathan Edwards," p. 154.

90. Fleischacker, "The Impact on America," p. 332.

91. THG to Ralph Emerson, 1816 Jan 11, transcribed in Humphrey, *Life,* pp. 45–48.

92. Chang, "Legacy of Jonathan Edwards," p. 156.

93. Valentine, "American Asylum for the Deaf," p. 108.

94. Dugald Stewart, *Collected Works,* vol. 4, pp. 332 and 337. The italics are Stewart's.

95. Stewart, *Collected Works,* vol. 4, pp. 6–18.

96. Stewart, *Collected Works,* vol. 4, pp. 238–245.

97. Benjamin Silliman to THG, 1816 Jun 1, GP LoC. Silliman was being kept informed about Gallaudet's doings in Europe by Daniel Wadsworth, Timothy Dwight, and Ralph Emerson. "Journal of Some Occurrences," 1815 Sep 30, GP LoC, mentions the visit to Stewart.

98. The letter is partly transcribed in E. M. Gallaudet, *Life,* pp. 89–90.

99. THG to Woodbridge, 1815 Sep 30, transcribed in Humphrey, *Life,* pp. 44–45.

100. Transcribed in Humphrey, *Life,* pp. 53–54. Humphrey gives the letter without a date and with the superscription "Edinburgh," but the content indicates clearly that it was written from London.

101. On Julia Brace and Lydia Sigourney's efforts on her behalf, see Sayers and Moore, ed., *Mrs. Sigourney of Hartford,* pp. 118–120.

102. "Journal of Some Occurrences," 1815 Nov 10, GP LoC, mentions Brown's lectures; for the number of lectures Gallaudet attended, forty, THG to Ralph Emerson, 1816 Jan 11, transcribed in Humphrey, *Life,* pp. 45–48.

103. Thomas Dixon, "Revolting against Reid," p. 23. The following discussion of Brown is indebted to Dixon's article and to his *Thomas Brown, Selected Philosophical Writings.* Quotations of Brown's contemporaries are from Dixon's remarks in *Selected Philosophical Writings,* p. 24. Gallaudet's remarks are in THG to Ward Woodbridge, [1815] Dec 6, transcribed in Humphrey, *Life,* pp. 50–51: this is the same letter appearing somewhat differently excerpted in E. M. Gallaudet, *Life,* pp. 82–84.

104. THG to Ralph Emerson, 1816 Jan 11, transcribed in Humphrey, *Life,* pp. 45–48.

105. Theodore Dwight Jr., *President Dwight's Decisions,* pp. 345–346.

106. This story is excerpted and discussed in Edna Edith Sayers and Diana Gates, "Lydia Huntley Sigourney and the Beginnings of American Deaf Education in Hartford," p. 381. The manuscript is in GP LoC.

107. "Journal of Some Occurrences," 1815 Sep 30, Oct 29, Dec 27, and 1816 Feb 3, GP LoC.

108. THG to Mason Fitch Cogswell, 1815 Oct 10, SMSS.

109. Alice Cogswell to Sarah L. Cogswell and Harriet B. Cogswell, 1815 Oct 17, CFP. One of the recipients has rather unkindly noted on the envelope, with underscoring, "Letter from Alice Cogswell the Mute."

110. THG to Mason Fitch Cogswell, 1815 Oct 10, SMSS.

111. THG to Mason Fitch Cogswell, 1816 Feb 21, GP LoC.

112. "Journal of Some Occurrences," 1815 Dec 27, GP LoC; also transcribed in Barnard, *Tribute,* p. 18.

113. Mary Shelley, *Frankenstein,* chapter 4.

114. Alice Cogswell to THG, 1815 Dec 13, GP LoC.

115. Gallaudet relates this visit and mentions the gift in a now-lost letter to Daniel Wadsworth. Wadsworth refers to these events in Daniel Wadsworth to THG, 1816 July 31, transcribed in Humphrey, *Life,* pp. 67–69.

116. Zachary Macaulay to THG, 1816 Apr 16, transcribed in Humphrey, *Life,* pp. 76–77.

117. John Tabak, *Significant Gestures,* p. 27. The controversial policy established by Gallaudet was, in the *Observer*'s view, the failure to engage in speech training.

118. John Quincy Adams to David Baillie Warden, 1816 Mar 2, Warden Papers, Maryland Historical Society.

119. THG to Ward Woodbridge, 1816 Mar 4, transcribed in Humphrey, *Life,* pp. 59–60.

FIVE "What's the Gaiety of Paris to Me?"

1. Mary Grant to Harriet Jackson, 1816 Feb 11, Mary Grant Correspondence 1810–1834, Massachusetts Historical Society.

2. THG to Mason Fitch Cogswell, 1816 Mar 14, GP LoC.

3. Gallaudet, "Journal of Some Occurrences," GP LoC. Gallaudet again credits Clerc with the idea of accompanying Gallaudet to Hartford in a letter to Sicard, 1816 May 21, GP LoC.

4. See Nathan Chang, "Legacy of Jonathan Edwards," p. 17, for discussion of Sicard as a Jansenist.

5. Jean Massieu, "Autobiography," p. 77.

6. Laurent Clerc, "Jean Massieu," *American Annals of the Deaf and Dumb* 2 (1849): pp. 85, 88, and Jean Massieu, "Autobiography," pp. 77–78.

7. Edmund Booth, "Thomas Hopkins Gallaudet," p. 25.

8. This is according to Clerc, in his remarks in J. M. Wainwright, "Institution at Hartford," p. 132.

9. Clerc's remarks in Wainwright, "Institution at Hartford," pp. 133–134.

10. Quoted in [F. A. P. Barnard], "Education of the Deaf and Dumb," *North American Review,* 1834 Apr, pp. 76–77.

11. Harlan Lane, *When the Mind Hears,* p. 62. See also Clerc's pupil Ferdinand Berthier's example of the five methodical signs needed to express the notion of unintelligibility in Lane, ed., *The Deaf Experience,* p. 197.

12. Roche-Ambroise Bébian, "Essay on the Deaf and Natural Language," in Lane, *Deaf Experience,* p. 140.

13. GP LoC.

14. Chang, "Legacy of Jonathan Edwards," pp. 171–177.

15. *Discourses on Various Points of Christian Faith and Practice.* This book was copyrighted in the United States in April 1818: GP LoC. The anonymous review is in the *Christian Observer,* 1818 Jul, pp. 456 ff.

16. Poems, GP LoC.

17. Both quoted passages are from THG to [Mason Fitch Cogswell], 1816 Mar 14, GP LoC. Gallaudet used the exact phrasing of the bulk of this letter in another letter written on the same day to Ward Woodbridge, transcribed in Humphrey, *Life,* pp. 60–62.

18. Benjamin Silliman to THG, 1816 Jun 1, GP LoC.

19. Joshua Kendall, *Forgotten Founding Father,* p. 334.

20. THG to Mason Fitch Cogswell, 1816 April 11, GP LoC.

21. THG to Sicard, 1816 May 21, GP LoC.

22. Clerc, *Diary,* p. 7; "Autobiography," p. 3. At the dedication of the monument to Gallaudet on the campus of the American Asylum, Clerc repeated the assertion that it was Gallaudet who originated the idea of Clerc accompanying him to Hartford as his assistant: "Clerc's Tribute to Gallaudet: Delivered at the Dedication of the Monument at Hartford,

Connecticut, in Honor of Gallaudet," GUA. "Journal of Some Occurrences," 1816 May 20, GP LoC.

23. Contract between Gallaudet and Clerc, GP LoC.

24. THG to Mason Fitch Cogswell, 1816 Jun 17, MFCP. Also transcribed in Root, p. 69, but Root misreads the month as January.

25. THG to Mason Fitch Cogswell, 1816 Aug 8, MFCP.

26. See Edith Nye MacMullen, *In the Cause of True Education*, p. 3, and William J. Broad, "How a Volcanic Eruption in 1815 Darkened the World."

27. Clerc, *Diary,* pp. 7, 9, and passim; Clerc, "Autobiography," p. 5.

28. THG to Mason Fitch Cogswell, 1816 Aug 8, MFCP.

29. Cogswell's remark recorded on THG to Mason Fitch Cogswell, 1816 Aug 8, MFCP.

30. Clerc, "Autobiography," p. 5. The following narrative of Gallaudet's fund-raising tour derives largely from this autobiography.

31. THG to Mason Fitch Cogswell, 1816 Aug 8, MFCP.

32. Nathaniel F. Moore to John McVickar, 1816 Aug 21, transcribed in E. M. Gallaudet, *Life,* pp. 112–115.

33. Ferdinand Bethier in Lane, *The Deaf Experience,* p. 191. Clerc, "Jean Massieu," *American Annals of the Deaf and Dumb* 2 (1849): p. 203. Valentine, "American Asylum," p. 115, gives John Carlin's statement on Clerc having to steel himself.

34. "Mechanics Institute, Cincinnati." Clipping in the Edward Miner Gallaudet scrapbook, GUA.

35. THG to Mason Fitch Cogswell, [undated: "Thursday afternoon"], MFCP.

36. Benjamin Silliman to THG 1816 Jun 1, GP LoC.

37. THG to Alice Cogswell, 1816 Mar 24, GP LoC.

38. Alice Cogswell to THG, [1816] April, GP LoC.

39. Alice Cogswell to THG, 1816 Dec 27, GP LoC.

40. Mason Fitch Cogswell to Mary Cogswell, 1816 Sep 7, transcribed in Bell, "Historical Notes," vol. 3, p. 348. *Poulsen's American Daily Advertiser,* 1816 Sep 13.

41. "Connecticut Asylum for the Deaf and Dumb: Prospectus," Broadside collection, CHS.

42. Fernandes, "Gate to Heaven," p. 116; Valentine, "American Asylum," p. 119.

43. Mason Fitch Cogswell to Mary Cogswell, 1816 Sep 7, transcribed in Bell, "Historical Notes," vol. 3, p. 348.

44. Fernandes, "Gate to Heaven," p. 100.

45. Heman Humphrey describes the subscription papers and attributes authorship to Gallaudet, *Life,* pp. 20–21. Fernandes, "Gate to Heaven," pp. 106–107, 111, 89.

46. Sheila C. Moeschen, *Acts of Conspicuous Compassion,* p. 19.

47. Mason Fitch Cogswell to Mary Cogswell, 1816 Oct 30, transcribed in Bell, "Historical Notes," vol. 3, p. 349.

48. Mason Fitch Cogswell to Mary Cogswell, 1816 Oct 30, transcribed in Bell, "Historical Notes" vol. 3, p. 349. Valentine provides a thorough discussion of this debacle in "American Asylum," pp. 128–133, and quotes the announcement, made in the *Courant,* concerning the refusal of charity pupils.

49. "The Deaf and Dumb," *Albany Daily Advertiser,* 1816 Nov 12, p. 2.

50. See letters from Cogswell to his wife dated Nov 4, Nov 6, Nov 10, and Nov 17, partially transcribed in Bell, "Historical Notes" vol. 3, pp. 350–357.

51. See Valentine, "American Asylum," p. 123, on this point. Gallaudet's words to Cogswell are from THG to Mason Fitch Cogswell, 1816 Dec 18, MFCP.

52. THG to Mason Fitch Cogswell, 1816 Dec 18, MFCP.

53. These matters are mentioned in THG to Mason Fitch Cogswell, 1817 Jan 14, transcribed in Bell, "Historical Notes," vol. 3, pp. 431–437. THG to Joshua Lacy Wilson, 1819 Jun 19, American Memory Collection, LoC.

54. The letter is partially transcribed in E. M. Gallaudet, *Life,* pp. 119–120. See also Lane, *When the Mind Hears,* p. 222.

55. Redford Webster to THG, 1817 Apr 24, GP LoC.

56. Daniel Sterner, *Vanished Downtown Hartford,* pp. 16–17.

57. Abraham O. Stansbury to Arthur Stansbury, 1817 July 12, transcribed in Bell, "Historical Notes," vol. 4, pp. 26–28.

58. Information on all pupils enrolled in the Asylum up to Gallaudet's death is given in a chart in Barnard, *Tribute,* pp. 225–254. See also Lane, *When the Mind Hears,* pp. 225–226. Edmund Booth, "Thomas Hopkins Gallaudet," p. 25, said that Loring and Whiton arrived together by coach.

59. Phyllis Valentine, "Thomas Hopkins Gallaudet," p. 64.

60. Gallaudet, "A Sermon Delivered at the Opening of the Connecticut Asylum for the Education and Instruction of Deaf and Dumb Persons."

61. "Mechanics Institute, Cincinnati." Clipping in the Edward Miner Gallaudet scrapbook, GUA.

62. "Mirth" is copied into his notebook of poems, GP LoC, immediately following the poem about the stranger he met in Paris in 1816, and he was still using the long *s,* which he gave up around the time the Asylum opened.

63. See Lane, *When the Mind Hears,* pp. 225–226 for discussion of pupils and their typical day.

64. Newspaper article regarding Monroe's visit to Hartford is reprinted in Daniel Preston and Marlena C. DeLong, eds., *The Papers of James Monroe,* vol. 1, pp. 130–135.

65. Goodrich, *Recollections,* vol. 2, p. 127; see also Lane, *When the Mind Hears,* pp. 224–225.

66. See Stanislaus M. Hamilton, ed., *Writings of James Monroe,* vol. 4, pp. 414–417, 480, and Bell, "Historical Notes," vol. 2, pp. 385–390.

67. Quoted in E. M. Gallaudet, *Life,* p. 124. See THG, "Recollections of the Deaf and Dumb," p. 55, on seating at the Center Church.

68. THG to Nathaniel Terry, 1817 Sep [no day], GP LoC.

69. Abraham O. Stansbury to Arthur Stansbury, 1817 Sep 17, transcribed in Bell, "Historical Notes," vol. 4, pp. 31–32.

70. *Oxford English Dictionary,* s.v. "Jesuit."

71. Letter to Editor, *Connecticut Courant,* 1817 Sep 16, p. 3; *New-York Daily Advertiser,* 1817 Dec 4, p. 2.

72. On Hawes, see George Leon Walker, *History of the First Church,* pp. 367–402.

73. GP LoC.

six Mission to the Deaf

1. THG to Board of Directors, 1818 Aug 3, ASD. For a discussion of the troubles the school brought on itself with its ill-considered age requirement, see Phyllis Klein Valentine, "Nineteenth-Century Experiment in Education of the Handicapped," pp. 364–367.

2. The classic study of deaf people and sign language on Martha's Vineyard is Nora Groce, *Everyone Here Spoke Sign Language.* See Joseph D. Stedt and Donald F. Moores, "Manual Codes on English and American Sign Language," p. 6, for a corrective to the assumption that large numbers of Vineyard signers were present at the Asylum.

3. Booth, "Thomas Hopkins Gallaudet," p. 24.

4. In "Original Letters of Pupils in the Connecticut Asylum, April 3rd, 1818," Lewis Weld Papers, GUA.

5. Word list, GP LoC; Exercise book, ASD; Alice Cogswell's notebook, MFCFP.

6. Original compositions by pupils, GUA.

7. Original compositions, GUA.

8. E. M. Gallaudet, *Life,* p. 148.

9. I. A. Jacobs to THG, 1848 Oct 12, GP LoC.

10. *Second Report of the Directors of the Connecticut Asylum,* p. 5. That Gallaudet composed every annual report signed by the directors or their clerk from 1817 to 1830 is attested in THG to Directors, 1830 Jan 11, ASD.

11. "Original Letters of Pupils in the Connecticut Asylum, April 3rd, 1818," Lewis Weld Papers, GUA.

12. William Willard to THG, 1844 July 1, GP LoC.

13. THG to Directors, 1818 Jun 1, ASD.

14. Memo from James H. Wells and Seth Terry to Directors, 1821 Apr 12, ASD; *Eighth Annual Report of the Directors of the American Asylum* (1924), p. 8.

15. Enoch Perkins to Thomas Perkins, 1818 Apr 19, Harriet Beecher Stowe Center.

16. All these matters are mentioned in Laurent Clerc to Mason Fitch Cogswell, 1818 May 7, MFCP.

17. THG to Board of Directors, 1818 Dec 7, ASD.

18. F. A. P. Barnard, "Education of the Deaf and Dumb," *North American Review* 38 (1834), p. 79; John Tabak, *Significant Gestures,* p. 25. See also Stedt and Moores, "Manual Codes on English and American Sign Language," for discussion of the fate of methodical signs in the United States.

19. John R. Burnet, "The Necessity of Methodical Signs Considered," *American Annals of the Deaf and Dumb* 7.1 (1854), p. 5, and "Colloquial Signs vs. Methodical Signs," *American Annals of the Deaf and Dumb* 7.3 (1854): p. 134.

20. Lane, *When the Mind Hears,* p. 233.

21. "Regulations for the Asylum," as drafted by the Committee of the Instructors, undated, and "Regulations for the Asylum," as drafted by the principal, 1830 Mar 1, ASD.

22. On Karl "Uncle Charlie" Jaekel, see "*In surdum memoriam*: Karl Jaekel," in Lois Bragg, ed., *Deaf World,* pp. xi–xxvii.

23. Valentine, "Thomas Hopkins Gallaudet," p. 63.

24. The first incident is told in Gallaudet's "Recollections of the Deaf and Dumb,"

American Annals of the Deaf and Dumb 2 (1849): pp. 54–57; the second in Henry Winter Syle, *Biographical Sketch,* p. 24. On Alcott, see Ann Douglas, *Feminization,* p. 127.

25. "Minutes of Board Meetings 1818 Jul 20–1819 Mar 16, ASD.

26. THG to Board of Directors, 1818 Aug 3, ASD.

27. Whittlesey to Directing Committee, 1822 Jun 14, Directing Committee to THG, 1822 Aug 23, ASD.

28. *Report of Committee on Asylum Difficulties,* 1823 Sep 15; THG to Directors, 1823 Sep 17, ASD. E. M. Gallaudet, *Life,* p. 139.

29. *Boston Recorder,* 1819 Jan 2: p. 2; *Third Report to the Directors,* 1819 May 15: the quotation is from page 10, although Sophia is not named here. The reports were signed by one or more of the directors or their clerk, but we know that Gallaudet composed and submitted these reports for their signature and that he had at times to plead with them not to change his text.

30. Eliza Clerc to Laurent Clerc, 1819 Oct 2, Laurent Clerc Papers, Stg MSSA.

31. Letters to the Editor signed "G." in the *Christian Observer,* 1819 Oct, pp. 646–650, and Dec, pp. 784–787.

32. This letter was printed in Sigourney's *Memoir of Phebe P. Hammond,* which is reprinted in Sayers and Moore, eds., *Mrs. Sigourney of Hartford,* pp. 92–107; Gallaudet's letter is on p. 103.

33. The American Antiquarian Society, Worcester, Mass., owns a number of P. W. Gallaudet's publications. His will is in the Gallaudet Family Papers, GUA.

34. THG to Mason Fitch Cogswell, 1820 Sep 18, MFCP.

35. Account Book, GP LoC.

36. Franklin Bowditch Dexter, *Biographical Notices,* vol. 6, p. 754.

37. "Journal of Some Occurrences," entry for 1818 Jan 25, GP LoC.

38. Booth, "Thomas Hopkins Gallaudet," p. 24.

39. "Original Letters of Pupils in the Connecticut Asylum, April 3rd, 1818," Lewis Weld Papers, GUA; George Turberville to Nathaniel Terry, 1818 Dec 9 and 1819 Jan 19, GP LoC.

40. Edwin Pond Parker, *History of the Second Church of Christ in Hartford,* p. 177. A good discussion of the social and political world of 1818 and beyond is Jarvis Morse, *A Neglected Period of Connecticut's History, 1818–1850;* the "triumph of Satan" is on p. 120. See also David Ludlum, *Social Ferment in Vermont,* on temperance and the Millennium.

41. See, for example, see Peter Dobkin Hall, *The Organization of American Culture,* pp. 83–91.

42. Jarvis Morse, *A Neglected Period,* quotations on pp. 140 and 171.

43. THG to Thomas Chalmers, 1818 Sep 29, transcribed in Humphrey, *Life,* pp. 86–88.

44. Quoted in Louise Hall Tharp, *Three Saints and a Sinner,* p. 145.

45. THG to Mason Fitch Cogswell, 1818 Aug 29, MFCP.

46. THG to Mason Fitch Cogswell, 1818 Aug 8 [copy], Francis C. Higgins Papers, GUA.

47. THG to Mason Fitch Cogswell, 1818 Aug 29, MFCP.

48. http://founders.archives.gov/documents/Jefferson/01-28-02-0310, accessed February 15, 2017.

49. THG to Directors, 1819 Jun 28, ASD.

50. *Third Report of the Directors,* Hartford (1819), pp. 7–8.

51. See Kathleen D. McCarthy, *American Creed,* p. 167.

52. Lincoln quoted in Harry V. Jaffa, *Crisis of the House Divided,* p. 405.

53. "Disgraceful," *Niles Weekly Register,* 1820 Feb 26, p. 441. See also the *Connecticut Courant,* 1920 Feb 29, p. 3.

54. From Section 1 of the Act in Behalf of the Connecticut Asylum for Teaching the Deaf and Dumb, reprinted in Anson T. McCook, ed., *Legislative History,* p. 9.

55. Fernandes, "Gateway to Heaven," p. 135, finds this quest to have been Gallaudet's "brain-child."

56. Minutes of a directors' meeting, 1820 Apr 19; William Ely to Directors, 1821 Feb 26, Mar 29, Apr 20, and 1829 May 14; John Boardman to [?], [no date], ASD.

57. *Fifth Report to the Directors* (1821), pp. 5–6.

58. Rachel L. Swarns, "Georgetown Confronts a Haunting Sale of Slaves."

59. E. M. Gallaudet, *Life,* p. 133; Humphrey, *Life,* p. 129.

60. *Third Annual Report,* pp. 4, 5.

61. THG to J. M. Sturtevant, 1839 May 28, Media Center Library, Illinois School for the Deaf. The *Annual Reports* show the specific dollar and cent figure "received by Fund Commission" that balances the books every year.

62. "Discourse, Delivered at the Annual Meeting of the Hartford Evangelical Tract Society," pp. 4, 10.

63. *Sixth Annual Report* (1822), p. 20.

64. "A Discourse, Delivered at the Dedication." Many of Gallaudet's themes in this discourse appeared in an earlier address reprinted in Humphrey, *Life,* pp. 163–169, although the "affections of the heart" business was new in the 1821 dedicatory address.

65. On David Seixas, see Lane, *When the Mind Hears,* pp. 242–243, and Linda Gerson, "The Pennsylvania School for the Deaf," pp. 6, 19, 53–61.

66. Thomas Gallaudet, "Sketch of My Life," Henry Buzzard Papers, GUA.

67. Mason Fitch Cogswell, "Account of an Operation for the Extirpation of a Tumour, in which a Ligature Was Applied to the Carotid Artery," *New England Journal of Medical Surgery* 13 (1824): 357–360.

68. P. W. Gallaudet to John Quincy Adams, 1824 May 15, Gallaudet Family Papers, GUA.

69. On the meeting house, see Sterner, *Vanished Hartford,* p. 121, and "Diamond Anniversary," *Hartford Courant,* 1901 Nov 11.

70. THG to Seth Terry, 1824 Nov 20, ASD. "A Sermon on the Duty and Advantages of Affording Instruction to the Deaf and Dumb," pp. 10, 11, 20.

71. "An Account of the Exhibition of Three Pupils in Montpelier, Vt.," in the *Eleventh Annual Report* (1827), p. 19.

72. *Tenth Annual Report* (1826), pp. 5, 6; a one-page undated memo filed as 1826, ASD.

73. *Twelfth Report of the Directors* (1828), p. 17.

74. Adams, *Memoirs of John Quincy Adams,* vol. 7, pp. 434–437. THG to Eli Todd, 1828 Feb 12, HBP CHS.

75. Resolution dated "the first Wednesday of May A.D. 1828," ASD.

76. Cyrus Swan to Seth Terry, 1828 Jun 7, ASD.

77. Seth Terry to David McKinney, 1828 May 13; THG to Directors, 1830 Jan 11: ASD.

78. "A Marriage Hymn," Correspondence and Papers of the Weld and Cogswell Families, Connecticut State Library.

79. Merrill H. Dooey, "Famous Visitors," p. 121.

80. THG to Seth Terry 1829 Feb [no day], ASD.

81. Memo in various hands dated "June 1829" but bearing notations made the previous year, ASD.

82. THG to Directors, 1830 Jan 11; THG to Messrs. Clerc, Turner, Peet, Brinsmade, Bartlett, and Rockwell, 1830 Mar 1, ASD.

83. William W. Turner to THG, 1830 Mar 25; William W. Turner to THG, 1830 Mar 25 evening; William W. Turner to THG, [1830] Mar 25; THG to Messrs. Clerc, Turner, Peet, Brinsmade, Bartlett, and Rockwell, 1830 Mar 25: copies, ASD.

84. THG to Messrs. Clerc, Turner, Peet, Brinsmade, Bartlett, and Rockwell, 1830 Mar 24; William W. Turner to THG, 1830 Mar 25; "Regulations for the American Asylum, proposed by the Principal," undated; Committee of the Instructors on a communication of the Principal, undated; "A Copy of the Regulations . . . submitted by the Principal," 1830 Mar 1; Chauncey A. Goodrich to THG, 1830 Mar 21: ASD.

85. THG to Directors, 1830 Jan 11, ASD.

86. [THG], un-headed and unsigned document beginning "List of the Duties" and filed as "Remarks of the Principal," 1830 Apr [?], ASD.

87. THG to Directors, 1830 Apr 7 and Apr 14; THG to Committee to Revise the By-Laws, 1830 Apr 19: ASD.

SEVEN Life after Deaf I

1. Humphrey, *Life,* pp. 252–257, 269; THG to William B. Fowle, 1827 Jan 30, William B. Fowle Papers, Massachusetts Historical Society, Boston.

2. On Dwight's influence on public education, see Peter Dobkin Hall, *The Organization of American Culture,* pp. 155–163. On Barnard, see Edith Nye MacMullen, *In the Cause of True Education,* p. 35.

3. E. M. Gallaudet, *Life,* pp. 225–226; Humphrey, *Life,* pp. 236–246. Deaf people are, in fact, regularly offered braille menus in restaurants today.

4. THG to James A. Mathews, 1830 Oct 5, New York University Archives; "New York Literary Convention," *American Annals of Education* 1.4 (1830 Dec): pp. 168 ff.; *Journal of the Proceedings of a Convention of Literary and Scientific Gentlemen,* New York: Leavitt & Carnill, 1831; "Report," *American Annals of Education* 1832 Oct: pp. 509–531; Elsie A. Hug, *Seventy-Five Years in Education,* p. 6; Theodore F. Jones, *New York University, 1832–1932,* pp. 32–33, 141; "Thomas Hopkins Gallaudet," *Cyclopedia of Education,* New York: Macmillan, 1911–1913; Theodore Dwight [Jr.] to THG, 1831 Feb 1, GUA; THG to Mathews, 1832 Jul 5, Rosenbach Museum, Philadelphia; I. M. Mathews to THG, 1832 Jul 6, GP LoC. See also Paul H. Mattingly, "Why NYU Chose Gallaudet," and Humphrey, *Life,* pp. 247–251. E. M. Gallaudet, *Life,* p. 227, believed that his father would have taken the job if it had been offered sooner, but there is no basis for such an assumption. Gallaudet told a correspondent that he was offered a $2,500 annual salary, which is nowhere else corroborated: THG to John H. Cocke, 1830 Dec 8, CFP.

5. THG to A. Alexander, 1829 Apr 4; THG to Sophia Gallaudet, 1829 May 5; A. Alexander to THG, 1829 Jun 13: GP LoC.

6. "Hartford Female Seminary," *American Journal of Education* 2.4 (1827 Apr 2): 252;

Kathryn Kish Sklar, *Catharine Beecher*, pp. 52, 59. On difficulties for girls, see Mae Elizabeth Harveson, "Catharine Esther Beecher, Pioneer Educator," pp. 41, 59.

7. "An Address on Female Education," pp. 24, 28, 29. Gallaudet also turned down an offer to superintend the Pittsfield (Mass.) Female Academy: see Charles Dillingham to THG, 1833 Sep 16, GP LoC.

8. "Female Teachers of Common Schools," *Connecticut Common School Journal*, 1838 Sep 1, p. 9; Oct, p. 17; Dec, p. 34; 1839 Jan, p. 49; Mar 1, p. 104; Mar 15, p. 105.

9. Barnard, *Tribute*, p. 29; E. M. Gallaudet, *Life*, p. 242.

10. "Intelligence," *American Annals of Education*, 1832 Apr 15: p. 55; THG to John Cocke, 1832 Sep 13, CFP.

11. Humphrey, *Life*, p. 218.

12. I had previously speculated that prior ill health was perhaps the case: Sayers and Moore, eds., *Mrs. Sigourney of Hartford*, p. 51. THG to Delafield, 1830 Dec 27, New York University Archives.

13. E. M. Gallaudet, *Life*, pp. 86–87.

14. Transcribed in Grace Cogswell Root, *Father and Daughter*, p. 75.

15. Thomas Gallaudet, "A Sketch of My Life," Henry Buzzard Papers, GUA. Thomas gives an example of being teased by the older boys in "Dr. Gallaudet's Lecture in Boston," *Deaf Mute Journal*, 1883 Apr 26.

16. THG to John Delafield, 1830 Dec 27, New York University Archives.

17. Sigourney's poem was published under a variety of titles and is reprinted in Sayers and Moore, ed., *Mrs. Sigourney of Hartford*, pp. 74–75.

18. All poems in GP LoC.

19. Theodore Dwight Jr. to THG, 1830 Oct 11, GP LoC. On Hartford publishers, see MacMullen, *In the Cause of True Education*, p. 7.

20. THG, *The Child's Picture Defining and Reading Book*, pp. iii–vi, 7, 21.

21. THG, *The Child's Picture Defining and Reading Book*, pp. 22–23, 34–35.

22. This was the nickname of Webster's popular textbook, entitled *A Grammatical Institute of the English Language*, published in 1783. It was named for its characteristic blue cover.

23. Gaskell, *My Lady Ludlow*, chapter 9. On Dilworth and Webster, see Joshua Kendall, *The Forgotten Founding Father*, pp. 78–81. Theodore Dwight Jr. to THG, 1833 Sep 10, GP LoC.

24. Charlotte Elizabeth [Phelan], *The Happy Mute*, pp. 7–8.

25. On whole-word instruction in Edinburgh, see Cyrus Peirce, *Lecture on Reading*, cited in *Remarks on the Seventh Annual Report*, by the Association of Masters of the Boston Public Schools, p. 58.

26. "Methods of Teaching to Read," *American Annals of Education* 1.1 (1830 Aug), pp. 49ff.

27. *Mother's Primer*, pp. 9, 17, 37.

28. Mary Tyler Peabody Mann, ed., *Life and Works of Horace Mann*, vol. 2, pp. 517, 521, and vol. 3, pp. 309–310, 318.

29. Association of Masters of the Boston Public Schools, *Remarks on the Seventh Annual Report*, p. 65.

30. "Rejoinder to the Third Section of the Reply," in Association of Masters, *Rejoinder to the "Reply" of the Hon. Horace Mann, Secretary*, pp. 39, 40.

31. Blumenfeld, *The New Illiterates*, p. 137; Rodgers, *The Case for the Prosecution*, pp. 44, 47; Updike, "Reading: Mind over Matter," *Washington Post*, 1976 Dec 19: pp. 29, B5. See also Allan C. Brownfeld, "Cause of Our Growing Illiteracy Rate Is No Mystery," *New York Tribune*, 1986 Nov 4.

32. Gallaudet's letter to the Andover classmate is transcribed in Humphrey, *Life*, p. 372.

33. "Philosophy of Language," *American Annals of Education*, 1830 Dec, pp. 156ff.

34. See Alan Richardson, *Literature, Education, and Romanticism*, pp. 109–147.

35. Maria Edgeworth, *The Parent's Assistant*, pp. 1–4. See Thomas J. Brown, *Dorothea Dix*, pp. 21, 33–34, on dialogue books.

36. Mrs. G. M. Sykes, "Reminiscences," pp. 43–45; Horace Hooker, "Thomas Hopkins Gallaudet, L.L.D." This explanation for Gallaudet's auctorial voice is also found in the *London Sunday School Teacher's Magazine:* see the endpapers of the 3rd edition of *Child's Book on the Soul* (Hartford: Cooke, 1833). Henry Barnard, *Tribute*, p. 51.

37. Quoted in [Lewis Tappan], *Letters Respecting a Book*, p. 6. The complaint that the passage was "discourteous" is from p. 4.

38. F. A. Packard to THG, 1848 Jan 28, GP LoC.

39. Quoted in [Tappan], *Letters Respecting a Book*, p. 13.

40. See Thomas J. Brown, *Dorothea Dix*, p. 50, for discussion.

41. According to Alcott, *Tall Oaks*, p. 292.

42. *Child's Book on the Soul: Two Parts in One*, p. 5.

43. *Child's Book on the Soul*, pp. 11, 13, 29. On translations, these are listed by Gallaudet in an 1845 letter to an Andover classmate collecting information on former students, transcribed in Humphrey *Life*, p. 370. THG to George Merriam, 1843 Oct 6, G. and C. Merriam Correspondence, CHS.

44. *Class Book of Natural Theology* (Madras: Hunt, American Mission Press, 1846), pp. 19, 182.

45. *Youth's Book of Natural Theology*, pp. 76–77.

46. Sheldon Dibble to THG, 1841 Jul 12; Statements from American Tract Society: GP LoC. Alcott, *Tall Oaks*, p. 292.

47. *History of Joseph*, vol. 2 of *Scripture Biography*, pp. 8–9, 12–13.

48. *History of Jonah*, pp. 9, 10.

49. Samuel Knox's "An Essay on the Best System of Education" and Noah Webster's "On the Education of Youth" in Frederick Rudolph, ed., *Essays on Education*, see pp. 67 and 333; Gallaudet's Preface to Henry Dunn, *School Teacher's Manual*, p. 1.

50. Gaskell's *My Lady Ludlow* (1858), chapters 4 and 10; Edgeworth, *The Parent's Assistant*, p. 2. Much of this paragraph is indebted to Alan Richardson's *Literature, Education, and Romanticism;* see especially pages 26–68. See James M. Banner Jr., *To the Hartford Convention*, p. 55, for more examples of the importance of teaching deference to one's betters. Boudinot is quoted in Paul C. Gutjahr, *An American Bible*, p. 10.

51. On adjustable seats, see MacMullen, *In the Cause*, p. 53. "Black Tablets," *American Journal of Education*, 1830 Jul, p. 296. THG to Benjamin Silliman, 1817 Apr [?], Microfilm, Stg.

52. THG to S. V. S. Wilder, 1824 Dec 10, reprinted in E. M. Gallaudet, *Life*, p. 196.

53. *Plan of a Seminary*, quotations from pp. 5, 7, 21, 37. On the origins of teacher training programs discussed here and below, see MacMullen, *In the Cause*, pp. 73–74, 157, 173, and

passim; Herbert Fowler, *A Century of Teacher Education*, pp. 12–19; Richard G. Boone, *Education in the United States*, p. 128; and Bernard C. Steiner, *The History of Education in Connecticut*, p. 43. For the biggest picture, see also Paul H. Mattingly, *The Classless Profession*.

54. On suspicion of state control, see Theodore Dwight Jr. to THG, 1841 Aug 20, GP LoC. On the School Fund, see Dorothy Ann Lipson, *Freemasonry*, pp. 85–89. On the Society, see "Society for the Improvement of Common Schools," *Connecticut Courant* 1827 Apr 2; Henry Barnard, *Tribute*, p. 30; Alcott, *Tall Oaks*, p. 276; MacMullen, *In the Cause*, p. 8; Bernard C. Steiner, *History of Education in Connecticut*, p. 37.

55. The teacher's convention is reported in "School Convention," *Connecticut Courant*, 1830 Nov 16, p. 3. On the Association, see "Common School Meeting," *Daily Courant*, 1839 Jan 21.

56. "Public Schools, Public Blessings," quotations from pp. 7, 10, 23, 11, 13–14, 17. Rush Welter, *American Writings on Popular Education*, p. 62. Theodore Dwight Jr. to THG, 1833 Nov 14, GP LoC.

57. "On Attention," *American Annals of Education*, 1839 Mar, pp. 111ff, and Apr, pp. 173ff.

58. "Co-operation of Parents in Improving Common Schools," *Connecticut Common School Journal*, 1839 Aug, p. 7; Oct, p. 38; Nov, p. 55, Dec, p. 71; 1840 Jan, p. 86. The September installment was repeated in October, so is not listed here. The quotation is from p. 55. Herbert E. Fowler, *A Century of Teacher Education*, p. 11. E. K. Hunt, a supervisor of the Hartford Retreat for the Insane, is quoted on this point in E. M. Gallaudet, *Life*, 283–84.

59. Barnard, *Tribute*, pp. 30–31; see also Alcott, *Tall Oaks*, p. 297. Will S. Monroe, *The Educational Labors of Henry Barnard*, p. 12; Frank Luther Mott, *A History of American Magazines*, pp. 694–695. On the origins of Barnard's family fortune, see MacMullen, *In the Cause*, p. 9.

EIGHT **Life after Deaf II**

1. On the home school, Barnard, *Tribute*, p. 29; on the piano, Philip E. Howard, *Life Story of Henry Clay Trumbull*, p. 130 (Trumbull married Alice Cogswell Gallaudet); on Sophie as teacher of Eddy, E. M. Gallaudet, "Memoir," GP LoC; on Sundays in the family pew, H. Clay Trumbull, *The Sunday-School*, p. 314; on Gallaudet's depression, "Dr. Gallaudet's Lecture in Boston," *Deaf Mute Journal*, 1883 Apr 26; on a deaf mother, Alcott, *Tall Oaks*, p. 296; on Sophia's aborted education, Amos Draper, "Sophia Gallaudet," *American Annals of the Deaf and Dumb* 22 (1877 Jul), pp. 8–9.

2. On five children under a doctor's care, THG to John Cocke, 1831 Apr 22; on Sophia's pneumonia, THG to John Cocke, 1830 Mar 10; on Thomas's scarlet fever, THG to John Cock, 1831 Jun 6; CFP. Catherine's baptismal certificate, GP LoC. On Gallaudet's scarlet fever, THG to John Cocke, 1831 Apr 22, and on his pneumonia, THG to John Cocke, 1832 May 19 CFP; on his horseback trip through Massachusetts, THG to James McFarland Matthews, 1832 July 5, Rosenbach Library, Philadelphia.

3. "Preliminary Essay," quotations on pp. 3, 6, 15, 1–2.

4. Daughter Sophia in a note appended to Sophia Gallaudet (mother) to Horatio N[elson] Fowler, 1835 22 Apr, ASD. Barnard, *Tribute*, p. 27.

5. *The Every-Day Christian*, pp. 43, 50, 57, 62 83, 85, 111, 121.

6. "Family and School Discipline," *American Annals of Education*, 1837 Oct, pp. 452, 454.

7. *Starting in Life*, pp. 15–16. Alcott, *Tall Oaks*, pp. 286–287.

8. "The Goodrich Association," *Connecticut Courant*, 1832 Feb 21; Alcott, *Tall Oaks*, p. 278. "On the Principle of Association, as Giving Dignity to the Christian Character," pp. 49, 56, 61, 62.

9. "Proceedings of the American Lyceum," *Daily Courant*, 1838 May 17, p. 3.

10. On Prussian schools, see Herbert E. Fowler, *A Century of Teacher Education*. Horace Mann, "Seventh Annual Report of the Secretary of the Board of Education," the *Common School Journal* 7.5 (1844 Mar 1): p. 75.

11. Association of Masters, *Remarks*, p. 75; "Mr. Weld's Report," in *The Twenty-ninth Report of the Directors of the American Asylum at Hartford*, pp. 129, 121.

12. THG to Horace Mann, 1844 May 13, extracts transcribed in Humphrey, *Life and Labors*, pp. 209–212. "Degeraldo" must be Humphrey's misapprehension of the name of linguist George Dalgarno. R. A. R. Edwards provides an interesting and cogent discussion of Howe's and Mann's theories and pronouncements on deaf education and on Gallaudet's 1844 letter in *Words Made Flesh*, pp. 143–159. William Willard to THG, 1844 Jul 1, GP LoC.

13. "On the Natural Language of Signs; and Its Value and Uses in the Instruction of the Deaf and Dumb," *American Annals of the Deaf and Dumb*, 1847 Oct, pp. 55–60, quotation from p. 56. Gallaudet quotes from Edwin James, compiler, *Account of an Expedition from Pittsburgh to the Rocky Mountains*, reprinted by University Microfilms, Ann Arbor, MI, 1966.

14. 1848 Jan: pp. 79–93. Quotations from pp. 80, 81, 88, and 93.

15. "Reminiscences of Deaf-Mute Instruction," *American Annals of the Deaf and Dumb* 2.2 (1849): pp. 190–196.

16. "On Family Devotions," *Mother's Magazine*, 1843 Feb, p. 31, 32; "On Domestic Education at the Table," 1839 Apr, p. 74; 1839 Jan, p. 7.

17. There has been a great deal of historical work on the reform movements of this period. See, for example, the opening pages of Gilbert Hobbs Barnes, *Anti-Slavery Impulse;* Perry Miller, *The Life of the Mind;* Robert E. Abzug, *Cosmos Crumbling;* and articles by Lois Banner, Richard D. Birdsall, and Clifford S. Griffin.

18. Objections to reform societies were made by Calvin Colton, on whom see Lorman Ratner, *Powder Keg*, p. 115; by many Unitarians, on whom see John R. Bodo, *The Protestant Clergy*, pp. 23–29; and by Francis Wayland, *The Limitations of Human Responsibility*. On the residents of Pleasant Valley, see Eric R. Schlereth, *An Age of Infidels*, p. 227.

19. Clifford S. Griffin, "Religious Benevolence as Social Control," p. 437.

20. Hartford Auxiliary Bible Society Constitution [no publication information: 1816]; *First Report* (Hartford: 1817); *Second Report* (Hartford: 1818), p. 4. Hume is cited in Ernest Campbell Mossner's *David Hume*, p. 234.

21. THG to Thomas Chalmers, 1817 Mar 2, and Zachary Macaulay to THG, 1818 Nov 7, transcribed in E. M. Gallaudet, *Life*, pp. 102–104 and 106–110. THG, "Connecticut Peace Society," *Connecticut Courant*, 1832 Nov 6, p. 2; THG, "Report of the Connecticut Peace Society," *American Advocate of Peace* 1.2 (1834 Sep): 89–95; "Connecticut Peace Society," *American Advocate of Peace* 1.7 (1835 Dec): 340–341.

22. On the Connecticut Mission Society, see Richard D. Shiels, "The Second Great

Awakening." On the ABCFM school, see John Demos's *The Heathen School.* For Gallaudet's remarks on his first visit, Hiram Bingham to Samuel Worcester, 1819 May 11, Bingham Family Papers, Stg MSSA. THG to Thomas Chalmers, 1820 Sep 20, transcribed in Humphrey, *Life,* pp. 97–99.

23. Hiram Bingham to THG, 1821 Feb 23, GUA.

24. "An Address, Delivered at a Meeting for Prayer," p. 9. On Fuller and Melville, see Ann Douglas, *Feminization,* p. 289.

25. See Charles Taylor, *The Language Animal,* for a discussion of the limitations of Hobbes's and Locke's linguistic theories.

26. "On Some of the Elementary Principles of Language," *Christian Observer,* 1826 Aug, pp. 464–470; "Remarks on the Oral Language and the Language of Signs," Sep, pp. 525–533. "Language of Infancy," *American Annals of Education,* 1831 Mar, pp. 99ff; Jul, pp. 321ff.; 1832 Apr, pp. 185ff. Quotations from pp. 101, 102, and 185. "The Mother's Face," *Mother's Magazine,* 1838 Feb, pp. 30–31.

27. "The Philosophy of Language," *American Annals of Education,* 1830 Sep, pp. 70ff, quotations on pp. 71, 74; "Remarks on Oral Language and the Language of Signs," *Christian Observer,* 1826 Sept, p. 528; "Language of Infancy, *American Annals of Education,* 1832 Apr., p. 188–189.

28. "The Language of Signs Auxiliary to the Christian Missionary," *Christian Observer* 26 (1826 Oct): pp. 592–599, quotations from p. 593; "American Asylum," *New Hampshire Repository,* 1823 Apr 7.

29. Prison Disciplinary Society, "First Report" (1826), in *Reports,* pp. 12, 24–25.

30. Prison Disciplinary Society, "Thirteenth Report" (1838), in *Reports,* p. 260; "Fourteenth Report" (1839), p. 364. *American Mercury,* 1832 Feb 6, p. 3.

31. On Gallaudet's "affection," see his letter transcribed in Humphrey, *Life,* p. 372, which was picked up in *Biographical Sketches of the Graduates of Yale University,* Stg MSSA.

32. Hartford Evangelical Tract Society, "Fourth Report" (1820).

33. Spring is quoted in Clifford S. Griffin, "Religious Benevolence," p. 442. William Cobbett, *Rural Rides,* p. 75; and, on Africans, *The Children's Friend,* quoted in Joanne Pope Melish, *Disowning Slavery,* p. 196.

34. This paragraph relies on W. J. Rorabaugh, *The Alcoholic Republic.* For Day and Terry, see "State Temperance Society," *Connecticut Courant,* 1820 May 26; for Edward Gallaudet, see Alcott, *Tall Oaks,* p. 264; for Gallaudet's views, see THG to John Cocke, 1840 Apr 27, CFP; on the Washington Temperance Society, see Robert H. Abzug, *Cosmos Crumbling,* pp. 103–104.

35. Lyman Beecher, *Six Sermons on the Nature, Occasions, Signs, Evils, and Remedy of Intemperance,* pp. 71–72.

36. Heman Humphrey, *Parallel between Intemperance and the Slave Trade.* Douglass, "American Slavery, American Religion, and the Free Church of Scotland: An Address Delivered in London, England, on May 22nd, 1846," in *The Frederick Douglass Papers,* vol. 1, p. 269.

37. On anti-Catholic overtones, see Harry V. Jaffa, *Crisis of the House Divided,* p. 246. Leonard Bacon [Address to the Christian Alliance].

38. The series was published in book form as *Foreign Conspiracy against the Liberties of the United States;* quotation from pp. 28–29.

39. Lyman Beecher, *A Plea for the West,* excerpted in David Byron Davis, *The Fear of Conspiracy,* pp. 85–94.

40. Samuel F. B. Morse, *Foreign Conspiracy,* p. 186. On the riot, see the contemporary account of Edward Strutt Abdy, *Journal of a Residence and Tour,* vol. 3, pp. 258–259.

41. Theodore Dwight [Jr.], *Open Convents.* Edward Beecher, *The Papal Conspiracy Exposed:* "with any regard," p. 147. For "morbid obsession," see Perry Miller, *The Life of the Mind,* p. 56. Examples of anti-Catholic hysteria are from Ray Allen Billington, *The Protestant Crusade, 1800–1860;* information on Unitarian pupils at the Charlestown convent school on p. 69, and remarks about Charlotte Elizabeth on pp. 347–348. On John Scudder, see contemporary observer Abdy, *Journal of a Residence and Tour,* vol. 3, p. 261.

42. E. M. Gallaudet, *Life,* pp. 243–245. Cash transfers to Bigelow are mentioned in THG to Sophia Gallaudet, 1835 Jan 22; American Tract Society statement of THG's account, 1834 Aug 11; and elsewhere in GP LoC. Also in that collection are notations, headed "Expenditures," concerning Gallaudet's six-month salary of $600 paid on March 25, 1836, payments to Seth Terry for boarding missionaries in July of that year, and the like, as well as receipts and expense accounts showing that Henry Hudson was also involved. See also Barbara Brown Zikmund, "UCC's 'Illogical Alliance.'"

43. Sophia Gallaudet to Horatio N. Fowler, 1835 Apr 22, ASD; THG to Henry Barnard, 1835 Mar 9, HBP Trty; Alcott, *Tall Oaks,* p. 278. The clipping quoted is found in Edward Miner Gallaudet's Scrapbook, GUA.

44. Kathryn Kish Sklar, *Catharine Beecher,* p. 115.

45. Edward Miner Gallaudet's Scrapbook, GUA, contains the clippings cited.

46. Carl E. Schneider, "In the Days"; Zikmund, "UCC's 'Illogical Alliance'"; "He Had Compassion on the Deaf."

47. See stjucc.org/wordpress/history/, accessed February 16, 2017.

48. http://www.glorecords.blm.gov/details/patent/default.aspx?accession=MO2210__. 182&docClass=STA&sid=j33l4p1j.4jm, accessed February 16, 2017. H. L. Ellsworth to THG, 1844 Oct 23. GUA.

NINE Toward a White Nation

1. Alcott, *Tall Oaks,* pp. 281–282. I refer to the intentions of the colonizationists, of whom Gallaudet was a leading advocate, as "deportation," a word perhaps first used of this effort in 1916 (see H. N. Sherwood, "Early Negro Deportation Projects"); Jefferson, who was also a supporter, called it "expatriation"; some historians use the term "negro removal." See discussion in Winthrop D. Jordan, *White over Black,* p. 547. Colonization was assuredly not "repatriation," since the people of color who were the intended "colonists" were largely native-born Americans. The settlement can properly be designated a "colony" because the colonizationists always intended the settlement to be controlled by white Americans. The remark on Roger Pearson's demeanor toward African Americans is from a private communication by a person who worked in his Washington office in the 1990s.

2. Quotation on the myth of the antislavery North is from Leonard L. Richards, *"Gentlemen of Property and Standing,"* p. 4. On colonial Connecticut's slave trade, New York's slave trade in Antebellum years, and trade with slave-labor plantations, see Farrow, Lang,

and Frank, *Complicity,* pp. 114–115, 121–126, 48, 23, and 13; on the Collins Axe Works, see Edward Baptist, *The Half Has Never Been Told,* p. 320; "jeopardize everything," Farrow, Lang, and Frank, p. 36.

3. On the black population in 1776, Edgar J. McManus, *Black Bondage,* pp. 169–170, 182. Bacon is quoted in Joanne Pope Melish, *Disowning Slavery,* p. 214–215; on slaves auctioned in New Haven, Hilary Moss, "'Cast Down on Every Side,'" p. 151. Mars is quoted in Christopher L. Webber, *American to the Backbone,* p. 131; James Mars, *The Life,* p. 37. Hawthorne is quoted in Wendy Warren, *New England Bound,* p. 251. Gallaudet signed a statement published by the Connecticut Colonization Society, "An Address to the Public," p. 9.

4. On Dwight, see Antony Dugdale, J. J. Fueser, and J. Celso de Castro Alves, *Yale, Slavery and Abolition,* p. 14. Silliman, "Some of the Causes of National Anxiety," *African Repository and Colonial Journal,* 1832 Aug, pp. 161ff., and Dugdale, Fueser, and de Castro Alves, pp. 14–15.

5. [Samuel Griswold Goodrich], *Peter Parley's Method of Telling about Geography to Children,* chapter 25; on blackface, Lorman A. Ratner, pp. 22–23; on broadsides, Melish, *Disowning Slavery,* p. 177; on newspapers, Shane White, *Stories of Freedom,* pp. 52ff.; on facial angles, Richard H. Colfax, *Evidence against the Views of Abolitionists,* p. 25; on the 1840 census and mulattoes, Farrow, Lang, and Frank, *Complicity,* pp. 185–187.

6. On God's election of the white race and polygenesis, Reginald Horsman, *Race and Manifest Destiny,* pp. 275, 148; William Jay, *Inquiry into the Character,* p. 19; Elizabeth Gaskell, *My Lady Ludlow,* chapter 10.

7. On the Constitution for whites only, Reginald Horsman, *Race and Manifest Destiny,* p. 238; on constitutional prohibition of abolition and the option of urging manumission, Francis Wayland, *Limitations of Human Responsibility,* pp. 169–174, 191, and Lorman Ratner, *Powder Keg,* p. 64; on property rights, Baptist, *The Half Has Never Been Told,* p. 188 and passim. See also Calvin Colton, *Abolition a Sedition:* Colton was a student at Andover at the same time as Gallaudet and Hawes. The statement Gallaudet signed was in Connecticut Colonization Society, "An Address," p. 6. Stowe, *The Minister's Wooing,* chapter 11; Catharine Beecher, *Essay on Slavery,* pp. 26–28.

8. On segregated neighborhoods, Katherine J. Harris, "The Rise of Communities," p. 59n1; on stagecoach waybills, Edward Strutt Abdy, *Journal of a Residence,* 3: 311; on segregated reform societies, Webber, *American to the Backbone,* pp. 141, 172.

9. On Hartford's black community, Craig Steven Wilder, *Ebony and Ivy,* p. 260; on Hartford's black schools, Webber, *American to the Backbone,* p. 128, and R. J. M. Blackett, *Beating against the Barriers,* pp. 15–17. David O. White discusses Ann Plato, pp. 48, 51, and passim. Plato published her *Essays; Including Biographies and Miscellaneous Pieces, in Prose and Poetry,* in Hartford in 1841. THG letter of reference for Amos Beman, 1838 May 26, Amos Beman Scrapbook, Beinecke Library, Yale.

10. On the Dixwell Avenue Congregational Church, Margo Johnson-Taylor. On the Talcott St. Church, Pennington, and the Underground Railroad, see Webber's biography of Pennington, *American to the Backbone,* and Blackett, *Beating against the Barriers,* passim. THG, "Private Journal," 1850 Aug 18, GP LoC.

11. On white resentment, see Beverly C. Tomek, *Colonization and Its Discontents,* p.

139; James Brewer Stewart, "Emergence of Racial Modernity," p. 192. On Pennington at Yale, Blackett, *Beating against the Barriers,* p. 11, Dugdale, Fueser, and de Castro Alves, p. 21, and Webber, *American to the Backbone,* p. 143. Quotation on rock throwing from Abdy, *Journal,* vol. 3, pp. 206–207. On resultant deaths, see Kathleen D. McCarthy, *American Creed,* p. 146. On Connecticut as having the most riots per capita, see Leonard L. Richards, *"Gentlemen of Property,"* p. 40.

12. THG to R. R. Gurley, 1830 Sep 24, ACSP. See Henry Mayer, *All on Fire,* p. 101.

13. J. K.'s letter is headlined "The Late Riots," the *Liberator,* 1831 Jun 4, p. 90. Rev. Wheeler's sermon is reported in "Diamond Anniversary," *Hartford Courant,* 1901 Nov 11. George R. Price and James Brewer Stewart, *To Heal the Scourge,* p. 22, outline some of the 1834 and 1835 riots. *Connecticut Courant,* 1835 Jun 15, p. 3.

14. This information about rioters in the 1830s is dependent on Richards, *"Gentlemen of Property and Standing."* See also Price and Stewart, *To Heal the Scourge,* p. 19 and passim, and Daniel Walker Howe, *What God Hath Wrought,* pp. 432–444. For an example of blaming black people for riots in their neighborhoods, see Joseph C. Hart's 1834 novel *Miriam Coffin; or, the Whale-Fishermen,* vol. 2, ch. 14.

15. Good discussions of the motivations of ACS members are P. J. Staudenraus, *The African Colonization Movement,* and David M. Streifford, "The American Colonization Society."

16. "Fascism and philanthropy" is from Katherine J. Harris, "The United States, Liberia, and their Foreign Relations to 1847," p. 129. Other quotations from Staudenraus, *The African Colonization Movement,* pp. 28, 30, and 137. On the ACS as a reform society, Howe, *What God Hath Wrought,* p. 265, and George M. Frederickson, *Black Image in the White Mind,* pp. 7–8, 12, 32. Garrison's satiric analogy is in *Thoughts on African Colonization,* pp. 55–56.

17. "Meeting of the Connecticut Colonization Society," *Courant,* 1829 May 26, p. 3; Humphrey, *Life,* p. 221; *Biographical Sketches of the Graduates of Yale College,* Stg MSSA; Thomas Robbins, *Diary,* vol. 2, p. 144. On the Independence Day drives, see Mayer's biography of Garrison, *All on Fire,* p. 61.

18. On Charles and Arthur Tappan's involvement, see Bertram Wyatt-Brown, *Lewis Tappan,* pp. 85–87. The following discussion of the prince relies on Terry Alford's biography, *Prince among Slaves.*

19. Peter Manseau, *One Nation, Under Gods,* p. 127; Christopher Martin, *The Amistad Affair,* p. 155.

20. THG to R. R. Gurley, 1828 Oct 14, ACSP.

21. THG to "the Moorish Prince," 1828 May 15, transcribed in E. M. Gallaudet, *Life,* pp. 203–206.

22. THG to R. R. Gurley, 1828 Oct 14, ACSP. The address is excerpted in E. M. Gallaudet, *Life,* pp. 201–203. Terry Alford's biography, *Prince among Slaves,* discusses Gallaudet's role on pp. 158–166.

23. *A Statement with Regard to the Moorish Prince,* quotations from pp. 4, 5, 6, and 8.

24. Arthur Tappan to THG, 1828 Nov 1, GP LoC; THG to R. R. Gurley, 1828 Nov 8 and Jun 8, ACSP.

25. Arthur Tappan to THG, 1829 Jun 30, GP LoC.

26. See Eugene S. Van Sickle, "Reluctant Imperialists."

27. "Summary of an Address," pp. 5–13.

28. Elizabeth M. Thomson to THG, 1832 Dec 23, 1833 Oct 25, 1835 Feb 26, and 1839 May 6, GP LoC; 1841 Sep 19, www.freemaninstitute.com/blackcm.htm, accessed February 16, 2017.

29. THG to W. McLain, 1848 May 11, GP LoC. On Ibrahima's children, see Alford, *Prince among Slaves,* pp. 186–187 and 200–203.

30. On Fenton Mercer, see Douglas R. Egerton, "Its Origin," pp. 469–470; quotation from CCS is from Christopher Collier, "In Search," p. 139; on Cresson, see Tomek, *Coloniza-tion and Its Discontents,* pp. 102, 108. Theodore Dwight Jr. to THG, [1834] Jun 4, GP LoC.

31. *African Education Society Report,* p. 8; E. M. Gallaudet, *Life,* pp. 209, 211; and on the Episcopal school, William Jay, *Inquiry,* p. 37.

32. On Tappan, Bertram Wyatt-Brown, *Lewis Tappan and the Evangelical War against Slavery,* pp. 87–89; on opposition, Hilary Moss, "'Cast Down on Every Side,'" pp. 150–152; on Bacon, Dugdale, Fueser, and de Castro Alves, *Yale, Slavery and Abolition,* p. 20; on thwarting colonization, Giles Badger Stebbins, *Facts and Opinions,* p. 82; Catharine Beecher, *An Essay,* p. 29; on resultant mobs, see Dugdale, Fueser, and de Castro Alves, p. 21; on the real reason for resistance in New Haven, Dugdale, Fueser, and de Castro Alves, p. 18. For Gallaudet's public relations suggestion, see R. R. Gurley to John H. Cocke, 1831 Sep 14, CFP.

33. Catharine Beecher, *An Essay,* p. 31; on church reactions, Bernard C. Steiner, *History of Slavery,* pp. 45–46, 51; quotation from Selectmen, Steiner, p. 48; on the Black Law, see John C. Hurd, *Law of Freedom,* pp. 45–46; *Connecticut Courant,* 1833 Jul 8, p. 3; on the silence of Connecticut colonizationists, see *Fruits of Colonizationism,* Boston: s.n., 1833 (NB: This pamphlet can be found in the May Anti-Slavery Collection at Cornell University, where its authorship is mistakenly attributed to the ACS; it was written and published by William Lloyd Garrison.). See also William Jay, *Inquiry,* pp. 32–33, 38, and passim.

34. Pupil dates, hometowns, and who paid their fees are given in an appendix to Barnard, *Tribute.* Race was never publicly stated and can be determined today only by examining intake forms archived at the American School for the Deaf. I rely for information about pupils of color on R. A. R. Edwards, *Words Made Flesh,* pp. 65–68 and 223–224n45.

35. Edwards, *Words Made Flesh,* suggests that the Black Law was ignored by the Asylum (pp. 67–68), but this does not seem to have been the case. Even if Horace Way were still a pupil on the day the law was enacted, he was soon gone, and no other black pupils were admitted while it was in force.

36. Edwards, *Words Made Flesh,* to take one recent example, assumes that Lewis Weld was "a committed abolitionist" (p. 67) and that Gallaudet "supported the abolitionist cause" (p. 66). Abdy, *Journal of a Residence,* vol. 1, pp. 222–224.

37. Theodore Weld's 1833 letter to Lewis is quoted in Robert Abzug, *Cosmos Crumbling,* p. 81.

38. THG to John H. Cocke, 1837 Aug 1, CFP.

39. On Theodore Weld's 1837 visit with Lewis and the Weld-Grimké wedding, see Abzug, *Cosmos Crumbling,* pp. 196–199, and Angelina Grimké to Theodore Dwight Weld, 1838 Mar 28, in Gilbert Hobbs Barnes and Dwight L. Dumond, eds., *Letters of Theodore Dwight Weld, Angelina Grimké Weld and Sarah Grimké,* p. 609.

40. On Cocke, see Henry F. May, *Enlightenment,* p. 331, and Bertram Wyatt-Brown, *Lewis Tappan,* pp. 134–136. THG to John H. Cocke, on niece's tutor, 1828 Dec 12, Dec ?, Dec 29, 1829 Jan 30, Mar 28, July 31; on proposed Monticello school, 1828 Nov 24, 1829 Jun 22, Nov 12, quotation from 1830 Jan 7; on Humphrey, 1829 Sep 10; on pigs and recipe, 1829 Dec 1: all letters in CFP. Dix is quoted in Thomas J. Brown, *Dorothea Dix,* p. 51.

41. Isaac Orr to John H. Cocke, 1830 Jan 12, Feb 22, Mar 29: CFP.

42. John H. Cocke to THG, 1834 Jul 15, GP LoC. Gallaudet's essay was enclosed in THG to John H. Cocke, 1837 Aug 1; the Bushnell sermon in THG to John H. Cocke, 1839 Feb 18.

43. The Alabama plantation mentioned in THG to John H. Cocke, 1840 Apr 27: CFP. Cocke's scheme for sending his slaves to a cotton planation is in John H. Cocke to THG, 1845 Jan 10, GP LoC.

44. THG to R. R. Gurley, 1831 July 26, enclosed in Gurley to John H. Cocke, 1831 Sep 14, CFP; Theodore Davenport Bacon, *Leonard Bacon,* pp. 235–236.

45. On death rates, see Tomek, *Colonization and Its Discontents,* p. 233; on "hygiene," Early Lee Fox, *American Colonization Society,* pp. 55–56; on rum, Tomek, p. 126. On Gallaudet's complaints, see, for example, THG to [?], 1939 Mar 20, GP LoC.

46. On Garrison's 1829 address, see Abzug, *Cosmos Crumbling,* pp. 142–144; on donations, see Richards, *"Gentlemen of Property,"* p. 26. On Garrison's simple message, see John R. Bodo, *Protestant Clergy,* pp. 136–137; on Garrison's *Thoughts,* see Lawrence J. Friedman, *Inventors of the Promised Land,* p. 221; on Tappan and Forten, see David Brion Davis, *The Problem of Slavery,* p. 186, and on Tappan and the Crandall riots, see David Grimsted, *American Mobbing,* p. 51; on Macaulay, see an 1833 letter he signed, quoted in Henry Mayer, *All on Fire,* p. 164.

47. On friendships with black people, see Tomek, *Colonization and Its Discontents,* p. 130; on Garrison's Baltimore contacts, see Davis, *The Problem of Slavery,* pp. 186–187, and Edward E. Baptist, *The Half Has Never Been Told,* p 194; on Weld's contacts with African Americans, see Abzug, *Cosmos Crumbling,* p. 160, and Gerda Lerner, *The Grimké Sisters,* pp. 158–159.

48. On the 1831 meeting in Hartford and Gallaudet's response, Louis R. Mehlinger, "Attitude of the Free Negro," p. 286; on newspaper silence, Davis, *The Problem of Slavery,* pp. 181–182; on unfilled ships, Tomak, *Colonization and Its Discontents,* p. 113; on making black Americans "unwelcome," Davis, *The Problem of Slavery,* p. 181. THG's advice on how to silence Garrison is in THG to R. R. Gurley, 1830 Sep 24, ACSP, also quoted in Stadenraus, *The African Colonization Movement,* pp. 193–194.

49. Garrison as a "low-life" and the strategy for gaining endorsements from the elite are from Mayer, *All on Fire,* pp. 139 and 156. On the split along denominational lines and over women's rights, see Gilbert Hobbs Barnes, *Anti-Slavery Impulse,* pp. 91 and 156, and Lorman Ratner, *Powder Keg,* p. 89.

50. Dix is quoted by her biographer Thomas J. Brown, p. 77; Child's sudden loss of book income is noted in Gerda Lerner, *The Grimké Sisters of South Carolina,* p. 99.

51. Leonard Bacon to Joel Hawes, 1836 Mar 22, and Hawes to Bacon, 1836 Jun 5 and 20, Bacon Family Collection, Stg MSSA.

52. Weld to Lewis Tappan, 1837 Jun 8; Barnes and Dumond, *Letters,* p. 398. On the 1838 meeting, see Ruth C. Douglass, "Possible Underground Railroad Houses in Hartford,

Litchfield and Tolland Counties, Connecticut," unpublished typescript, CHS; Douglass, or her source, get both Hawes's and Mars's names slightly wrong. THG to Leonard Bacon, 1838 May 14, Bacon Family Papers, Stg MSSA.

53. On Bacon, see Theodore Davenport Bacon, *Leonard Bacon,* pp. 164–166; on Hawes, Webber, *American to the Backbone,* p. 132; on George Day, Roland H. Bainton, *Yale and the Ministry,* pp. 154–155, John Barber, *History of the Amistad Captives,* and, on his use of Gallaudet's textbook, Marcus Rediker, *Amistad Rebellion,* p. 140. Lewis Tappan to THG, 1839 Oct 21, Stg. microfilm. On Judson, Rediker, p. 148. Quotation on carnival atmosphere, Webber, p. 122.

54. Assertions that Gallaudet, and even Clerc, assisted the Africans can be found in popular accounts such as Bruce A. Ragsdale's "'Incited by the Love of Liberty,'" and children's books such as Susan Dudley Gold's *United States v. Amistad,* both of which assert, erroneously, that Gallaudet was brought in by Yale professor Josiah Gibbs before Gibbs found a Mende interpreter. Gold's portrait of THG is actually that of the younger Thomas Gallaudet, p. 48, who was a teenager at the time. Works of Deaf history also frequently demonstrate a conviction that Gallaudet and even Cogswell were "very supportive of the black community" and that Gallaudet and Clerc rallied to the captive Africans. See, for example, "The ASD-Amistad Connection," http://www.deafis.org/history/how_why/asd .php (accessed February 16, 2017), and Kim A. Silva, "Deaf Connections to the Amistad Story," in *Telling Deaf Lives: Agents of Change* (Washington: Gallaudet University Press, 2014), both of which claim sign-language stories passed down in the Deaf community for two hundred years. The sole contemporary documentation of Gallaudet's contact with the Amistad captives is "An Incident," *New York Commercial Advertiser,* 1839 Sep 16; a later article that was published in Gallaudet's lifetime affirms the newspaper report and adds nothing new: "Primary Instruction of the Deaf and Dumb," *American Annals of the Deaf and Dumb* 1 (1848): pp. 3–55, see p. 54.

55. THG to John Quincy Adams, 1840 Nov 16, Adams Family Papers, Massachusetts Historical Society.

56. Humphrey, *Life,* p. 220; R. R. Gurley to THG, 1830 Jun 21, Aug 20, and Nov 29, and Elliott Cresson to THG, 1830 Jun 25 and 1839 [May or June]—this 1839 offer gives Gallaudet the option of keeping his appointment secret—GP LoC; THG to R. R. Gurley, 1831 Jul 26, ACSP. Gallaudet told Bacon that he preached and collected donations at four churches in two days of July, 1830: THG to Leonard Bacon, 1830 Jul 8, GP LoC.

57. Gallaudet's delusive statements on the ACS are from "Colonization Meeting," *Hartford Daily Courant,* 1844 May 31, p. 2, and THG to W. McLain, 1848 May 11, GP LoC. His recommendation of the Fosters is in "Colonization," *Hartford Daily Courant,* 1850 Dec 12, p. 2. On the Washington Monument cornerstone, Lawrence J. Friedman, *Inventors of the Promised Land,* p. 216. On the Divinity School debate question, Dugdale, Fueser, and de Castro Alves, *Yale, Slavery and Abolition,* p. 23.

58. Amos Kendall to Andrew Jackson, 1835 Aug 7, and Jackson to Kendall, 1835 Aug 9, in John Spencer Bassett, ed., *Correspondence,* vol. 5, pp. 359–361.

59. On Adams and Martineau, see Kathleen D. McCarthy, *American Creed,* pp. 136–137; On Webster, see Barnard C. Steiner, *History of Slavery in Connecticut,* p. 74. Broadside, "A Declaration of the Sentiments of the People of Hartford," 1835, CHS.

60. This glance at Kendall's life relies on Donald B. Cole, *A Jackson Man;* quotations of Kendall's remarks to Tappan on p. 239 and of E. M. Gallaudet's on Kendall as his "second father" on p. 286. See Russell B. Nye, *Fettered Freedom,* pp. 56–65, for more on the post office and abolition mail, and Kendall's *Autobiography,* pp. 555–559, for his views of the "deaf-mute college."

TEN The Last Years

1. On demographics, factories, and finances, see Christopher L. Webber, *American to the Backbone,* pp. 126–127; Edward Baptist, *The Half Has Never Been Told,* p. 323; J. Eugene Smith, *One Hundred Years,* pp. 168, 195. On the Panic of 1837, see Clifford S. Griffin, "Religious Benevolence as Social Control," p. 441, and Ray Allen Billington, *The Protestant Crusade,* pp. 199–200.

2. See Thomas J. Brown's biography, *Dorothea Dix: New England Reformer,* pp. 91–92 and passim. The definitive history of the Retreat is Lawrence B. Goodheart, *Mad Yankees.*

3. Quotation on fund-raising committee from THG, "Discourse Delivered at the Dedication of the Chapel of the Connecticut Retreat for the Insane, January 28th, 1846," *Connecticut Common School Journal and Annals of Education,* 1852 Mar/Apr, p. 207. Story told by Mrs. Henry Leavitt Ellsworth is given in E. M. Gallaudet, *Life,* p. 266. "Retreat for the Insane," *Connecticut Courant,* 1821 June 12, p. 1.

4. This story is told in Barnard, *Tribute,* pp. 33–35; Alcott, *Mighty Oaks,* pp. 285–288; and in letters transcribed in Humphrey, *Life,* pp. 340–347.

5. On state funding, Jarvis Morse, *A Neglected Period,* pp. 178–180, and Gerald N. Grob, *Mental Institutions in America,* p. 350; on the Retreat's pretexts, Grob, pp. 78–79 and 246–248. Cocke to THG, 1845 Jan 10, and "Private Journal," GP LoC. Retreat superintendent John S. Butler is quoted on the needs of wealthy patients in Grob, p. 79. Opium addiction and the DTs are mentioned in an 1838 entry in a now-lost diary, transcribed in Humphrey, *Life,* p. 363.

6. Amariah Brigham's denial that mental illness was divinely caused is mentioned in Lawrence B. Goodheart, *Mad Yankees,* p. 6; Barnard states his beliefs in *Tribute,* pp. 42–43; Gallaudet's views and the incident with Dr. Fuller are from his lost diary, transcribed in Humphrey, *Life,* p. 352. *Annual Report of the Retreat for the Insane* for 1842, pp. 34–36.

7. The chapel floor plan is from Barnard, *Tribute,* p. 40. Goodheart describes Brigham's views of religious enthusiasm in *Mad Yankees,* p. 6. *Annual Report of the Retreat for the Insane for 1847,* pp. 29–31. Gallaudet's narrative of the woman who walked to the men's side of the chapel was recorded in his now-lost diary in 1841, transcribed in Humphrey, *Life,* p. 367. Thomas Robbins's remarks were recorded in his *Diary* on 1845 Apr 20.

8. Teaching the finger alphabet is mentioned in the now-lost diary in 1838, transcribed in Humphrey, *Life,* pp. 352. Taking patients to observe the deaf school is from Alcott, *Mighty Oaks,* p. 290. Gallaudet's ideas for patient activities were listed in an 1839 entry, transcribed in Humphrey, pp. 359–360. The story about the patient who wanted to jump off the roof was told by Dr. John S. Butler to Gallaudet's granddaughter Grace Gallaudet Closson, as related in her 1939 article, p. 2.

9. Gallaudet's paternal feelings for the insane are given in Alcott, *Might Oaks,* p. 289. McEwan's story was recorded in Gallaudet's diary in 1838, transcribed in Humphrey, *Life,*

p. 355; the McEwans' state support comes from the pupil list in an appendix to Barnard, *Tribute.* "Discourse Delivered at the Dedication of the Chapel," *Connecticut Common School Journal and Annals of Education,* 1852 Mar/Apr.

10. Gallaudet's home school accounts in GP LoC; E. M. Gallaudet, *Life,* p. 288.

11. Gallaudet's accounts in the GP LoC. On the Chinese boys, Anita Marchant, "Yung Wing and the Chinese Educational Mission at Hartford," and Shao Yuen Carol Chen, "Yung Wing, the First Chinese Student in the United States." Yung Wing's remarks are from E. M. Gallaudet, *Life,* p. 295. S. R. Brown to THG, 1847 Jan 17 and Sep 17, GP LoC. On the deaf seamstress and the spare room, E. M. Gallaudet, *Life,* pp. 291 and 292.

12. On the piano from Alfred Smith, see E. M Gallaudet, *Life,* pp. 297–298. Eddy's rabbits are mentioned in THG to Edward Miner Gallaudet, 1846 Aug 18, reprinted in Humphrey, *Life,* pp. 326–327.

13. On the 1841 flood, Christopher L. Webber, *American to the Backbone,* p. 148. On Dickens's visit, Merrill H. Dooey, "Famous Visitors"; THG on novels, from his review of A. S. Roe, *James Montjoy,* in the *Hartford Daily Courant,* 1850 Feb 11, p. 2. P. W. Gallaudet's Will, proved 1843 Jan 3, GUA; comments on it from Robert Munro Erwin to Katherine Gallaudet, 1938 Sep 11, GP LoC. The Philadelphia offer is made in A. S. Barnes to THG, 1844 Sep 3, GP LoC.

14. The letters Gallaudet wrote to his children during his trip to Montreal are reprinted in Humphrey, *Life,* pp. 321–329. Assessments of the religious state of the children are given in the opening to his "Private Journal," GP LoC.

15. The story of Thomas's career and Gallaudet's role in (thwarting) it is told in Thomas Gallaudet, "Sketch of My Life," Henry Buzzard Papers, GUA, and "Recollections of My Father," GP LoC.

16. On Onderdonk, see Patricia Cline Cohen, "Ministerial Misdeeds."

17. Quotations from THG to Thomas Gallaudet, 1844 Nov 29, reprinted in Humphrey, *Life,* pp. 318–319. On the wedding, "An Interesting Ceremony," *New York Commercial Advertiser,* 1845 Jul 16. Thomas's IOU is copied into Gallaudet's "Account Book," GP LoC.

18. Entry for 1848 Nov 7 in "Private Journal," GP LoC; E. M. Gallaudet, *Life,* p. 312. On Taylor's lack of express commitment regarding his presumed advocacy of containment of slavery, see Henry Mayer, *All on Fire,* p. 381.

19. "Private Journal," GP LoC.

20. Will of Daniel Wadsworth, Sterling Library, Yale.

21. "Reform in the Navy—Meeting at American Hall," *Hartford Courant,* 1849 Aug 24, p. 2.

22. "Private Journal" and a loose sheet of paper headed "House in Buck. St.," GP LoC: E. M. Gallaudet, *Life,* pp. 301–302.

23. "Private Journal" and "Account Book," GP LoC. The convocation and presentation of the silver-plated gifts are related in all three nineteenth-century biographies and Harvey Prindle Peet's "Tribute," *American Annals of the Deaf and Dumb* 4.2: 65–77. Addresses delivered on the occasion are reprinted in Christopher Krentz, ed., *A Mighty Change.* Thomas Brown to THG, 1851 Mar 1, GP LoC.

24. "Private Journal," GP LoC; THG to Caroline Gallaudet, 1851 Jan 27, transcribed

in Humphrey, *Life,* p. 335; Robbins, *Diary,* 1851 Feb 13; Allen McLean, *My Farewell to the World and All It Contains,* p. 46.

25. "Private Journal" and Sophia Gallaudet "Account of her Father's Death," GP LoC. The heat is given as cause in *Biographical Sketches of the Graduates of Yale College,* Stg MSSA. THG to the Convention of American Instructors of the Deaf and Dumb, 1851 Aug 28, printed in the *American Annals of the Deaf and Dumb* 4.1: p. 26.

26. On Western Reserve College, Mayer, *All on Fire,* p. 140. E. M. Gallaudet, *Life,* p. 319.

27. Thomas Gallaudet to Heman Humphrey, 1857 Jul 28, GP LoC. E. M. Gallaudet, *Life,* p. 311.

28. Lewis Weld, "Death of Mr. Gallaudet," *American Annals of the Deaf and Dumb* 4.1 (1852): 57–62; "Account Book," GP LoC.

29. H[enry] B[arnard], "Thomas Hopkins Gallaudet: Description of the Monument: The Public Ceremony," *Connecticut Common School Journal and Annals* (1854 Dec): p. 377.

30. E. M. Gallaudet, "The Prenatal History of the College: Address Delivered on Presentation Day, May 6, 1914," *Buff and Blue* 32.7 (1924 Apr), GUA.

31. "Memorial Windows," typescript, 1950, First Church of Christ in Hartford, archives.

NB: Citations of present-day reference dictionaries and of articles in eighteenth- and nine-teenth-century newspapers and journals are all given in full in the endnotes and do not appear here. Citations of eighteenth- and nineteenth-century novels that are available today in various editions are given in the endnotes with reference to chapters, not pages, and do not appear here.

Abdy, Edward Strutt. *Journal of a Residence and Tour in the United States of North America: From April, 1833, to October, 1834.* 3 vols. London: John Murray, 1835.

Abzug, Robert H. *Cosmos Crumbling: American Reform and Religious Imagination.* New York: Oxford University Press, 1994.

Adams, John Quincy. *Memoirs of John Quincy Adams,* ed. Charles Francis Adams. Philadelphia: Lippincott, 1875.

African Education Society Board of Managers. *Report of the Proceedings at the Formation of the African Education Society.* Washington, D.C.: African Education Society, 1830.

Alcott, William A. *Tall Oaks from Little Acorns; or, Sketches of Distinguished Persons of Humble Origins.* New York: Carlton and Phillips, Sunday School Union, 1856.

Alford, Terry. *Prince among Slaves: The True Story of an African Prince Sold into Slavery in the American South.* Oxford: University Press, 1977.

[Alsop, Richard, et al.] *The Echo, with Other Poems.* New York: Porcupine Press, 1807.

Association of Masters of the Boston Public Schools. *Remarks on the Seventh Annual Report of the Hon. Horace Mann, Secretary of the Massachusetts Board of Education.* Boston: Charles C. Little and James Brown, 1844.

————. *Rejoinder to the "Reply" of the Hon. Horace Mann, Secretary of the Massachusetts Board of Education, to the "Remarks" of the Association of Boston Masters, upon the Seventh Annual Report.* Boston: Charles C. Little and James Brown, 1845.

Bacon, Leonard. [Address to the Christian Alliance.] In *Addresses of Rev. L. Bacon, D.D., and Rev. E.N. Kirk at the Annual Meeting of the Christian Alliance.* New York: S. W. Benedict, 1845, pp. 9–19.

Bacon, Theodore Davenport. *Leonard Bacon: A Statesman in the Church.* New Haven: Yale University Press, 1931.

Bainton, Roland H. *Yale and the Ministry: A History of Education for the Christian Ministry at Yale from the Founding in 1701.* New York: Harper, 1957.

Banner, James M. Jr. *To the Hartford Convention: The Federalists and the Origins of Party Politics in Massachusetts, 1789–1815.* New York: Knopf, 1970.

Banner, Lois "Religious Benevolence as Social Control." *Journal of American History* 60 (1973 Jun): 23–39.

Baptist, Edward E. *The Half Has Never Been Told: Slavery and the Making of American Capitalism.* New York: Basic Books, 2014.

Barber, John. *A History of the Amistad Captives: Being a Circumstantial Account.* New Haven: Barber, 1840. Reprint New Haven: Amistad Committee, Inc. [1993].

Barbour, Lucas Barnes. *Families of Early Hartford, Connecticut.* Baltimore: Genealogical Publishing Co., 1977.

Barnard, Henry. *Tribute to Gallaudet: A Discourse in Commemoration of the Life, Character and Services of the Rev. Thomas H. Gallaudet LL.D.* Hartford: Brockett & Hutchinson, 1852.

Barnes, Gilbert Hobbs. *The Anti-Slavery Impulse, 1830–1844.* Gloucester, Mass.: Peter Smith, 1957.

Barnes, Gilbert Hobbs, and Dwight L. Dumond, eds. *Letters of Theodore Dwight Weld, Angelina Grimké Weld and Sarah Grimké.* 2 vols., continuously paginated. New York: Appleton-Century [ca. 1934].

Bassett, John Spencer, ed. *Correspondence of Andrew Jackson.* 7 vols. Washington, D.C.: Carnegie Institution of Washington, 1926–1935.

Beecher, Catharine E. *An Essay on Slavery and Abolitionism with Reference to the Duty of American Females.* Philadelphia: Henry Perkins, 1837.

Beecher, Charles, ed. *The Autobiography Correspondence, etc. of Lyman Beecher, D.D.* New York: Harper and Bros., 1865.

Beecher, Edward. *The Papal Conspiracy Exposed, and Protestantism Defended, in the Light of Reason, History, and Scripture.* New York: M. W. Dodd, 1855.

Beecher, Lyman. *Six Sermons on the Nature, Occasions, Signs, Evils, and Remedy of Intemperance.* Boston: T. R. Marvin, 1827.

Bell, Alexander Graham. "Historical Notes." *Association Review* 2 (1900): 33–70, 113–126, 257–172, 385–409, 489–519; 3 (1901): 329–335; 4 (1902): 19–41, 139–151, 439–454; 5 (1903): 370–378.

Billington, Ray Allen. *The Protestant Crusade, 1800–1860: A Study of the Origins of American Nativism.* New York: Rinehart, 1938.

Birdsall, Richard D. "The Second Great Awakening and the New England Social Order." *Church History* 39.3 (1970): 345–364.

Bishop, Abraham. *Proofs of a Conspiracy, against Christianity, and the Government of the United States, Exhibited in Several Views of the Union of Church and State in New England.* Hartford: J. Babcock, 1802.

Blackett, R. J. M. *Beating against the Barriers: Biographical Essays in Nineteenth-Century Afro-American History.* Baton Rouge: Louisiana State University Press, 1986.

Blumenfeld, Samuel L. *The New Illiterates—And How You Can Keep Your Child from Becoming One.* New Rochelle, N.Y.: Arlington House, 1973.

Bodo, John R. *The Protestant Clergy and Public Issues, 1812—1848.* Princeton, N.J.: Princeton University Press, 1954.

Boone, Richard G. *Education in the United States: Its History from the Earliest Settlements.* New York: Appleton, 1914.

Booth, Edmund. "Thomas Hopkins Gallaudet." *North Dakota Banner* 53.3 (1943 Dec): 1–3. Originally published in the *Iowa Hawkeye*, 1881; also reprinted in *American Annals of the Deaf and Dumb* 26.3 (1881 Jul): 200–202.

Bragg, Lois. "Visual-Kinetic Communication in Europe before 1600: A Survey of Sign Lexicons and Finger Alphabets Prior to the Rise of Deaf Education." *Journal of Deaf Studies and Deaf Education* 2 (1997): 1–25.

Bragg, Lois, ed. *Deaf World: A Historical Reader and Primary Sourcebook.* New York: New York University Press, 2001.

Broad, William J. "How a Volcanic Eruption in 1815 Darkened the World but Colored the Arts." *New York Times,* 2015 Aug 25.

Brown, Thomas J. *Dorothea Dix: New England Reformer.* Cambridge, Mass.: Harvard University Press, 1998.

Brown, William. "An Oration Spoken at Hartford, in the State of Connecticut on the Anniversary of American Independence, July 4th, A.D. 1799." Hartford: Hudson and Goodwin, printer, 1799.

Buel, Richard Jr. *America on the Brink: How the Political Struggle over the War of 1812 Almost Destroyed the Young Republic.* New York: Palgrave MacMillan, 2005.

Buggeln, Gretchen Townsend. "Elegance and Sensibility in the Calvinist Tradition: The First Congregational Church of Hartford, Connecticut." In Paul Corby Finney, ed., *Seeing beyond the Word: Visual Arts and the Calvinist Tradition,* 429–453. Grand Rapids, Mich.: William B. Eerdmans, 1999.

Burstein, Andrew. *The Original Knickerbocker: The Life of Washington Irving.* New York: Basic Books, 2007.

Carey, Mathew. *A Short Account of the Malignant Fever, Lately Prevalent in Philadelphia.* Philadelphia: Printed by the author, 1793.

Chang, Nathan W. "The Legacy of Jonathan Edwards in the Founder of American Deaf Education: An Historical Theology of Thomas Hopkins Gallaudet." PhD dissertation, Trinity Evangelical Divinity School, 2016.

Chen, Shao Yuen Carol. "Yung Wing: The First Chinese Student in the United States." *Connecticut Education History Series,* No. 4. Storrs: University of Connecticut, 1987.

Child, Mrs. [Lydia Maria]. *The American Frugal Housewife.* New York: Samuel S. and William Wood, 1838.

Clerc, Laurent. "Autobiography." In Lois Bragg, ed., *Deaf World.* 1–9. Originally published in Henry Barnard, *Tribute to Gallaudet.*

———. *The Diary of Laurent Clerc's Voyage from France to America in 1816.* West Hartford, Conn.: American School for the Deaf, 1952.

Closson, Grade Gallaudet. "Thomas H. Gallaudet as Chaplain for the Insane." *Just Once a Month* [magazine of the Kendall School, Gallaudet University] 19.3 (1939 Dec): 1–2, 12.

Cobbett, William. *Rural Rides.* E. Fitch Daglish, ed. New York: Dutton, 1932. First published 1830.

Cohen, Patricia Cline. "Ministerial Misdeeds: The Onderdonk Trial and Sexual Harassment in the 1840s." In Susan Juster and Lisa MacFarlane, eds., *A Mighty Baptism: Race, Gender, and the Creation of American Protestantism,* 81–106. Ithaca, N.Y.: Cornell University Press, 1996.

Cole, Donald B. *A Jackson Man: Amos Kendall and the Rise of American Democracy.* Baton Rouge: Louisiana State University Press, 2004.

Colfax, Richard H. *Evidence against the Views of the Abolitionists, Consisting of Physical and Moral Proofs, of the Natural Inferiority of the Negroes.* New York: Bleakley, 1833.

Collier, Christopher. "In Search of an Education, Seventeenth to Nineteenth Centuries." In Elizabeth J., Normen et al., eds., *African American Connecticut Explored,* 137–147.

Colton, Calvin. *Abolition a Sedition.* Philadelphia: G. W. Donohue, 1839.

Connecticut Colonization Society. "An Address to the Public." New Haven: Treadway and Adams, printers, 1823.

Davis, David Brion. *The Fear of Conspiracy: Images of Un-American Subversion from the Revolution to the Present.* Ithaca, N.Y.: Cornell University Press, 1971.

———. *The Problem of Slavery in the Age of Emancipation.* New York: Knopf, 2014.

Davis, Hugh. *Leonard Bacon: New England Reformer and Antislavery Moderate.* Baton Rouge: Louisiana State University Press, 1998.

———. "Northern Colonizationists and Free Blacks, 1823–1837: A Case Study of Leonard Bacon." *Journal of the Early Republic* 17 (1997 winter): 651–675.

Demos, John. *The Heathen School: A Story of Hope and Betrayal in the Age of the Early Republic.* New York: Knopf, 2014.

Dexter, Franklin Bowditch. *Biographical Notices of Graduates of Yale College, with Annals of the College History.* New York: Holt, 1885–1912.

———. "Student Life at Yale College under the First President Dwight." In Dexter, *A Selection from the Miscellaneous Historical Papers of Fifty Years,* 382–394. New Haven: [no publisher], 1918.

Dixon, Thomas. "Revolting against Reid: The Philosophy of Thomas Brown." In Gordon Graham, ed., *Scottish Philosophy in the Nineteenth and Twentieth Centuries,* 23–46. Oxford: University Press, 2015.

Dixon, Thomas, ed. *Thomas Brown: Selected Philosophical Writings.* Charlottesville, Va.: Philosophy Documentation Center, 2010.

Dooey, Merrill H. "Famous Visitors and Distinguished Guests of Hartford, 1645–1936." MA Thesis, Trinity College, 1958.

Douglas, Ann. *The Feminization of American Culture.* New York: Knopf, 1977.

Douglass, Frederick. *The Frederick Douglass Papers.* John W. Blassingame and John R. McKivigan, eds. Series 1; 5 vols. New Haven: Yale University Press, 1979.

Dugdale, Antony, J. J. Fueser, and J. Celso de Castro Alves. *Yale, Slavery and Abolition.* [New Haven]: Amistad Committee, Inc., 2001.

Dunn, Henry. *The School Teacher's Manual; Containing Practical Suggestions on Teaching and Popular Education.* Prepared for publication in this country, with a preface, by T. H. Gallaudet. Hartford: Reed and Barber, 1839.

Dwight, Theodore. *A History of the Hartford Convention, with a Review of the Policy of the United States Government, which Led to the War of 1812.* New York: N & J White, 1833.

———. "An Oration Spoken at Hartford, in the State of Connecticut, on the Anniversary of American Independence, July 4th, 1798." Hartford: Hudson and Goodwin, printers, 1798. New Haven: Thomas and Samuel Green, 1798.

Dwight, Theodore [Jr.]. *Open Convents, or, Nunneries and Popish Seminaries Dangerous to the Morals and Degrading to the Character of a Republican Community.* New York: VanNostrand & Dwight, 1836.

———. *President Dwight's Decisions of Questions Discussed by the Senior Class in Yale College, in 1813 and 1814.* New York: Jonathan Leavitt, 1833.

Dwight, Timothy. "A Discourse on Some Events of the Last Century, Delivered in the Brick Church in New Haven, on Wednesday, January 7, 1801." New Haven: Ezra Read, printer, 1801.

————. "The Duty of Americans, at the Present Crisis, Illustrated in a Discourse, Preached on the Fourth of July, 1798." New Haven: Thomas and Samuel Green, 1798.

————. "The Folly, Guilt, and Mischiefs of Duelling: A Sermon, Preached in the College Chapel at New Haven, on the Sabbath Preceding the Annual Commencement, September, 1804." Hartford: Hudson and Goodwin, printers, 1805.

————. "A Sermon Preached at the Opening of the Theological Institution in Andover, and at the Orgination of Rev. Eliphalet Pearson, LL.D., September 28th, 1808." Boston: Farrand, Mallory, and Co., 1808.

Edgeworth, Maria. *The Parent's Assistant, or Stories for Children.* Reprint, London: Macmillan, 1907.

Edwards, R. A. R. *Words Made Flesh: Nineteenth-Century Deaf Education and the Growth of Deaf Culture.* New York: New York University Press, 2012.

Egerton, Douglas R. "'Its Origin Is Not a Little Curious': A New Look at the American Colonization Society." *Journal of the Early Republic* 5 (1985): 463–480.

Farrow, Anne, Joel Lang, and Jenifer Frank. *Complicity: How the North Promoted, Prolonged, and Profited from Slavery.* New York: Ballantine Books, 2005.

Fernandes, James John. "The Gate to Heaven: T. H. Gallaudet and the Rhetoric of the Deaf Education Movement." PhD dissertation, University of Michigan, 1980.

Fiedler, Leslie. *Love and Death in the American Novel.* New York: Criterion, 1960.

Fitzmier, John R. *New England's Moral Legislator: Timothy Dwight, 1752–1817.* Bloomington: Indiana University Press, 1998.

Fleischacker, Samuel. "The Impact on America: Scottish Philosophy and the American Founding." In Alexander Broadie, ed., *The Cambridge Companion to the Scottish Enlightenment,* 316–337. Cambridge, United Kingdom: Cambridge University Press, 2003.

Fowler, Herbert E. *A Century of Teacher Education in Connecticut: The Story of the New Britain State Normal School and Teachers College of Connecticut, 1849–1949.* s.l.: Teachers College of Connecticut, 1949.

Fox, Early Lee. *The American Colonization Society, 1817–1840.* Baltimore: Johns Hopkins Press, 1919.

Franklin, Wayne. *James Fenimore Cooper: The Early Years.* New Haven: Yale University Press, 2007.

Frederickson, George M. *The Black Image in the White Mind: The Debate on Afro-American Character and Destiny, 1817–1914.* Middletown, Conn.: Wesleyan University Press, 1987.

Friedman, Lawrence J. *Inventors of the Promised Land.* New York: Knopf, 1975.

Fuess, Claude M. *An Old New England School: A History of Phillips Academy, Andover.* Boston: Houghton Mifflin, 1917.

Fulton, John, ed. *Memoirs of Frederick A. P. Barnard.* New York: Macmillan, 1896.

Gallaudet, Edward Miner. *The Life of Thomas Hopkins Gallaudet, Founder of Deaf-Mute Instruction in America.* New York: Henry Holt and Co., 1888.

Gallaudet, Thomas Hopkins. "An Address, Delivered at a Meeting for Prayer, with Reference to the Sandwich Mission, in the Brick Church in Hartford, October 11th, 1819." Hartford: Lincoln and Stone, printers, 1819.

————. "An Address on Female Education, Delivered, Nov. 21st, 1827, at the Opening of the

Edifice Erected for the Accommodation of the Hartford Female Seminary." Hartford: Huntington, 1828.

——— . *The Child's Book on the Soul: Two Parts in One.* New York: American Tract Society, n.d. Originally published 1836.

——— . *The Child's Picture Defining and Reading Book.* Hartford: Huntington, 1830.

——— . *The Class Book of Natural Theology for the Use of Schools.* Madras: P. R. Hunt, American Mission Press, 1846.

——— . "A Discourse, Delivered at the Annual Meeting of the Hartford Evangelical Tract Society, in the Baptist Meeting-House, in Hartford, January 5, 1820." Hartford: Hudson & Co., printer, 1820.

——— . "A Discourse, Delivered at the Dedication of the American Asylum for the Education of Deaf and Dumb Persons, May 22nd, 1821." Hartford: Hudson & Co., printer, 1821.

——— . *Discourses on Various Points of Christian Faith and Practice; Most of which Were Delivered in the Chapel of the Oratoire in Paris, in the Spring of M.DCCC.XVI.* New York: P. W. Gallaudet, 1818.

——— . *An Elementary Book for the Use of the Deaf and Dumb, in the Connecticut Asylum.* Hartford: Hudson & Co., printers, 1817.

——— . *The Every-Day Christian, No. 1: General Principles, Temperance, the Family State.* New York: Leavitt, Lord and Co., 1835.

——— . *History of Jonah: For Children and Youth.* New York: American Tract Society, 1833.

——— . *The Mother's Primer to Teach Her Child Its Letters, and How to Read.* Hartford: Daniel Burgess, 1836.

——— . "On the Principle of Association, as Giving Dignity to the Christian Character." In *Lectures, on the Literary History of the Bible, by Rev. Joel Hawes; on the Principle of Association, as Giving Dignity to the Christian Character, by Rev. T. H. Gallaudet; and on the Temporal Benefits of the Sabbath, by Rev. Horace Hooker, Originally Delivered before the Goodrich Association.* Hartford: Cooke, 1833.

——— . *Plan of a Seminary for the Education of Instruters [sic] of Youth.* Boston: Cummings, Hilliard, 1825.

——— . "Preliminary Essay." In T. Babington, *A Practical View of Christian Education.* Hartford: Cooke, 1831.

[———]. *Public Schools, Public Blessings.* New York: New York Public School Society, 1833. Reprinted in Welter.

——— . *A Scriptural Catechism, Designed Principally for the Deaf and Dumb in the American Asylum.* Hartford: Case, Tiffany and Co., 1848. Previously published as *A Catechism of Scripture History, Designed Principally for the Deaf and Dumb in the American Asylum.* Hartford, Hudson and Skinner, printers, 1829.

——— . *Scripture Biography for the Young: With Critical Illustrations and Practical Remarks.* 7 vols. New York: American Tract Society, 1833–1843.

——— . "A Sermon Delivered at the Opening of the Connecticut Asylum for the Education and Instruction of Deaf and Dumb Persons." In *Discourses on Various Points,* pp. 221–239.

——— . "A Sermon on the Duty and Advantages of Affording Instruction to the Deaf and Dumb." Portland, Maine: A. Shirley, printer, 1824.

——— . *Starting in Life; or, Hints Addressed to an Elder Scholar to which is Added "Going Apprentice."* Philadelphia: American Sunday-School Union, 1862.

———. *A Statement with Regard to the Moorish Prince, Abduhl Rahhahman*. New York: Daniel Fanshaw, printer, 1828.

———. "Summary of an Address." In American Colonization Society, *The Proceedings of the Public Meeting, Held in the Middle Dutch Church, Together with Addresses Delivered on That Occasion*. New York: Protestant Episcopal Press, printer, 1829.

[———.] Valedictory Address. *The Panoplist and Missionary Magazine* 10.10 (1814 Oct).

———. *The Youth's Book on Natural Theology*. New York: American Tract Society, 1932.

Gallaudet, Thomas Hopkins, and Horace Hooker. *A Practical Spelling-Book with Reading Lessons*. Hartford: Hamersley, 1866. Originally published 1840.

Garrison, William Lloyd. *Thoughts on African Colonization, or An Impartial Exhibition of the Doctrines, Principles, and Purposes of the American Colonization Society*. Boston: Garrison and Knapp, 1832.

Gerson, Linda. "The Pennsylvania School for the Deaf, 1820–1892, with a Focus on David G. Seixas." MA thesis, Temple University, 1978.

Goodheart, Lawrence B. *Mad Yankees: The Hartford Retreat for the Insane and Nineteenth-Century Psychiatry*. Lowell: University of Massachusetts Press, 2003.

Goodrich, Samuel Griswold. *Peter Parley's Method of Telling about Geography to Children*. Burlington, CT: Chauncey Goodrich; Hartford: Huntington, 1830.

———. *Recollections of a Lifetime*. 2 vols. New York: Alvord, printer, 1856.

[Green, Francis]. *Vox Oculis Subjecta . . . by a Parent*. (Published anonymously.) London: Benjamin White, 1783.

[Green, Francis, trans.]. "Preface of the Translator." In Abbé de l'Épée, *The Method of Educating the Deaf and Dumb; Confirmed by Long Experience*, i–xxiv. London: T. Cadell and W. Davies, 1801.

Griffin, Clifford S. "Religious Benevolence as Social Control, 1815–1866." *Mississippi Valley Historical Review* 44.3 (1957 Dec): 423–444.

Grimsted, David. *American Mobbing, 1828–1861: Toward Civil War*. New York: Oxford University Press, 1998.

Grob, Gerald N. *Mental Institutions in America: Social Policy to 1875*. New York: Free Press, 1973.

Groce, Nora. *Everyone Here Spoke Sign Language: Hereditary Deafness on Martha's Vineyard*. Cambridge, Mass.: Harvard University Press, 1985.

Gutjahr, Paul C. *An American Bible: A History of the Good Book in the United States, 1777–1880*. Stanford, Calif.: Stanford University Press, 1999.

Haggerty, George E. "Satire and Sentiment in *The Vicar of Wakefield*." *The Eighteenth Century* 32.1 (1991): 25–38.

Hall, Peter Dobkin. *The Organization of American Culture, 1700–1900*. New York: New York University Press, 1984.

Hamilton, Stanislaus Murray, ed. *The Writings of James Monroe*. 7 vols. New York: Putnam, 1898–1903.

Harris, Katherine J. "The Rise of Communities and the Continued Quest for Freedom for All." In Elizabeth J. Normen et al., eds., *African American Connecticut Explored*, 51–63.

———. "The United States, Liberia, and their Foreign Relations to 1847." PhD dissertation, Cornell University, 1982.

Harveson, Mae Elizabeth. "Catharine Esther Beecher, Pioneer Educator." PhD dissertation, University of Pennsylvania, 1932.

"He Had Compassion on the Deaf." *Sunday School Times* (1957 Apr): 324–325.

Hofstadter, Richard. "The Paranoid Style in American Politics." In *The Paranoid Style in American Politics, and Other Essays.* Boston: The Beacon Press, 1965.

Hooker, Horace. "Thomas Hopkins Gallaudet, L.L.D." In William Buell Sprague, ed., *Annals of the American Pulpit,* vol. 2, 609–614. New York: Arno Press, 1969. Originally published 1856.

Hopkins, Robert H. *The True Genius of Oliver Goldsmith: A Georgian Study.* Baltimore: Johns Hopkins University Press, 1969.

Horsman, Reginald. *Race and Manifest Destiny: The Origins of American Racial Anglo-Saxonism.* Cambridge, Mass.: Harvard University Press, 1981.

Howard, Leon. *The Connecticut Wits.* Chicago: University of Chicago Press, 1943.

Howard, Philip E. *The Life Story of Henry Clay Trumbull, Missionary, Army Chaplin, Editor and Author.* Philadelphia: Sunday School Times, 1905.

Howe, Daniel Walker. *What God Hath Wrought: The Transformation of America, 1815–1848.* Oxford: Oxford University Press, 2007.

Hudson, Winthrop S. *The Great Tradition of the American Churches.* New York: Harper [1953].

Hug, Elsie A. *Seventy-Five Years in Education: The Role of the School of Education, New York University, 1890–1965.* New York: New York University Press, 1965.

Humphrey, Heman. *The Life and Labors of the Rev. T. H. Gallaudet, LL.D.* New York: Robert Carter and Bros., 1857.

———. *Parallel between Intemperance and the Slave Trade, An Address Delivered at Amherst College, July 4, 1828.* Amherst, Mass.: J. S. & C. Adams, printers, 1828.

Hurd, John C. *The Law of Freedom and Bondage in the United States.* Vol. 2. Boston: Little, Brown, 1862.

Jaffa, Harry V. *Crisis of the House Divided: An Interpretation of the Issues in the Lincoln-Douglas Debates.* University of Chicago Press, 1982. Originally published New York: Doubleday, 1959.

Jay, William. *Inquiry into the Character and Tendency of the American Colonization and American Anti-Slavery Societies.* 6th ed. New York: R. G. Williams, 1838.

Jenks, William. "Memoir of Rev. Louis Dwight." In *Prison Discipline Society Reports,* vol. 1: 1826–1835. Boston: T. R. Marvin, 1855. Separately paginated.

Johnson-Taylor, Margo. "Dixwell Avenue Congregational Church, UCC." www.scribd.com/doc/81233674/Dixwell-Avenue-Congregational-Church-UCC, accessed February 17, 2017.

Jones, Theodore F. *New York University, 1832–1932.* New York: New York University Press, 1933.

Jordan, Winthrop D. *White over Black: American Attitudes toward the Negro, 1550–1812.* New York: Norton, 1977. Originally published University of North Carolina Press, 1968.

Keller, Charles Roy *The Second Great Awakening in Connecticut.* New Haven: Yale University Press, 1942.

Kendall, Amos. *Autobiography of Amos Kendall.* William Stickney, ed. New York: P. Smith, 1949.

Kendall, Joshua. *The Forgotten Founding Father: Noah Webster's Obsession and the Creation of an American Culture.* New York: Berkley Books, 2010.

Kettell, Samuel, ed. *Specimens of American Poetry, Specimens of the American Poets.* 3 vols. Boston: S. G. Goodrich, 1829.

Kilmeade, Brian, and Don Yaeger. *Thomas Jefferson and the Tripoli Pirates: The Forgotten War That Changed American History.* New York: Sentinel, 2015.

Krentz, Christopher. *A Mighty Change: An Anthology of Deaf American Writing, 1816–1864.* Washington, D.C.: Gallaudet University Press, 2000.

Ladd, Paddy. *Understanding Deaf Culture: In Search of Deafhood.* Buffalo, N.Y.: Multilingual Matters, 2003.

Lane, Harlan. *A Deaf Artist in Early America: The Worlds of John Brewster, Jr.* Boston: Beacon Press, 2004.

———. *When the Mind Hears: A History of the Deaf.* New York: Vintage Books, 1989.

Lane, Harlan, ed. *The Deaf Experience: Classics in Language and Education.* Franklin Philip, trans. Cambridge, Mass.: Harvard University Press, 1984.

Leffler, Christopher T., and Puneet S. Braich, "The First Cataract Surgeons in Anglo-America." *Survey of Ophthalmology* 60.1 (2015): 86–92.

Lerner, Gerda. *The Grimké Sisters of South Carolina: Pioneers for Women's Rights and Abolition.* New York: Oxford University Press, 1998.

Lipson, Dorothy Ann. *Freemasonry in Federalist Connecticut.* Princeton, N.J.: Princeton University Press, 1977.

Loew, Ruth C., C. T. Akamatsu, and Mary Lanaville. "A Two-Handed Manual Alphabet in the United States." In Karen Emmorey and Harlan Lange, eds., *The Signs of Language Revisited: An Anthology to Honor Ursula Bellugi and Edward Klima,* 245–259. Mahwah, NJ: Erlbaum, 2000.

Loring, George H. "Address to Laurent Clerc." Reprinted in Christopher Krentz, ed., *A Mighty Change: An Anthology of Deaf American Writing, 1816–1864,* 147–148. Washington, D.C.: Gallaudet University Press, 2000.

Ludlum, David M. *Social Ferment in Vermont, 1791–1850.* New York: Columbia University Press, 1939.

MacMullen, Edith Nye. *In the Cause of True Education: Henry Barnard and Nineteenth-Century School Reform.* New Haven: Yale University Press, 1991.

Mann, Mary Tyler Peabody, ed. *Life and Works of Horace Mann.* 3 vols. [s.l.]: [n.p.], 1865–1868.

Manseau, Peter. *One Nation, Under Gods: A New American History.* New York: Little, Brown, 2015.

Marchant, Anita. "Yung Wing and the Chinese Educational Mission at Hartford." MA thesis, Trinity College, 1999.

Martin, Christopher. *The Amistad Affair.* London: Abelard-Schuman, 1970.

Massieu, Jean. "Autobiography." Excerpted in Harlan Lane, *The Deaf Experience: Classics in Language and Education,* 73–80. Franklin Philip, trans. Washington, D.C.: Gallaudet University Press, 2006.

Massieu, Jean, and Laurent Clerc. *A Collection of the Most Remarkable Definitions and Answers of Massieu and Clerc, Deaf and Dumb, to the Various Questions Put to Them, at the Public Lectures of the Abbé Sicard in London.* J. H. Sievrac, ed. London: Cox and Baylis, printers, 1815.

Matthewson, Tim. "Abraham Bishop, 'The Rights of Black Men,' and the American Reaction to the Haitian Revolution." *Journal of Negro History* 67.2 (1982): 148–154.

Mattingly, Paul H. *The Classless Profession: American Schoolmen in the Nineteenth Century.* New York: New York University Press, 1975.

———. "Why NYU Chose Gallaudet." *New York University Education Quarterly* (1981 fall): 9–15.

May, Henry F. *The Enlightenment in America.* Oxford: Oxford University Press, 1976.

Mayer, Henry. *All on Fire: William Lloyd Garrison and the Abolition of Slavery.* New York: St. Martin's, 1998.

McCarthy, Kathleen D. *American Creed: Philanthropy and the Rise of Civil Society, 1700–1865.* Chicago: University of Chicago Press, 2003.

McCook, Anson T., ed. *Legislative History of the American School, at Hartford, for the Deaf.* West Hartford, Conn.: Printed at the American School, 1924.

McLean, Allen. *My Farewell to the World and All It Contains.* Hebron, CT: G. M. Milne, 1981. Originally dictated by the author between 1851 and 1861 and printed privately.

McMahon, Sarah F. "'All Things in Their Proper Season': Seasonal Rhythms of Diet in Nineteenth Century New England." *Agricultural History* 63.2 (1989); 130–151.

———. "A Comfortable Subsistence: The Changing Composition of Diet in Rural New England, 1620–1840." *William and Mary Quarterly,* 3rd series, 42.1 (1985): 26–65.

McManus, Edgar J. *Black Bondage in the North.* Syracuse, N.Y.: Syracuse University Press, 1973.

Mehlinger, Louis R. "The Attitude of the Free Negro toward African Colonization." *Journal of Negro History* 1.3 (1916 Jun): 276–301.

Melish, Joanne Pope. *Disowning Slavery: Gradual Emancipation and "Race" in New England, 1780–1860.* Ithaca, N.Y.: Cornell University Press, 1998.

Miller, Perry. *The Life of the Mind in America: From the Revolution to the Civil War.* New York: Harcourt, Brace & World, 1965.

Moeschen, Sheila C. *Acts of Conspicuous Compassion: Performance Culture and American Charity Practices.* Ann Arbor: University of Michigan Press, 2013.

Monroe, Will S. *The Educational Labors of Henry Barnard: A Study in the History of American Pedagogy.* Syracuse, N.Y.: C.W. Bardeen, 1893.

Montgomery, Susan J., and Roger G. Reed. *Phillips Academy, Andover: An Architectural Tour.* New York: Princeton Architectural Press, 2000.

Morse, James King. *Jedidiah Morse: A Champion of New England Orthodoxy.* New York: Columbia University Press, 1939.

Morse, Jarvis. *A Neglected Period of Connecticut's History, 1818–1850.* New Haven: Yale University Press, 1933.

Morse, Jedidiah. "A Sermon, Delivered at the New North Church in Boston, in the Morning, and in the Afternoon at Charlestown, May 9th, 1798, Being the Day Recommended by John Adams, President of the United States of America for Solemn Humiliation, Fasting and Prayer." Boston: Samuel Hall, 1798.

Morse, Samuel F. B. [Brutus, pseud.] *Foreign Conspiracy against the Liberties of the United States*. New York: Leavitt, Lord, & Co., 1835.

Moss, Hilary. "'Cast Down on Every Side': The Ill-Fated Campaign to Found an 'African College' in New Haven." In Elizabeth J. Normen et al., eds., *African American Connecticut Explored*, 148–154.

Mossner, Ernest Campbell. *The Life of David Hume*. 2nd ed. Oxford: Clarendon Press, 2001.

Mott, Frank Luther. *A History of American Magazines, 1741–1850*. Cambridge, Mass.: Harvard University Press, 1957.

Newman, Eric P. "The Continental Dollar of 1776 Meets Its Maker." The *Numismatist* 72.8 (1959): 914–925.

Normen, Elizabeth J., et al., eds. *African American Connecticut Explored*. Middletown, Conn.: Wesleyan University Press, 2013.

Nye, Russell B. *Fettered Freedom: Civil Liberties and the Slavery Controversy, 1830–1860*. East Lansing: Michigan State College Press, 1949.

[Odgen, John Cossens]. *A View of the New-England Illuminati, Who Are Indefatigably Engaged in Destroying Religion and Government of the United Sates under a Feigned Regard for Their Safety—and under an Impious Abuse of True Religion*. Philadelphia: James Carey, printer, 1799.

Parker, Edwin Pond. *History of the Second Church of Christ in Hartford*. Hartford: Belknap and Warfield, 1892.

[Phelan], Charlotte Elizabeth. *The Happy Mute; or, the Dumb Child's Appeal*. New York: American Tract Society, n.d.

Preston, Daniel, and Marlena C. DeLong, eds. *The Papers of James Monroe*. 5 vols. Westport, Conn.: Greenwood Press, 2003.

Price, George R., and James Brewer Stewart, eds. *To Heal the Scourge of Prejudice: The Life and Writings of Hosea Easton*. Amherst: University of Massachusetts Press, 1999.

Prison Discipline Society. *Reports*. 2 vols. Boston: T. R. Marvin, 1855.

Purcell, Richard J. *Connecticut in Transition: 1775–1818*. New ed. Middletown, Conn.: Wesleyan University Press, 1963.

Rae, Luzerne. "Review of *A Tribute to Rev. Thomas H. Gallaudet*, Henry Barnard, ed." *American Annals of the Deaf and Dumb* 4.3 (1852): 193–199.

Ratner, Lorman A. *Powder Keg: Northern Opposition to the Antislavery Movement, 1831–1840*. New York: Basic Books, 1968.

Rediker, Marcus. *The Amistad Rebellion: An Atlantic Odyssey of Slavery and Freedom*. New York: Viking, 2012.

Richards, Leonard L. *"Gentlemen of Property and Standing": Anti-Abolition Mobs in Jacksonian America*. New York: Oxford University Press, 1970.

Richardson, Alan. *Literature, Education, and Romanticism: Reading as Social Practice, 1780–1832*. Cambridge, United Kingdom: Cambridge University Press, 1994.

Robbins, Thomas. *Diary*. 2 vols. Boston: Beacon Press, 1886–1887.

Rodgers, Geraldine E. *The Case for the Prosecution in the Trial of Silent Reading "Comprehension" Tests, Charged with the Destruction of America's Schools*. College Station, Tex.: Virtualbookworm.com, 2007.

Root, Grace Cogswell. *Father and Daughter: A Collection of Cogswell Family Letters and Diaries (1772–1830)*. West Hartford, Conn.: American School for the Deaf, printer [1924].

Rorabaugh, W. J. *The Alcoholic Republic: An American Tradition*. New York: Oxford University Press, 1979.

Rourke, Constance Mayfield. *Trumpets of Jubilee*. New York: Harcourt, Brace, 1927.

Rudolph, Frederick, ed. *Essays on Education in the Early Republic*. Cambridge, Mass.: Belknap Press, 1965.

Sayers, Edna Edith, and Diana Gates. "Lydia Huntley Sigourney and the Beginnings of American Deaf Education in Hartford: It Takes a Village." *Sign Language Studies* 8.4 (2008): 369–411.

Sayers, Edna Edith, and Diana Moore, eds. *Mrs. Sigourney of Hartford: Poems and Prose on the Early American Deaf Community*. Washington, D.C.: Gallaudet University Press, 2013.

Schereth, Eric R. *An Age of Infidels: The Politics of Religious Controversy in the Early United States*. Philadelphia: University of Pennsylvania Press, 2013.

Schneider, Carl E. "In the Days of Our Fathers." The *Messenger* 8.17 (1906): 15–16.

Seigel, Jules Paul. "The Enlightenment and the Evolution of a Language of Signs in France and England." *Journal of the History of Ideas* 30 (1969): 96–115.

Sharp, James Roger. *American Politics in the Early Republic: The New Nation in Crisis*. New Haven: Yale University Press, 1993.

Sherwood, H. N. "Early Negro Deportation Projects." *Mississippi Valley Historical Review* 2.4 (1916): 484–508.

Shiels, Richard D. "The Second Great Awakening in Connecticut: Critique of the Traditional Interpretation." *Church History* 49.4 (1980): 401–415.

Shorter, Edward. *Before Prozac: The Troubled History of Mood Disorders in Psychiatry*. Oxford: University Press, 2008.

Sigourney, Lydia H. *Letters of Life*. New York: Arno Press, 1980. Originally published New York: Appleton, 1867.

Silverman, Morris. *Hartford Jews, 1659–1970*. Hartford: Connecticut Historical Society [1970].

Simmons, Amelia. *American Cookery*. Hartford: Hudson and Goodwin, 1796.

Sklar, Kathryn Kish. *Catharine Beecher: A Study in American Domesticity*. New York: Norton, 1976.

Smith, Billy G. *Ship of Death: A Voyage That Changed the Atlantic World*. New Haven: Yale University Press, 2013.

Smith, J. Eugene. *One Hundred Years of Hartford's* Courant; *From Colonial Times through the Civil War*. New Haven: Yale University Press, 1949. Reprinted Archon Books, 1970.

Sparks, Jared, ed. *The Works of Benjamin Franklin: Containing Several Political and Historical Tracts Not Included in Any Former Edition and Many Letters Official and Private, Not Hitherto Published: With Notes and a Life of the Author*. Boston: Hilliard, Gray, 1840.

Staudenraus, P. J. *The African Colonization Movement, 1816–1865*. New York: Columbia University Press, 1961.

Stauffer, Vernon. *New England and the Bavarian Illuminati*. New York: Columbia University Press, 1918.

Stebbins, Giles Badger. *Facts and Opinions Touching the Real Origin, Character and Influence of the American Colonization Society*. New York: Negro Universities Press, 1961.

Stedt, Joseph D., and Donald F. Moores. "Manual Codes on English and American Sign

Language: Historical Perspectives and Current Realities." In Harry Bornstein, ed., *Manual Communication: Implications for Education*, 1–20. Washington, D.C.: Gallaudet University Press, 1990.

Steiner, Bernard C. *The History of Education in Connecticut*. Washington, D.C.: Government Printing Office, 1893.

———. *The History of Slavery in Connecticut*. Baltimore: Johns Hopkins Press, 1893.

Sterner, Daniel. *Vanished Downtown Hartford*. Charleston, S.C.: History Press, 2013.

Stewart, Dugald. *Collected Works*. 11 vols. William Hamilton, ed. Edinburgh: T. Constable, 1854–1860.

Stewart, James Brewer. "The Emergence of Racial Modernity and the Rise of the White North, 1790–1840." *Journal of the Early Republic* 18 (1998): 181–217.

Stokes, Anson Phelps. *Memorials of Eminent Yale Men*. New Haven: Yale University Press, 1914.

Stokes, Anson Phelps, and Leo Pfeffer. *Church and State in the United States*. Revised ed. New York: Harper and Row, 1964.

Streifford, David M. "The American Colonization Society: An Application of Republican Ideology to Early Antebellum Reform." *Journal of Southern History* 45.2 (1979 May): 201–220.

Strong, Nathan. "Political Instruction from the Prophecies of God's World—A Sermon, Preached on the State Thanksgiving, Nov. 29, 1778." Hartford: Hudson and Goodwin, 1798.

Swarns, Rachel L. "Georgetown Confronts a Haunting Sale of Slaves." *New York Times* (2016 Apr 17): 1, 16.

Sykes, Mrs. G. M. "Reminiscences of the Late Rev. Thomas Hopkins Gallaudet." *Mrs. Whittelsey's Magazine* 3 (1852): 42–47.

Syle, Henry Winter. *A Biographical Sketch of the Rev. Thomas Hopkins Gallaudet, LL.D., the First Great Educator of the Deaf in America*. Philadelphia: Cullingworth, 1887.

Tabak, John. *Significant Gestures: A History of American Sign Language*. Westport, Conn.: Praeger, 2006.

Tappan, David. "A Discourse Delivered in the Chapel of Harvard College, June 19, 1798." Boston: 1798. Excerpted in David Brion Davis, *Fear of Conspiracy*, 49–52.

[Tappan, Lewis.] *Letters Respecting a Book Dropped from the Catalogue of the American Sunday School Union in Compliance with the Dictation of the Slave Power*. New York: American and Foreign Anti-Slavery Society, 1848.

Taylor, Charles. *The Language Animal: The Full Shape of the Human Linguistic Capacity*. Cambridge, Mass.: Belknap Press, 2016.

———. *A Secular Age*. Cambridge, Mass.: Harvard University Press, 2007.

Tharp, Louise Hall. *Three Saints and a Sinner: Julia Ward Howe, Louisa, Annie, and Sam Ward*. Boston: Little, Brown [1956].

Thornton, William. "Cadmus, or a Treatise on the Elements of Written Language, Illustrating, by a Philosophical Division of Speech, the Power of each Character, Thereby Naturally Fixing the Orthography and Orthoepy." *Transactions of the American Philosophical Society* 3 (1793): 262–319.

Tice, Larry E. *American Counter-Revolution: A Retreat from Liberty*. Mechanicsburg, Pa.: Stackpole, 1998.

Toczé, Claude, and Annie Lambert. *Les Juifs en Bretagne*. Rennes, France: Presses Universitaires de Rennes, 2006.

Tomek, Beverly C. *Colonization and Its Discontents: Emancipation, Emigration, and Antislavery in Antebellum Pennsylvania*. New York: New York University Press, 2011.

Trumbull, H[enry] Clay. *The Sunday-School: Its Origin, Mission, Methods, and Auxiliaries*. Philadelphia: Wattles, 1888.

Valentine, Phyllis Klein. "American Asylum for the Deaf: A First Experiment in Education, 1817–1880." PHD dissertation, University of Connecticut, 1993.

———. "A Nineteenth-Century Experiment in Education of the Handicapped: The American Asylum for the Deaf and Dumb." *New England Quarterly* 654.3 (1991): 355–375.

———. "Thomas Hopkins Gallaudet: Benevolent Paternalism and the Origins of the American Asylum." In John Vickery Van Cleve, ed., *Deaf History Unveiled: Interpretations from new Scholarship*, 53–73. Washington, D.C.: Gallaudet University Press, 2002.

Van Sickle, Eugene S. "Reluctant Imperialists: The U.S. Navy and Liberia, 1819–1845." *Journal of the Early Republic* 31.1 (2011 spring): 107–134.

Wainwright, J. M. "Institution at Harford for Instruction the Deaf and Dumb." *North American Review and Miscellaneous Journal* 7.1 (1818): 127–136.

Walker, George Leon. *History of the First Church in Hartford, 1633–1883*. Hartford: Brown and Gross, 1884.

Warren, Wendy. *New England Bound*. New York: Liveright, 2016.

Wayland, Francis. *The Limitations of Human Responsibility*. New York: D. Appleton, 1838.

Webber, Christopher L. *American to the Backbone: The Life of James W. C. Pennington, the Fugitive Slave Who Became One of the First Black abolitionists*. New York: Pegasus, 2011.

Welter, Rush. *American Writings on Popular Education: The Nineteenth Century*. New York: Bobbs-Merrill, 1971.

White, David O. "Hartford's African Schools, 1830–1868." *Connecticut Historical Society Bulletin* 39 (1974 Apr): 47–53.

White, Shane. *Stories of Freedom in Black New York*. Cambridge, Mass.: Harvard University Press, 2002.

Wilder, Craig Steven. *Ebony and Ivy: Race, Slavery, and the Troubled History of America's Universities*. New York: Bloomsbury Press, 2013.

Wilentz, Sean. "Confounding Fathers: The Tea Party's Cold War Roots." *The New Yorker* (2010 October 18).

[Williams, Job.] "Brief History of the American Asylum at Hartford, for the Education and Instruction of the Deaf and Dumb." Hartford: Case, Lockwood and Brainard, 1893.

Wilson, Jean Taylor Kimball. "Account of the Gallaudet Family," 1953. gallaudetfamily.com/files/gallaudet%20book.pdf, accessed February 17, 2017.

Woods, Leonard. *Memoirs of American Missionaries, Formerly Connected with the Society of Inquiry Respecting Missions, in the Andover Theological Seminary*. Boston: Peirce and Parker, 1833.

Wyatt-Brown, Bertram. *Lewis Tappan and the Evangelical War against Slavery*. Cleveland: Case Western Reserve, 1969.

Zikmund, Barbara Brown. "UCC's 'Illogical Alliance' May Have Been Foreshadowed by Earlier Events." http://ucc.org/uccs-illogical-alliance-may, accessed February 9, 2017.